ZANE GREY

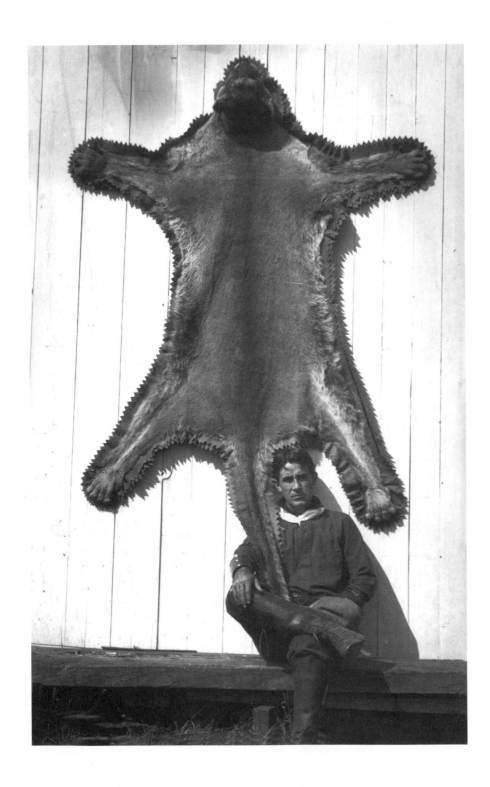

ZANE GREY

His Life, His Adventures,

His Women

THOMAS H. PAULY

University of Illinois Press

Urbana and Chicago

Frontispiece: Zane Grey and mountain lion pelt, ca. 1909

C 5 4 3 2 1
Library of Congress Cataloging-in-Publication Data

Pauly, Thomas H.
Zane Grey : his life, his adventures, his women /
Thomas H. Pauly.
p.   cm.
Includes bibliographical references and index.
ISBN-13: 978-0-252-03044-4 (cloth : acid-free paper)
ISBN-10: 0-252-03044-3 (cloth : acid-free paper)
1. Grey, Zane, 1872–1939.
2. Novelists, American—20th century—Biography.
3. Adventure and adventurers—United States—Biography.
4. Grey, Zane, 1872–1939—Relations with women.
5. Western stories—History and criticism.
I. Title.
PS3513.R6545Z83   2005
813'.52—dc22   2005009413

For Suzie (my wife),
and Anne (my sister),
and our adventures together.

Contents

Acknowledgments

One of the best parts of this project was all the kind, interesting people who aided my search for information. Early on, while I was deliberating whether to write this biography, I decided that I needed to meet with Loren Grey, Zane's son and the current head of Zane Grey, Inc., and find out what he thought about this possibility. During our first luncheon together, which lasted over three hours, he was remarkably open about his father's secret life and very interested in what I had learned so far. He reassured me that he and the rest of the family no longer wished to suppress the truth about Zane. So long as he could read the finished result and did not object to my treatment, he would allow me to quote from the unpublished writings of his father and mother. Several years later, after more lunches and memorable conversations, he granted me this permission.

Although Loren did not allow me immediate access to his holdings of photographs, letters, and journals, he informed me that his materials and those owned by his sister, Betty, had already been photocopied by professors Candace Kant and Joe Wheeler, and he encouraged me to contact them. Both responded warmly to my letters and agreed to share what they had. Candace did an enormous amount of photocopying and mailed me several huge boxes that included many helpful books and articles. Joe invited me to visit him, and provided me a room in which to examine his carefully catalogued materials. Not only was his library impressive, but he freely shared with me all that he had found and learned as well.

Further investigation carried me to Pat Friese, the daughter of Claire Wilhelm Carlin. When I contacted her and asked if she knew about Claire's relationship with Zane Grey, she said that she indeed did and was positively excited that I was interested in her mother. She told me immediately about her many letters and photographs as well as the ten journals that Claire had written during her trips with Zane. She invited me to see everything and, shortly after I arrived, I learned that Elma and Dorothy had been frequent visitors to her home while she was growing up. Pat recalled their animated conversations with her mother and convinced me that they lost little of their spunk as they aged. She spent a whole summer with her aunt Lillian in Arizona. She was pleased that I thought her mother and her friends were remarkable women. Better still, as I cautiously informed her about their unconventional lives, she grew even prouder of them.

George Houle and Dan Brock were equally generous. George has bought and sold Grey materials for years. I explained that I was a scholar and not a collector, and he nonetheless allowed me first to examine his extensive holdings and later to quote from them. Dan Brock and his friend Stan Vath are collectors of tackle and own many rare and unusual items. When I called for information about Grey's 18/0 reel, I learned that he had a large collection of Grey materials that ranged far beyond tackle. I was lucky enough to visit him during a major exhibition of his fishing tackle. Bridget McMahon not only enlightened me about the typescript that launched my investigations but also showed me many letters that she had not included. However, the high point of my peregrinations was the day that X (who asked that his name be withheld) allowed me to see his collection of photographs and journals that confirmed and far exceeded my long-standing suspicions.

Although very few of Grey's letters and journals were in library archives when I initiated my research, I nevertheless incurred a huge debt to librarians along the way. Ben Helle promptly answered my early questions about the Grey materials at the Ohio Historical Society and Liz Plummer responded quickly to more recent appeals from me. At the Beinecke Library, George Miles and Leigh Golden did all they could to ensure that my visits went smoothly and gained me the information I was seeking. I also wish to thank the staff at the Cline Library at the University of Northern Arizona; Gail Morshower, the librarian at the IGA Museum; Mary Francis Travelli at the

Los Angeles Maritime Museum; Leila Wiles at the library of the Izaak Walton League; Dorothy Moon at the Zane Grey Museum (Lackawaxen); Frank Slaughter at the Archives of the Church of Christ of the Latter Day Saints; Edna Smith at the Altadena Historical Society; Ralph Getson at the Maritime Museum, Lunenburg, Nova Scotia; Gail Myker, local history librarian in Middletown, N.Y.; Tim Miller at Flatsigned Books; and especially the interlibrary loan staff at the library of the University of Delaware. The Free Library was an invaluable resource for rare books and obscure periodicals and I hope that the city of Philadelphia will continue to fund this magnificent cornerstone of its cultural heritage.

Many individuals contributed to this book. Professor Philip Rulon, who published a sampling of the letters of Dolly and Zane in the *Missouri Review* and then mailed me a photocopy of Bridget McMahon's typescript, belongs at the top of this list, but I am grateful as well to Donna Ashworth, Robert Ebbeskotte, Mike Farrior, David Karpeles, Harvey Leake, Charles Mangnum, Ed Pritchett, Rose Jane Rudicel, Anthony Slide, Jon Tuska, and my colleagues George Basalla, Carl Dawson, Kevin Kerrane, Drury Pifer, and Stan Weintraub who read portions of my book and offered helpful suggestions. Jerry Beasley, who gave generously of his precious time, provided exceptional advice and encouragement at a low point in this project. I am also indebted to several students who uncovered valuable information that I have used: Karen Baltz, Eliza Cogbill, Julie Goodwin, Jennifer Herst, Brian Packett, Carly Riskus, Joanna Schumacher, and Danielle Sepulveres.

Finally I want to acknowledge the financial support I have received from the University of Delaware and my three travel grants from the Historical Society of Southern California. I don't know what I would have done without my good friend Keith Markolf who always let me stay with him during my visits to Los Angeles and had to listen to ever more about Zane.

Illustrations

ZANE GREY

Introduction

"Most people are as they are. You can't change them.
I change always. But then I am not normal,
not ordinary in any sense."

—Zane Grey, Letter to Claire Wilhelm Carlin,
    September 3, 1932

On October 22, 1939, Zane Grey's wife of thirty-four years, Dolly Grey, responded to a note of condolence from Dan Beard, a distant friend, who had written when he learned about Zane's death:

> My thanks to you and Mrs. Beard for your letter of sympathy. Zane's passing was so sudden and unexpected that I can't realize it. Somehow, it seems to me that he is just away on one of those adventurous trips he loved so much—and perhaps he is.
>
> It was splendid of you to say that you considered Zane a man of great genius. I know that he was, but I also know that it takes a man of great genius to recognize one of his ilk.[1]

Given the remarkable success of her husband's career, the defensiveness in Dolly's comment about her husband's "genius" is surprising. Grey was *the* best-selling author in America during the 1920s and a major contributor to the Western genre's rise in popularity. In nine of the ten years from 1915 through 1924, Grey had a new novel among the top ten best-selling novels for the entire year.[2] Moreover, Westerns of his from before and after these dates achieved the monthly list.[3] At the time of his death, Harpers, his publisher since *The Heritage of the Desert* (1910), estimated that sales of his novels exceeded 17,000,000 copies.[4] "The greatest selling author of all time," its press release of this information claimed. "In sales Zane Grey is exceeded only by the Bible and the Boy Scout Handbook."

The extraordinary commercial demand for Grey's books did not bring commensurate critical respect. Reviewers regularly condemned his novels, and their hostility was intensified by his success. By the time of his death, this animus was so virulent that it infected his obituaries, and made Dolly grateful for Beard's kind praise for her husband. Grey's obituary in the *New York Times* included this negative appraisal from fifteen years before: "His art is archaic, with all the traits of archaic art. His style . . . has the stiffness that comes from an imperfect mastery of the medium. It lacks fluency or facility; behind it always we feel a pressure toward expression, a striving for a freer and easier utterance."[5] The overlap of Grey's death with that of Opie Read, another Western author, moved Burton Rascoe to write a reflection for the prestigious *Saturday Review* in which he praised Read and bludgeoned Grey: "It is difficult to imagine any writer having less merit in either style or substance than Grey and still maintaining an audience at all."[6]

The mean spirit of these last respects gave the *New York Times* second thoughts, and elicited a special editorial in defense of Grey—one, however, that did not relinquish its low opinion of his novels: "Grey's novels were immensely popular. It is easy to sniff at his work; nonetheless it was honest work. He thought and wrote clearly. Whatever of the conventional melodramatic lay in his subject or his method, his books are of the clean and bracing outdoors. Therefore they are as odious as tracts to those who want their literary diet copiously peppered. Wouldn't a little tolerance in these matters be useful?"[7] Although it had ignored his work for years, the *New Yorker* was likewise bothered by this ill will in Grey's death notices, and countered with praise that was less qualified and more appropriate: "We do not like the haughty tone the *Herald Tribune* has seen fit to adopt in speaking of the late Zane Grey. The critics, it remarks loftily, will eventually reduce him to the position of one 'who also wrote.' Come, gentlemen. This was a great writer, rich in invention, prodigal with his action, juicily romantic."[8]

Contrary to the negative assessments of these critics, Grey was, in fact, a skillful writer who combined easy readability with artful embellishment. He was justifiably wounded by negative appraisals of his work. In the Western, he found an outlet for his considerable talent and strong beliefs in the spiritual value of the outdoors. Grey did not invent the Western, but he did profoundly influence both the popularity of the genre for most of the twentieth century and the more durable appeal of the West as alternative culture. Other writers like Bret Harte and Frank Norris wrote about the West before him, but Grey's romantic stories ranged beyond the actual locales and authentic history and made the region fabled and legendary. His fantasies became those of the nation.

Public libraries keep Grey's Westerns on their shelves today because their patrons regularly check them out, but few of them realize that when he started to write, the Western was not the genre we take for granted, and the Southwest was still a vast wasteland devoid of water, people, and cultural value for those who lived elsewhere. He was neither the first nor the only writer to see the rich potential in these limitations, but he was without equal in transforming the area's hot, dusty landscape into grand, colorful settings for exciting, eventful dramas. One of the reasons his stories were more believable and compelling when they first appeared than today is because their locus then was so far away from and so unlike the developed, humdrum, workday world of the East.

His poetic descriptions of desert conditions and the myriad changes wrought by the sun's movement and quick shifts in weather rendered them variably wondrous and menacing. His chases and stampedes, in conjunction with his gunslingers and outlaws, transformed this atmospheric stage set into a gymnasium where men were tested and cured of ailments acquired from too much civilization. His books showed that one of the greatest benefits of this locale was its prospect for romance: the recurring likelihood that his rehabilitated hero would find there a woman who was his equal, whose interests and capabilities had been similarly enlarged, and whose responsiveness and loyalty inspired confidence that their love would be fulfilling and would endure.

Although Grey's Westerns were seminal in getting people all over the world to believe that the arid American Southwest was especially panoramic and conducive to vigorous activity and romance, he could never have accomplished this Herculean feat by himself. He can only be understood and appreciated in terms of his connection to an emerging popular culture that was bigger and more influential than any individual writer. A large measure of his achievement came from being ahead of a mammoth wave of popular in-

3

terest in his material. Behind his work and looming over it was a formidable entertainment industry just discovering the value of best sellers and the appeal of movies. This carnival of entertainment showered Grey with wealth, but shackled him to its demands. He was repeatedly frustrated by a publishing industry that disliked his attempts at innovation as much as his critics. Early on, he recognized the cinematic potential of his work, but he never understood the filmmaking industry. He deeply regretted his outright sale of film rights to his early Westerns, and failed to grasp how much his novels benefited from the multiple remakes that his "mistake" made possible. The filmmaker whom he initially entrusted with his stories was a hustler whom Jesse Lasky and Adolph Zukor, the wily founders of Paramount, had already outmaneuvered and doomed to failure. When Zane Grey Pictures lurched toward bankruptcy, Paramount took over the foundering company and shrewdly marketed Grey's work like chilled soft drinks for a thirsty audience.

Despite the many hours he spent writing his books in longhand, Grey's life was as "juicily romantic" as any of his novels, and far more unusual. Had he not been a talented baseball player, he never would have attended college—an education that trained him to be a dentist. In 1903, at the age of thirty, he quit dentistry to become a writer. His first five years of feverish work yielded meager pay, and five more brought only a living wage. His black depressions over his slow progress were alleviated by a passionate love of the outdoors and adventure. In 1906, Grey and his wife took a honeymoon trip to the Grand Canyon, and saw it during the early stages of its development into a tourist attraction. In 1907 and 1908, at a critical juncture in his early career and prior to Arizona's achievement of statehood, he returned to the Grand Canyon for two hunting trips for mountain lions and was among the first to travel its new backcountry trails. These trips started him writing Westerns and inspired many more return visits. He was one of the first white men to reach the Rainbow Bridge, and more than twenty years before John Ford discovered the magnificence of Monument Valley, Grey actively campaigned to have his Westerns filmed there.

Grey also avidly pursued saltwater fishing in Tampico, Mexico; Long Key, Florida; and Catalina, California. During the 1920s, his lust for "virgin seas" and his determination to catch the biggest fish carried him to Nova Scotia, the Galapagos Islands, New Zealand, Tahiti, and Australia. These trips garnered him a dozen world records; he was the first person to land a 1,000-pound fish on sporting tackle. His nine books about these adventures, all entitled "Tales of . . .," contain some of his best writing; they remain in print and deservedly so.

Grey in Arizona, 1920. (Courtesy of Loren Grey.)

Left to right: Mildred Fergerson, Lillian Wilhelm, Claire Wilhelm, and Zane Grey at Long Key, 1916. (Courtesy of Pat Friese.)

For a person of such range and accomplishment, it is remarkable that his life remains so little-known and misunderstood. Currently, the chief source of information is a biography that is outdated and long out of print—Frank Gruber's *Zane Grey: A Biography* (1970).[9] Gruber started his project as an ailing author of popular Westerns and actually died before the biography was published. Gruber made little effort to distinguish the specious and anecdotal from the true; important information was sloppily handled and intentionally ignored. Gruber was also recruited to write this biography by the Grey family, which pressured him to uphold the wholesome image of the author promoted by his publishers and to gloss over or suppress the problematic aspects of his life.

Grey had a troubled youth, and he was deeply scarred by his father's slide into poverty and his family's decline from its distinguished heritage. As a young man, he was sensitive, reserved, and antisocial, and later he became outspoken and reactionary. He disliked cities, vehemently opposed drinking and smoking, and repeatedly criticized modern development.

Grey was profligate with his money and often used overspending as an incentive to work. In 1913, after renting a spacious apartment in New York City for the upcoming winter, he wrote to Dolly, "I've got to touch Rome [Zane's brother] or somebody for some coin, and then work like hell and I'm grimly settled in mind on the latter."[10] By 1920, when his annual income surpassed $100,000, he was so pleased with his two-year experiment with California living that he purchased a grand residence in Altadena. That same year, he acquired another house in Catalina, a ranch in Arizona, and an expensive new boat. Five years later, when Zane purchased a grand schooner and initiated costly renovations, Dolly indignantly wrote to him:

> Now about the ship. Never knew you were even looking at more than one so your telegram was somewhat puzzling. However, the part about depositing the $10,000 for you by Sept. 1st was clear enough. I'll do it, tho it will pretty well clean me out. Not a cent came in since you left and the only money you have given me in months is that $9,000 just before you left . . . According to the N.Y. Times you are having your boat refitted in N.Y. Why? When labor was so infinitely cheaper in Nova Scotia? Did anyone ever tell you that it would cost you a fortune to bring that boat through the canal? It cost the *Manchuria* $11,000 for a single trip. Well, Pa's rich and Ma don't care! That is, if the children don't starve.[11]

Her irony and ire could not constrain his determination to have what he wanted.

Zane Grey in front of the house in which he grew up, during his 1921 visit to Zanesville. (Courtesy of Loren Grey.)

By the Depression, Grey's profligate spending was so ingrained and so excessive that it almost ruined him. Despite widespread signs of a national financial crisis, an unmistakable drop in demand for his work, and objections from his wife, he purchased another yacht for $50,000 in 1930 and then spent $300,000 on renovations. This would be approximately three and a half million in today's dollars, but an even better measure of this sum might be the $80,000 that Babe Ruth earned in 1931, a salary that provoked controversy because he was paid $5,000 more than the president of the United States.[12] Added to the debt that Grey was already carrying, this yacht decimated his finances and necessitated that he cut short his most ambitious fishing trip, intended to circle the world. For the next four years, he hovered precariously close to breakdown and bankruptcy.

Over the course of his life, Grey also offended many people. He so antagonized members of the prestigious Tuna Club in southern California that they conspired to drive him away. After the citizens of New Zealand staged an extravagant welcome for him on the occasion of his visit, he publicly de-

8

nounced their primitive methods of fishing. When Arizona refused him a special exemption from its hunting regulations, he angrily proclaimed that he would never again return to the state in which so many of his novels had been set. Inevitably, and inexorably, his dark moods, competitiveness, and self-absorption drove away almost everyone he ever befriended. Laurie Mitchell served him longer than any of his other boat captains, but his seven years of loyalty did not prevent Grey from summarily firing him. Grey was so grateful to Alvah James for his example and advice when he started out as a writer that he allowed him to occupy his Lackawaxen residence for years, but his abrasive letters to James suggest that their friendship only endured because they were never around each other. Grey's deep attachment to his younger brother extended from childhood outings through many trips together as adults, but even R. C. eventually had to distance himself.

Dolly was the one person who remained steadfastly loyal to Grey, and her observation to Beard that it took "great genius to recognize one of [Zane's] ilk" was at once self-congratulatory and characteristically self-effacing. She understood better than anyone else the full measure of her husband's uniqueness and its staggering demands. During their courtship, she initially won his love by supporting his ambition to write and allaying his crippling doubts. In one of his earliest letters, Grey wrote to her:

> On the stone I shall engrave:
> Here lies a man, to fame unknown;
> Who on the wings of love was blown,
> To suffer for the sins he'd sown.
> What an epitaph for the greatest might-have-been in
>   American letters.[13]

Dolly approved of Zane's wrenching decision to quit dentistry and ably assisted his ferocious struggle to get his work published. Her modest inheritance financed the two Arizona trips that transformed him into an author of Westerns.

Dolly accommodated herself to "those adventurous trips he loved so much." From the East in the spring of 1922, Zane wrote to her: "We are not going to see a great deal of each other this year, I'm sorry to say. And this letter is to ask you to help me make the best of what we have. A little time in April—in August—in November."[14] His ensuing voyages to New Zealand, Tahiti, and Australia kept him away six to nine months each year thereafter, and much of his time back in the United States was also spent away from home.

Most extraordinarily, Dolly accepted "the girls." With this, more than with all the other things that she did for Zane, she demonstrated that she possessed the "great genius to recognize one of his ilk" and that her genius was as peculiar as her husband's. Grey was extremely handsome and charming to women. He had many sexual adventures while growing up and during his years as a baseball player. At sixteen, he was arrested in a brothel, and several years later he was charged with a paternity suit. He had affairs with other women throughout his five-year courtship of Dolly and after their marriage. In 1913, he took two female cousins of Dolly on his first trip to the Rainbow Bridge, perhaps the most memorable trip of his life. With an outfitter he trusted and an Indian who pioneered the route, he and his companions traversed a labyrinth of canyons and treacherous terrain in northern Arizona to a remote natural arch first seen by whites only four years before. He perceived the awesome Rainbow Bridge as validation for the adventure in his novels, for the spiritual transcendence he associated with the West, and for his yearning for romance.

Thereafter, women regularly accompanied him on his trips, sometimes as many as four. The few scholars aware of these relationships have assumed that they were paternal and platonic,[15] but they were, in fact, romantic and sexual. There exists an enormous, totally unknown cache of photographs taken by Grey of nude women and himself performing various sexual activities, including intercourse. Of the women discussed in this book, only Nola Luxford and Lola Gornall are not in this collection. These photographs are accompanied by ten small journals, written in Grey's secret code, that contain graphic descriptions of his sexual adventures.[16]

Dolly knew about these relationships and accepted an "open marriage" long before the term existed. She and Zane never divorced and each professed love for the other up to their deaths. Their marriage was not only unusual, but also crucial to his fragile health and his success as a writer. Dolly supervised the business side of Zane's career for years, and her decisions averted bankruptcy during the 1930s. She accepted his suspect claims that his trips and women alleviated his depressions and inspired him to write. Although these affairs provoked considerable anguish and sharp-tongued complaints, Dolly consistently accepted them, sometimes in ways that were remarkable. She remained close friends with some of his companions, and even allowed several to stay in her home. She intervened on Zane's behalf when the romances foundered, and maintained friendships with some of these women for many years after his death. She was faithful Penelope, steadfastly loyal to her restless, driven Odysseus.

Obviously, Dolly was an unusual woman, and most of the "other women" were too. Contrary to the easy assumption that they were foolish, weak, or exploited, Grey's paramours were usually vivacious, outgoing, broad-minded, and unconventional. In an era when marriage was the rule and alternatives were limited and unappealing, these women chose to be different. They had a relish for adventure that Dolly lacked, but admired. Their openness to sex came with an enthusiasm for primitive conditions and outdoor sports that only men were supposed to like. Grey's published accounts of his adventures seldom mention these women, in part to mask his involvement with them, but also to uphold the prevalent belief that outdoor sports were a male preserve.

If the unusualness of these women was greatest in their capitulation to Zane's needs and wants, none was as accepting as Dolly. Some balked at his uncompromising need for others. Some needed other partners too. Some objected to the time he spent away from them; others were offended by his returns home. Some could not endure the inconsistency of his attention to them; others left because of the stifling heat, seasickness, and poor food. Dolly outlasted them all because she best understood Zane and effectively used her knowledge to help and hold him. She realized that human nature, common sense, and the world conspired against his grandiose dreams. As she once confessed to a mutual friend: "I must admit that I am looking at the book [a new Zane novel] through the bias of Zane's hurt. Don't laugh! The man has always lived in a land of make-believe, and has clothed all his own affairs in the shining garments of romance, and it is as if these were rent and torn and smirched."[17]

Zane's depressions were such that, had he yielded to them, they could have prevented him from completing a single novel. That he endured so much anguish and completed so many books is remarkable. Set against his enormous investment in trips and women, his output is amazing. Grey's unquenchable need for escape, inspiration, and romance kept him searching for more Rainbow Bridges. Dolly accepted his women and travel as necessary and therapeutic, but she also realized that they could aggravate his depressions, and did so many times. Thus when her Ulysses returned with his garments "rent and torn and smirched," loyal Penelope put aside her misgivings and repaired the damage so that he could resume his unending quest.

I

Wayward Youth: 1872–90

"We all have in our hearts the kingdom of adventure.
Somewhere in the depths of every soul is the inheritance
of the primitive. I speak to that."
—My Own Life

Pearl Zane Gray's pioneer heritage was imprinted on his consciousness with the name his parents gave him at his birth on January 31, 1872. Anecdotal histories report his given name of Pearl as derived from the mourning attire of Queen Victoria that newspapers regularly described as "pearl gray." Although Pearl may also have been named after a distant relative, his unusual, female name caused much taunting and embarrassment. Eventually he dropped it, though not until his twenties, and long after the spelling of his last name had been changed from Gray to Grey. His middle name of Zane, by which he would be known as a writer, did come from his family background. His mother was a Zane—and proud of her family lineage that extended back to Ebenezer Zane, a patriot colonel during the Revolutionary War, and his heroic sister Betty.

Although Grey believed that his ancestry was Danish, Robert Zane, a Quaker, carried the family name to the New World in 1673 from England, and he resided at various locations in New Jersey. His grandson William Zane chose to marry outside the religion and he was so ostracized that he relocated to Hardy County, West Virginia, not far from that state's current border with Virginia. Ebenezer, William's second son, was born on October 7, 1747, and three more sons followed—Silas, Jonathan, and Isaac. The Zane brothers became explorers and quickly adapted to the fluctuating alliances of local Indian tribes—mainly the Wyandots and Delawares. Around 1757–58, Jonathan and Isaac were kidnapped by Indians and lived with them for several years. Following a successful escape, Isaac returned and married Myeerah, the daughter of a Wyandot chief.[1]

In 1768, Ebenezer married Elizabeth McColloch. She and her four brothers, who were also adept woodsmen, were reputed to be half-Indian and instilled in the young Zane a lifelong belief that he carried Indian blood.[2] A year later, following the birth of the first of the couple's twelve children and ratification of a treaty that opened southeastern Ohio to settlement, Ebenezer, Silas, and Jonathan explored and claimed two miles of property on each side of the Ohio River near Wheeling, West Virginia.[3] In 1770, Ebenezer brought his family to Wheeling, and he participated in the construction of Fort Fincastle there in 1774. During the Revolutionary War, he led a successful defense of the fort, renamed Fort Henry, against several British and Indian attacks. A final assault on September 12, 1782, exhausted the defenders' stock of gunpowder, and Betty Zane saved the day by running a gauntlet of gunfire and returning with a new supply.[4] Grey's first three novels would memorialize the heroism of these distant relatives.[5]

Following the Revolutionary War, Ebenezer hunted and did little to develop his property. A New England merchant who visited him in 1789 observed that he made "money very fast but live[d] poor." Twenty years after his original claims, his holdings were still characterized as "fronttear," and he had acquired a bad reputation for his foul temper.[6] When his seventeen-year-old daughter Sarah received a marriage proposal from John McIntire, who was eighteen years older, Ebenezer forbade the marriage and huffed off for an extended hunting trip. During his absence, the two married anyway.

Despite these faults, Ebenezer stayed vigilant for commercial opportunity. He shrewdly perceived the 1795 Treaty of Greenville as a golden opportunity for "a good Wagon road." He petitioned Congress to establish a major throughway from Wheeling, West Virginia, to Maysville, Kentucky, and to compensate him for his military service with parcels of land suitable for ferry crossings on the Muskingum, Hocking, and Scioto rivers. Approval of these requests in 1796 produced two memorials to his name—Zane's Trace and the town of Zanesville on the Muskingum River. Ensuing modification of the original route, along with extensive improvement over the next twenty years, created the National Road, the country's first highway. The National Road established Zanesville as a commercial center for outlying farms, and it remained so when Zane's parents moved there around the time of the Civil War.[7]

Alice Josephine Zane, Zane's mother, was born on September 5, 1835, to Ebenezer's son, Samuel Zane, who inherited property from his father in Ohio across the river from Wheeling.[8] Little is known about Samuel's life beyond entries in local records that eleven of his twelve children were born there and that he served for several years on the local school board. Alice met her future husband, Lewis Gray, when she was visiting a sister who had married and relocated to Westmoreland County, where Grays had worked as farmers for several generations.

Liggett Gray, Zane's paternal grandfather, grew up in Westmoreland County, and resettled to a farm near Zanesville shortly before his marriage to Nancy Guttridge on April 3, 1816.[9] In June of the following year, they had the first of their thirteen children. Lewis, their eighth child, was born July 10, 1831.[10] He and his three older brothers worked Liggett's farm with the expectation that they too would be farmers. The two children who preceded Lewis and the one who followed were daughters, and a brief family history written years later by Ida Grey, Zane's sister, claimed that Lewis was "petted and spoiled" by his sisters.[11]

Lewis undoubtedly met Alice Josephine through relatives in Westmoreland County. They married on February 5, 1856, and did not have their first child until five years later.[12] Their life together was a far cry from the eventfulness and glory of Ebenezer's. Ida's family history claims that her father owned a "fine farm" at the time of his marriage, but sometime around the birth of their first son Ellsworth in 1861, Lewis made a momentous, life-altering decision that foreshadowed a similar one by Zane: Lewis hated farming so much that he quit to become a dentist instead. Prior to the Civil War, dentistry was more a trade than a profession, and so Lewis moved to Zanesville to apprentice himself to John Hobbs, who had been a gunsmith prior to taking up dentistry.[13] When he completed his training, Lewis opened an office on Main Street. Though he changed his Main Street address several times, he remained in Zanesville for the next thirty years, and his next four children were born there. Ella (1867), who came a year after Ida (1866), was beautiful and a favorite of her parents, but she died suddenly on February 7, 1871. An entry in the record book of the town cemetery communicates the family's

Earliest photograph of Zane Grey. Taken by a professional photographer in Delphos, Ohio, ca. 1893. (Courtesy of Loren Grey.)

grief with its notation that she was "four years and twenty days old."[14] Pearl Zane Gray was born a year later on January 31, 1872. Romer, nicknamed "R. C." and Zane's closest friend for many years, followed on April 8, 1875.

Having been raised in rural Ohio, Lewis, like Ebenezer and his brothers, was a hunter, and he introduced Zane to the woods at an early age. Though he was marginally literate ("I never [k]new a card"), he wanted to write, as a surviving poem about his dead mother and an account of his woodland walks verify.[15] Religion was also important to Lewis. He attempted to be an itinerant preacher prior to taking up dentistry, and he taught regularly at the Mission Sunday School while Zane was growing up. A surviving three-page autobiography attests to his fundamentalist beliefs. In this curious document, which may have been written for a church event, Lewis announces his trust in the Lord, the importance of moral training, and the triumph of his faith and hard work over his lack of education. He states that at the age of seven, he resolved to "be good, do good, and make something of his life," and that at twelve, he vowed never to swear or drink. He maintains that temperance, morality, and religion enabled him "to rise in the world." "I love cultured, talented society," he admits, "but have had a hard struggle to get there. What I am I made myself, a self made man."[16] Despite Lewis's fervent efforts to appear humble, his testimony contains telltale hints of the resolve and sternness that Zane would later resent.

Through his drive and hard work, Lewis was able to develop a successful dental practice and to construct a modest residence in one of the most desirable areas of Zanesville. In Zane's earliest attempt at autobiography, a 1918 letter to a clairvoyant named Anna Andre, he claimed that he grew up in "comparative poverty" and initiated a misleading impression of deprivation that has persisted in accounts of his life since. From his birth in Zanesville until he was seventeen years old and the family relocated to Columbus, Zane lived in the family residence that was constructed in 1871 at 303 Convers Avenue (currently 705). This area of Zanesville was originally named "McIntire Terrace" after John McIntire, the son-in-law whom Ebenezer initially disliked, but later favored over all the other members of his family. In 1799, Ebenezer had him lay out the town of Zanesville. Called simply "the Terrace" by the time the Grays moved there, this large hilltop plateau overlooked the Muskingum River and the historic bridge connecting it to the town center. This was prime real estate, and it remains so to this day. Across the street and on both sides of the Gray house are large historic dwellings built of brick and stone that are attractive and still command high prices. By comparison, the two-story clapboard Gray home looks plain and austere—that of an interloper aspiring to status its owner cannot afford. Twentieth-century photographs of this house do suggest impoverishment, but they also fail to convey the affluence of the surrounding area or to hint at the respectable salary Lewis was making while the family lived there.

The year before his death, Zane drew upon this letter and several other short articles about his life and expanded them into a little-known autobiography entitled "The Living Past." Not published until forty-five years later in an obscure journal, this unfinished account covers his life through his first year of college, and it is the primary, almost exclusive, source of information about his early years.[17] For an author of fiction, Grey was unusually honest and reliable in writing about himself, but he was also an accomplished storyteller sensitive to the expectations of his audience and anxious that his life appear colorful and attractive. His candid admission that he was wayward and delinquent as a boy capitalized on the fact that these traits in a boy were widely regarded as healthy and normal. He exploited the image of the young roughneck so successfully that readers are more likely to notice his prowess and potential and to miss the pain. His presentation resembles *The Adventures of Tom Sawyer* so much that Grey appears to have used Twain's classic as a model; the young Zane has an uncanny number of Sawyer's traits. Like Tom, he dislikes school and is a poor student. His enthusiasm for manly stories suggests that his scholastic aptitude is misrepresented by his failing grades. He too commits petty thefts, feuds with rivals, and disobeys adults. His thirst for adventure carries him away from school and home. His flights to the woods express rebellion and enable him to escape misunderstanding, unwanted responsibilities, and damaging criticism. There he finds the one place where he can be himself and do as he pleases. Twain had done such a good job of convincing adults that this kind of behavior was the stuff of boyhood that the young Zane and his experiences seem normal, even conventional. However, Grey's account is much darker and depicts a seriously troubled boy.

"The Living Past" does not hide the fact that Zane was alienated from others, with more enemies than friends. Although he enjoyed privilege, he was inclined to befriend those lower on the social scale. Zanesville's modest size made it necessary for him to attend grade school at the Eighth Ward School along with working-class children who "did not think much of the boys from the Terrace." He preferred "these rough appearing boys" and their unruly conduct, but their surly response to him and his superior status made acceptance impossible (1, 7). This friction was worsened by his enthusiasm for baseball and the formation of local teams by district. Grouped with boys from the Terrace, he strove to best opponents and did not bond with his teammates. Grey comments, "I knew I was misunderstood and unappreciated and the object of jealousy to some of the boys of the best families" (5, 5).

Zane's many fights worsened this displacement. He hurled himself into combat with disturbing relish and ferocity, flinging stones without regard for potential injury. He relates how he toppled a boy with a brick (3, 5), and another one was lucky to survive a rock bounced off his temple (5, 9), yet this good fortune did not prevent Zane from striking another behind the ear and sending him to the hospital (6, 7). He knocked a rival into a ravine so that he "plunged down in a most alarming manner" (3, 5), and he kicked another in the face "with all my might" (3, 8). He so enraged one adversary that he returned with a rifle intent upon shooting Grey (3, 8). This penchant for violence spilled over into his thievery. He chased down a neighbor's chickens, clubbed them to death, and cooked them in tin cans over an open fire.[18] Years later, a female classmate wrote to him, "I am truly glad to know that 'the wild boy' I once knew has outlived that wildness."[19]

Lewis Grey, date unknown. (Courtesy of Loren Grey.)

Any parent would have faced a formidable challenge with a son like this, but Zane's father obviously made matters worse. His demanding work ethic antagonized his son. Zane disliked having to clean the office, mow the yard, and work as a shoe salesman. His resentment over the obligations imposed by his father outweighed the value of whatever money he received. Moreover, his father's harsh response to his delinquency aggravated it. At the outset of his account, Grey recalls how his father insisted on being fanned during his Sunday naps and punished his son for slipping away when he went to sleep. In winter, his father sent him to gather fresh snow for a drink, and he was so displeased with what he brought back that Zane was sent for more until after dark and he became frightened (1, 5).

Grey recalls, "I had many a poignant acquaintance with the apple switch" (3, 1), and some of these beatings were harsh and abusive. In one egregious example of his father's harshness, Zane relates how he and his friends built a pirate's club and there, during idle hours, he wrote a short narrative called "Jim of the Cave" on pieces of wallpaper. When his father discovered Zane's hideout, he angrily hurled this first story into the campfire and then inflicted "the worst [whipping] I ever had" (6, 11). Another time, Zane was so outraged over "a terrific whack with a good stiff willow stick" that he fled up a seventy-five-foot tree. When his father threatened a worse beating, he furiously bounced on a large limb until it cracked and nearly broke, terrifying both of them (3, 4). These beatings are never linked to Zane's many fights, but it is hard for a modern reader not to connect them. Years later, when his own son Romer announced that he was going to run away from home and steal a horse, Zane was intimidated by the threat "because I had made worse to my father, and carried it out."[20]

Lewis's anger was not directed only at his wayward son. His father so abused visiting salesmen that Zane was deeply embarrassed (7, 5). An obituary affirms this harshness in its characterization of Lewis as "rather peculiar," "very positive in his likes and dislikes," and "somewhat cranky."[21]

Zane's characterization of his father in "The Living Past" contrasts with his affectionate references to his understanding mother. Though she is mentioned only in passing, his comments about her are uniformly positive. Her "soft dove eyes" and "gentle smile" (1, 8) communicate nurturing support. "My mother was sweeter and kinder than ever" (6, 10), he observes at one point, and earlier notes how she "divined my feelings and sought to comfort me" (5, 5). An observation by Dolly in a letter from their courtship reveals more about Zane's feelings than any of these comments: "I fell all over in love with you again when I saw how nice you were to your mother."[22]

An aged fisherman named Muddy Miser is presented as even more of a foil to Lewis Gray. Miser was an obvious vehicle for discussing his early interest in fishing, but Grey accentuates his difference from his stern, hardworking father. During a trip when he was only eight, Zane saw his first fish. From his excited conversation with his mother, he learned about Miser. When she characterized the stream containing the fish as "a bad place," Zane pressed for more explanation. Groping for "the unfavorable impression that she knew would have pleased my father," she informed him that Miser, who frequented the stream, was "a lazy, good-for-nothing fisherman" (1, 6). During a later outing, Lewis directed Zane's attention to a poorhouse frequented by Miser and warned, "If you don't learn to like work and study that's where you will end up" (1, 7).

Zane's building resentment toward his father discredited these negative appraisals and attracted him to this fellow outcast. Grey's description of his first sighting of Miser is both poetic and mythic:

> I was amazed to look up and see the strange figure of a man standing way out there where the water poured over the long fall. He stood up to his bare knees in the current that foamed around his legs. He was an old man, gaunt and bowed, and he pointed a long pole out over the swift water (1, 9).

Later, when boys from the Terrace taunted the old man for his poverty and hurled rocks at him, Zane impulsively rushed to his defense and got into one of his most violent fights (3, 7). In the meeting with Miser that followed, Zane fastened upon the old man's "weary sad eyes" and "mild and soft-spoken" demeanor (3, 8–9), so different from his father's "piercing gray eyes" (1, 7) and abrasiveness. Thereafter, from their many conversations about fishing, Zane learned so much about life that he judged Miser to be his best teacher. The old man encouraged him to admit his animosity toward work, dentistry, and, most of all, his father. Miser's approval of the fishing and writing that his father condemned helped Zane to follow his heart, disregard the expectations of the Terrace, and trust that he would "become somebody someday" (4, 7). This portrait of Miser suggests that he also strongly influenced the alternative fathers depicted in Zane's novels.

If Muddy Miser was the father he preferred and someone who approved of his wishes, there was more Lewis in Zane than he acknowledged. He too would be opinionated, irascible, and antisocial. Later, with his fishing, he sought advancement and distinction as well as relaxation; his articles about his adventures were written for money and to augment his reputation. Even his criticisms of his father and his unreasonable expectations served to make him likewise "a self-made man." As he admitted in his 1918 letter to Anna Andre, "I did inherit much from him [Lewis]."[23]

If Zane's battles with his rivals and his father differentiate his youth from Tom Sawyer's, this distinction is even more striking in his response to the opposite sex. Most readers of "The Living Past" are struck by Zane's preoccupation with fishing, but, oddly enough, do not notice the attention lavished upon his girlfriends. Twain, of course, gave Tom Becky Thatcher, but he scrupulously avoided sexuality. Grey, on the other hand, makes his sexual experience central and important.

The earliest surviving example of Zane's writing is a verse he wrote in an autograph book for Anna Oldham at the age of twelve:

> Friend Anna
> Remember this and bear in mind
> A good beau is hard to find.
> But if you find one gentle and gay
> Hang to his coat tail night and day.
> But if your hand should choose to slip
> Catch another and let him rip.
>> Yours truly
>> Pearl Gray[24]

Despite the obvious flirtation in this exercise of wit, Grey claims in "The Living Past" that that he was not interested in the opposite sex until he was fourteen. At this age he suddenly developed "an unaccountable fascination" with social functions that opened to him "all that was wonderful and mystical and alluring about girls" (3, 9). One of his first parties involved a parlor game in which a girl with a pillow selected a boy from those encircling her, dropped her pillow before him, knelt upon it, and received a kiss. This game produced Grey's first kisses, and his extended description of them makes clear that they were uplifting, upsetting, and momentous. A kiss from "Pet" transfixed him until he was rudely jolted from his reverie by everyone's laughter. As the game continued, Grey was bypassed several times. Eventually, a girl named Alice hesitantly approached, dropped her pillow before him, and looked up sweetly for a kiss. Although he had never spoken to her, he knew from others that she had never been kissed. Her kiss, he writes, "burned like sweet fire on my lips," but this time the crowd's jocular reaction upset him so much that he fled home early (3, 9–10).

Later that same summer, Grey attended another party at which "the boys were wilder [and] the girls freer." Instead of playing games, they danced, paired up, and left for walks in the woods. "Somehow I liked this better," he confesses. There he met Maud, who was a year older, had "audacious hazel eyes," and wore a "tight fitting dress of blue." When they left for the woods together, she "met my timid hand more than half way" and so too his "further advances." His transport over this experience ended when he learned that Maud was a flirt who "acted precisely the same" with other boys (3, 10).

Zane was confused and troubled by his intense attraction to girls who were so different from each other. Muddy Miser counseled him that he could either support the "noble ideal of womanhood" or turn women into a "great evil" (4, 8). Unfortunately, his smoldering desires made Miser's advice hard to follow. Grey remarks, "I could not cast the girls out of my heart" (3, 11), admitting a defeat that was worsened by its betrayal of his fundamentalist morality. His "contemptible weakness for girls" (3, 11) made kissing both shameful and irresistible. When his lust overcame his reservations, he discovered that the virtuous Alice and flirtatious Maud harbored similar desires and were equally receptive to his advances. But "this company of girls, seductive and alluring as was Maud and bewildering and sweet as was Alice, did not satisfy like a lonely walk in the woods or like fishing beside the running stream" (3, 9–10). This flight from temptation helped, but did not last. By the time Zane was sixteen, Alice looked "prettier than ever" (4, 11). Unfortunately, an accidental soiling of her dress during a classroom brawl turned her against him and sent him after "companionship with new and more attractive girls who made eyes at me and wrote me notes and waylaid me after school" (5, 5). These overtures ended his solitary walks, worsened his academic performance, and embroiled him in more fights. Although his fundamentalist upbringing gave him a lifelong opposition to drink and smoking, he allowed himself to join a dancing club and quickly became one of the best dancers. This involved him with three girls and "a predicament." Nelly, one of the three, had a jealous brother named Ralph who used his friendship with the club president to circulate lies about Zane and get him expelled. Outraged at this injustice and the consequential loss of his girlfriends, Grey thrashed Ralph. He then sought out Nelly, explained Ralph's lies, and informed her that he "*cared* terribly," but she was unmoved (5, 5–6). Years later, she would reenter his life and provoke even greater distress.

When another Nell spurned Zane because of false rumors about them and turned her two friends against him, he searched out and thrashed the boy she blamed. These conflicts led to his first serious depression and the greatest humiliation of his Zanesville years. Eventually Nell and Pet softened, but Margaret, the third girl, haughtily persisted in ignoring him. Determined to win her over, he confronted her and appealed for a hearing, but was coldly rebuffed. As Grey explains: "It seemed that something youthful and fine in me died a violent death. I was ashamed of her for her false pride and of those who had made her wish to shame me. But the finer feelings gave place to fury. I would show her how little I cared for her, or Nell, or anyone" (6, 8). With a pair of friends, Zane stormed off to a brothel and was arrested in a police raid.

23

Frank Gruber's biography totally ignores this event despite Grey's claim that "this calamity marked a great difference in my life in every way" (6, 10). In "The Living Past," Grey offers his arrest as the climax of his years in Zanesville and as a momentous reckoning with his budding sexuality. Whether they were so at the time, his intense feelings of sexual excitement, confusion, and humiliation are depicted as interlaced with an aggrieved sense of injustice and mistreatment. Grey acknowledges that his brothel visit was motivated by "a dark excitation of spirit [and] enticing sensation of forbidden fruit." The prostitute there was "shockingly beautiful" (6, 8). Later, mired in the disgrace and depression of his jailing, he thought to himself, "I had not done any harm" (6, 9). When asked by a fellow inmate if he realized that he was going to "a donie-castle," he replied, "I'm afraid I didn't think of it in that way; I was excited—carried away—terribly thrilled" (6, 9). Grey leads his reader to believe that he did not deserve to be jailed, in part because he had not bedded anyone, but also because his wayward desires were instinctive and natural. This estimate is further supported by his revelation that the "poor" owner of the brothel was driven by her arrest to commit suicide. Grey also references a kind, sympathetic teacher who reassured him, "You were not bad. You were just wild and foolish," and he reveals that she too committed suicide when an affair of hers was exposed (6, 10). Grey believed that his arrest was not for a legitimate crime or even a bad decision. On the contrary, it was the culmination of many narrow-minded, small-town judgments that left him alienated and resentful.

Shortly after this incident, Grey's father abruptly left Zanesville and relocated to Columbus. Existing records reveal that Lewis Gray sold his residence on McIntire Terrace on October 24, 1889, and a 153-acre parcel of undeveloped land on December 4, 1889.[25] "The Living Past" reports that Lewis took a trip to Washington, D.C., that same fall and was there either cheated or robbed of a large sum of money (7, 5). Ida Gray's brief family history mentions this same disastrous loss in Washington, but claims that her father "got in with some women who fleeced him out of most of his money."[26] While this alternative explanation opens the possibility that Zane's attraction to women was inherited,[27] both explanations were almost certainly cover-ups for worse humiliation: Lewis probably lost his money in a way that compelled him to leave Zanesville. The Washington disaster that Lewis claimed is too simple and leaves too many questions unanswered. Why was he traveling with so much cash? If he was exploring a possible relocation to Washington, why did he not assess the prospects and then arrange any purchase through banks? Presumably his lost funds were from the sale of the home and land parcel. If so, what prompted him to sell both his nest and his nest egg? Even more baffling, why did he decide to give up his thriving dental practice? In short, Ida and Zane were probably presented their father's excuse for his misfortune without explanation. Following an observation that his father was uncharacteristically happy and making "lots of money" during most of his high school years, Grey mentions that he suddenly began to look worried and dejected (6, 10). He attributes this change to the desertion of his brother Ellsworth from the navy and his own brothel arrest, but Lewis undoubtedly had worries of his own. The humiliation caused by his sons could have harmed his practice, but probably would not have destroyed a livelihood that had been built up over so many years. A more likely explanation, one Lewis may have been hiding with his contrived story, is a disastrous investment or ruinous bout of gambling that devoured his assets, decimated his reputation, and forced him to relocate.[28] This would explain the related facts that Lewis left Zanesville with little money from the sales of his property and that he immediately changed the spelling of his name from "Gray" to "Grey."[29] Previous explanations have attributed this name change to dates and events long after it actually occurred.[30]

Zane cried as he looked at Zanesville from the window of the train that carried him and his family to Columbus (7, 5). Uppermost in his mind was his parting with Muddy Miser, Licking Creek, Joe's Run, and Dillon's Falls. Into these poignant memories intruded the shame of his poor performance in school, his anguish over the girlfriends who did not understand him, and the humiliation of his arrest. Now without even a home, he felt more alone and displaced than ever.

2

Quest for Direction: 1890–1905

I made up my mind today. I didn't load myself with
too much. This is how wise I was. I did not say I
shall never look into another woman's eyes again,
or run from any pretty girl, or tease you any more.
But I did say I would study and read all that I could . . .
[and] write literature, not thoughtless, careless books,
but throbbing, red-blooded histories of life.
—September 27, 1904, to Lina Roth

By the precocious age of fifteen, Pearl was already "very expert in extracting teeth" (5, 8). Rural Ohio was so sufficiently free of regulation that he was able to practice dentistry even *before* his relocation to Columbus. In Zanesville, Lewis employed cocaine, but this sedative still necessitated a deft removal of the tooth to prevent pain. From his baseball and fishing, Pearl had developed a powerful grip and sure hand that made him a valuable assistant. One Saturday as Pearl was cleaning the office, Lewis enlisted his help with an extraction and was so pleased with the result that he began using him regularly and increased his pay to seventy-five cents (5, 8). Shortly after the move to Columbus, Pearl sought to convert his limited training into a necessary source of income.

The first six months in Columbus were very trying, and Lewis had so little money that he needed help from relatives to rent a house. His new practice fared poorly. Though he hated promotion and considered it unethical, the emptiness of his office forced him to run newspaper ads and to circulate handbills. R. C. started eighth grade, but quit after only three days to drive a delivery wagon. Meanwhile, Pearl worked as an usher in a large theater. During this difficult period, Lewis received a letter from Frazeysburg, a small country town outside Columbus. An elderly woman in pain from bad teeth requested that he come to treat her and assured him additional business. Reluctant to pursue this long-shot opportunity but also unwilling to lose it, Lewis sent his son, even though the boy had so far done only extractions. When he arrived, Pearl learned that the woman wanted all her teeth removed, and every one of them was decayed or broken off to the gums. With open mouth and no questions, she had absolute confidence in his competence. He, on the other hand, quaked at the challenge before him. After administering a stout dose of cocaine that turned her gums white, he groped with his forceps for a promising nub. With a silent prayer, he pulled hard. When the first tooth came out cleanly and his patient felt nothing, he proceeded to extract the remaining twenty-six "without breaking one" (7, 6).

This success impressed the locals, and they invited Pearl back to Frazeysburg. He quickly initiated once-a-week visits and was soon traveling to other towns nearby. These trips yielded several memorable experiences. On a visit to Warsaw, Grey's first customer requested that he extract his only tooth, which was enormous and felt "like a solid nail in hard oak." When he gave it a powerful twist and vigorous pull, "there came a sound like a pistol shot, the forceps were knocked out of my hand, and the big tooth flew across the room like a bullet and cracked the window pane" (8, 6). This experience was undoubtedly on his mind when a village blacksmith with a massive square jaw insisted that he remove a perfectly sound tooth and would not be dissuaded. After a futile struggle that broke his largest instrument, Grey sheepishly admitted defeat and learned that he was the fourth tooth-puller to fail (8, 6). Another time he disregarded his father's warning against the use of cocaine on frail people because his elderly patient appeared to be in good health. When he administered the sedative, the old man suddenly went limp, slid to the floor from his seat, and appeared dead. When he determined that the man's heart was still beating, Grey sent for a doctor and hastily left town (8, 6).

Over the course of these experiences, Grey learned that dentistry without certification was illegal and worried that his lucrative practice could land him in jail. His father reassured him that other dentists would have to report him, and since he was not competition, they were unlikely to do so. Nonetheless, in late fall an official from the Ohio State Dental Association contacted Lewis and Zane and explained that no action would be taken if the young man stopped practicing or entered a program for qualification.[1] By this point, professionalized dental schools, many associated with universities, had supplanted the apprentice system under which Lewis was trained. Unfortunately, Lewis's financial problems placed this education beyond reach.

Whether he was ushering or pulling teeth, Zane's mind was on the baseball diamond. The numerous stone-throwing episodes in his autobiography were meant to establish that he had a strong arm and natural talent for pitching long before he tried the game. Pick-up games at the Madden Hill playground in Zanesville honed his talent and gave him a repertoire of pitches. At fourteen, he was the only boy who could throw a curve ball. The summer before the move to Columbus, he pitched for a Terrace team that lost a close game to a team of older boys from the Eighth Ward, but the experience bolstered his confidence in his pitching skill.

Zane and R. C. were so committed to baseball that they immediately sought opportunities to play in Columbus. Their performance in pick-up games led to an association with the team for the Town Street School.[2] This team's nine victories and several Zane shutouts qualified him and R. C. for the Capitals, a strong team in the semiprofessional City League of Columbus that were league champions that year (7–11).[3]

Zane's success with the Capitals led to a memorable game during a dental trip to an outlying area. To salvage a day of slow business in Baltimore (Ohio), he contacted the local team, cited his association with the Capitals, and offered to pitch its upcoming game against a formidable, undefeated Jacktown team. In his autobiography, Grey awarded this contest the fullest description of all his games—by far. Part of this was due to the quaint setting and dramatic outcome. With hundreds of wagons parked around the infield and a towering crop of corn as a fence for the outfield, he and the star for Jacktown staged a tense pitching duel through seven scoreless innings. The two teams were helpless against Zane's curves and the fastballs of the other pitcher until Grey advised his fellow players to bunt. This strategy produced two runs, loaded the bases, and brought him an opportunity to blast a grand slam into the cornfield. As he prepared to mow down the six remaining batters, the gaudily attired umpire, partial to Jacktown, suddenly

Grey in Penn baseball uniform, ca. 1895. (Courtesy of Loren Grey.)

stopped the game; he declared Grey a "ringer" and forfeited the game. During the uproar that ensued, Zane grabbed his clothes and fled into the corn to hide his escape (8, 7–8).

Grey originally told this charming story in an earlier account entitled "Breaking Through," but he deleted this rationale from his autobiography. "Now the point of this baseball narrative," he explains, "is that a University of Pennsylvania man saw me pitch this game, hunted me up in Columbus, and assured me that Pennsylvania was the college for me to pick. So that very fall I found myself enrolled as a student there."[4] Grey dropped this explanation from "The Living Past" in order to tell about a talented local team with which he played in Columbus. After initial victories over Capitol University and the Panhandlers, this presumptuous group of amateurs with no college affiliation was able to schedule a game with the Ohio State team and won by a lopsided score. This victory included a grand slam by R. C. and earned the team games with other colleges, including Ohio Wesleyan, Oberlin, and Kenyon. The team's many victories earned it a season finale against Dennison that was attended by several college scouts, and Zane's best pitching effort produced a close 3–2 victory. Over the weeks that followed, he was contacted by representatives from Ohio Wesleyan, Vanderbilt, the University of Michigan, and the University of Pennsylvania (8, 7–8).

In "The Living Past," Grey says little about the summer baseball that he played while he deliberated which college to attend. In early May, Zane, R. C., and George Kihm, a mute who was a better hitter than the Greys, journeyed to northwest Ohio to play for the Delphos Reds. The opponents of this semiprofessional team presented Zane his stiffest competition and brought him more success. The Reds lost three of their first four games. In the fifth game against Finlay, the team broke out on a 35–8 romp and followed with twenty-one victories in the next twenty-three games. A game against the Toledo Auburndales drew the greatest crowd of the season. In a 23–0 blowout, Zane allowed only four hits, struck out ten, hit three doubles, and added a final home run. At least twice more, large crowds gathered with anticipation for close contests that the Reds turned into routs; the team went on to win the regional championship. Although Zane did not remain for the entire season, he compiled an impressive .419 batting average and an 8–0 pitching record.[5] The *Delphos Herald* reported that Grey went back to Columbus early in order "to resume his studies,"[6] but this partial truth glossed a more problematic reason. Grey pitched a Sunday game for the Reds that violated city ordinances, and a warrant was issued for his arrest. Realizing that an arrest would not look good on his college application, he hopped a freight train and fled (8, 8–9).

Following a brief stay in Columbus, Zane departed for dental school at the University of Pennsylvania. A reader of Grey's autobiography is rather surprised by this decision, given his previously expressed hatred for his father, his office, and his profession. Early in "The Living Past," while discussing his boyhood, Grey claims to have sworn that he "would rather be a tramp fisherman than the best dentist in the world" (3, 5). Actually, this conviction and animus came years later and misrepresented his thinking at the time.

When he left for Philadelphia, his opinion of dentistry was more complicated and less negative. As a prestigious Ivy League school, Penn offered a welcome escape from his stern father and his family's humiliating drop in status. For Zane, these advantages were overshadowed by the golden opportunity of its baseball team. With its winning record against the country's best collegiate teams, its metropolitan exposure, and the National League Phillies across town, Penn was a far more promising gateway to professional baseball than any of the small-town Ohio teams on which he had played (even though Cy Young rose to fame from them several years later).

Dentistry was something Zane needed more than wanted. His decision to attend the dental school was influenced by uneasiness over his failure to finish high school. The two and a half years he completed in Zanesville were a sorry record of dismal grades.[7] Though both he and R. C. played on the Town Street School team in Columbus, neither actually attended the school. Lewis's decimated finances had prevented Zane from resuming high school and compelled him to work. Even though his baseball skills opened the way for college acceptance and funding, he still had to pass demanding courses in conventional academic disciplines. Dentistry was an attractive field of study because it was a practical subject in which he had a solid grounding. Conversely, the other colleges that had recruited him had mediocre teams and an intimidating array of traditional courses.[8]

Grey's three years in Columbus made him twenty-one when he entered Penn. Although the dental school accepted older students as well as entering freshmen, he was so uneasy over the hiatus in his education that he presented his birth date as 1875 rather than 1872 (and retained this amended date for years). Ironically, Grey's acceptance did not compromise the school's entrance requirements. The "Conditions for Admission" in the university catalogue for 1893–94 required an applicant to write an essay attesting to his competence in orthography and grammar and to pass an examination on arithmetic, history, and geography. But it added: "A candidate who has received a collegiate degree, or passed the matriculate examination of a recognized college, or who has a certificate from a normal, high or grammar

31

school, or a teacher's certificate, properly attested, may enter without examination."⁹ In other words, Grey's graduation from grammar school was sufficient. At the time, Penn's dental school was only fifteen years old.¹⁰ In providing the standardized, verifiable education promoted by boards of certification, Penn was sensitive to its intrusion upon the traditional apprenticeship system and required that an entering student have a sponsoring "preceptor," the conventional term for an apprentice's mentor. Zane's preceptor was "L. M. Grey."¹¹

Zane's dental experience was strong support for his application, but it was his athletic prowess and Penn's desire for winning teams that got him accepted. By the 1890s, college athletics were big-time sports and vital to a school's reputation. The Ivy League had the best teams, the largest crowds, and the greatest alumni support. The year that Grey enrolled, Penn's Board of Trustees approved plans for building a $100,000 stadium at Franklin Field. Conceived as "the most complete athletic facility in the country," this structure was for football, baseball, and track, and it was designed to provide covered seating for 10,000 spectators, open seating for 10,000 more, and temporary stands for another 25,000.¹²

When he stepped off the train in Philadelphia, Zane immediately faced a formidable gauntlet of tests. Unlike today's ball players, he did not arrive with a guaranteed commitment from either Penn or its baseball team. The representatives from Penn who saw him play against Jacktown and Dennison were impressed and encouraging, but they only arranged for the baseball team to expect him: his scholarship was contingent upon his performance at a tryout. Thus he was told to report for a baseball game that weekend against a strong Riverton club of college graduates that had beaten Penn's varsity team the year before. At the end of the fifth inning of a close contest with Penn down 4–2, Grey was tapped to pitch. This decision dismayed the veterans, who did not want a greenhorn ruining their chances to win. With "great speed, perfect control, [and] a wonderful curve ball," Grey held Riverton hitless for three innings. After his team tied the score and sent the game into a tenth inning, Grey yielded a hit but not a score. When Penn came to bat, he rapped a double that scored the winning run (8, 10–11). Confident that he had passed his trial, he purchased his bat and started his collection of memorabilia that in later years outgrew the storage space of his mansion.

Grey's performance against Riverton exempted him from the dental school's entrance exams, got him accepted, and earned him a $100 scholarship for tuition, but he was responsible for housing and food. He located a cheap rooming house, ushered at football games, and ate as little as possible.

32

His ordained slate of courses was more of a problem. His background experience made the classes on operative dentistry and mechanical dentistry relatively easy, but the other courses demanded academic skills and discipline that he sorely lacked.[13]

Despite fervent vows, Zane had difficulty making class and spent more time at a nearby poolroom. There he picked up games and side bets that earned him badly needed rent and food money. He passed long hours in the library—not reading or preparing for exams, but savoring the tranquility and relief from academic pressure. "I seldom read anything," he once recollected, "there I seemed to escape from the turmoil of college, and from myself."[14] When he made class, his attention usually did not. The classes he liked were ones that matched *his* expectations. His lifelong aversion to alcohol caused him never to forget Professor Wormley's pouring it upon an egg that curdled and illustrated its chemical effects upon the human brain. He liked Formad's class best because he complimented Grey's sketches (9, 5–6).

A significant amount of Grey's difficulty came from fellow students who were "beyond my understanding" (9, 1). These well-to-do Easterners were prepared for mores and traditions that were meaningless to him. During the first week of classes, he unwittingly sat in a section of a lecture hall reserved for upper classmen. When they hooted his mistake, he defiantly refused to budge. An uproar ensued and he was branded a rebel. In order to avoid more confrontations, he stayed away from class (9, 5–6).

The day of reckoning for this dereliction was delayed until the second semester, but came sooner than he expected. Two months before finals, he learned about a new university rule that required freshmen to pass all courses in order to be eligible for spring baseball, thereby forcing him to contact his professors and take his finals early. This sudden preemption of badly needed study time proved to be a stroke of good fortune. Several professors perceived him as a promising athlete and unfortunate victim of circumstances beyond his control and awarded him a passing grade, either without testing or in spite of deficient work. These acts of generosity left him still shy of the requisite grade point average of sixty. "In a state of mind that anyone could readily see was little short of desperation," he explained his quandary to Professor Formad—who smiled, granted him a 99, and wished him well (9, 7).

Much to his surprise, his hardest test awaited him. He won his scholarship to Penn as a pitcher. When spring practice began, he learned that home plate would be ten feet further away. On March 7, 1893, the National League decreed that henceforth, pitchers would have to position themselves at a fixed 12" x 4" rubber 60' 6" from the plate instead of within a 6' x 6' box whose forward edge was 50' 10" away, almost ten feet further away.[15] When Grey arrived at Penn, the old rule still governed collegiate play, but the new one was adopted for the 1894 season. The Penn coach, Arthur Irwin, was not present for Grey's initial tryout, but happened to observe him hurling potatoes in a student melee, and was so impressed that he invited him to spring practice for the varsity. However, the new distance deprived Zane of the drop curve that was his favorite pitch. Fortunately, his batting was impressive enough that Irwin repositioned him in the outfield and kept him on the team.

Penn had a wealth of talent for the 1894 season. The team was one of Penn's finest; Grey was lucky to be a substitute and played very little. It won eighteen of its twenty-seven games and outscored its opponents 430 runs to 190.[16] The team's star, Danny Coogan, went on to play professional baseball for the Washington Nationals and Arthur Irwin was tapped to replace the popular Harry Wright as manager for the Phillies.[17]

Following his first year at Penn, Grey returned to Columbus to work for his father and to play for local teams. In late May, the *Columbus Dispatch* listed "Grey, lf and p" on the roster of the Barracks team.[18] By July, "Pearl Zane" was playing for the Defiance, and for the remainder of the summer he used this name to evade a college mandate against "summer nines." Following the Defiance's loss to Delaware (Ohio), he defected to that team for its upcoming game against Finlay, which had a twenty-eight-game winning streak. Having already been Finlay's nemesis once before, "Zane" hit a grand slam in the fourth inning of a scoreless contest that was the difference in Delaware's 5–3 victory. Nine games later, his batting average stood at an impressive .482.[19]

At a moment when he appeared to have moved beyond the disappointments and upheavals of the past few years, everything went haywire. On August 8, the *Delphos Herald* reported, "Pearl Grey of Columbus, who has been playing left field with the Delaware team under the name of Zane, was quietly arrested after to-day's game on a telegraph from Delphos, Ohio stating that a warrant was issued there for his arrest on a paternity charge."[20] In "The Living Past," Grey acknowledges his involvement with a "belle of Delphos" during his previous summer with the Reds. He even mentions how R. C. "broke rudely into my romance" one morning to inform him about the arrest warrant that had been issued for playing baseball on Sunday (8, 8). While it may have been coincidental that his unfinished autobiography stopped just before this paternity suit, it is also possible that he wanted to avoid the episode. In any case, this paternity suit posed a formidable problem. Up to this point, Grey had been exceptionally open and honest for an author of fiction, and he had even admitted his brothel arrest. Most of the discrepancies in the account of his early years were understandable lapses of memory or were warranted by his narrative. On the other hand, a paternity suit on top of his brothel arrest bespoke a worrisome pattern of behavior. If he chose to drop it, how many more excisions would he make, and would these liberties not transform the account of his life into another one of his stories?

Following his arrest, Zane thought immediately about the dire consequences should Penn officials learn of it. Initially, he claimed that the charge was blackmail, but later agreed to settle with the girl for $100. His father followed Zane to Delphos and posted $133.40 to cover the full cost of the case. Upon his release, Zane returned to Delaware.[21]

On the same page of the *Delphos Herald* that announced this settlement, an entry in another column informed readers, "Pearl Grey will probably be signed on the local team and the fans are glad, as he is not only a great ball player, but a gentlemanly one."[22] Days later he rejoined the Delphos team, and he performed so well over the next month that scorecards sold at the games carried his photograph. Still, neither he nor the team was as successful as the year before. The team record of 17–13 did not approach its previous 33–12.[23] In mid-September when he left for school, Grey sought to hide evidence of his summer play by informing the *Herald* that he was returning to Ohio Wesleyan University.[24]

That fall a group from Penn's athletic teams organized a new chapter of Sigma Nu and invited Zane to join. Though he had been only a substitute, varsity players knew him, and this invitation altered his outsider status. Game programs from the era listed him at 5' 9" and 150 pounds, which increased his actual size by more than an inch and ten pounds. (During a later period of illness, Zane wrote to Dolly that his weight had dropped to 120 pounds, and on his 1907 visit to the Grand Canyon, he reported that he was down to 116 pounds.) By either measure, he was only average in size and smaller than his athlete friends; he gained their respect with his competitive intensity and brash confidence. His dental classes were now more practical and less intimidating. He ceased to worry about passing and trusted that his baseball play would compensate for his academic mediocrity.

After Irwin left for the Phillies, the baseball team had difficulty finding a new manager. The players and university officials decided that the current team captain, John Blakeley, should handle these responsibilities, and he picked Grey to start in right field. The loss of so many players from the year before dimmed the team's prospects. The season was scheduled to open against the Giants at the polo grounds in New York, and Grey eagerly awaited this opportunity to compete against professionals. Unfortunately, Penn lost 21–4 and he went hitless. Next, rain forced the cancellation of games against strong teams from Wesleyan, State College (Penn State), and Georgetown, and Princeton and Yale had already been dropped from that year's schedule. Franklin Field opened on April 10 for the Penn Relays according to plan, but the field was so muddied by persistent rain that the baseball team was unable to play there until its May 4 game against Columbia. "It is very seldom," an editorial in the university newspaper reflected, "that any base-ball team meets with as much discouragement as has Pennsylvania's team this year."[25]

Over May, the weather improved, and so did the team's fortunes. After a close 7–6 loss to powerful Georgetown, Penn had impressive victories against Virginia, Harvard, and Lehigh. But Zane went into a slump. After four hits and four runs against Columbia, he went hitless against Georgetown, Harvard, and Cornell and had only single hits against Virginia and Lehigh. For the Lehigh game, he was dropped to the bottom of the batting order. Following losses to Lehigh and Harvard, both Grey and Penn finished strong. The team's record of seventeen victories and four losses approximated that of the year before, even though everyone acknowledged that the team was inferior. Grey, however, was pleased with his overall batting average of .292.[26]

That summer, Zane stopped working for his father and concentrated on baseball. The upcoming year would be his last at Penn, and he wanted it to be his best. Both he and R. C. started with the Finlay team that they had repeatedly beaten in the past. R. C. had already played thirty games by June 15 when Zane joined the team, and he arrived just in time to see his brother blast a game-winning slam at the bottom of the ninth. Over the next twenty-one games, as "Pearl Zane," he hit .295. By mid-August, the town of Jackson, Michigan, was so demoralized over a mid-season disbanding of its team that it enticed the Finlay team into replacing it. During the twenty-seven games he played there, Zane increased his batting average to .398.[27]

Since he had survived the paternity scare and improved his hitting, Grey started his final year at Penn in high spirits. His years of loneliness and anonymity were behind him, and he had performed well enough the previous season that he was expected to be the star of the baseball team. Early hopes that the 1896 team might surpass that of 1894 were suddenly dashed by a ruling of the faculty athletic committee. At a meeting on January 25, 1896, the committee announced that all players who had participated in "summer nines" would be ineligible and banished all returning members of the 1895 team except Grey and Blakeley.[28] Grey's modification of his name success-

Grey at the time of his graduation from Penn, 1896. (Courtesy of Loren Grey.)

fully hid his own summer play, but he was really saved by having played in distant Ohio; the ineligible players had remained nearby in Pennsylvania or New Jersey, where their illegal play got noticed. Grey was lucky to escape this harsh judgment, but his team was ruined and its hopes were dashed. The athletic committee also canceled two early season games against the Phillies and eliminated Grey's last chance to play against major leaguers.[29]

Contrary to expectations, the first six games of the season were lopsided Penn victories that exhilarated fans. Georgetown and Brown then routed Penn and exposed the team's vulnerability. Grey's five hits against Georgetown included a home run, a triple, and three singles and were impressive enough that the *Philadelphia Inquirer* turned the team's humiliating 19–7 loss into a story of achievement that included a woodcut drawing of him and a headline proclaiming "Grey was the hero."[30] His three hits against Brown validated his improvement and established him as the team's best player. In an 11–7 victory over Lehigh, he made "two sensational catches" and batted in two runs. During the rematch with Georgetown, he had two hits and again scored two runs in a tough 14–13 loss. He figured prominently in Penn's two victories over a strong Cornell team. The *Pennsylvanian*'s account of the second victory observed, "At the bat Grey carried off the honors making five singles in six times at the bat."[31] Local newspapers agreed that Penn's 3–2 win over Virginia was its best game and that Grey's hits were the margin of difference.[32] One portrayed his second hit as the stuff of legend:

> Two men were put out and one University of Pennsylvania man was on second base when Pearl Grey went to bat for the last time. As Pearl picked up his bat to try his luck, Dr. White, one of the leading professors of the institution called Grey to him and said; "Grey, the honor of the University of Pennsylvania rests with you."
> Virginia's pitcher had been too much for the Keystone boys, and the latter had not been hitting the ball, but young Grey was equal to the occasion and sent the ball out of reach, making a home run and letting in the man on second base. Two thousand students and 500 beautiful girls jumped to their feet and rent the skies with their wild yells. Pearl Grey was a hero. The crowds yelled his name, [and] carried him all over the field.[33]

Ensuing losses to Harvard, Brown, and Chicago disappointed everyone. In his final game, which Lehigh won 7–6, Grey went hitless and dropped a ninth-inning fly that allowed Lehigh to tie the score and sent the game into extra innings.[34]

On June 11, 1896, "Pearl Zane Grey" graduated from Penn's School of Dentistry.[35] He left Philadelphia immediately and played summer baseball for the Orange Athletic Club in Orange, New Jersey. The previous season, Penn had played the OAC because its roster included several of its graduates; the team's best player was Roy Thomas, a teammate of Grey's from two years before. Local newspapers hailed Grey as "the most valuable accession to the field this year" and "one of the best players the club has ever had," and he quickly justified this advance billing. After seventeen games, he had six homers, two triples, seven doubles, and twenty singles; he went hitless only once. The newspaper that tallied these achievements concluded, "It is perhaps no exaggeration to say that this is the best OAC team ever, with Grey in left field."[36]

Grey continued to play for the OAC through the 1897 and 1898 seasons. For him, this team was an alternative route to the big leagues and not merely an opportunity for more baseball. Though he received a modest stipend, the Orange Athletic Club was not a professional team, but it did have close connections to several nearby teams with salaried players. The same year that Zane graduated, R. C. broke into professional baseball with a team in Fort Wayne, Indiana, and from 1897 to 1903, played with pro teams in the Eastern League.

Grey's other activities during these years are less clear and harder to track. Although baseball was his priority, he did practice dentistry. An undated, unidentified clipping in his baseball scrapbook reported him as "engaged in dentistry in New York." However, another reported that he had closed his office in Newark, New Jersey, and was now associated with Dr. R. M. Sanger in East Orange.[37] Whether he practiced dentistry in New Jersey only during baseball season or throughout the year as well, he always planned to practice in New York City when his baseball days were over. Prior to his graduation from Penn, the dental board for the State of New York established procedures for certification that required education, experience, and examination.[38] The work he did in New Jersey gained him both necessary experience and a location near the OAC. Until he obtained his license, he could not afford to live in New York City, and he was not certified until October 14, 1897, almost a year and a half after graduation.[39]

Grey performed even better during his second season with the OAC, and he came very close to the break for which he had been hoping. Midway through the season, reports surfaced that a Newark team had signed him. The manager confirmed that the team had offered Grey "a handsome salary" and compensated the OAC. Several days later, Grey informed the press that he opposed Newark's Sunday games and preferred to remain with the Orange team, which did not play on Sundays.[40] That he would have rejected this opportunity for such a reason is highly unlikely, since he had already played on Sundays in Delphos. The actual reason was probably money. Since Grey was currently the OAC's best hitter (with a batting average just shy of .400), an accomplished outfielder, and a major factor in the team's success, the syndicate in control of the OAC may have decided to match Newark's offer in order to keep him with the team. Frank Gruber has stated that Grey was making more money at this time from baseball than dentistry; this estimate cannot be verified, but it is probably true.[41] Later that season, a local newspaper reported: "It can be stated on very good authority that the following players will be declared professionals, and consequently will be ineligible to compete in amateur sports: Nichols, Grey, Smith, Grissinger, Horner, and Murphy."[42] These claims were never substantiated and nothing came of them.

During the off-season, Grey did sign with Newark. He played on its team through the April preseason and started at right field when the regular season began on April 27.[43] Newark's grueling schedule of more than four games a week in locations like Norfolk, Richmond, Allentown, Hartford, and Lancaster left Grey no time for dentistry. On June 14, after thirty-eight games, he and the team parted ways. Though he may have been cut, it is more likely that he quit due to Newark's financial troubles. Three weeks after his departure, several players publicly complained about not being paid and the whole team quit.[44] Scant funding may indeed have influenced his rejection of the team's original offer. Whatever the reason, Grey's batting average with Newark was more than a hundred points below that of his previous season with OAC, and this decline snuffed his fading hopes for a professional career.[45] On June 25, he rejoined the OAC team for the remainder of the season.[46]

Although he continued to play for OAC the next season, Grey shifted his priority to dentistry. He moved to New York City and opened a cramped office at 117 W. Twenty-first Street. This was an impoverished area of the city heavily populated with immigrants who came to him with acute dental problems and little money. Because their income was meager, his was too. During this period, he was so destitute that he once went four days without eating. He withdrew into his office to avoid the congestion and squalor outside, and he went out only when necessary.[47] For the first time in years, he became an avid reader.[48] To alleviate his acute loneliness, he attended several reunions with fraternity brothers, but he found these gatherings crude and offensive and decided his bleak office was preferable.

Grey turned to women to alleviate his pained sense of isolation, and the photographs of them interspersed among the newspaper clippings in his baseball scrapbook suggest that there were more than a few of them. One was a young seamstress named Doris who signed her letters "Diosus." Zane had become involved with this woman in Orange during the 1897 season, and he continued to see her for eight years. Her sixteen surviving letters to him reveal her life to have been as hard as his. She lived at home, sang at church, and made dresses for scant, intermittent pay. Her father earned so little that the family had to rent rooms, and Grey met her during his stay in one. "I know how you must feel when not working," she wrote to him in an 1899 letter, "and pity you profoundly because I have been there myself." The pair seldom went out in public together, and relied on letters and covert meetings to sustain their relationship and escape the misery of their daily lives. Her affectionate salutations to "Dearest Muddy" evidence an informed understanding of his past life and psychological wellsprings. As their affair deepened and intensified, strains developed and worsened their anguish. In another section of the same 1899 letter, Diosus reveals how distressing and unsure their relationship was:

> I think that we were both in fault. I most; because I acted like a fool. You were a little strange to me yesterday. I can not explain how. If there is anything to pardon, you may be sure of my complete forgiveness, but *I* am the one to be sorry, and ask your pardon. . . . I am right in saying that I am changing. I am growing bitter and restless; and such feelings must have no place in a heart which I have given to you to keep. Sometimes I feel as if that heart would burst with mingled emotions, and there, sometimes I am conscious of a hard, bitter, dissatisfied feeling that used never to be there. . . . Let us make these last few months that are left to us a time to be remembered, because of its fullness of love and happiness, and not a period to think of as dark and fraught with misunderstandings. We can do better and we know it. When we do not, our love suffers, and it is not our fault, and it is too beautiful, too perfect a love to wound by a careless remark or a frown.[49]

Two months earlier, Diosus had expressed her hope that R. C. might come east and stay with Zane because he was "terribly lonely." In early April, before he rejoined his team in Toronto, R. C. did visit Zane and tried to lift his spirits. After the season was over, R. C. returned and they went camping together in the upper reaches of the Delaware River near Lackawaxen. Both were uneasily aware that baseball was a young man's game, and their days as players were dwindling. They went to Lackawaxen seeking emotional uplift and liberation from pressures to take jobs and make money. The game that made them close as youths was now keeping them apart, and they looked to camping and fishing as an opportunity to reconnect. Zane badly needed a respite from bad teeth, foul breath, and six long days of work, and he hoped their outing would alleviate his dejection.

When Zane and R. C. arrived at Lackawaxen, the surrounding area of the upper Delaware River was a popular destination for summer vacationers. The rugged rolling hills and lazy, twisting river between heavily wooded banks formed a lush, inviting, pastoral landscape. The ferry ride from New York City to Hoboken and the hour-long train ride past several convenient stops made it readily accessible for city dwellers, who relished it most. Each year, thousands of visitors flocked to the area. A dozen hotels had accommodations for a hundred or more guests, and many farmers and homeowners rented rooms. A few miles south of Lackawaxen in Shohola, there was a large amusement park that attracted crowds in excess of 10,000 during peak season.[50]

This wave of vacationers, who came seeking a respite from work, were also rebelling against long-standing taboo. Early in the nineteenth century, as the country converted from Calvinism to capitalism, good citizens still believed that they had to work hard and save. Industry, productivity, and perseverance determined the success of the individual and the nation. Leisure and idleness, on the other hand, were vices fraught with moral, financial, and political danger. However, the new and enlarged middle class that emerged following the Civil War had the capital and the initiative to challenge this harsh distinction. Conceding that work was necessary and good, these upright citizens argued that it was also tiring, stressful, and unhealthy. Was it not better to take time off as protection against these damaging effects? According to this reasoning, vacations were not indulgence or dereliction. On the contrary, they restored physical and psychological vitality; workers became happier and more productive. As one scholar on the subject has argued, "Reconciling their need and desire for extended periods of rest and recreation with their commitment to work remained a central struggle for middle-class Americans."[51]

By 1899, when Zane and R. C. first visited Lackawaxen, they encountered fellow vacationers who shared their enthusiasm for camping. Wealthy New Englanders first popularized camping with well-supplied outings during the 1880s. For the less affluent who followed, camping made vacation affordable. The exposure to fresh air, the spiritual uplift of nature, and liberation from work also made it therapeutic.[52] Away from the claustrophobia, loneliness, and punishing routine of his New York office, Zane discovered that camping and fishing rejuvenated him.

Following his return, Grey relocated his office to a "dingy flat" on 100 W. Seventh-fourth Street.[53] Actually, this Upper West Side location brought more room and better patients. He bought new curtains and furnishings to make his studio-office more attractive and accommodating. He then mailed engraved announcements stating that "Dr. Zane Grey" was open for business and offering "all modern methods and latest appliances for painless dentistry."[54] He affixed a plate on the front door that likewise dropped the Pearl and proclaimed his pen name before he had a novel to go with it.[55]

The next summer, the Grey brothers went for a longer stay in Lackawaxen. Earlier, when the baseball season opened in early May, Zane was again with the Orange Athletic Club and appeared in box scores until the end of September. However, from August 11 to September 8, he disappeared from the team's roster for another visit to the upper Delaware that was longer than the year before. On August 28, 1900, while he was at the Westcolong railroad station, the next stop beyond Lackawaxen, he encountered an attractive young woman leaving the train. He initiated a casual conversation and learned that the buxom, dark-haired, brown-eyed girl called herself "Dolly."[56] Her full name was Lina Elise Roth, and her warm response to his overture initiated their lifelong relationship.

At the time, Dolly was seventeen, eleven years younger than Zane, and she had recently finished her freshman year at the New York Normal College (later renamed Hunter College), where she was preparing to become an elementary school teacher. Weighing 122 pounds, she thought of herself as a "living skeleton."[57] Although she was only 5' 4", she played on the women's basketball team and was an active thespian. Her ebullient temperament and outgoing personality got her accepted into the Gamma Tau Kappa sorority and later elected vice president of the Alpha Beta Gamma Honorary Society. Her membership in the "Old Maid" club announced her availability, and her round-faced good looks guaranteed that she would not be single for long.[58]

In his 1918 letter to Anna Andre, Zane stated that Dolly came from an "old New York family [that] had no use for me."[59] Her father and paternal grandfather were successful doctors, and her maternal great-grandfather was the first coroner for New York City. Dolly and her widowed mother were currently living on Edgemont Avenue, and were about to move into a stately old residence at 701 St. Nicholas Street, near the southern tip of Manhattan. A series of untimely deaths had destabilized the prosperity and stability of

Lina Elise Roth, ca. 1900. (Courtesy of Loren Grey.)

the Roth-Battenhausen line and was weighing down Dolly's spirits. Her father, Julius Roth, died in 1899 from a prolonged bout with Bright's disease. Her paternal grandmother, Margarethe Roth, died more suddenly in February 1904. These misfortunes carried some benefit. Starting in March, 1904, when she was twenty-one, Dolly received a series of distributions from these estates that brought her $10,626 by January, 1906.[60] This inheritance did not make Dolly wealthy, but it ensured her a comfortable, privileged life and freed her from having to sustain it by taking a job or marrying. However, her status-conscious relatives were suspicious of the older stranger from Ohio and openly questioned her association with him.

During a stroll the day after their meeting in Westcolong, Zane boldly kissed Dolly.[61] Since she had to leave a few days later, there was little time for more kisses, but they continued to meet and correspond when Zane returned to New York City, and their relationship quickly grew more intimate. Surviving letters from October and November of 1900 begin "Dear Dr. Grey," but one from December 5 suddenly opens "Dear Pearl."[62] Early the next year, she began calling him "Doc," a nickname that persisted through the hundreds of letters that followed. In the December letter with the changed salutation, Dolly frankly speculated whether or not she loved her new suitor. Concluding that she probably didn't, she hastily added, "but sometimes, Oh dear!"[63]

This blossoming romance did not stop Zane from continuing to see other women. In May of 1902, Diosus wrote to him, "Dear old sweetheart. I'm so glad that you love me. Everything looks brighter and better to me when I think of you."[64] Other letters reveal that Diosus's feelings for Zane carried no expectation of faithfulness. In one, she explained that worsening financial pressures had compelled her parents to rent "your little room with all its memories." Acknowledging that his own shortage of funds further constrained their options, she added, "You know just as well as I do that any idea of marriage is ridiculous, not to be even thought of." She proposed that they confront their circumstances with an open mind and agree to go out with others.[65] However, an earlier letter betrays feelings of jealousy: "Don't dare to take Reddy [R. C.] to see any of your other girls before you bring him here."[66] How many "other girls" there were can only be guessed, but Zane once admitted to Dolly that he had "loved" Nell, Kate, Maud, Alice, Loma, Visa, Edith, Daisy, Mabel, Emily, Madge, and Betty.[67] A surviving letter from "Gertrude," a showgirl to whom Zane sent a copy of his first novel, reveals at least one more who was very interested. "The other day I asked Madge," she teased, "if you make love as you wrote in your book. She just laughed and didn't tell me—so you must enlighten me—Do you?"[68]

When Zane left the OAC on July 13, 1901, for another trip to the Lackawaxen area, he left for good. That Christmas, when he returned to Columbus, he was surprised to be recognized as a Zane by an old woman whom he did not know.[69] Conversations with his mother rekindled memories of her stories about the Zanes, and of his boyhood reading about them in *Our Western Border* (1879) by Charles McKnight as well as his enthusiasm for Cooper's Leatherstocking novels and the adventure stories of Harry Castleman.[70] If there was any single epiphany that transformed the has-been baseball player and unhappy dentist into a writer, this was it. After he returned to New York and the drudgery of his dental practice, he found himself reflecting on the difference between the purposefulness of his distinguished ancestors and his discontent with his own life. Initially, their uplifting example sparked daydreams, but he soon decided to write about them during the evening in order to take his mind off his drab, wearying routine.

Grey's initial efforts were almost certainly hampered by a consciousness that he had always been a poor student, especially in English classes. His letters reveal that he conscientiously read and reread writing guides like John H. Gardiner's *The Forms of Prose Literature* (1900), Herbert Spencer's *Philosophy of Style* (1873) and *Principles of Psychology* (1858), and later Clayton Hamilton's *Material and Methods of Fiction* (1908). Dolly was also there to reassure him. She had taken many English courses, understood the fundamentals of good writing, and was willing to help. Her reading of his tentative efforts gained him approval and helpful suggestions, and encouraged him to continue. Unlike Diosus, who could only comment "I suppose you are writing for dear life,"[71] Dolly's letters from 1902–4 contain discussions of authors, books, and the craft of writing that were often naïve, sometimes even foolish, but they reassured him that someone was interested in his work and eager to discuss the process with him.

What Zane actually learned from Dolly and these guides is impossible to identify and document. He did not begin his first journal until 1905, more than three years after he started writing. In his love letters to Dolly, as in the many journals and letters that followed, he frequently mentioned that his writing was going well or poorly, but seldom explained the reasons why or discussed matters of importance to his craft. One surviving example of his early work, a transcription, enclosed in a letter to Dolly, of his opening to a new novel to be entitled *Shores of Lethe,* exemplifies the deficiencies and wrong turns of his early efforts:

> Folly, thou hast cost me dear; the light of women's eyes—Ah! Wine—thou mocker! Outcast am I, thrown from my father's house hard upon the world, after an idle, luxurious, improvident youth. Better, surely to yield to the strain of suicide blood in me and seek forgetfulness in the embrace of cold dark death. What makes life worth living? Indefinable, for me, is the unpardonable sin. Yet to give it up, at twenty five, when the blood burns, for the unknown—No. I will see this game of life to its bitter end. I will try again, and yet again. Men may rise on stepping-stones of the dead selves to higher things.[72]

Since this overwrought passage is so different from anything in his early novels, one hesitates to ascribe it much significance beyond its exemplification of his tortured self-consciousness and the error of this stylistic experiment. But even this can be a distortion. In his love letters, his early novels, and his first journal, Grey writes far better than this example and rarely lapses into such archaic diction. Not only are his sentences grammatically sound and even graceful, but he also seldom crosses out a word or rewrites a sentence—a practice that extends through the many handwritten manuscripts of his novels. Like many other American writers, Grey's woeful lack of formal training in writing was not the liability it would be for most people. Despite false starts like this, he was able to write easily and well, almost naturally.

What Grey needed more than training in sentence formation and paragraph structure was an outlook and subject matter quite different from that of *Shores of Lethe.* Here again, his first journal is instructive. Anyone coming to this journal for information about Zane's daily life or insights into thinking can be frustrated by its many pages of scenery description; he rarely mentions the novels on which he is working, the criticisms that accompanied rejections of his work, or rewriting that he may or may not have attempted. On the other hand, these descriptions read like conscientious exercises in the variant moods created by different seasons, weather conditions, or times of day. It is as though Grey's primers had advised him to move away from himself and his feelings as the point of reference, and to locate an effective equivalent in the circumstances around him. These descriptions anticipate the poetically rendered scenes of his later work that set the tone for the upcoming drama and action. These early efforts contain little of the awkwardness of the *Lethe* passage. They also show him downplaying and externalizing his own feelings, a tactic that invigorated his early fiction.

One early sign that Dolly's support of Zane's literary efforts was gaining her an edge on her competition was a hasty January 31, 1903, note from Zane informing her, "I will come up for you about 7:30 tomorrow eve. Mr. Shields has invited me to bring (no, fetch) a pretty girl down to his place. . . . Dress up and look the part. I would not wear that low-necked and shaped lopped-off dress; but something suitable for music and dancing."[73] By this point, Grey had been writing for more than a year and he was taking Dolly to meet the editor who provided crucial support for his earliest efforts. "Shields" was George O. Shields, the current editor of *Recreation.* Shields's commitment to the outdoors and the cause of conservation led him to found the Camp Fire Club in 1898.[74] He then started *Recreation* to promote the club and to circulate news of interest to the membership. As editor of the magazine, he accepted

47

Grey's first article, "A Day on the Delaware," which appeared in the May 1902 issue. Shortly after the event to which Zane escorted Dolly, Shields accepted his "Canoeing on the Delaware" for the June 1903 issue. Grey's invitation for Dolly to meet Shields expressed confidence that she would make a favorable impression. Since he had already enlisted her help with his writing, the invitation may have also been an expression of gratitude. Even more revealing about his feelings toward Dolly was his willingness to appear in public with her, in contrast to his covert relationship with Diosus.

By writing every moment he could spare over the fall and winter of 1902–3, Grey was able to complete several articles and his first novel. In spring, he dispatched the finished manuscript of *Betty Zane* to various publishers, including Harper and Brothers, and was promptly sent back demoralizing rejections. Unwilling to accept defeat or give up on his investment of time and hope, he contacted the Charles Francis Press, a small firm with shaky finances, and explored paying for publication. Since the fee of $500 exceeded his meager resources, he had to enlist help. Dolly has been frequently identified as his benefactor, but it was actually Reba Smith, who was romantically involved with R. C.[75] They too had met in Lackawaxen, and when R. C. finally quit baseball after the 1903 season, they became engaged. Reba was sympathetic toward her fiancé's appeals on behalf of his unhappy brother. The coal mines owned by her family in Blairsville, Pennsylvania, furnished her ample funds; her trust was large enough that R. C. never worked after their marriage.[76] Dolly, on the other hand, was not yet receiving distributions from her trusts and was therefore unable to help with the publication bill. But Zane was grateful enough for her encouragement and suggestions that he proudly presented her one of the first copies of *Betty Zane* as a Christmas gift.[77]

Betty Zane (1903) was an exercise of compensation by an unhappy dentist hoping to overcome his despondency by writing about ancestors whose lives were more eventful and more satisfying than his own. In the dim light over the kitchen table in his "dingy" office late at night, Grey imagined them to be "reckless bordermen [who] knew not the meaning of fear" and for whom "daring adventure was welcome" (vii). In his novel, Zane's maternal great-grandfather, Col. Ebenezer Zane, along with Ebenezer's sons, the McCullochs, and Wetzels, are portrayed as resourceful pioneers who battled Indians and cleared the way for settlement. Grey wanted his readers to be as impressed as he was by their heroic feats. Isaac Zane's capture and daring escape from Indians, Col. Samuel McCulloch's bold flight from them over a precipice, Lewis Wetzel's cool victory in a shooting contest, and the climactic defense of Fort Henry were depicted as exciting and important. Grey believed that a significant amount of these men's greatness came from simply doing what they had been raised to do. To prevent their imagined humility from being misunderstood or diminished, Grey used Betty's suitor, Alfred Clarke, as a mouthpiece for his personal estimate:

> Alfred honored courage in a man more than any other quality. He marveled at the simplicity of these bordermen who, he thought, took the most wonderful adventures and daring escapes as matter of course, a compulsory part of their daily lives. He had already, in one day, had more excitement than had ever befallen him; and was beginning to believe his thirst for a free life of stirring action would be quenched long before he learned to be become useful in his new sphere (48–49).

Given the manly achievements in this story, it is strange that Grey made his chief character a woman, but he did so not just to show Betty as equal to the men around her. His large cast of males challenged and occasionally overcame his ability to sustain a coherent narrative. As much as he admired his ancestors, he did not know enough about their actual lives to develop them into full, rounded characters. His descriptions of tracking drew heavily upon his own hunting experience and offered some of his best writing, but they also strained his limited knowledge and threatened to exhaust his reader's interest.

He introduced Betty as a colorful variation. Unlike conventional women of her day or Grey's own, Betty is bold, independent, and daring. She is an accomplished rider, likes to fish, and skillfully maneuvers her own canoe. Indians have inscribed her craft with the appropriate motto, "The race is to the swift and strong" (85). This affinity for male activities endows her with male traits. She is intent upon having her way and defies those who attempt to restrain her. Told repeatedly not go riding alone, she does so anyway and is nearly captured by Indians.

The reader learns that she hails from a Philadelphia background of "luxury, society, parties, balls, dances, [and] friends, all that the heart of a girl would desire" (69). She favors her life on the frontier because it allows her to be the person *she* wants to be. She is grateful that locals tolerate her assertiveness and openly proclaims her affection for their way of life. However, she is not blind to its limitations. She notices that men enjoy greater privilege, and she resents it. She complains at one point, "It is always a man that spoils everything" (35). Men are a nuisance because they take their superiority for granted. "I rather envy your being a man," she confesses to Alfred. "You have a world to conquer. A woman—what can she do?" (69). Later she rephrases this question:

"But what can women do in times of war? . . . Few women have the courage for self-destruction" (270). Later, when Fort Henry is surrounded by the British and their Indian allies and its defenders face looming defeat, she dashes for a new supply of gunpowder, affirming that she possesses as much courage as any man and discrediting conventional assumptions about women.

Nonetheless, Betty only *appears* equal to the bordermen around her. Grey made Betty his chief character in order to introduce a romance and enlarge the appeal of his adventure, especially to female readers. Love attracts men to her and becomes an alternative measure of worth. Within this small but diversified society, courage and resourcefulness separate the admirable from the ignoble, the hero from the villain, but so too respect for women—and tolerance for their presumed weakness. When courtship takes over the stage from coping with the woods and Indians, Betty is revealed to be considerably less confident and brave than she seems. Betty's heritage is supposed to make her both a bold woman and a responsive lover: "Betty was a Zane and the Zanes came of a fighting race. Their blood had ever been hot and passionate; the blood of men quick to love and quick to hate" (141). Though "quick to love," Betty is notably reluctant to assert herself when love arrives. Alfred's display of interest flusters and unnerves her. When he encounters her in the woods after she has badly twisted her ankle, she is understandably wary and defensive, but her refusal of help and subsequent burst of tears perplexes him. Before a later encounter, she resolves not to dance with him, but then accepts his offer because she "lacked courage" to say no. Her tongue-tied inability to communicate her true emotions and expectations produces more erratic behavior and more confusion. Grey needs these miscues to complicate their relationship, but they also transform his strong-willed heroine into a genteel, submissive woman. Ironically, after her heroic dash saves Fort Henry, Betty agrees to marry Alfred and is described as "brave even in her surrender" (286).

Grey, of course, realized that romance was an alternative form of adventure that broadened his novel's appeal, but one cannot help suspecting that his involvement with Dolly influenced his story as much as his ancestry. Because of the eleven-year difference in their ages, Dolly was initially an awed admirer, but she quickly became aggressive in her appeals for Zane's attention. Silently, he registered her social pedigree and her familiarity with metropolitan life but was even more impressed by her open displays of love for him and the woods. Within a year of their meeting, she relished their outings in Lackawaxen and, like Betty, enjoyed canoeing and fishing. The dell with the large sycamore where Alfred and Betty frequently meet was

Dolly and Zane, camping near Lackawaxen, ca. 1904. (Courtesy of Loren Grey.)

probably based upon a special woodland spot of theirs. Though Dolly usually stayed at the Delaware House during her visits to Lackawaxen (and wrote many letters on its stationery), she also went camping with him and was not constrained by the era's standards of propriety. A year before their marriage in 1905, on the occasion of their fourth anniversary as a courting couple, Dolly rejoiced that they were "not merely lovers, but companions, friends, mentally and physically if I might so state it."[78] Though close to her own family, she defied their status-conscious estimate of Zane as a suspect provider and unworthy suitor.

Like Betty and Alfred, Dolly and Zane had misunderstandings, and they exposed gaps in Dolly's boldness as well. By their second year together, conflicts arose and rapidly grew stormier and more contentious. Some were provoked by Zane's turbulent emotions, which were worrisome and sometimes frightening. "I don't know what's the matter with me, but *anything* would be preferable to this," he wrote to her in 1901. "If I spent another two such days & nights I would either go insane or kill myself."[79] Later, Dolly objected to the girlfriends that he refused to conceal and to relinquish. In 1903, she complained to him, "But seriously, Pearl, can't you give up other days than Thursday to stray girls. I look forward to that all week and it's a great disappointment. And it means that you'd rather see someone else. I'm not angry, but the green-eyed monster is rampaging a bit."[80] A year before, she had a dream in which she and Zane were in a hammock together, and another woman sat down alongside. Grey put his arm around the other woman and kissed her. When Dolly told the woman that Zane did not care for her, he said, "Shut up Dolly, don't be a fool," and Dolly awoke screaming.[81]

Zane urged her to "fight" her jealous spells and agreed to see "fewer" girls the upcoming winter. "As far as is possible I am yours," he reassured her. "Whether I can ever be wholly yours is a question the future alone can answer."[82] He found it easier to apologize for his hurtful behavior than to change it. "Now there was no earthly sense in me talking to you as I did; that is, scolding and nagging you," he wrote to her following a disagreement. "I am always ashamed of it; I am sorry for it now. I believe it is my own discontent; my haste and fire to do something immortal, and the realization of how futile that ambition may be, or rather how useless. I have to say something and you always get it. That's because you are the only person who understands me."[83]

Dolly was more outspoken than Betty about her feelings and even pressured Zane to reveal his. Her understanding and reassurance made him secure enough to do so, and he confessed to her:

> Were my temperament and disposition such that I could be satisfied and content with work, and work all the time, without any real life, there might be a bright side to things.
>
> But I love to be free. I cannot change my spots.
>
> The ordinary man is satisfied with a moderate income, a home, wife, children, and all that.

That is all right and just what man ought to be.

But I am a million miles from being that kind of man and no amount of trying will ever do any good.

I want to be somebody. I want fame. I do not want much money, but I want enough to keep me from worrying to death all the time, as I have for years.[84]

Though Dolly often doubted her power over him, she argued that she could help him realize his potential if he would allow her to do so:

I felt as if I had things in me which if I could express, would make me great. I felt as if I could write a great book. Please do not laugh, it may sound ridiculous, to you, but I had the feeling. I know I could never do anything like that, as I have *not* the power to express. Whether I ever will have it, I do not know, and besides I do not care for myself. My ambition is for you, and I shall expend all my energy & all the power I possess to make *you* a great man.[85]

Over time, Zane accepted more and more of Dolly's help. Her insistence upon dialogue mollified their misunderstandings, and made correspondence a crucial component of their relationship. "I like our talks now almost as much as I liked to be kissed," she confided. "I almost think our intellectual intercourse is the sweetest part of our love. If that were not there, I don't think I could care as much for you."[86] Despite her refusal to be diffident and tongue-tied like Betty, Dolly was conventional enough to believe that love should lead to marriage and told Zane so. "Oh, Pearl, I hope I'll always be to you what the letter expressed," she responded to one of his love letters. "But strange to say, rather than be your ideal, I'd be your *wife,* for an ideal cannot participate in all the every sweetness of such a relation."[87] To her dismay, Zane persisted in thinking of himself as different from those "ordinary men" who wanted only "a home, wife, children, and all that."

In May 1904, Grey returned to Columbus and Zanesville for some public appearances on behalf of his new novel.[88] He also wanted to confer with his father about his deepening wish to quit dentistry and to concentrate upon writing. Instead of his usual disagreement, Lewis urged that Zane stay with dentistry for income and write during his free time. Zane resisted this strategy. First, he had already experimented with this for two years, and the experience only intensified his longing for a complete break. Also, there was the negative example of Lewis himself, who had worked hard for many years but was currently too destitute to provide for Zane's mother and unmarried sister. For months, Zane had been receiving emotional appeals from Ida for rent money.[89] These circumstances may have been the chief reason for his visit.

When he returned to New York City, Zane informed R. C. that their mother and sister were in dire need of help. Lewis's dark mood and foul temper were driving away the last of his patients and making his family miserable. This situation spurred Zane to "cross my Rubicon," as he later characterized the momentous decision before him.[90] Why continue with a profession that he detested when he could see that it had left his father impoverished and deranged? Would it not be better to do something he truly wanted to do? Concluding that he *would* leave dentistry and write, he decided to purchase a residence in Lackawaxen and to convert it into a family haven.

The one deterrent was money. Mary Hobart wanted $1,425 for her residence and three acres of land at the confluence of the Lackawaxen and Delaware rivers. Since he could not even afford the $500 for publication of *Betty Zane,* he could pay no more than a small portion of the asking price. His father's financial situation left his mother and sister without anything to add. Nonetheless, Zane closed on the property on September 27, 1904.[91] Reba undoubtedly contributed, since she and R. C. constructed a residence for themselves there a year later.[92] Since distributions from Dolly's inheritance began the spring before, she also contributed; shortly after closing, Zane wrote to her, "In regard to the investing of your money, I consider your place an excellent one."[93]

A U.S. Park Service landscape treatment plan has characterized the site as "a family retreat from urban living."[94] Grey viewed his new home in just this way—as liberation from New York City, a return to unspoiled nature, and a refuge for his beleaguered family. In the same letter in which he acknowledged Dolly's investment, he observed that "the air, the rivers, the pines and freedom make it most desirable for someone who wants these things." Grateful that she had urged him to remain longer than he intended, he informed her that he had read "Mr. Wagner's Simple Life," and found the book "beautiful, instructive, and good," but also "distress[ing]" in exposing "the shams and faults of my own life."[95] Charles Wagner was a French clergyman whose *The Simple Life* (1901/1904) attacked modern development and advocated a return to traditional values. When the book was translated into English in 1904, it was enormously popular in the United States. Like many Easterners, including Derek Bok, the editor of *Ladies' Home Journal* who strongly recommended it to his readership, Wagner believed that the recent surge in wealth and urbanization was worrisome and that a more austere life was healthier and preferable.[96] He proposed a Thoreauvian reassessment of "our complex life," and argued that very little was required for a satisfying, fulfilling life. Focusing upon the centrality of money to modern existence, he proclaimed that it "complicates life, demoralizes man, [and] perverts the cause of society."[97] His argument dealt with the discontents that drove Grey away from dentistry and New York City, and furnished strong support for his Lackawaxen purchase.

Following the September closing, Zane worked hard on his new property; *Shores of Lethe,* his critique of contemporary thinking and behavior; and *Peaceable Village,* a much delayed sequel to *Betty Zane.* He then summoned Ida and his mother to leave Columbus and join him. By the end of the year, he had both a house and a family, but was still resistant to marriage and a wife. At thirty-two, he was no longer the promising bachelor Dolly had first met; his baseball days were behind him, and he had recently quit his only other source of status and income. His one novel had yet to recover its costs and his two unfinished manuscripts were long shots at best. His modest "new" home lacked winter insulation and was in the middle of nowhere, and his mother, sister, and brother were living there with him. Were Dolly to marry him, she would have to go against her family and her privileged New York existence and accept both his isolation and his family. Nonetheless, she was willing, but Zane was not.

During the spring of 1905, Dolly was tormented by more jealousy over Zane's girlfriends. In a May letter she informed him of mysterious pains in her head, back, and stomach. Straining to appear upbeat, she praised the progress of his writing: "When I compared the difference in you now and two, three, even one year ago, it makes me very happy, and very confident that you will accomplish something in the literary field."[98] A week later, she revealed that her ailments were persisting, but again accentuated the positive. "I am in a very cheerful frame of mind. I haven't been jealous or blue once," she reassured him. In the lengthy discussion of writers that followed, she maintained that prose writers had "greater stability" than poets, who were more inclined to pursue their imaginings. She then presumed upon this assessment to urge that Zane not act on his attraction to women. "I do not blame you & hope I never shall for what has happened or for what may happen," she explained, "for I think I understand your nature and how you are handicapped." To ensure that this appeal not be construed as faultfinding, she conceded her own jealousy and maintained that it too was "a primal instinct." Hoping to be a positive example for him, she resolved that her jealousy "must be pulled out by the roots."[99]

Dolly's next letter announced that she "never for a moment doubted your word in saying you wanted to marry me," but she now defended her jealousy as natural and justified: "I hated the thought of your being with other women and the reactions which in the nature of things would exist between you and them." Charging that his need for women was an illness warranting treatment, she again stopped short of demanding that he change. Cryptically and prophetically she concluded, "I have realized some things in the last four months which will be of life long service to me and which I probably could not have gained any other way."[100] Despite the careful concessions in these circumspect appeals, Grey continued to see and correspond with Diosus. Her letters to Zane after May, however, betray a pained realization that he was withdrawing and she was losing out to Dolly.[101]

The sudden, unexpected death of Lewis Grey that summer toppled Zane's crumbling resistance to marriage. On July 15, Lewis was overcome by heat and taken to the Mt. Carmel Hospital in Columbus. Six days later, he died from heart failure. Ellsworth, Zane's brother, was tapped to represent the family and to escort the body from Columbus to Zanesville for burial in Woodlawn Cemetery.[102]

On the day of his father's collapse, Zane started his first journal and his first entry is a description of an approaching thunderstorm that reads like a scene from one of his novels and opens, "Dark and forbidding came the fast-scudding broken clouds." His second entry declares, "My father died today," and follows with a vague, impressionistic poem. The following day, he added:

> My thoughts go back to the days I climbed the hills with my father when I was a lad eager and gay, with no thought of tomorrow, no understanding of the sadness of human life. And today he is gone. I shall never see him again. Somewhere in the darkness and silence, alone, stone-cold, he lies.
> If only I might have done more.[103]

Clearly his father's death was very upsetting, but for an author whose novels would accentuate emotion, he was notably reserved about his own feelings. The man who had sternly judged him all his life and harshly punished his many mistakes was gone. Even though his ties to his father had been fraying for years and had finally broken months before, it took death to end the force of his influence.

Zane was now entirely free to make his own decisions and to move forward with his new life. In October, Zane informed Dolly that he had "come

to the point where I intend to marry" and accompanied his announcement
with this explanation:

> My blood is red, I know, pure I hope and believe, but as it was born of
> woman so it will never be free of that softness. . . . I shall never lose the
> spirit of my interest in women. I shall always want to see them, study
> them, interest them. I never grow tired of women. Even my development
> has added tenfold to this fateful thing. *Every* woman rouses my antago-
> nism, excites my instinct of wonder, and fear, and pity. Where I once
> wanted to break a girl's heart—with that horrible cruelty of the young
> and ignorant—now I want to help, cheer, uplift, develop, broaden, show
> things and at the bottom still a little of that old fateful vanity.
>
> Am I wrong? Am I only a monster? I love you truly, if such a man can
> love truly. I know I can quake your heart with a look, but I fear you some-
> times with a *trembling* soul. I fear your strength.[104]

That Zane needed to discuss his love for Dolly in terms of "my interest in
women" is both strange and fraught with significance. His explanation was
supposed to justify his decision to marry, not to prepare her for the women
in his future. Furthermore, his acknowledgment of Dolly's strength and of
his indebtedness to women in general was communicated as an admission
of weakness. The softness and sensitivity of women were not just alluring
to him; they drew out similar traits within himself, making women both
impossible to resist and a threat to his manliness. This thinking anticipated
his theory, admitted years later to his son Loren, that his body contained
an abundance of female cells that normal men did not possess.[105] He would
also believe that his black depressions and need for romance were driven by
emotions that normal men either did not have or learned to master. Women,
on the other hand, understood and often shared them.

A letter from Dolly to Zane written from early in 1905 is equally revealing about deep-seated beliefs that she brought to their impending marriage.
"There are times when I myself feel some power stirring in me which seems to
drive me to impossible things (for me). It makes me dissatisfied with myself
and my surroundings. At such times I wish I were a man, but after a while it
usually turns into the channel of wishing to inspire and help *you* to do great
things. What is that feeling—ambition? I think it is higher, more."[106]

The crippling ailments that sent Dolly to doctors and sometimes to bed
over the spring of 1905 were aggravated by Zane's reluctance to give up his
girlfriends and commit to marriage, but they were also worsened by her
course work at Columbia Teachers College where she was working on a mas-

ter's degree in education. Classes there were more difficult than the ones she had taken at the New York Normal College. Long hours of studying and writing intensified her worry of failing. Defensively, she concluded that she was in a "strained social atmosphere" and that her fellow students were "dried out, old maid school teachers."[107] Her doctors' advice that she quit school reinforced her wish to marry. Lacking confidence in herself and her own abilities, she believed that men did not have such doubts. Zane's distress made him unusual—simultaneously a kindred spirit and a worthy project. With her teaching career in doubt, she consoled herself that she was not like the unfeminine women who were performing better, but she did share their manly longings to succeed and make something of themselves. She determined that inspiring Zane and helping him to succeed was a "higher" ambition and one more appropriate for the kind of woman she preferred to be and was raised to be. As much as she wanted to be strong like Betty Zane, she too was submissive around the man she loved.

On September 20, R. C. and Reba were married in New York City, and two months later, on November 21, 1905, the wedding of Zane and Dolly ended their five-year courtship. Afterward, they returned to Lackawaxen and settled into the cottage that they would call "honeymoon house."

3

Adventurous
Apprentice: 1906–10

*"If you want fame or wealth or wolves, go out and hunt
for them"*
—*The Last of the Plainsmen*

In one of the few reviews of *The Last of the Plainsmen* (1908), *Forest and Stream*
offered the following information about the work's little-known author: "Dr.
Grey hails from Pike county, Pennsylvania. A couple of years ago he had in
contemplation a trip to South America; a cruise in a small boat around the
Peninsula of Labrador to Hudson Bay; and a journey through the Arizona
desert country. He chose the latter."[1]

These comments reveal that, long before Grey became famous, the editors
of this magazine were aware of both him and his plans. Even though *Forest
and Stream* did not publish any of his early articles, he did submit several and,
by way of support, arranged to meet the editorial staff and to present himself
as an adventurer. When he visited Zanesville in May 1904 to promote *Betty
Zane,* he informed the local paper of his intent to summer in British Columbia.[2] Clearly he wanted to impress editors and readers with his ambition and
daring. The fact that he did not get to these places does not make his plans

deceptions or pipe dreams; like many plans, they got changed. Nonetheless, they are a revealing indication of intent and direction. For someone who had traveled little beyond Ohio, New Jersey, and Pennsylvania and who had recently converted to the simple life, these were ambitious hopes to extend his range, but he was as uncertain as he was restless. Getting going and coping were the hard part.

Although he was thirty when he decided to become a writer and thirty-three when he married, Grey still thought of himself as young, and he harbored intense longings for adventure and excitement. He shared his age's enthusiasm for the outdoors and sporting activities. Roughing it exposed the drawbacks of modern conveniences, provided healthy conditioning, and fostered self-sufficiency. Back in 1893, Frederick Jackson Turner had journeyed to the Columbian Exposition in Chicago and had informed his fellow historians that the frontier era had ended; but, thirteen years later, Grey could see that pristine wilderness and large stocks of wild game still existed, even if they were far away from life in the East. Fastening initially upon the access this expansion provided and disregarding its menacing potential, he construed the problem as one of money and time.

Grey refused to believe that his career change and recent marriage placed opportunity beyond his grasp. He could see that sporting magazines needed fresh, interesting accounts. Most of these magazines were spawned by recent industrialization, which lowered the cost of production, increased their attractiveness, and exploited the outdoors to sell manufactured goods. Even though the pay for authors was poor, sometimes nothing at all, these journals covered expenses and facilitated trips that could gain him experience and reputation. He wanted to be an explorer—of places first and then of materials, issues, and attitudes crucial to his writing.

Starting came first, and the author who wrote with such admiration for his venturesome ancestors was surprisingly reluctant to leave home. Dolly campaigned for a cross-country trip as a honeymoon and she was willing to pay for it. She proposed that they take a train to the Grand Canyon, travel leisurely from San Diego to San Francisco, and sightsee in Colorado on their way back. In a journal entry on the eve of his departure, Zane confessed reservations about the upcoming trip, and more than a little uneasiness about his own reluctance:

> Tonight I leave for California with my wife. *I really don't want to go.* I
> don't seem to have the right feeling. I'd rather stay at home. . . . What
> will be the result of this trip? Shall I come back with a wider Knowledge, a

deeper insight, a greater breath, or shall I simply be the same? I say—No! But then I've said no to too many things. There is something wrong with me, with my mind, with my soul.[3]

Dolly, on the other hand, initiated her journal for the trip with the following entry; "In almost a week we'll be 'over the hills and faraway.' What a new experience that will be for me, who has done absolutely no traveling."[4]

This trip during January and February of 1906 dented Zane's reluctance. On January 15, he and Dolly arrived at the first destination on their itinerary: the Grand Canyon. In 1901, when the Santa Fe and Grand Canyon Railroad completed a spur from Williams to the South Rim, visitors no longer had to take a long, hard stagecoach ride, and the Canyon immediately became more accessible and less costly. The convenience of this railroad connection was bolstered by the construction of the elegant El Tovar hotel in 1905. Two years later, in January 1906, Theodore Roosevelt invoked the Antiquities Act of 1906 and declared the Canyon a national monument, although it did not become a national park until 1919.[5]

When Zane and Dolly checked into El Tovar, they were the early beneficiaries of an unfolding commercialization that soon became as integral to the experience as the breathtaking views. The Kolb Brothers studio that opened in 1904 was ideally positioned near the entrance to the Bright Angel Trail and there they purchased photographs and film. On January 16, after a storm that left a foot of snow, they went down into the Canyon on the mule ride to Indian Gardens and Plateau Point. Although these rides commenced in 1891, the extension of Bright Angel from this midpoint to the Colorado River at the bottom was completed only three years before.[6] This excursion left the couple with aching bones and colds that kept them close to the hotel for the next two days.[7] Zane was captivated by the Canyon's vast, desolate scenery, and, as he strolled the walkways and paused at the overlooks, he dreamed of exploring and camping in the shadowy recesses in the distance below, little realizing that his writings would one day influence the way visitors perceived this landscape.

From the Grand Canyon, the newlyweds journeyed to southern California for two weeks. In San Diego, they stayed at the Coronado Hotel and Zane caught a shark while he was fishing from a nearby pier. "This was the beginning of Zane Grey's sea fishing," Dolly appended in a 1937 notation to her honeymoon journal. When Doc went fishing several more times, Dolly noted that she did not "like to be alone among so many people as there are here. I have no self-confidence."[8] From Los Angeles, the couple took a day trip that passed through Altadena, where they would settle fifteen years later, to the narrow-gauge railroad that ran to the top of Mount Lowe. The major attraction for Zane was Catalina Island, an acclaimed center for sportfishing, where he and Dolly stayed for a week. There, in 1898, Charles Holder, a former curator of the American Museum of Natural History and son of its cofounder, landed the first 100-pound tuna to be taken with rod and reel. More accurately, Holder's many articles about this catch earned him this distinction. This and Col. Morehouse's much larger 251-pound tuna that same year sparked interest in angling for saltwater game fish with tackle, and attracted fishermen from the East and England.[9] Having been an avid bass fisherman for many years, Grey was eager to catch one of the fabled tuna.

The abbreviated entries in Dolly's honeymoon journal discreetly veil the disappointment of this first visit:

Feb. 1: This morning early we left Los Angeles for Santa Catalina. First we took the train for San Pedro, then a really fine-looking boat for the island.

Feb. 2: This morning Doc went fishing on the ocean, but I, dreading my first experience, remained here. At noon the fishing boats began to come in and all seemed to have had pretty good luck.

Feb. 3: Today we took another fishing trip, but with no material luck.

Feb. 4: Doc went fishing but I remained at the hotel.

Feb. 5: Today I caught my big albacore.

Feb. 6: This morning Doc took Mr. Clausen out fishing.

Feb. 8: Today we left Catalina Island. Doc went out and attempted to catch a yellow tail.

In a marginal aside to the February 8th entry, Dolly wrote, "Notice *attempt*—That's why we left."[10] This notation implies that Dolly was the only one to catch a large fish.

Grey's avoidance of Catalina for nine years afterward was not due to this initial disappointment.[11] There were other factors in his long-delayed return. His experience taught him that the tuna season did not really start until May and that the numbers of tuna around Catalina had dropped sharply following the catches by Holder and Morehouse. He also learned the critical importance of a skilled boatman and the steep rates to hire them. Even more of an obstacle was the Tuna Club, which dictated how the fishing should be done and was already a bastion of wealth and snobbery. Its rules on tackle and technique and its prized buttons for large catches fostered intense competition. These conditions made the fishing expensive and intimidating, and Grey was neither the first nor the last to be put off by these drawbacks.[12]

From southern California, Zane and Dolly journeyed to the San Gabriel Mission in Santa Barbara and then to Santa Cruz, where they visited a nearby grove of giant redwoods. After a stay in San Francisco, they took the train across the Nevada desert and stopped overnight in Salt Lake City, which struck Dolly as populated with the "most pathetic set of people." On February 16, they arrived in Denver and from there took a final excursion to the Royal Gorge, Pike's Peak, and Garden of the Gods.[13] Ten days later, when they returned, Zane recorded his mixed feelings about the experience in his journal: "I may say traveling has some pleasant features, among which may be named the greed of people."[14]

Zane was eager to resume his writing. The year before, he had finished *The Spirit of the Border* and A. L. Burt, a reprint house with a strong line of books for juveniles, agreed to publish it. Although Grey was relieved not to have to pay, he knew that Burt was well down the ladder of publishers and realized that the prospects for his book were not bright. *Spirit* had come out while he was away, and his first concern now was to rework his manuscript of "Peaceable Village." This work would be rejected many times over the next three years and would be retitled *The Last Trail* when it finally appeared in 1909.

Over the summer of 1906, the paucity of reviews and dismal sales for *Spirit* sent Zane on a searching reevaluation of his efforts so far. He worried that his completed novels were set too far in the past and focused too much upon his ancestors. His guidebooks on writing stressed the importance of personal experience and intensified his awareness of the need for change. Was there worthwhile material for a novel somewhere in his honeymoon trip? Or should he search elsewhere? Should he take more trips? Where should he look to find more promising material? Viewed from this alternative line of thinking, British Columbia, South America, Labrador, and Arizona contained an underlying resemblance: all were exotic and wild. The kind of challenge and opportunity that Zane's ancestors discovered in Ohio so long ago still existed in these distant areas.

When he spoke to the editors of *Forest and Stream*, Grey was seeking the kind of support he initially received from the Camp Fire Club. His second publication, "Canoeing on the Delaware," was originally presented as a talk at a club meeting. George Shields encouraged him to write it up for *Recreation*, the club magazine that he owned and edited, and he accepted it. By 1905, however, Shields's autocratic manner had so strained his relations with the club's membership that he resigned, sold *Recreation,* and started *Shields'* magazine. [15] As Zane experimented and evolved, Shields continued to believe in him. In the late summer or early fall of 1906, he accepted for his new magazine an article by Grey entitled "A Hunter's Change of Heart" that ran in the March 1907 issue. The next issue carried a notice revealing how Grey had solicited more advice from Shields for a trip to Mexico:

> Dr. Zane Grey, the author of "Betty Zane" and several other popular books, went to Mexico some months ago, and in a conversation a few days before leaving he asked me what I wanted from there in the way of stories.
>
> I told him he might get a good story by spending a night in the jungle . . . The Doctor went up into the foot hills, about 100 miles from Tampico, got off at a lonely little station, went into the forest. . . . But why spoil a good story by telling it beforehand? It is a corker and will be published in the May number of this magazine. [16]

Five obscure articles and some faded photographs contain the little available information about a second trip taken by Zane and Dolly, this time to Tampico, Mexico, over January 1907. They make clear that a jungle visit was not his main objective. [17] He was more interested in the area's large concentrations of tarpon. Although anglers had caught some of these large acrobatic fish on rod and reel back in the 1890s, the Tuna Club and its innovative tactics increased its popularity. Much of this interest gravitated to the gulf coast from Florida over to Port Aransas, Texas, which quickly became the Catalina for tarpon fishing. In 1903 the then-secretary of the Tuna Club visited Port Aransas and was so impressed by its tarpon that he established a satellite club with similar rules. Had Grey been seeking only tarpon, he could have visited Port Aransas for less time and money.

Two factors influenced Grey's decision to head for more distant Tampico. First his aversion for the Tuna Club and its influence sent him looking for somewhere less developed and less regulated. Second, Tampico was far less known and therefore a more promising opportunity for articles about it. So far, the published information about the area consisted of an informative letter to the editor that appeared in the March 1905 issue of *Forest and Stream.* In it, J. A. L. Waddell reported that there were only a dozen boats fishing during peak season and that these were dispersed over a vast area teeming with large tarpon. Visitors stayed at a single hotel, the Hildago, whose rooms were small but accommodating and inexpensive. So far there had not been enough visitors for another hotel or a better one. On the other hand, boats and knowledgeable operators could be rented for low fees.[18]

The greatest drawback was the slow, hot, dusty train trip necessary to get there. Until 1900, when Edward Doheny was attracted to the region's rich reserves of oil, Tampico was an isolated seaside village backed by densely foliaged mountains. The lazy outflow of the nearby Panuco River created a large estuary that was ideal habitat for tarpon. Doheny's need for transportation speeded the 1903 completion of a railroad spur from San Luis Potosi to Tampico. This connection to the Mexican Central Railroad made Tampico accessible and deseminated news of its fabulous fishing.[19] Although the oil industry eventually polluted the estuary and destroyed the fishing, the area was still pristine and untapped in 1906. The exhausting three-day train ride from Lackawaxen to San Luis Potosi and the punishing final leg to Tampico were formidable obstacles, especially for Dolly, but the prospects for fabulous fishing and saleable articles fired Zane's determination.

Grey wrote three articles about the tarpon fishing—"Byme-by-Tarpon," "Three Strikes and Out," and "The Leaping Tarpon." These avoided the informational detail of Waddell's letter and sought instead to dramatize the experience. In these apprenticeship efforts, Grey consciously strove to develop his fishing adventures into stories or "Tales," as he entitled the books that later reprinted his articles on sport. All these articles celebrate the natural beauty of the area and the excitement of the fishing, but were consciously crafted as reckonings with defeat.

"Byme-by-Tarpon" recounts Grey's first attempt at tarpon fishing and opens with a colorful portrait of the setting that establishes an upbeat note of anticipation:

> Under the rosy dawn the river quivered like a restless opal. The air, sweet with the song of blackbird and meadow lark, was full of cheer; the sun, rising, shone in splendor on the water, and on the long line of graceful palms lining the opposite bank, and the tropical forest beyond, with its luxuriant foliage festooned by gray moss. Here was a day to warm the heart of any fisherman; here was the beautiful river (613).

The boatman Attalano is accomplished and optimistic, and Grey soon hooks a large tarpon. The fish makes unbelievable jumps, a powerful run, and a long fight ensues. Near the point of exhaustion himself, Grey realizes that the tarpon is also spent. As he prepares to boat the fish, it makes one final desperate lunge, snaps the frayed line, and escapes.

With the title of "Three Strikes and Out," Grey employs the familiar phrase learned from his baseball experience to characterize a similar setback—he gets and misses three very promising strikes. The tarpon are described as numerous, large, and game, but the emergent theme is again failure. In this case, Grey acknowledges that he is not a novice, but admits that he also lacks wisdom. "Every fisherman of wide experience knows that when a day starts badly, it almost invariably ends badly," he observes. "This thought has occurred to me often, at times when, if I had accepted the fatalistic portent, I might have been spared much pain" (201). Not only does Grey respond poorly to his three strikes, but his disregard for his bad luck and his refusal to quit worsen the day for him.

"The Leaping Tarpon" offers a third variation of this thinking. Grey recounts a series of missed tarpon, but here disappointment compensates him with a valuable lesson in the importance of a positive attitude. Grey and an unnamed companion from Chicago encounter two disappointed fishermen and one of them complains about his lone catch of a "five-foot minnow." Zane's friend sarcastically inquires whether the two anglers are "in the fish business" (156–57). When this same friend catches nine tarpon the next day, he furnishes the article's conclusion with his triumphant exclamation: "Tampico no good for tarpon? The fishing here is the best in the world. I've been around some, and I know" (157). This obvious allusion to the disgruntled fisherman from the day before encourages Grey to look beyond his disappointments and to appreciate Tampico's uniqueness.

Since all three articles present Grey failing to catch a tarpon, a reader might conclude that he fared poorly. However, several badly faded photographs of mammoth tarpon, especially one of Grey standing alongside a fish that is longer than he is tall, verify that he actually had terrific success. Another, of Dolly posing with a pair of large tarpon, suggests that she did well too. So why did Grey dwell on his failure? Part of the explanation lies with the fish. Grey wanted his readers to believe that Tampico's tarpon were very challenging; his failure made his adversary appear more formidable and the fishing more exciting. Since his articles were read mostly by men who had never fished for tarpon, they could relate more readily to his defeat than to his success. As a newcomer to tarpon fishing, Grey was aware of his limited skills and truly believed that the main goal of fishing should be appreciation. Grey was also enough of a newcomer to writing about sport that he felt more comfortable with the identity of a deficient enthusiast.

"A Night in a Jungle," Grey's account of his overnight trip into the jungle, cultivates a variant strategy. During his train ride over the mountains to Tampico, he beholds a dazzling expanse of wild jungle and decides that it would be perfect for the outing that Shields had proposed. Another friend and advisor, Alvah James, also influenced this decision. James was a recognized adventurer who went down the Amazon River in a raft in 1902 and published a serial about his trip in *Field and Stream*.[20] Grey met and befriended James during a meeting of New York sportsmen and was thrilled when he accepted an invitation to Lackawaxen.[21] Grey decided to take James on a canoe trip down an unexplored tributary of the upper Delaware River, and wrote an account of the experience entitled "James' Waterloo." James helped Grey to place this article with *Field and Stream,* which published it four months before his Tampico trip. The account characterizes James as a veteran adventurer disdainful of the canoe trip that Grey has proposed. He believes that the lazy waters of the side stream offer little challenge. This skepticism is overturned by hair-raising obstacles and plunges that are exaggerated until they become comic. Bruised and exhausted, James judges the trip to be one of his worst experiences, and Grey is embarrassed over his foolhardy suggestion. Any sense of accomplishment is dispelled by his inept planning and anticipation.

"A Night in a Jungle" recycles both the adventure of his river trip and Zane's self-deprecation. Since he knew nothing about jungle conditions or the area, Grey found it easy and honest to portray himself as a naïf. After he gets off the train at a remote village and surveys the dense foliage beyond, he sheepishly acknowledges, "My intention was somewhat hazy." He violates his original agreement not to carry a gun because "a hunter who would venture into the jungle unarmed was crazy" (296). Unfortunately, his gun compounds his problems. Following an encounter with a jaguar that "checked my communion with nature," he shoots a menacing javelina (wild boar). This provokes its companions to charge and chase him up a tree. "Happily," he observes, "I was a good climber, though I dare say my conquest of that special coconut palm was essayed at the expense of athletic grace and dignity" (297). Later that night, when another jaguar is attracted to the dead javelina, Grey again reaches for his gun, but his nervousness mars his shot and jams his weapon. Luckily, the wounded cat flees. He is relieved when morning arrives and his humiliating outing is over.

Grey's comic presentation spoofed conventions of macho achievement and finessed his lack of qualification. As much as he wanted to be a daring, venturesome explorer, his aspiration was checked by the hard fact that he was merely an ex-baseball player, ex-dentist, and recreational camper. His qualifications were a good-natured enthusiasm and a willingness to learn. Being a greenhorn adventurer and fledgling writer, Grey succeeded by mocking his longings for achievement, but he silently worried about the limited life for this identity.

Tampico was a beneficial introduction to adventure, but not promising material for a novel. Grey did not want to write a novel about fishing. His jungle trip was too brief and his limitations were too pronounced. His discussions with Shields and James carried him to uncharted territory, but sent him elsewhere for the opportunity he needed. Two months after his return, he was off again, this time for an outing into the Grand Canyon. Already thirty-five years old and a tenderfoot from the east, he understood that this would be a more grueling test. Assured of the scenery's magnificence by his honeymoon trip, he knew it would also be equally demanding and dangerous. The water that was so plentiful on all his previous outings would be scarce and challenging to locate. Riding a horse would be hard and controlling it effectively would be even harder. Having suffered the pitfalls of going alone into the jungle, he realized that, first and above all, he needed a reliable guide.

Grey's return to Arizona was inspired by a fortuitous encounter with C. T. "Buffalo" Jones. He met Jones in New York City when Alvah James took him to hear Jones's lecture about capturing live animals out West. Even though the date and place of this talk have never been established, it occurred either during the late fall of 1906 or just after his return from Tampico the following spring, and this event was probably sponsored by the Camp Fire Club, which hosted presentations like this and had Jones, Grey, and James as members.[22] In his discussion of this fateful meeting in "My Own Life," Grey concentrated upon the audience's reaction to Jones's lecture. "He was pretty much hurt," Grey explained, "by the fact that New York sportsmen ridiculed his claims as to the lassoing of wild animals."[23] Jones's lecture was given at a time of exacerbated sensitivity to specious claims about nature and the outdoors. In an article entitled "Real and Sham Natural History" that appeared in the March 1903 issue of *Atlantic Monthly,* John Burroughs offered a six-page denunciation of Ernest Thompson Seton for excessive fabrication in his animal stories. He argued that the animals in his popular stories were depicted as humans preferred to think of them rather than as they actually were. This attack and an article of support by President Roosevelt launched a heated debate about "nature-fakers."[24]

Grey was so impressed by Jones that he went to visit him in his hotel room. There he found Jones despondent over the criticism he had received and grateful for Grey's interest. He asked Jones to include him on his next trip and proposed to write an account that would prove both Jones's claims and his daring.[25] This request represented another important step away from his reluctance to travel. At a May 1906 meeting of sportsmen, Zane encountered a man who had gone to Cuba to write a story about the Bay of Fundy and wrote to Dolly, "This sort of thing, in so many men, seems odd to me. I understand their wandering, or desire to see, hear, watch, study life, but Lord! To go one place to get far away from another to write about it makes me a little tired."[26]

Grey's proposal also contains a couple of puzzling incongruities. First, Grey says that Jones's lecture was criticized even though it was accompanied by "motion pictures of wild animals he had caught."[27] Apparently his film showed only the animals and not the capture. On this next trip, Jones took not only Grey but also Grant Wallace, who was a skilled photographer and the owner of a motion picture camera. He was responsible for film footage that later showed Jones in action and verified his claims.[28]

Even more surprising is Grey's plan to write a book that would discredit Jones's detractors, since his two novels so far were romanticized history. Still, here and with the Westerns that followed, Grey consciously vindicated his stories with claims that they were based upon personal experiences or actual history. Charles Schreyvogel would construct his narrative paintings about the West from figures posing on New York City rooftops. Frederick Faust would write his Max Brand Westerns in a villa near Florence. Karl May imagined most of his popular Westerns for Europeans before his brief visit to the United States in 1908. Grey, on the other hand, believed that firsthand knowledge of his material was essential and that he had to experience the West in order to write about it. For this trip, he acquired the best portable camera that money could buy. The thousands of photographs that he would take over the years that followed were motivated by a deeply rooted need for a record and proof. Although he took photos to aid his memory, he valued them even more as verification. The photographs that always accompanied his articles on sport were the result of technological advances that made photographic reproductions possible and popular, but they also involved a hypersensitivity to "nature faking" and a conviction that they authenticated both his experiences and his writings. For such a romantic writer, Grey's lifelong commitment to photography was as peculiar as it was compulsive.

In 1906, Jones had acquired a ranch in the House Rock Valley on the eastern perimeter of the Grand Canyon, and at the time of his lecture, he had scheduled a lion hunt into the North Rim area. He agreed to include Grey if he paid. Grey claimed that this demand exhausted Dolly's inheritance. Jones's fee of $200–300 was a substantial sum, but it certainly did not deplete Dolly's $10,000 inheritance.[29] Grey was too intent upon avoiding the plight of his father or an enforced return to dentistry to gamble everything. Nonetheless, this investment was as momentous for him as his decision to finance the publication of *Betty Zane,* and his prospects for turning a profit were not any better.

Jones himself was in no position to help a needy writer. Until 1900, his life had been a series of unprofitable experiments with politics and ranching. At this time, he noticed the distressing fact that the once vast herds of buffalo had dropped to less than 1,000 survivors and began campaigning for the establishment of refuges. When he learned of plans to use Yellowstone National Park as a preserve for buffalo, he applied to be the park's first game warden, and won the appointment. In this position, he arranged transportation for specimens from the Goodnight Ranch in Texas and supervised construction of a compound for them. His ensuing indifference to the details of management and bureaucratic procedures turned other administrators into enemies and led to his resignation in September 1905.

Deciding that his best prospect for income was raising cataloes, a crossbred of buffalo bulls with Galloway cattle, Jones obtained a federal land grant for his House Rock Ranch in the Kaibab range north of Lee's Ferry, and quickly established a herd there. When the Grand Canyon Game Preserve was established in November 1906, Jones arranged for Jim Owens, his assistant in Yellowstone, to be appointed its game warden. Since this position brought Jim Owens a meager salary and Jones's cataloes left him in debt, they collaborated on a plan for capturing mountain lions alive and selling them to zoos and private preserves. The terms of the preserve's establishment stipulated that deer inside its boundaries were protected from hunting, but mountains lions, coyotes, wolverines, and wolves were designated predators and bounties were paid for them.[30] That is to say, Grey was going hunting in a federal reserve with the game warden, and its regulations allowed, even encouraged, killing some of its wild animals.

Jones needed Grey's fee to defray his own expenses. Both he and Owens had already hunted mountain lions in Yellowstone, but they had not been in Arizona long enough to be comfortable with its much different terrain and weather conditions. Consequently, Jones enlisted Jim Emett, a prominent but controversial local, and agreed to pay him $5 a day per person to guide and outfit his party. Whether Grey paid this cost or a higher fee to Jones is unclear.

Grey's book was as important to Jones as his money. Jones did not expect it to convert his skeptics, but he believed it would be good publicity and he had always wanted that. Jones's grandstanding factored prominently into his feud with the administration of Yellowstone. He situated corrals for buffalo near Mammoth Hot Springs, then the park's busiest entrance, so that tourists would have convenient access, instead of using a remote area that would have better served the buffalo.[31] Jones then slighted their care and concentrated upon public appearances. When Theodore Roosevelt visited the park, Jones took his hounds and joined the party uninvited. He then pushed his agenda so hard that Roosevelt had to enlist help to be rid of Jones.[32]

Grey did not notice Jones's flaws until he was under way and apprehensive. En route to the Grand Canyon, he dispatched Dolly a letter proclaiming "I miss my girl . . . [and] do not want to go away at all." He reassured her, "Barring some unfortunate event I shall come back soon, and be better for my work," but admitted, "I am groping. I am discouraged because of my insufficient training, not because of my gifts. It is a terrible handicap."[33] He arrived at the South Rim in a blizzard and complained to Dolly, "I am about sick and wish I were home with you. I hurt my back a little carrying my baggage."[34] Deciding that the outing should be delayed until the weather improved, the group opted for the warmth and sunshine of Los Angeles. From there Grey wrote to Dolly, "I am afraid that this trip started wrong, and will be a failure. . . . Col. Jones is such a selfish, forgetful old fool. He doesn't know where he is half the time." Jones was also "horribly stingy," insisting upon coach fare and refusing to join Grey in the Pullman car on the train. In Los Angeles, he refused to pay twenty-five cents for a bus and Grey had to cover the fare for both of them.[35]

When Arizona's wintry weather improved sooner than they expected, the group hurried back to Flagstaff and the imminent start of the trip lifted Grey's spirits:

> I am positively quivering with joy at the prospect of the trip. I have lost all my blues, and I'm actually happy. I need this wild life, this freedom, and I'll come home to love you to death. The spirit of my ancestors is dominant in me at this time. I don't want to kill. I simply want the broad open free wilderness, to be alive, to look into nature, and so into my soul.[36]

Other problems had to be settled first. Grey learned that Jim Emett was being tried for stealing cattle and could be jailed. Since 1896, when Mormon Church elders appointed him to supervise the Colorado River crossing at Lee's Ferry, Emett had been embroiled in disputes with local cattle and sheep ranchers. The most recent one involved a 1906 charge of rustling cattle from the Bar Z Ranch. Emett maintained that the cattle were actually his. Luck-

Jim Emett, ca. 1907. (Courtesy of Loren Grey.)

ily, key witnesses for the plaintiff were elsewhere when the trial started and Emett had strong support for his claims. The two-day trial ended with a verdict of not guilty and gave Grey a memorable introduction to the rough-and-tumble of life in the West.[37]

On April 12, Grey, Jones, Owens, Emett, and several Mormon elders departed Flagstaff for Lee's Ferry. "You ought to see this crowd of Mormons I am going with," he boasted to Dolly. "If they aren't a tough bunch, I never saw one. They all pack guns. But they're nice fellows."[38] In an earlier letter, he had reassured her, "Do not worry about me. I am at home in the woods. I'll take to the thing like a duck takes to water."[39] On the second day, when the party reached the Moenkopi Wash, he was already stiff and sore. His lips were cracked, his tongue swollen, and his eyes burned painfully. The alkali water made him sick. Two days later he wrote in his journal, "I am a sight to behold. Never thought I would get so dirty, or hungry, or cold."[40] A discussion of religion with a Mormon president and bishop went so poorly he resolved to keep his mouth shut. The final sixteen miles to the Colorado River were "hell," and the ferry crossing even worse. The run-off swollen river did not crest until June, but it was already a chocolate torrent when Grey arrived. He did not bother to record the details of his crossing because "I shall remember—rather I shall never forget" (21).

During the group's two-day stay at Lee's Ferry, Emett told Grey about his predecessor, John D. Lee, who started the ferry when he was exiled there for his involvement in the Mountain Meadows Massacre. On September 11, 1857, Lee led a group of Indians and fifty Mormons in an attack upon a wagon train of California-bound settlers that left all 120 dead. Until Lee was finally executed in 1877, he maintained and operated his ferry. In 1898, Mormon elders approved Emett's petition to take over and restore the abandoned crossing.[41] Grey was intrigued by the hard lives of Lee and Emett. He learned that Emett came from Mormon parents who settled Utah, and was born in a wagon during a desert crossing. His mother had climbed steep trails three days later, and lived to be ninety-three. By the time Grey met him, Emett had broad shoulders, a great shaggy head, and a bushy white beard that emanated dignity and virility. He was also a polygamist with two wives and twenty children. In 1890, when his first wife, Emma, was thirty-eight, he married Electra Jane Gruell, who was eighteen. In 1893, when Electra had their first child, Emma gave birth to her eleventh and final one. Despite his large family, Emett slept out in the open most nights and possessed an encyclopedic knowledge of the surrounding area.[42] To the impressionable tenderfoot, this resourceful, strong-willed, self-reliant outdoorsman was as impressive as the

Zanes and Wetzels and presented him reassuring proof that hearty settler stock still existed.

Dee Wooley, who was among the "crowd of Mormons" accompanying him, likewise impressed Grey. Zane learned that Wooley was a polygamist and told Dolly, "Mr. Wooley wants me to go to Kanab to study the Mormons. He has two families and 15 handsome unmarried girls."[43] When he visited Kanab several weeks later, he did not mention whether he met Wooley's families, but he encountered another Mormon there who had five wives and fifty-five children, and so fascinated Zane that he told others about the man for years afterward.[44]

When the group finally arrived at the House Rock Ranch on April 19, Grey's legs were so sore from riding he could not sit down. When he recovered, he explored a primeval forest near the Persia sheep camp and discovered some Indian pictographs at Snake Gulch, but confessed to his journal, "I am afraid that I am not getting as much out of this trip as I might get" (34). Days later, he beheld a big white mustang racing ahead of a pack of wild horses. On April 29, the group established its hunting camp high in the Siwash with an expansive view of the Powell's Plateau and the distant San Francisco peaks. Though the Grand Canyon itself was not visible, Point Sublime was nearby and offered one of the most dramatic views from the North Rim. The next day Jones treed his first mountain lion, but it escaped. Grey dropped another one weighing 350 pounds with what Jones called "the finest shot I ever saw." He gloated, "My first lion was the King" (59–60).

Since the group's North Rim location was three thousand feet higher than the South Rim, the weather was cold with frequent snow squalls. On May 6, the hunters awoke to falling snow that evolved into a blizzard and left them frozen and disoriented. Wallace returned from the long day "torn, ragged, bloody, and haggard," and Jones's leg was injured when his horse fell. Five lions were sighted, but all escaped. The group finally captured a female lion, but the bound, helpless beast left Grey feeling dejected. "And I could feel for her," he wrote in his journal. "Give me liberty or give me death" (103).

On May 9, the men broke camp and headed west for a return to El Tovar and the South Rim. Exhilarated by his experiences, Grey was confident that he had gained a wealth of material and was eager to resume his writing. To his surprise and dismay, the trip's greatest ordeal lay ahead and, for some reason, he never published a word about it. A person familiar with the Grand Canyon today would expect the group to have headed down the Kaibab trail, crossed the river, and ascended the historic Bright Angel Trail. However, in May 1907, this route was not yet possible. Prior to leaving for Los Angeles,

Jones and Grey met with David Rust, the son-in-law of Dee Wooley, about guiding them. Grey informed Dolly that Rust "was to have charge of our trip."[45] Unfortunately, Rust had to withdraw in order to complete a trail on which he had been working all spring. This was the Kaibab trail, which was initially named after him, and the high water of the spring runoff stalled his cable crossing over the Colorado River and kept him from completing his trail until June, long after Grey's trip was over.[46]

When Rust had to withdraw, he informed Jones about another trail further to the west that had been established the year before by William Bass. The north side of this trail, called the Shinumo, was little more than an intermittently marked route, and no one in the group had ever taken it. Several times during the descent, the trail disappeared and the group had to dispatch scouts in different directions to locate the way. About halfway down, Grey left his horse to explore and arrived at a dead-end precipice. He was so hot and exhausted when he returned, he had difficulty remounting. When the terrain became treacherous again, he was too fatigued to dismount and his overburdened horse fell. Luckily he escaped unharmed. A cliff outcropping provided a view that confirmed that the group was on course, but it sent them along a perilous, foot-wide shelf of loose shale. Further on, the horses had to make a series of dangerous jumps ranging from two to four feet. "The sheer drop was tremendous," Grey jotted in his journal, "It was appalling. Once, my heart stopped beating." A gushing spring furnished badly needed water and prompted a decision to follow the drainage that proved to be *the* worst stretch so far. "When I say bad, I mean BAD," Grey noted (111–14).

Acknowledging that his nerves were shot and his body was spent, Grey relied on grim determination to continue. With a ragged scrawl that graphically registered the toll of the ordeal, he imagined that Bass might not be there. "What on earth could I do?" he speculated. "I could not get over this horrible monstrous river and I could not go *back*." When they finally did reach the river and spied the cable, no one was there. Reflecting later on his devastation, Grey wrote, "How I hated the river, the place! I cursed it" (116). Before he and the others could muster energy to discuss their plight, they heard a shout and spotted Bass waving to them from the other side. Later they learned that Bass never saw the fire that was supposed to signal him because they positioned it in the wrong place. Minor repairs and sheer luck had carried Bass to the river that day.

Back in Lackawaxen by mid-May, Grey worked feverishly developing his notes. The opening pages of *The Last of the Plainsmen,* his completed account, effectively convert the novice fisherman of the Tampico articles into a dude tenderfoot, and present him so that the reader expects change and improvement. Grey reduced the many hardships in his journals and associated them with this potential:

> So I sat down and wondered what Jones and Emmett,[47] and these men would consider really hazardous. I began to have a feeling that I would find out; that experience for me was but in its infancy; that far across the desert the something which had called me would show hard, keen, perilous life. And I began to think of reserve powers of fortitude and endurance.[48]

This thinking reconfigures his suffering into a series of tests that make him stronger and more skillful. His persistence against adversity effectively closes the gap between his deficiencies and the prowess of his companions.

Over the course of his narrative, Grey develops into a confident, capable hunter. During his first lion chase, he finally understands when to rein in his horse and when to let him run (91). Several chases later, he confidently asserts, "Here I wore out my soreness of muscle, and gradually overcame my awkwardness in the saddle" (106). These advances diminish his outsider status, and he finally gains the group's acceptance when he spots a prank intended to embarrass him and turns it against the perpetrators (194–98).

This progress dissolves his self-conscious sense of alienation, and soon afterward he ceases to be merely a detached observer of his surroundings: "I started to run as if I were a wild Indian. My running had no aim; just sheer mad joy of the grand old forest, the smell of pine, the wild silence and beauty loosed the spirit in me so it had to run, and I ran with it till the physical being failed" (209). This transformation qualifies him to hunt Old Tom, a lion legendary for his elusiveness (232–33). When he finally bags a wolf (substituted for the lion he actually killed) with a perfect shot (248), he is so pleased with his accomplishment that he jubilantly proclaims, "If you want fame or wealth or wolves, go out and hunt for them" (249).

Personal development was neither Grey's only theme nor even his main one. Frequently in his account, he presents animals so that they upstage him. The herds of buffalo and wild horses exhilarate him and leave him feeling fortunate. They grace the scenery and animate it, especially the mountain lions that bound effortlessly across the treacherous terrain and adroitly blend in. His highest regard is reserved for animals that are not wild. He is awed by the horses and dogs that are so integral to the hunt. He truly cares for the horse that transports him long distances and charges through dense underbrush after the quarry. Though smaller and less endowed for combat, the dogs inspire Grey with the way they spring to life at a fresh scent, race howling after lions, and then fearlessly attack.

Buffalo Jones is the centerpiece of the story, the person behind the title, and the outdoorsman that Grey admires most. Throughout the trip and afterward, Grey was continually reminded of Jones's defects,[49] but he decided that an accurate record of Jones's faults and deficiencies was inappropriate and chose instead a romantic depiction, a choice of momentous importance for his future novels: instead of presenting the actual person who created so many problems, he crafted a slick portrait of an accomplished hunter and leader. He reconfigured the facts of his personal experiences so that his reader was presented with a figure that was larger than life, and the result was more than a little contrived. Jones was sixty-three years old at the time of the trip, but Grey presented him as spry enough to ride long distances, to climb trees after lions, and to endure rude camps and adverse weather. Grey made him equal to the heartiest member of the group and the best hunter. The Jones in his story assesses situations and issues commands. He is deadly serious and aloof, indisputably the group's leader. Frank, Jim, and Wallace are subordinates who interact comfortably with each other, but are indistinguishable.

One consequence of this ennoblement of Jones was Grey's elimination of Jim Emett. Except for the long description of his compound at Lee's Ferry, Emett is mentioned only in passing and the reader is wrongly led to believe that he remained there when the group departed. In a 1926 article entitled "The Man Who Influenced Me Most," Grey memorialized this rugged Westerner who outfitted his earliest trips and inspired many characters in his Westerns. This account clarifies Grey's deep indebtedness to Emett on this outing and was undoubtedly meant to correct his slighting in the original account. Grey states that he had "the marvelous good fortune" to have had him as a "constant companion." Emett is commended as a knowledgeable guide, an accomplished hunter, and an adept tree climber. Grey credits Emett with securing his sighting of Silvermane, the leader of a pack of wild horses that would reappear in several of his Westerns. Unlike Jones who was preoccupied with subduing animals, Emett is presented as a lover of animals and scenery, and an enormous influence upon Grey's high regard for both.[50] When he was writing *The Last of the Plainsmen,* Grey realized that any such acknowledgment would have diminished Jones's stature and kept Emett offstage. The same fate befell Jim Owens, who was as adept as Jones at hunting mountain lions.

Grey also aided Jones's exploitation of Buffalo Bill Cody. His appropriation of "Buffalo" in his name communicated the fact that he too had killed many buffalo, but also signaled an important distinction. Buffalo Bill Cody

had achieved wealth and renown for his Wild West show celebrating construction of the railroad and settlement of the West; he killed buffalo and
Indians in order to pave the way for civilization. Buffalo Jones preferred to
think of himself as an enlightened visionary who recognized the wanton
destruction of Cody's actions and dedicated himself to saving the buffalo
from extinction. As Grey explained in his preface:

> For years necessity compelled him to earn his livelihood by supplying the
> meat of buffalo to the caravans crossing the plains. At last, seeing that the
> extinction of the noble beasts was inevitable, he smashed his rifle over
> a wagon wheel and vowed to save the species. For ten years he labored,
> pursuing, capturing and taming buffalo, for which the West gave him
> fame, and the name Preserver of the American Bison (v).

Grey conspired to make Jones's hunt an extension of his Yellowstone work in
his quest to capture mountain lions alive and relocate them to zoos. (Ironically, the difficulties of transportation killed most of the lions they caught).

Grey and Jones presumed Cody's outlook to be mercenary, old-fashioned,
and behind the times. Cody's dedication to progress blinded him to the
defects in his cause and its disastrous consequences. Unlike Cody, Jones
represented those pioneers who appreciated the value of the undeveloped
West, and campaigned to preserve it. Grey's first three novels memorialized his ancestors as virile, resourceful, self-reliant outdoorsmen. Believing
at the time that these kind of men disappeared with their deaths, he tentatively entitled the final novel of his Ohio trilogy *The Last of the Bordermen*.
However, his exposure to Jones, Emett, and Owens persuaded him that men
like this *did* exist, even if they were an older generation and lived only in
remote, desolate areas like Arizona, which was a "territory" until 1912, the
last of the contiguous states to be granted statehood. To Grey's perception,
they and their adventures made them as threatened as the buffalo, and his
account consciously strove to preserve their stories. However, the title he
transferred from his Ohio novel and applied to these living examples caused
a problem. Ned Buntline earned Buffalo Bill his first fame back in 1869 with
a serial entitled "Buffalo Bill, King of the Border Men" that became a popular
dime novel.[51] Grey needed a title that would sharpen, rather than blur, the
important distinction between Buffalo Jones and Buffalo Bill. This modification of *The Last of the Bordermen* to *The Last of the Plainsmen* may seem slight,
but it expresses Grey's developing perception of the West.

At the time that he was writing his account of Jones, Grey worried that he
and his book might be condemned and dismissed as harshly as Jones was at

Pawnee Bill, Buffalo Bill (seated), and Buffalo Jones (standing), ca. 1909. (Courtesy of the Buffalo Bill Historical Center, Cody, Wyoming.)

the time of his lecture, and this fear added another dimension to his depiction of Jones as an endangered species. Critical indifference to his first two novels had strained his commitment to writing. Following his difficulties with *Betty Zane,* he arranged for Daniel Murphy, the son-in-law of the poet Edwin Markham, to become his literary agent, and Murphy's advice and encouragement moved Grey to write this letter of gratitude:

> You wrote in your last letter "D— the critics!" . . . To be sure I was as much surprised as delighted, and told my wife so. She didn't believe it so I had to prove it to her, and then she expressed her sorrow, not only that you could use a cuss word, but because of my unholy glee. . . . These critics have the power. They know it; they are proud of it,—and in my instance if they do recognize something latent and powerful, it does not move them to encourage me. I know you will take exception to my view, and perhaps you will be right. I think already you have tempered and softened my rebellious spirit, and I may say earnestly that I have got so I do not care at all.

But, of course, he did care. This concern exacerbated his worry that his trip and his book about it might not fulfill his literary aspirations. Jones's stoic endurance of hardship became even more inspiring as Grey contemplated the real possibility that his account might be little read, and perhaps might not even be published. As he went on to explain in the same letter to Murphy:

> The thing was wonderful, and[,] strange to say[,] that which made [the] most impression on me had nothing to do with sport. I starved on the desert, was lost on the desert, buried in sand on the desert, and I lived on the desert. I met some real men, men who live lonely terrible lives, who are silent, who perform heroic deeds as a matter of course and men who have hearts, who have loved and lost. . . . I want to justify Buffalo Jones. It seems many of these nature writers ridiculed his story last winter, when he claimed to have lassoed and tied a mountain-lion all by himself. Well, he did. I can prove it. I have photographs to show it. And I believe as Wallace said that we have a story which will make these same sit-in-the-hotel-parlor-writers crawl under their beds.[52]

Behind his sensitivity to the "lonely terrible lives" of these men who had "loved and lost" lay his lack of confidence in his literary talent and his thwarted yearnings for recognition. His loneliness and rejection became theirs. The many hours and long days Grey invested in writing up his Arizona experiences only deepened this brooding. Over the summer, he sank into a deep depression, and in a journal entry on the first of September, he wrote:

> The summer is over. I write those words with mingled feelings of relief, shame, regret and pain. For in my long experiences this has been the saddest summer I have ever lived. Words are cold dead things. I need not put here in detail my wildness, my savage intensity of passion, my humiliation, my pain. For they have been burned indelibly into my heart.[53]

Only continued encouragement from both Dolly and Murphy enabled him to complete his book. In his preface, he explained, "As a man I came to see the wonder, the tragedy of their lives, and to write about them" (vii).

Unfortunately, Dolly and Murphy could not shield Zane from publishers and their frank estimate of his work. In January 1908, the manuscript was submitted to Harper and Brothers. Like his two previous novels, it was quickly rejected, but this time the editor Ripley Hitchcock delivered this brutal evaluation: "I don't see anything in this to convince me that you can write either narrative or fiction" (4). In the section of "My Own Life" in which he describes this devastating setback, Grey claims that Hitchcock's estimate so shell-shocked him that he did not register its full impact until he reached the street and suddenly had to grip a lamppost to keep from falling.

Grey also recalls that by day's end, his confidence had returned and that he started work on a new novel to prove Hitchcock wrong (5).[54] This self-serving commentary about his determination downplayed the prolonged devastation of this rejection. The novel he claimed to have started would have been *The Heritage of the Desert,* but he was unable to write this first Western until *after* he completed two more trips. The first was another hunt for mountain lions with Jones from mid-March to mid-May 1908, and the second was a return to Tampico from January to March 1909. After more rejections from Dodd, Mead, and Barnes, Murphy persuaded Outing Publishing to accept *The Last of the Plainsmen* the month before Grey's departure for Arizona, but the relief of this news was short-lived. The December before, Murphy had placed an excerpt from the book entitled "Lassoing Lions in the Siwash" with the highly regarded *Everybody's* magazine. Grey was so pleased that he wrote in his journal, "This is the first substantial appreciation that I have received in the four years I have been working at the gates of literature,"[55] and he hastily granted the magazine the rights to his photographs. The editors at Outing decided that these photographs were so important that they demanded use of them as a condition of acceptance. For several weeks, Grey agonized that his carelessness had ruined all his hard work.[56]

Outing was best known for its sport magazine with the same name, and few literary critics noticed its books. Moreover, the $200 Grey received in royalties for *The Last of the Plainsmen* barely surpassed the $100 *Everybody's* paid for his excerpt. However, sportsmen had enough respect for Outing's books that this work, when it was published, gained Grey a reputation as a daring and accomplished outdoorsman. Certainly *Field and Stream* thought so. Previously this magazine had merely been receptive to Grey's offerings, but after publication of his book it began to feature and promote them. Its backing of Grey at this critical moment of need sprang from its ambitious quest to become *the* premier magazine of sport. In 1906, ten years after the magazine's start in St. Paul and ambitious relocation to New York City in 1898, the owners of *Field and Stream* were strapped with a debt of $18,000 and a meager circulation of only 10,000. They approached Eltinge Warner, then a printing salesman and circulation manager, and offered him 50 percent of the magazine to be its general manager. Within two years, he had achieved enough momentum to obtain financing to purchase the remaining 50 percent.[57]

Under Warner's stewardship, *Field and Stream* published three of Grey's Tampico articles and "Tige's Lion." Although Warner paid a pittance for these, he saw Grey as an upcoming writer whose unusual experiences and engaging style would attract new readers and boost subscriptions. He also believed in aggressive promotion. After reading *The Last of the Plainsmen,* Warner contacted Grey and encouraged him to take another lion hunt and write a long serial. Over the eight months between Grey's April 1908 departure for Arizona and the publication of the first installment of "Roping Lions in the Grand Canyon" in the January 1909 issue, Warner labored to build anticipation. First, he ignored his policy against book reviews and ran a very positive one of *The Last of the Plainsmen* in the October issue. In bold contrast to *The Nation,* which denounced the story's "hero worship" as "so pronounced that one can hardly read it without suspecting an unconscious over-coloring,"[58] *Field and Stream* maintained:

> It will stand unchallenged as the most graphic and interesting description yet written of the wonderful region of desert and mountain bordering the Grand Canyon of the Colorado. The author has that happy art, shared by so few, of losing himself in his subject, rising superior to hackneyed tricks of style or expression, and writing as the men of the West talk, straight from the heart, forcefully, yet with an easy swing.[59]

Two months later, the magazine came out with an announcement of the upcoming serial that greatly exaggerated the importance of Grey and the success of his book:

Next month we shall commence publication of Zane Grey's new serial, "Roping Lions in the Grand Canyon." . . . Ours is the story of a second expedition to the wilderness of desert and mountains in northern Arizona, the wildest and most picturesque in America, so nearly inaccessible that it still teems with big game as in the days when the first white man gazed upon its wonders. The first lion hunt met with success and was chronicled in Grey's book 'The Last of the Plainsmen,' which met with a phenomenal sale—an entire edition being required to fill an order from London . . . he has a second hunt to tell about, more successful, more exciting, and with double the interest of the first. We can promise our readers a rare treat in this serial. It will be more widely read and discussed than any feature ever presented by a sportsmen's magazine.[60]

For the first installment, Warner fashioned a profile of the author that quickly evolved into a standard practice; beneath a large photograph of Grey, Warner offered this colorful characterization of his experience:

This is the newest of sports, strenuous and replete with peril, but alive with the thrills which sportsmen accept as full payment for their toils and risks. But few men have as yet shared in its delights, and one of these few is Zane Grey. . . . "Roping Lions in the Grand Canyon," commencing in this issue, is the true account of a notable hunting expedition—the most notable ever undertaken by American sportsmen.[61]

Whatever misgivings Warner harbored over Grey's return to the same area of the Grand Canyon for more mountain lion hunting were quelled by trust that his variation would be interesting and successful. More accurately, he was betting on it.

During his two-month trip over the spring of 1908, Grey kept another journal.[62] Its more abbreviated entries reveal that he followed a similar route and relied more on memory than notations. The trip from Flagstaff to Lee's Ferry and on to the ranch at the House Rock Valley was the same except for an overnight excursion to Tuba. From the ranch, Grey, Jones, Owens, and Emett crossed the Utah desert to Kanab and Fredonia. They headed south through Snake Gulch and established their lion-hunting camp at Rock Creek. "Roping Lions" dispenses with routing and concentrates instead upon the hunting. There is no mention of the day trip he took on April 20 to a cliff overlooking the Surprise Valley of the Thunder River. During his previous visit, Grey learned about this inaccessible, little-known area from David Rust, and he wrote Dolly about his excited wish to visit it:

Mr. Rust knows of a canyon where no man, except prehistoric, besides himself has ever put a foot. He reached it after a long, though not hard, climb over the Marble Walls below. This is a most beautiful place. There are great cottonwood trees, grass, and flowers, a great spring and stream, and deer and beaver.

No one suspects this. No one has ever seen it save him. From here the canyon looks like a dark thread.

Well, you and I are going to camp in that canyon alone for two or three months. Mr. Rust will get some men to carry our outfit up on their backs— a burro can't go—and we will stay there, and invite our souls.

Think of it! All alone amid the silence and grandeur of the canyon, far from the fretting world, and noise and distraction.[63]

The trail construction that kept Rust from serving as his guide prevented Grey from reaching this wondrous destination until his second trip. Curiously, he did not mention his momentous visit in his published account, even though he mailed Dolly an enraptured description of it. "Heart broken" because there was no access to the valley floor, he located a cliff overlook that unfolded to him the lush vegetation and towering walls that made the valley special. A wondrous river sprang from the side of a distant cliff, plunged 2,500 feet, and twisted its way through the center of the valley. (Thunder River is not only one of the world's shortest rivers, but also one of the few that empties into a stream—Tapeets Creek.) After describing how he had launched a boulder that took an amazing eighteen seconds to reach the bottom, he repeated, "I expect to find my way down there, and some day take you in and camp a couple of weeks."[64] This memory would inspire the famous ending to *Riders of the Purple Sage* in which Lassiter topples a precariously balanced boulder that seals himself, Jane Withersteen, and young Fay in the story's valley hideaway, making his romantic plans for himself and Dolly as important to this ending as the valley and his boulder.

Neither Warner nor Grey anticipated the most striking result of this trip: Grey's emergence as an adroit adventurer. With his first trip behind him, he realized that he was no longer a tenderfoot. His eventual acceptance as an equal by the other hunters blocked him from replaying the role of novice and recycling his self-consciousness and self-deprecation. His previous experience demanded that he present himself as a veteran who understands what to expect and how to respond.

In "Roping Lions," Grey dispenses with saddle soreness and horse control. Little is made of the discomforts of sleeping on hard ground and enduring cold nights and undesirable campsites. Although Grey's year away from Arizona necessitated difficult reconditioning and readjustment, he copes with hardship as his companions do—without comment. Competence frees Grey from having to rely on others and diminishes his awe for their resourcefulness and prowess. The characterization of Jones is most affected by this change. He continues to be the consummate outdoorsman and undisputed leader, but Grey now notices when he falters and even has him fail. At one point in the account, a treed lion lashes out and tears Jones's pants. Pulling away, he loses his balance, tumbles from the tree, and provokes everyone to laugh. The deaths of several lions cause him to question openly his abilities and goals.

Grey's abandonment of his tenderfoot identity necessitated an alternative measure of the trip's meaning. Since Jones is no longer his role model, Grey makes besting his lingering fears his objective. As he remarks several pages into his account, "I knew I had to be cured of my dread, and the sooner it was done the better."[65] Later, when he is near a lion, he explains, "I had to steel my nerve to keep so close" (75). These remarks prepare for the climactic moment when he matches Jones by climbing a tree after a lion without a gun. Proudly he asserts, "Fear of them [lions] was not in me that day" (149).

Grey linked this emotional reckoning to his heightened sensitivity to his awesome surroundings. "Roping Lions" presents fuller, more artful descriptions of the desert's beauty. Dan Murphy sent Grey a copy of John Van Dyke's *The Desert* (1901) while he was writing *The Last of the Plainsmen,* and he was so impressed by the verbal artistry of this art critic that he consciously studied his example.[66] However, the allure of the desert for him involved more than aesthetics. His fascination with the panoramic colors sunlight elicited from this forbidding landscape included a therapeutic confrontation with elemental conditions and needs. However beautiful it might appear, this rugged, parched terrain made survival both a paramount concern and a significant component of his reckoning with fear. The hunt in this treacherous landscape occasions a complex thrill that breaks down his civilized inhibitions, projects him beyond the confines of selfhood, and integrates him into the vastness of his surroundings:

> Something swelled within my breast at the thought that for the time I was part of that wild scene. The eye of an eagle soaring above would have placed me as well as my lion among the few living things in the range of his all-compassing vision. Therefore, all was mine, not merely the lion— for he was only the means to an end—but the stupendous, unnamable thing beneath me, this chasm that hid mountains in the shades of its cliffs, and the granite tombs, some gleaming pale, passionless, others red and warm, painted by a master hand; and the wind-caves, dark portaled

under their mist curtains, and all that was deep and far-off, unapproach-
able, unattainable, of beauty exceeding, dressed in ever-changing hues,
was mine by the right of presence, by right of the eye to see and the mind
to keep (109).

His activity and the setting awaken a wildness at the core of his being that
triumphs over fear, and even consciousness itself. As he explained more
clearly in his later article "What the Desert Means to Me" (1924): "Nothing in civilized life can cast the spell of enchantment, can grip men's souls
and terrify women's hearts like the desert. It has to do with the dominating
power of wild, lonely desolate places. . . . Men love the forbidding and desolate desert because of the ineradicable and unconscious wildness of savage
nature in them."[67]

This romantic transport could easily have been shattered by a careless mishap or a mauling by a lion, but it is not. Grey presents it glibly as a stimulus
to hunt that sends him racing across fields of scree and down steep drops
with total abandon. When he spots a lion in the distance, he charges after it,
oblivious to danger. With "sheer delight" and no heed for safety, he pursues
it along a narrow ledge. When the trail leads to a dead-end, he coolly photographs the cornered beast. "What would follow had only hazily formed
in my mind," he explains. "But the nucleus of it was that he should go free"
(130–36). Unfortunately, the lion does not comprehend this intent and attacks. Suddenly aware of danger for the first time, Grey draws his pistol and
shoots the beast between the eyes.

This death and that of another strangled lion intrude a dissonant note of
loss that qualifies his triumph over fear and liberated wildness. Grey leads
the reader to believe that he was so intoxicated with the emotional effect of
his experience that he was oblivious to consequences. However, the seeds
for future change are planted early in the account when he has an opportunity to examine closely a lion that has been captured and bound. Gazing
into the eyes of this magnificent creature, he suddenly beholds that the same
wildness that Aldo Leopold, the renowned naturalist, discovered years later
in the eyes of a dying wolf:

> I wanted to see a wild lion's eyes at close range. They were exquisitely
> beautiful, their physical properties as wonderful as their expression. Great
> half globes of tawny, amber, streaked with delicate wavy lines of black,
> surrounding pupils of intense purple fire. . . . Deep in those live pupils,
> changing, quickening with a thousand vibrations, quivered the soul of
> this savage beast, the wildest of all wild Nature, unquenchable love of life
> and freedom, flame of defiance and hate (75).

In his recounting of a similar experience in his landmark conservationist essay "Thinking Like a Mountain," Leopold would claim that the "fierce green fire" in the eyes of a dying wolf turned him against the policy of extermination for so-called predators.[68] Having depicted how his wild surroundings and the wild animals awakened the wildness within him, Grey does not comprehend this allied threat until late in his account when several lions end up dead and he, in his conclusion, offers a troubled reflection that hunting "taught mutely, eloquently, a lesson of life—that men are still savage, still driven by a spirit to roam, to hunt, and to slay" (168). Though his surroundings provoke and license this lust "to slay," he agonizes over the consequential loss of life and threat to wildness. When the wild activates a similar desire "to slay" in his novels, the results are much worse, and Grey dispenses with second thoughts.

When the first installment of "Roping Lions" appeared in the January 1909 issue of *Field and Stream,* Grey was back in Tampico. Warner was so pleased with this serial and the steady growth in subscriptions to his magazine that he invited Grey to contribute another serial about Tampico.[69] However, Will Dilg and the Ward line helped as much to make this trip possible. The friend in "The Leaping Tarpon" whom Grey characterized as "the best angler in Chicago" was Dilg, who worked as a publicist for a large advertising company in Chicago.[70] He had been visiting Tampico for several years prior to meeting Grey there in 1907, and in an article about these visits, his wife revealed that they were introduced to Tampico by a "vice-president of the Mexican-American S. S. Company."[71] This would have been the Ward line (also known as the New York and Cuba Mail Steamship Co.) whose steamships carried passengers from New York to Cuba and several other Caribbean locations. Whether or not Dilg worked for this company, his friendship with its vice president was undoubtedly responsible for two little-known Grey pamphlets entitled *Tarpon, the Silver King* (1908) and *Nassau, Cuba, Mexico* (1909) that were financed and distributed by the Ward line as promotion.[72] For writing these booklets, Zane received free passage for himself and Dolly to visit Tampico a second time.

This trip was supposed to be an escape from winter in Lackawaxen and a splendid opportunity to relax and fish, but it was far less romantic than Dolly and Zane had expected. Dolly was pregnant, and the travel aggravated her morning sickness and made her miserable. While they were in Merida, Zane pushed for a fishing trip to the Alacanes reef off the coast of Yucatan. The boat trip was very hard and their accommodations were wretched. Afterward, Dolly urged Zane to continue and she returned to the United States via Havana.[73] "I must have been a brute to drag you out there," Zane wrote to her following their separation. In order to complete his research for his travelogue, he headed for Mexico City. In San Luis Potosi, he discovered that his trunk was missing and then came down with a vicious case of diarrhea when he reached Mexico City.[74] "What a miserable farce this whole trip has been. I wish I were home," he complained to Dolly.[75]

Grey's commitment to his serial carried him back to Tampico and to the material he had tentatively assessed in "A Night in a Jungle." "Down an Unknown Jungle River" starts from the same remote village of Valles, and recounts his journey down the unexplored Panuco River from its headwaters high in the mountains, over a long stretch of uncharted, impenetrable jungle, to the river's outflow into Tampico's estuary. Although this boat trip represented an enlargement of "Canoeing on the Delaware" and "James' Waterloo," it was serious adventure with true risk. George Allen, an American then living in Tampico, helped Grey to locate a usable boat and a guide named Pepe, who misrepresented his outdoor experience and knowledge of the area. Grey was hoping these men would save him from the fiascos of his night in the jungle, but they only compounded his problems. George fired his rifle at everything that moved and seldom hit anything. At one point he put holes in the boat when he missed his quarry and then broke one of Grey's favorite fishing rods. Pepe was pitched overboard when he made a bad decision to stand up in the boat. The many wild animals terrified him. Both were so inept through a challenging stretch of rapids that they almost destroyed the boat.

At various points in his account, Grey exploits this incompetence for comic relief, but it provokes enough concern that he has to take over and serve as leader. In striking contrast to the bumbling novice of "A Night in a Jungle," he emerges as both skillful and resourceful. His deft maneuvering through the difficult rapids compensates for the mistakes of the others. Pepe proclaims him "grande mozo," and both men quickly learn that when Zane reaches for his rifle, the perceived threat will be eliminated. As in "Roping Lions," ordeals bring out the adventurer in him, but here they show him to be superior to the others. As he explains:

> This was a dare-devil trip, and the dare-devil in me had not been liberated. It took just the nervous dread, hard work, blunders and accidents, danger and luck to unleash the spirit which alone could make such a trip a success. Pepe and George by this time had a blind faith in me. They could scarcely appreciate the real hazard of our undertaking and I had no desire to impart it to them.[76]

Over the course of the trip, the group has to cope with many dangerous situations and a few that are harrowing. They encounter hungry alligators and an unnerving disappearance of the river into dense overgrowth that compels them to lie down in order to pass under low-lying limbs encircled with large snakes. A herd of javelinas attack, but Grey evades them by adeptly scaling a nearby tree. A wounded jaguar occasions the trip's most dramatic moment when his charge brings him close enough to cough blood onto Grey's shirt before dying from gunshot wounds. By the time the battered boat approaches its destination, the dangers, ticks, bad water, and sweltering heat have drained the trio and left them seriously ill. Fifteen years later, Grey would continue to suffer from ailments he incurred. Needless to say, *this* trip was a major accomplishment.

When Grey returned to Lackawaxen in March 1909, he was so sick and spent that he started with the easy job of completing his travelogue and rewriting *The Short Stop*.[77] Casting about for opportunity and money, he originally wrote this first of his books for boys as a serial but was unable to place it. In early May, McClurg agreed to bring out his rewrite as a book. Unsure of how to convert his travel experiences into a novel, Grey experimented with a series of short stories set in Mexico and Arizona that were conceived as market tests for a new novel without the Zanes or Ohio. "Tigre," "Don," and "The Rubber Hunter" were published over the next couple years. "Naza," "Old Walls," and "Thunder River and Buffalo Jones' Hardest Escape" either disappeared or were renamed. It is possible that "Yaqui" and "The Great Slave" originated during this period even though they were not published until the 1920s. Between May and June of 1909, nine of his ten offerings were rejected and he wrote in his journal: "I do not know what way to turn. I cannot decide what to write next. That which I desire to write does not seem to be what the editors want. This mood is distressing. I am full of stories and zeal and fire; yet I am inhibited by doubt, by fear that my feeling for life is false, that my imagined characters are not true, that my outlook is not sane."[78]

This uncertainty was worsened by the financial collapse of Outing, which was unable to pay Grey royalties for 5,000 copies of *Plainsmen*.[79] By mid-July, he was so demoralized that he ceased writing for the remainder of the summer.[80] By fall, Dolly's impending delivery spurred him to resume, and then deepened his depression when his efforts again faltered. In New York City, following the birth of his son Romer on October 1, he was bedridden and "out of my head."[81]

In mid-November, Zane mounted a desperate rebound and hurled himself into writing a new novel with a crazed determination to finish. Long days of writing that sometimes extended into the evening and even past midnight enabled him to complete his first Western on January 23, 1910.[82] Initially, he entitled his novel *Mescal,* the name of the Indian maiden involved in the story's romance.[83] Originally he may have conceived of this book as a *Betty Zane* with an Arizona setting, but the writing shifted his focus to Mescal's suitor and produced a quite different result. The finished novel, which was published as *The Heritage of the Desert* in September 1910, introduces the reader to a twenty-four-year-old Easterner named John Hare, who has journeyed to Salt Lake City to recover from a vaguely defined ailment that has left him as weakened and vulnerable as Zane was when he started his novel. Mistaken as a spy by local outlaws, he is forced to flee to the southern desert where he loses his way and finds himself "alone in the world, sick, and dependent upon the kindness of these strangers."[84] Grey intrudes an ominous foreboding upon Hare's plight and future with a riveting scene that evidences how quickly the competence of his Tampico description evolved into artistry. Rhythmic, sinuous sentences masterfully transform particulars of landscape into powerful images and portentous mood. Eerily and impressively, the first pages of his first Western flourish full development of his hallmark skill at converting scenery into a grand stage set for his unfolding drama.

> The desert, gray in the foreground, purple in the distance, sloped to the west. Eyes keen as those of hawks searched the waste, and followed the red mountain rampart, which sheer in bold height and processional in its craggy sweep shut out the north. Far away little puffs of dust rose above the white sage, and creeping specks moved at a snail's pace. . . . A broad bar of dense black shut out the April sky, except in the extreme west, where a strip of pale blue formed background for several clouds of striking color and shape. They alone, in all that expanse, were dyed in the desert's sunset crimson. The largest projected from behind the dark cloud-bank in the shape of a huge fist, and the others, small and round, floated below. To Cole it seemed a giant hand, clutching, with inexorable strength, a bleeding heart. His terror spread to his companions as they stared (2–3).

Hare's struggle to survive introduces him to the therapeutic redemption in the desert's menace and desolation: "The wildness of it all, the necessity of peril and calm acceptance of it, stirred within Hare the call, the awakening, the spirit of the desert" (53). A significant amount of this rehabilitation is due to the people who aid him. August Naab, a devout Mormon elder, is an imaginative synthesis of Jones and Emett. Even though Naab suspects that Hare has ties with his enemies, he is so steeped in the Bible that he feels compelled to help. He hides Hare from his pursuers, furnishes rest and nourishment, and introduces him to the Mormons' simple, antimodern values, like the battered silver cup, generously left at a water hole years before, that has been much used and never taken. Naab discerns Hare's potential and introduces him to the outdoors and hard work that develop it.

Naab's strength of will and resourcefulness includes a resolute opposition to killing that handicaps him against Holderness, who threatens everything for which he stands. Holderness is a selfish, acquisitive businessman wholly committed to an ethic of owning, developing, and profiting.[85] Hare's evolution into a compensatory son for Naab, a foil for his corrupt real one, prepares him to confront Holderness, though Hare has to become a gunman to do this.

Mescal, whose Indian name means "desert flower," completes this rehabilitation. Hare is introduced to her through a feigned involvement that diverts the men hunting him, but the couple discovers that their love is real when Hare goes off with Mescal to herd sheep on a verdant high plateau. Her Indian sensibility introduces him to the spirit within their environment that intensifies their romance and completes his recovery:

> He [Hare] saw himself in triumphant health and strength, earning day by day the spirit of this wilderness, coming to fight for it, to live for it, and in far-off time, when he had won his victory, to die for it . . . but it was Mescal who made this wild life sweet and significant. It was Mescal, the embodiment of the desert spirit. Like a man facing a great light Hare divined his love. Through all the days on the plateau, living with her the natural free life of Indians, close to the earth, his unconscious love had ripened. He understood now her charm for him; he knew now the lure of her wonderful eyes, flashing fire, desert-trained, like the falcon eyes of her Indian grandfather. The knowledge of what she had become to him dawned with a mounting desire that thrilled all his blood (89–90).

Grey glosses the primal emotion that Mescal awakens in Hare, but hints that it is more elemental than love.

This idyll is shattered when Mescal reveals that she is supposed to wed the already married Snap, Naab's prodigal son. In order to avoid the injustice of Mormon polygamy, she flees into the desert on the day of her marriage. Grey likens her to a captured mustang that must live free or die. Hare initiates a belated, implausible search over a vast expanse of desert, through a punishing sand storm, and into a maze of slot canyons until he arrives at a secret oasis that resembles the Surprise Valley of Thunder River. There he finds Mescal gravely ill and near death. He remains with her and nurses her back to health and this second exposure to the wild teaches him the desert's final lesson—"to strike first and hard" (251). This lust to slay completes his Zane-like initiation, and he returns to kill Holderness. Hare's encounters with the patriarchal Naab, the mystical Mescal, and the rugged, majestic landscape transform him from a sickly fugitive from the East into a potent avenger who guns down the menacing exemplar of modern commercialization.

In her critical study of the Western, *West of Everything* (1992), Jane Tompkins observes that Grey's prose doesn't sound like he had been reading Thackeray, Austen, or even Owen Wister. "It's wonderful writing, but not in good taste," she asserts. "For sheer emotional force; for the capacity to get and keep his readers, absolutely, in his grip; for the power to be—there is no other word for it—thrilling."[86] Although this estimate is hyperbolic, it has merit and warrants attention. At the time that Grey wrote his first Western, he was, in fact, reading Matthew Arnold, Tennyson, and Ruskin,[87] but his own writing does not evidence the stylistic refinement of these Victorians. Instead, it consciously evokes a world of charged emotion.

Tompkins makes another important point in noting that his books were not read by the elite who favored these writers. Grey's presentation was influenced more by the rising authority of journalism and its insistence upon concrete information and leaner sentences, but *Shores of Lethe* furnishes an important reminder of his indebtedness to the contrived emotion of nineteenth-century popular literature. Thrilling the reader was one of many emotions that Grey consciously strove to evoke. The one writing guide that he read and reread many times was *The Forms of Prose Literature* by John H. Gardiner, and the part he revered most was the seventy-page section on "Literature of Feeling."[88] Gardiner maintained that this kind of writing was more personal than the "Literature of Thought" and was distinguished by the manner in which the author recollected and represented his experience. Gardiner catalogued the many ways authors could put "emotional coloring" into plot and description, but insisted that the ways were not as important as the one principle that this coloring be the main objective. From Gardiner as his tutor, Grey was receiving old-fashioned advice and it left an old-fashioned patina upon his efforts. His subject matter, on the other hand, possessed a freshness and timeliness that editors and critics missed in their quick dismissals of his writing as overwrought and passé.

Grey was decidedly not the first writer to detect literary promise in the West. Since the Civil War, many dime novelists had experimented with it. Moreover, in the decade before Grey's arrival, Roosevelt, Wister, and Remington had already celebrated it. Their attraction, like Grey's, was that of outsiders, and they blazed a trail that he developed into a highway. In his groundbreaking investigation into the meaning of the West for Roosevelt, Wister, and Remington, G. Edward White discovered a pattern of uncanny resemblances in their personal lives. All three came from distinguished Eastern families, attended Ivy League universities, and originally went West to escape emotional or health crises. There they had memorable experiences that alleviated their problems and helped them to achieve successful careers that stressed both the West and its invigorating effect. For these three men to suggest that the raw, undeveloped West was preferable to the refined, class-conscious Eastern establishment from which they came constituted a betrayal of their heritage, and it was. The West exposed them to attitudes and skills that impressed them while they were there, but then dismayed them when they realized how little their peers respected these values. Convinced that this was a mistake, even a fault, they campaigned for change and acceptance.[89]

Although Grey's immediate family was different, his experience and thinking conformed to this pattern, but moved beyond this kinship in associating the West's therapeutic effect with an illness contracted in the East. Grey's protagonists were so repeatedly afflicted with an ailment that it bespeaks his own debilities, but he also used these ailments to express the welling doubts among Easterners about their long-standing commitment to manners, industrialization, civilization, and cultural superiority. Increasingly aware of the physical and psychosomatic ailments caused by these forces, they, along with Wagner and Shields, were beginning to view the forces themselves as a form of sickness. According to this revisionist thinking, Buffalo Bill's efforts on behalf of the railroad and progress destroyed not only Indians and buffalo but also the simpler, healthier way of life that engendered prowess, appreciation, and happiness.

By the time that Wister's *The Virginian* achieved the best-seller list in 1902, it was clear that the West was outgrowing its narrow circle of privileged supporters like Roosevelt, Remington, and himself. Moreover, their West was that of the northern plains and the 1880s, and this area had changed radically between their original visits and their nostalgic recollections. In his introduction to *The Virginian,* Wister wrote, "Had you left New York or San Francisco at ten o'clock this morning, by noon tomorrow you could step out at Cheyenne. There you would stand at the heart of the world that is the subject of my picture, yet you would look around you in vain for the reality. It is a vanished world. No journeys, save those of which memory can take, will bring you to it now."[90] Grey's Southwest, on the other hand, remained undeveloped and unspoiled. This area already had a paradoxical reputation

93

for being both more forbidding and more therapeutic than the rest of the country. Easterners suffering from commonplace bronchial ailments were noticing how the aridity of the Southwest improved their health. Although the summer heat could be withering, the milder climate of the other seasons was likewise gaining appeal. Visitors judged its air to be pure, not just because it was dry but also because it was far away from Eastern industrialization and pollution. This belief that lack of development made the desert healthier rapidly acquired psychological significance. In *The Desert* (1901), John Van Dyke maintained that desert inhabitants "have never known civilization, and never suffered from the blight of doubt. Of a simple nature, they have lived a simple way, close to their mother earth, beside the desert they loved."[91] In her influential *The Land of Little Rain* (1903), Mary Austin enlarged upon this estimate:

> If one is inclined to wonder at first how so many dwellers came to be in the loneliest land that ever came out of God's hands, what they do there and why stay, one does not wonder so much after having lived there. None other than this long brown land lays such a hold on the affections. The rainbow hills, the tender bluish mists, the luminous radiance of the spring, have the lotus charm . . . there is the divinest, cleanest air to be breathed anywhere in God's world. Some day the world will understand that, and the little oases on the windy tops of hills will harbor for healing its ailing, house-weary broods. . . . For all the toll the desert takes of a man it gives compensations, deep breaths, deep sleep, and the communion of the stars.[92]

At the outset of *The Heritage of the Desert,* Hare is near death from his desert trek, due in part to a "soreness of his lungs" and "one sensitive spot" that made breathing difficult. This physical ailment is accompanied by an "old settled bitterness" that erodes his wish to live. This vague illness conflated Grey's own discontents, disappointments, and depressions into ones commonplace in the East and already associated with its formality, development, and crowding. Conversely, Hare's experience out West was sufficiently connected to emergent assumptions about the Southwest's climate, awesome scenery, and lack of development to make his transformation into a manly, adventurous outdoorsman both engaging and believable.

4

Pursuit of the Dream: 1911–14

The tourist, the leisurely traveler, the comfort-loving motorist would never behold it. Only by toil, sweat, endurance and pain could any man ever look at Nonnezoshe. It seemed well to realize that the great things of life had to be earned.
—"Nonnezoshe"

In March 1911, four months after the publication of *The Heritage of the Desert*, *Field and Stream* presented the first installment of "Down an Unknown Jungle River." For this issue, the editors prepared a special, bright-red cover with a huge *Z* slashing from top to bottom of the page, like the famous mark of Zorro. A photograph of Zane appeared center left of the *Z*, with his name completed in block letters to the right. Although Warner, the magazine's owner, shrewdly calculated the benefit of this promotion to his magazine, his backing came when Grey badly needed it, and earned Warner his gratitude and loyalty. At the time, few editors were so accepting of his work. Grey's articles for *Field and Stream* financed trips that alleviated his crippling depressions, and these trips furnished material that enabled him to move beyond his Ohio novels, solidifying his stature as an outdoorsman and endowing his Westerns with authenticity.

"Down an Unknown Jungle River" appeared almost two years after the trip that it described, and Grey felt so pressured to write over this period that his travel was restricted to overnights in New York City and other places nearby. *The Heritage of the Desert,* completed between early November 1909 and late January 1910, was a product of his first complete winter in Lackawaxen. Snow came early that year and Grey wrote in a small cottage that had only a small stove and no insulation. The penetrating cold necessitated heavy clothing and every few minutes he had to hold his hand near the fire in order to continue writing.[1] In June, when Dan Beard invited him to Connecticut for a visit, he had to decline because he was straining to meet an August deadline on a book for young people.[2] *The Young Lion Hunter,* published in October 1911, appeared six months after *The Young Pitcher.* This was a simplification of "Roping Lions in the Grand Canyon" and Grey speedily followed with a conversion of "Down an Unknown Jungle River" into *Ken Ward in the Jungle* (1912), his last book for juveniles. Although Grey did his five boys' books for money and as insurance against failure with his novels, they were invaluable training in the development of a simple, accessible style that complemented his Westerns and appealed to adolescents, who would be a significant component in his later readership.

Grey's self-imposed confinement in Lackawaxen enabled him to complete these diverse projects, and it stimulated a compensatory daydreaming that he recorded in the pages of his journal. On March 10, 1911, he wrote:

> I seem to live so much in the future. I am always anticipating something, looking forward to this trip, or planning that one. I am haunted by a yearning to go afar, into the wilds mostly, and yet I know that when I do go, I never find content. Then I long for my home, my books, my family. It is a strange thing, this unrest, this insatiate desire to find the place and the happiness that seem forever just beyond the horizon. But they never are. They are in the depths of my own soul, and I never yet mined that deep.[3]

Frequently this daydreaming involved women and his powerful attraction to them. In an entry from two years before, he reflected, "For many years it has been my way to *look at* women, *judge* them, know them from the side which affected me personally."[4] Women were on his mind when he described the actress Lina Cavalieri, whose photograph he kept on his desk:

Cover of Field and Stream, *March 1911.*

Of all the lovely women whose pictures have fascinated me this one is the most perfect. She is dark, sweet, passionate; her face is oval and pure, her lips exquisite, her eyes like night. She is slender, svelte, voluptuous; her arms are round, her breast is full, her hips are swelling. . . . Are the laws of natural selection alone responsible for those eyes of fire, those lips of love, those breasts of pearl, those arms of Aphrodite?[5]

He penned another, much longer reflection on how women stimulated his thinking and inspired stories:

I like to climb the mountains with a girl, and picture her on mossy stones, in lichen-covered cliffs, or rugged trunk of twisted pine or oak. . . . I feel all the phases of the sex sense in man. I love youth and beauty free and wild in the mountain tops. The flush of cheek, the flash of eye, the peal of real laughter, the waving of hair, the action, the reality, the charm—these I feel with all the power there is in me.

Then there is more, infinitely more. The wonder of it all will never cease to hold me. The thousand thousand changes of mood, of feeling! To walk alone in the solitude under the pines with a girl with all life before her or a woman already beginning to look backward! That is what I hold as a wonderful privilege of life. . . . I do not deny the sweetness of clasped hands or the fragrance of wind-blown hair. But these things, the physical and the sensual, are not in any sense as memorable as the spiritual. I walk the mountain tops in dreams. . . . By women men live! A man is drawn unto a woman. What [is] more portent, intelligible, appalling than these two simple facts? So at the bottom of all the great stories lies the power of a woman.[6]

A reader of these entries cannot help wondering about affairs that might have contributed to these musings. In addition to the passage above, his journals mention two meetings with women other than Dolly.[7] The likelihood of extramarital involvements is increased by bizarre admissions to Dolly like this one from his first trip to Arizona: "I am quite sure if Helen herself should come back from the shadows and unveil herself to me, that while I might, I suppose I would, rave over her beauty and perhaps yield to it, but she could never hold me, nor any other woman. You see I cannot wash out that taint in me."[8]

Whether or not Grey did have liaisons at this time, his isolation in Lackawaxen and his immersion in his writing left little time for them, and made the *absence* of other women a more powerful influence upon his musings. Moreover, his strong commitment to his family also helped to confine his wanderings to daydreaming. Finances pressured his mother and sister to live with him and Dolly, but having these family members nearby fulfilled deep-seated emotional and psychological needs. When he and Dolly stayed with his brother for several months in Middletown, Grey wrote in his journal, "Just now the only bitter drop in my cup is the separation from mother and the rest of the family."[9] The birth of his first child deepened his attachment to his family. On one occasion when he found himself "fighting again and again the old battle," he went to the room of baby Romer, lay down next to the crib, and happily watched him play.[10] Six months later, the proud father elaborated upon his deep love for his young son:

> My boy was nine months old yesterday. He is beautiful, sturdy, unusu-
> ally strong and active, a picture of health and wonderful life. . . . Day by
> day I learn wisdom from this baby, and something else I cannot name. I
> watch him sometimes when he lies asleep, in some cozy natural position,
> half on his face perhaps, with little hands outspread and little pink heels
> pointed up. . . . So I am to learn through a child. To feel the pride and the
> life, the fear and the dread, the ambition and the longing, the sorrow and
> the love that come to those who are blessed with the blood of their blood,
> and the love of their love. It is the way of life. Through him, perhaps, I
> shall feel the bond between men, and understand the mother-longing
> of women, and see the scroll of humanity unrolled.[11]

These competing attractions to family and to other women would profound-ly influence *Riders of the Purple Sage,* his next novel, but he did not begin it until after two more trips that were brief but significant.

In the fall of 1910, Grey estimated his earnings for the year at $3,500. This represented a substantial improvement over his $439 for 1909. He received only $150 for *The Last Trail,* but he got the same amount more for two articles. Warner paid him $340 (and a rifle) for "Down an Unknown Jungle River" and published a notice in *Field and Stream* informing readers that the twelve-part serial "cost us no small penny to get all this for our readers."[12] *Popular Magazine* paid $1,800 for serial rights to *The Heritage of the Desert.* The novel came out in September 1910 and ensured Grey more royalties during the next year. In order to avoid the miserable winter of the previous year, Grey rented a house large enough for his family, mother, and sister at 103 Albion Place in Atlantic City from Thanksgiving until the end of March 1911.

Next, he organized a third trip to Tampico for himself and R. C. Over the summer, George Allen sought his opinion about a second boat trip down the Panuco River. "I would advise you not to, strictly *not,*" Grey responded.

"I can see where we had more luck than sense. And if I had not known how to pick out channels and guide the boat, we would be still there; and your little wife would be wearing black. It was a d— fool trip." Along with more advice about tarpon fishing, Grey mentioned that he would be returning to Tampico that winter. In mid-January 1911, he wrote that he and R. C. would be arriving on February 5 and requested that Allen scout locations for them to hunt jaguar, deer, and turkey.[13]

When their ship reached Cuba, Zane and R. C. learned about an outbreak of smallpox in Tampico and immediately altered their plans. During several days of poor fishing in Nassau, they heard about a new resort in Long Key, Florida, where the fishing was supposed to be outstanding.[14] The camp's collection of bungalows and central dining room originally housed workers during the construction of Henry Flagler's railroad from Miami to Key West. When the line finished in 1909, the facility was transformed into a camp for fishermen.[15] Zane and R. C. only had a week left when they reached Long Key, and it did not go very well. Initially, the weather was perfect, and their hopes were high. Their first day out, no one on their boat got a strike, but another boat returned with 350 pounds of fish. The next day, they had a better guide and located fish, but their lack of experience and deficient equipment kept them from landing any. The third day the wind kicked up and prevented boats from going out. "Rome is plainly discouraged, and as for me, I'm simply steeped in gloom," Zane related to Dolly. "After all my talk about trips and years of waiting to get Rome to come with me, and at last planning for months on this one, to have it turn out this way is simply heart-sickening. . . . There is absolutely nothing to do here when you can't fish. It is only a barren strip of island, and the ceaseless wind and shallow roar of the reef remind me of Alacanes."[16]

Zane converted this experience into "The Sea-Tigers of the Florida Keys," which ran in the December 1911 issue of *Field and Stream.* Beneath a photograph of a large display of freshly caught fish and following a prefatory characterization of his article as "a vivid account of great fishing," the piece opened: "The greatest places to fish are those where the watery denizens are most powerful and savage, surest to baffle the fisherman, and leave him with a broken line or a ruined rod—and a story."[17] Although Grey mentions tangled lines, broken equipment, and "fish-hog" anglers, he uses these incidents to make the camp appear to be both a fishing mecca and a Shangri-la. He captures the beauty and allure of Long Key in a sprightly conclusion that is cleverly cryptic:

Suffice it to add that Long Key is a place to thrill and to invite one's soul. At night, if no breeze blows, there is not a quieter place on earth. The sun burns white all day and the stars burn white all night. The spell of the south is upon this white strip of coral. The mystery of the place is the same as that of the little hermit-crab, which trails across the coral-sand in a stolen shell, and holds to his lonely course, and loves his life so well. And that secret no man knows.[18]

Both Dolly and R. C. knew that the secret of this inscrutable crab was the veiled truth of his account: Zane's first visit to Long Key was a crushing disappointment.

Two months before this trip, Grey approached David Rust about serving as his guide and outfitter for a late spring trip to southeastern Utah. He hoped that this alternative to Jones and Emett would help him find new material for a book. "I shall not write anything about the Mormons that would hurt anybody's feelings," he explained. "I simply want to tell of the wonder and beauty of their desert struggle as I see it." Originally, Grey's plans called for a return to Powell's Plateau, Kanab, and Fredonia, and a search for a route down into the Thunder River valley. Rust intrigued Grey with a proposal that they also visit "the Navajo Natural Bridge." Stating that R. C. and his wife would be accompanying him, Zane asked that Rust find him "a dandy horse to ride, one that will look good in pictures and that can run & climb."[19]

Unexpected developments altered these plans as well. When he returned to Atlantic City from Long Key, Grey and the rest of his family were devastated by a virulent strain of flu. Next, the fiasco of the Long Key outing turned R. C. against the Utah trip. Grey replaced his brother with Charles MacLean, the editor of *Popular Magazine,* who had purchased the serial rights to *The Heritage of the Desert.* Since MacLean could spare only three weeks, Grey had to scale back the three-month visit he had in mind. His quibbling over Rust's rate of $10 per day caused him to be greeted in Flagstaff not by Rust, but by a letter in which Rust claimed that spring runoff had made Lee's Ferry impassable and prevented him from reaching Flagstaff, their agreed-upon starting point.[20] Determined to salvage his investment of time and money, Grey located a local guide named Al Doyle who proposed a trip to northeastern Arizona that did not necessitate fording the Colorado.

These hastily amended plans left Zane nervous and uneasy. In a hasty letter to Rust, he complained about his alternative guide,[21] but Doyle quickly put these doubts to rest. Prior to establishing a guide service for tourists, he had worked on the transcontinental railroad, hunted buffalo, mined, and ranched. Doyle possessed a wealth of knowledge about local history and area residents, and he knew almost as much about its topography and geography. Grey soon realized that Doyle could find him promising subject matter.

Sensitive to Grey's expectations, Doyle took him and MacLean on a week-long journey toward Kayenta. According to a Flagstaff newspaper, their objective was "Marsh Pass, Navajo mountain, the natural bridges and other points of interest on the Navajo reservation."[22] Back in 1909, Byron Cummings, the dean of the School of Letters and Science at the University of Utah and a scholar of Indian culture, recruited John Wetherill, the knowledgeable owner of a trading post on the western edge of Monument Valley, to guide him on an ambitious quest for an enormous natural arch known only by rumor and called Nonnezoshe by the Navajos. The interest of Wetherill's wife in Navajo culture and her command of their language led to a conversation with One Eyed Man that furnished her husband and Cummings valuable information about the arch. Over most of the summer of 1909, Cummings conducted research on the Anasazi cliff dwellings at Keet Seel. Two days before his scheduled departure for Nonnezoshe, he discovered the equally impressive ruins of Betatakin.[23]

Armed with a crude map and an instinctive understanding of the landscape's twisting hills, washes, and canyons, Wetherill set out with Cummings and his party on August 11 to locate the fabled Navajo shrine. Meanwhile, W. B. Douglass from the U.S. Land Office had also heard about the bridge and was mounting a search of his own. To prevent these investigations from becoming a competition, the leaders agreed to join forces.

Though Wetherill led most of the way, a Piute named Nasjah Begay[24] caught up with the group at a critical moment of need and guided it through the final and most difficult leg. On August 14, they reached Nonnezoshe, subsequently renamed Rainbow Bridge.[25] Their measurements established the arch to be 308 feet high and 275 feet between the two base supports, making it the largest of all the known natural arches. Following the group's return, Cummings wrote an account of it and two other natural bridges for the January 1910 issue of *National Geographic*. Five months later, President Taft signed a bill designating Rainbow Bridge a national monument, as the Navajo Mountain had been on November 20, 1909. That summer, Wetherill and Nasjah Begay went to the Bridge again with a party from the U.S. Geological Survey consisting of H. E. Gregory, the leader, and Joseph Pogue from the National Museum. Pogue published an account about the Bridge itself in the *National Geographic,* which included five impressive photographs

Grey and Nasjah Begay, 1913. (Courtesy of Loren Grey.)

of the arch.[26] Rust's reference to "the Navajo Natural Bridge" in his letter to Grey may have been prompted by this burst of publicity.

Grey remembered the Bridge when Rust failed to show and he had to amend his North Rim itinerary. On April 16, 1911, Grey, MacLean, and Doyle left Flagstaff for the barren, desolate terrain of northwestern Arizona. Three days later, they arrived at the Tuba Trading Post, which Sam Preston and the Babbitt brothers had controlled since 1902. Preston informed them that Wetherill was away from the trading post that he had recently opened at Kayenta, and showed them photographs of the Rainbow Bridge, Keet Seel, and Batatakin. This was the first time that Grey distinguished the Rainbow Bridge from the other natural bridges of Utah and Arizona, and he judged it to be large enough that "the flatiron building could easily stand under the arch."[27] Efforts to find a local Indian to guide them to the site were unsuccessful, and they had to abandon their hopes of getting there. At the time, Grey was sufficiently impressed with his journey and the desolate landscape, but back in Lackawaxen, he concluded that he had "missed the grandest sight in the world" and vowed to return and see it.[28]

From Tuba, the group continued to a trading post at Red Lake that was also owned by the Babbits and Preston. Grey got badly sunburned during the slow, grinding uphill ascent and found the trading post "a horribly lonely place." When they reached Black Mesa, he was so saddle-sore he could hardly walk, even though he had been riding more than a week and had not experienced any discomfort until then.[29] Because the remaining pages of his unpublished account have disappeared, the details of the final leg of the trip are unknown. He and MacLean almost certainly reached Kayenta, but Wetherill's absence, Grey's limited time, and the significant distances separating Betatakin, Keet Seel, and Monument Valley probably prevented them from seeing all three.[30]

Grey returned via El Tovar and was back in Lackawaxen by May 6. On May 11, he wrote in his journal, "This time, out in the Painted Desert, something came to me and changed me. Only time will tell how."[31] He immediately began work on his next novel and finished it in August 1911.[32] Today, *Riders of the Purple Sage* (1912) is Grey's best-known and most often read novel, but the novel's personal wellsprings have never been explored beyond its connection to his outings with Jones because his journals were unknown and inaccessible. Like his account of Long Key, *Riders* was a romantic conflation of his experiences that cryptically veiled the true sources of Grey's inspiration.

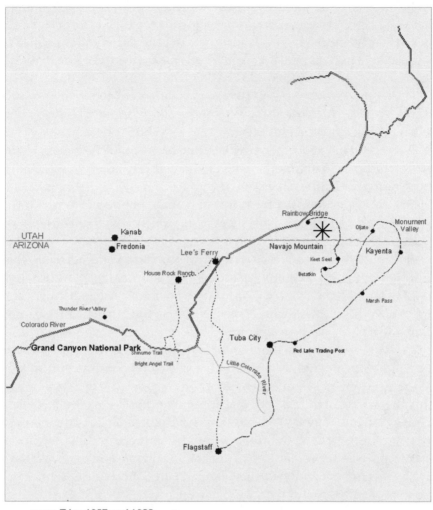

UTAH
ARIZONA

Kanab
Fredonia
Lee's Ferry
House Rock Ranch.
Thunder River Valley
Colorado River
Grand Canyon National Park
Shinumo Trail
Bright Angel Trail
Little Colorado River
Tuba City
Flagstaff
Rainbow Bridge
Navajo Mountain
Keet Seel
Betatkin
Oljato
Monument Valley
Kayenta
Marsh Pass
Red Lake Trading Post

········ Trips 1907 and 1908
------ Trips 1911, 1913, 1922, 1923, 1929

Map of Zane Grey's northern Arizona trips. (Map by Shelly McCoy, University of Delaware Library, 2003.)

The novel is set in Cottonwoods, a fictionalized site whose rugged, mountainous terrain and narrow, intersecting canyons possess the North Rim's immensity and grandeur, but the landscape is so generalized and so poetically rendered that its basis is unclear, and it is even hard to say for sure that Cottonwoods is north of the Colorado River. On the first page, Grey more specifically dates the unfolding events sixteen years after the Mountain Meadows Massacre and six years before the execution of John D. Lee, and draws upon actual history more than his previous Western did. As he explains, "That year, 1871, had marked a change which had been gradually coming in the lives of the peace-loving Mormons of the border . . . [who] had risen against the invasion of Gentile settlers and the forays of rustlers."[33] This conflict is crucial to Grey's story as is the Mormon practice of polygamy, which the U.S. Congress had outlawed in a series of enactments extending from 1862 to 1887.[34] His original vow "not [to] write anything about the Mormons that would hurt anybody's feelings" was reaffirmed in a letter informing Rust that he would *not* "roast the Mormons," despite the offer of a large advance to do so.[35] But he changed his mind. The finished book is a harsh indictment and reversion to his 1907 estimate: "I met Mormons and I hate them. I learned something of their women and I pity them."[36]

Grey's decision to make Mormons the villains of his novel boldly asserts itself in the opening scene in which a band of elders comes to punish Jane Withersteen and her gentile friend for their transgression of Mormon law. This chapter was startlingly original at the time, but it has been reenacted so many times that today its classic traits have been drained of their power. In characteristic fashion, Grey utilizes impressionistic landscape description to embellish the scene, but here the unfolding drama dominates. Well-orchestrated entrances and terse dialogue exchanges create abrupt shifts, but Grey masterfully sustains the scene's tension.

As a result of her father's death, Jane Withersteen has inherited a large ranch, but the area around her is controlled by Mormons. They oppose outsiders and support Elder Tull's wish to marry her, despite the fact that he already has several wives. Her compassion toward those in need has caused her to befriend an impoverished outcast named Venters. "Jane Withersteen, your father left you wealth and power," Tull tells her when he and his band of Mormon gunmen corner them together. "It has turned your head. You haven't yet come to see the place of Mormon women" (5). As he prepares to horsewhip Venters, a solitary figure appears in the distance silhouetted against the setting sun. All eyes fix upon the leather-clad stranger who appears to be "forever looking for that which he never found" (8). Calmly he rides up and politely asks Jane for permission to water his horse. When Tull proclaims that he is meddling with Mormon law, he responds, "To hell with your Mormon law!" During the tense uncertainty that follows, Jane beseeches the stranger to save Venters. With an uneasy laugh, Tull starts to leave with Venters and is told, "Mormon, the young man stays" (10). Tull now demands his name and learns that he is *Lassiter,* the legendary gunfighter. The chapter ends:

> Tull put out a groping hand. The life of his eyes dulled to the gloom with which men of his fear saw the approach of death. But death, while it hovered over him, did not descend, for the rider waited for the twitching fingers, the downward flash of the hand that did not come. Tull, gathering himself together, turned to the horses, attended by his pale comrades (12).

Although most of Grey's novels were converted into movies, it was not until the 1950s and long after his death that any would successfully replicate the prolonged menace of this scene in which violence and death constantly threaten but never happen.

This powerful scene is energized by Grey's personal involvement in it. The Mormons who lecture Jane and threaten Venters echo Zane's in-laws, who likewise judged him to be an outsider, unworthy of Dolly and a threat to the wealth and position that her dead father had bequeathed her. Venters recycles the weakness and rehabilitation of Hare in *The Heritage of the Desert.* Lassiter, on the other hand, is a wholly new character who imaginatively converts Grey's lower-class status, athletic prowess, and interest in the outdoors into a charismatic figure of enormous potency who defends Jane against the onerous expectations of her enclosed society. As Grey remarked in his journal following completion of *Riders,* "I love to idle—to dream impossible stories of which I am the central figure."[37]

This conflation of Zane's personal experience and wishful thinking underpins the remainder of the story. Back at her ranch, Jane tells Venters that "men like Lassiter and you have no home, no comfort, no rest, no place to lay your weary heads" (23). At this point the reader expects Jane and Venters to become romantically involved and Lassiter to aid them and move on. In the original manuscript, Tull's visit is prompted by Jane's sexual involvement with Venters. Although Grey eliminated this pesky complication and the guilt and self-condemnation Venters suffers when he later falls in love with Bess,[38] he retained his story's two romances, which complicated the focus and flow of his narrative because they absorbed the deep conflict within himself. Into the one involving Bess and Venters he channeled his wayward dreaming of other women. The one between Jane and Lassiter expressed his contrasting commitment to home and family.

Venters's involvement with Bess, a legendary outlaw whose true identity is hidden behind a mask, is downright prurient with its steamy eroticism and coy avoidance of actual sex. It begins during a gunfight with rustlers of Jane's cattle, in which Venters shoots the lead rider of Oldring's gang. When he realizes the person is not dead, he investigates the chest wound and discovers "the graceful, beautiful swell of a woman's breast!" (53). He discreetly covers this revelation, and decides that he must save the woman's life. His quest for a haven carries him to the tops of the highest ridges, past a site of cliff dwellers like Betatakin and Keet Seel, and to a secret entrance to Surprise Valley with a natural arch and large balanced rock nearby. The verdant foliage and cold, swift-flowing stream in the valley below, developed from Grey's romantic memories of the Thunder River, furnish the couple a perfect hideaway. There Venters nurses Bess back to health, and he falls in love:

> He had nursed what seemed a frail, shrunken boy; and now he watched a girl whose face had become strangely sweet, whose dark-blue eyes were ever upon him without boldness, without shyness, but with a steady, grave, and growing light. Many times Venters found the clear gaze embarrassing to him, yet, like wine, it had an exhilarating effect (134).

"Well, Bess, the fact is I've been dreaming a lot," Venters later observes, echoing Grey's journal admissions. "This valley makes a fellow dream" (194).

Venters's romance with Bess frees Jane for an involvement with Lassiter into which Grey channeled equally strong feelings and misgivings about his marriage. "I'm a man of strange beliefs an' ways of thinkin'," Lassiter says, repeating Zane's confessions to Dolly. "The trail I've been followin' for so many years was twisted an' tangled" (73). Jane's interaction with this powerful stranger is overtly sexual, but sex is decidedly not its objective. She wants him to give up his restless, violent life: "If she were to influence him it must be wholly through womanly allurement . . . if Lassiter did not soften to a woman's grace and beauty and wiles, then it would be because she could not make him" (74). Jane is twenty-eight years old, the same age as Dolly when Zane wrote this story. Her caring, maternal nature has moved her to adopt the orphan child Fay Larkin, and she and Fay team up to change Lassiter. Fay's childish play with Lassiter's ornamented clothing and imposing guns gives Jane an idea, and a few pages later she too goes for his weapons. Although Grey's description bristles with sexual implications, Jane's objective is emphatically a sublimation of sex with a forthright objective of suppression:

> "Lassiter! . . Will you do anything for me?"
>
> In the moonlight she saw his dark, worn face change, and by that change seemed to feel him immovable as a wall of stone.
>
> Jane slipped her hands down to the swinging gun-sheaths, and when she had locked her fingers around the huge, cold handles of the guns, she trembled as with a chilling ripple over all her body.
>
> "May I take your guns?"
>
> "Why?" he asked, and for the first time to her his voice carried a harsh note. Jane felt his hard, strong hands close round her wrists. It was not wholly with intent that she leaned toward him, for the look of his eyes and the feel of his hands that made her weak.
>
> "It's no trifle—no woman's whim—it's deep—as my heart. Let me take them?"
>
> "Why?"
>
> "I want to keep you from killing more men—Mormons. You must let me save you from more wickedness—more wanton bloodshed——" (146–47).

Though not immediately, Lassiter does yield, and he becomes gentler and kinder. Jane's appeals, his doting interaction with Fay, and the fruits of domesticity prevail over his proclivity toward gunplay and wandering.

Romance carries Venters and Lassiter in opposite directions, and the ensuing course of events expresses grave reservations about Lassiter's decision, with ominous overtones for Grey's relationship with Dolly. Lassiter's involvement with Jane and Fay drains him of the strength and purpose that distinguished him in the opening scene. On the other hand, Venters's nursing of Bess restores his masculinity and, amazingly, transforms him into Lassiter's equal and an implacable killer. As Venters and Bess explore the valley and the site of the cliff dwellers, he grows increasingly aware of the deeper meanings of wilderness and the limitations of civilized thinking. After an earthshaking thunderstorm sensitizes him to the power of love, Venters tells Bess, "Saving you, I saved myself," and announces his readiness to fight to save her (196).

The changes Lassiter and Venters undergo reach a simultaneous fruition that reverses their earlier roles. Lassiter is described as "sadder and quieter in his contemplation of the child, and infinitely more gentle and loving," but Jane grows increasingly uneasy over the force of her influence. Shortly after she experiences a "cold, inexplicable sensation of dread" (201), Lassiter hears shots, goes to investigate, and is wounded by outlaws lurking in the woods. "Have you no desire to hunt the man who fired at you—to find him—and—and kill him?" Jane asks, and he replies, "Well, I reckon I haven't any great hankerin' for that" (204). These circumstances of threat and hesitation recall those of the opening scene, but this time it is Venters who arrives from the Surprise Valley just in time to help the weak and needy:

> Like rough iron his hard hand crushed Jane's. In it she felt the difference she saw in him. Wild, rugged, unshorn—yet how splendid! He had gone away a boy—he had returned a man. He appeared taller, wider of shoulder, deeper-chested, more powerfully built. But was that only her fancy—he had always been a young giant—was the change one of spirit? He might have been absent for years, proven by fire and steel, grown, like Lassiter, strong and cool and sure (205–6).

Jane notices this change in part because she had previously convinced Venters to give up his guns, and thereby contributed to his weakness in the opening scene. A significant part of his rehabilitation, it turns out, has been overcoming the crippling effects of Jane's influence. "Had Venters become Lassiter and Lassiter Venters?" (208) Jane wonders, and her question is answered when Venters proceeds to shoot Oldring, the man responsible for so many of her problems.

Of course, Lassiter's submission to Jane does not last. When he learns that his sister Milly was destroyed by Dyer, another Mormon allied with Oldring and Tull, his thirst for revenge returns. He fastens on his guns and shoots Dyer and several of his henchmen. With two of the main enemies dead and their henchmen in hot pursuit, both couples flee for their lives. In a major reversal of expectations, Bess and Venters head east for civilization. Lassiter and Jane, reunited with Fay, ride for the Surprise Valley. When they reach its mountaintop entrance, Lassiter strains to topple the balanced stone onto Tull and his gang below, but cannot. The problem is not his five wounds; rather, it appears to be more psychological, perhaps an uneasiness, that he, Jane, and Fay will be left sealed in the valley. *Roll the stone! . . . Lassiter, I love you!* (335) Jane cries, and he finally succeeds. This ending leaves their future to the imagination of the reader. Lassiter and Jane have never excited each other the way Venters and Beth did—will the valley make it happen for them too? Or will Lassiter revert to his happy/unhappy domestication?

In early September 1911, when Grey submitted his completed manuscript to Harpers, he was filled with "hope, enthusiasm, energy, [and] fire" because

110

he believed that it was superior to *The Heritage of the Desert*.[39] When *Heritage* was accepted, he suspected that Ripley Hitchcock, his editor at Harpers, may have done him a favor because his rejection of *The Last of the Plainsmen* was handled so poorly and pained Grey so deeply. His dealings with Hitchcock had taught him that this editor favored a circle of young, new writers and the acceptance of *Heritage* encouraged him to believe that he had been admitted. Thus he was stunned and devastated when Hitchcock speedily rejected *Riders* "with the same chill, aloof, stereotypical advice" that accompanied his rejection of *Plainsmen*.[40] Unwilling to accept this judgment, Grey appealed to Hitchcock's superior, Frederick Duneka, through his agent Dan Murphy, who got Duneka's wife to read the manuscript. She was impressed, and told her husband so; he then urged Hitchcock to accept the book.[41] "I really feel I did not lay sufficient stress on my appreciation," Hitchcock wrote back to Grey on September 15. "And my conscience reproaches me for having possibly been too critical. . . . Of course, as I said to you, we wish to publish it."[42]

When the manuscript was shopped to magazines as a serial, there was more rejection, and it was adamant; no one wanted the story. After their Arizona trip together, Grey was especially pained by MacLean's curt letter of rejection stating that "the interest is centered too much in the women."[43] Finally, *Field and Stream* broke another of its policies, this time against publishing fiction, and accepted the novel, though Grey received considerably less for the serial rights than he was expecting. The serialization of *Riders* commenced in January 1912, and by July 1913, when it ended, *Field and Stream* had included a piece by Grey in every issue since March 1911, twenty-eight consecutive issues.

More disappointments followed. Over the fall of 1911, Murphy reshopped Zane's collection of short stories and it too was rejected by everyone. In December, Zane returned from a discussion with one publisher "unable to see what use there was in me writing." His efforts at "swift action" and "keen dramatic life" were condemned as "melodrama." Like countless writers before and afterward, he was left with "a suspicion that they do not know what a big story is until it has been printed and proved by the test of time and many readers."[44]

In an effort to settle his dismay and confusion, Grey arranged a long meeting with Hitchcock, but the advice he received left him even more embittered and resentful. Hitchcock counseled him to analyze a current best seller. Having already read the book, Grey boldly told Hitchcock that it was "poor wooden writing" and that he "would be ashamed to have my name on such a book." Afterward, he reflected:

I have confided a great deal in this man. I have trusted him, have believed him and tried to learn from him, to do many things because he advised them. I looked up to him. But I cannot ever do that any more.

I understand him now, and I cannot blame him. His idea is the commercial one. He would sacrifice genius for the "best-seller." It is simply that appalling thing commercialism.

I have been bitterly hurt. . . . My work is not to be what this critic advises, or that publisher wants. It is to be what I cannot help but make it. I am driven. I've got to write what I feel and see and think. But I am not yet an artist. In so far I thank these men who are torturing me. The best I can do is to study anew as if I really thought they were right. But I think they are wrong. I believe they have not even suspected my power. I have faith in myself. I stand alone. I can get no help from anyone.[45]

Despite repeated rejections and disappointments, Grey's annual income continued to rise, and he elected to rent a New York City apartment for the winter of 1911–12. Since Dolly was pregnant with their second child and expecting in April, they wanted to be near good medical help for the delivery. In October, he signed a lease on a flat at 550 W. 157th Street. A few days later, he wrote George Allen in Tampico about the serialization of "Down an Unknown Jungle River" that was nearing conclusion. "You will observe that I made George a little funnier than he really was, and also a darn sight poorer shot than he was," he explained. "But I had to put in some fun. And, of course, I exaggerated other things."[46] The purpose of the letter was not only to maintain their friendship, but also to inform Allen that he would not be returning to Tampico.

Instead, Grey persuaded R. C. and Reba, his wife, to accompany him to Long Key for three weeks over late January and early February 1912. Again, lovely weather greeted their arrival and their hopes soared. Grey was especially pleased to learn that his article about his previous visit had been much noticed and had significantly increased the number of guests.[47] However, the weather again turned windy and they were able to fish only three days. While he was there, Grey received his first batch of reviews on *Riders,* and they were disappointing. "I didn't think so much of the reviews, and that one in the *Sun* just about floored me," he admitted to Dolly. "You know the *Sun* did not give me a good review on the *Heritage.*"[48]

Despite the negative appraisals of editors and reviewers, *Riders of the Purple Sage* was the first of Grey's books to make the best-seller list. This achievement requires some explanation, since the list then was quite different from today's. The American best-seller list originated with the first issue of *Book-*

man in February 1895. In a section entitled "The Book Mart," this journal published a list of novels "in order of demand." Extending to the United States a system that originated in England, *Bookman* contacted bookstores in nineteen cities and ranked the six most popular books in each one. In 1899, when the original list of cities was expanded to thirty, the magazine added another list of "Best Selling Books" for the entire year, calculated by the number of times a given book made the monthly lists with a weighting for the positions it achieved.

This system was little noticed and little questioned until the era of *Riders*. At this time, "best seller" first became an understood, commonly used term. In 1911, *Bookman* ran a series of articles about "best sellers" from the past, and the 1910–14 volume of the influential *Readers' Index of Periodical Literature* added the term as a category for entries. In 1912, *Publishers Weekly* initiated a rival listing of the sixteen most popular novels. This "Books of the Month," which appeared irregularly at first, likewise polled bookstores around the country, but found differing results. Over the five years that followed, this competition sparked debate over the accuracy of the lists, spurred *Publishers Weekly* to amend its method of computation, and moved *Bookman* to discontinue its lists for several years, leaving *Publishers Weekly* the dominant source. Even more significant was a related debate over the differences between "high brow" and "low brow" literature.[49] The only point on which everyone agreed was that best sellers were attracting more notice, undermining the authority of critics, and altering the way publishers sold books.[50]

The March 1912 issue of *Bookman* positioned *Riders of the Purple Sage* at number two in Cleveland and number one in New Haven for the month of January.[51] The April issue, which ran February's results, placed it on the lists for Buffalo, Pittsburgh, Cleveland, and Toledo.[52] The month following, its ranking at number four in New Orleans and number two in Birmingham showed that its appeal had extended to the south. That same month, it reached number three for New York City.[53] Although Grey was too busy and too far away to notice, it probably would have surprised him to learn that his novel appealed most to readers in urban centers of the industrialized northeast and did not make the list of any city west of Ohio.

During the poor weather of Long Key and long days of writing, Grey's mind returned to women and the thrill of imagined encounters. In early February, he wrote Dolly about his ruminations and, with surprising candor and less sensitivity, he confessed:

> I don't seem to be satisfied. I want so much, and I don't know what *all* of what I want is. Can you understand that? There is always the perfectly

clear knowledge and happiness that I want to spend nine tenths of my time with you & Baby & my work. But that other tenth haunts me. I wish there was some beautiful worldly woman here or some slip of a silly pretty girl, so that I could talk to her & walk with her along the beach. Don't fail to understand that, Dolly. I insist that that can be true and all right even when I know I am a better man than I was and that I love you a million times more than when we were engaged, or even after we were married. There is something provocative & stimulating in this habit of mine. Even the poor vain silly girl friends you choose to pity and despise are *good* for me. What wouldn't I give now for one of my old friends I used to neglect![54]

This preoccupation with other women persisted after his return to his apartment in New York City. "Yesterday I saw a perfectly, wonderfully beautiful woman," he wrote in his journal in early April. "She was a Russian. I was so moved by her grace and beauty that I cannot remember just what she looked like. But I shall go again to see her and then, perhaps, I may dare attempt a description." The next day Zane did go, and afterward recorded this description:

She was regally tall, a slender woman of perfect form, hair a golden brown, eyes wonderful dark blue, an exquisite mouth. Yet these tell the least of her charm. It was nameless. I thought of something noble, gracious, patrician. I have seen many beautiful women, but none like this Russian. She was so new, so strange, so startling, so natural. . . . I remember once before in my note book I wrote of a beautiful woman—Lina Cavalieri. I have now seen one infinitely more lovely than the Italian beauty. . . . I did not think of any lover for this flower-faced Russian. It seemed to me, if I were to think of that, that the idea would be presumptuous. I cannot imagine the heaven there would be for the man she loved. Yet I know it would be so.

I have no wish to meet this woman, to know her. I want to have her *always* as my possession in fancy. I have looked at her: I have her face engraved forever upon my *mind;* I do not want to change in the least that image. Perhaps to know her would hurt the beauty, the purity, the nobility. She was just a splendid gleam of light, and I never want a shadow to darken its memory. . . . She touched a divine chord and the melody will haunt me all my life.[55]

Over the months spanning these two reflections, Grey completed *Desert Gold,* another story with two romances set on the Mexican-American border and meant to capitalize on the unfolding civil war in Mexico.[56] Gold does not factor into the story until the final pages, and the only character who rises above convention is the intuitive, mystical Yaqui who anticipates Indian characters who would be more important in Grey's future novels.

On April 22, 1912, Dolly gave birth to a daughter named Betty. This pregnancy made her even sicker than she was with Romer, and the delivery was especially taxing. Zane wrote this vivid description of the event:

> I left the room just before the child came, and it was at this time that she had the severest pains. I crouched in my chair in the next room, and listened to the first real cries of mortal agony that I ever heard. She called for me—my name—in a voice low, vibrant, deep, poignant, terrible in its racking power. Powerless to help her I trembled there, suffering through that cry, realizing through it what she really meant to me, what I was to her, and I sweated and shuddered in my own agony. I heard the baby squirt out—heard the last shrill shriek of the mother—heard the doctor slapping the infant—and then its faint wail. "It's a girl," said the doctor. And then I knew. Elizabeth Zane Grey had been born to me. A Betty Zane![57]

The child was healthy, but Dolly's difficulties were more severe than Zane realized. She developed phlebitis and doctors worried about blood clots and a possible stroke. She could not walk for weeks, and months later she was still weak and recuperating. The persistence of her ailments into the fall provoked a traumatic dream in which a doctor informed her that she had terminal cancer. In her diary account, she explained, "I had no fear but there was an awful horror in my soul—I cannot describe it—a feeling of doom, the feeling which can be caused by one thing alone—the certainty of death."[58] Zane had intended to have Wetherill take him to the Rainbow Bridge, but Dolly's prolonged recovery kept delaying and altering his plans. In July, he canceled a six-week trip he had scheduled and wrote Hitchcock that he would instead take a much shorter trip involving a plane ride both ways.[59] This would have been Zane's first time in an airplane and his cancellation of this trip as well postponed his eventual first flight for twenty-five more years; he flew in an airplane for the first and only time the year before his death.

In the same July letter to Hitchcock in which he mentioned his plans to go West, Grey explained that he was well into a novel to be titled "Under Western Stars."[60] He expected to finish it that fall, and he was writing it for both serialization and dramatization. Five months before, Robert Davis had suggested both the topic and a strategy for his story. Since 1903, Davis had been editor of *Munsey's* and he had recently accepted three articles by Grey for *Munsey's*—"Horses of Bostil Ford," "Tiger," and "Phantoms of Peace." Davis was sufficiently impressed with Grey's potential that he agreed to serve as his agent for film and play rights. During their conversations, Davis suggested that his next novel be about "a splendid girl, an American Beauty, developing and finding herself in the west."[61] Grey liked this idea because it encouraged him to indulge his dreaming about women and to have a woman discover the uplifting power of the West.

Madeline Hammond, the chief character in *The Light of Western Stars* (1914), Grey's final title for his novel, is beautiful, wealthy, and refined. She comes from a distinguished Eastern family accustomed to status, privilege, and comfort. Unlike the Eastern males in Grey's previous Westerns, she is neither ill nor in need of rehabilitation. Rather, she is "tired of fashionable society" and wants more from life.[62] Too restless and headstrong to be the indolent, dependent woman esteemed by her class, she goes to see her brother in New Mexico and exhibits remarkable enthusiasm for Grey's interests.

Madeline embraces life in the West and adapts quickly. Despite her lack of experience, she is eager to ride. On her first try, she allows her horse to go as fast as it can, and finds the experience thrilling. Later, when she stops at the top of a hill and surveys the magnificent scenery that extends for miles, she beholds her destiny. "She felt a mighty hold upon her heart. Out of the endless space, out of silence and desolation and mystery and age, came slow-changing colored shadows, phantoms of peace, and they whispered to Madeline" (87). Madeline decides not to return to the East and to purchase a ranch instead. This decision is tested when her sister and some old friends come to visit her. Most of these women have trouble riding, complain of their discomfort, and are unimpressed with the West.

Until *The Light of Western Stars,* all Grey's heroines tended to be strong women and enthusiastic for outdoor activities, but diffident lovers. Jane Withersteen represented a tentative movement away from the submissiveness of Mescal and Bess. She resisted Mormon demands that she marry, but was notably reluctant to challenge the authoritarian Mormon elders and even felt guilty when her actions violated their expectations. She relied on Lassiter to protect her and even addressed him as "master" (286). Having noticed how Grey had used the West to make weak men stronger and more resourceful, Davis suggested that he do the same for a woman. Davis realized that both Grey and the culture of his day were gravitating toward women with greater vitality and independence, and he urged Grey to depict a woman who developed these traits from her contact with the West.

Grey's Madeline is less intimidated by men than his previous female characters. Her experience in the West convinces her that she could never again be happy with a man from the East. Boyd, who has been a close friend for years, journeys from New York to New Mexico with a marriage proposal. He is "handsome, young, rich, well born, pleasant, cultivated—he was all that made a gentleman of his class" (256). However, Madeline is uninterested in these traditional male attributes. His skin does not tan, his hands are soft, and riding is distasteful to him. Madeline wraps up her catalogue of his drawbacks with an observation that his flaccid children would resemble him and be "a generation more toward the inevitable extinction of his race" (256). Needless to say, they do not marry.

This encounter with Boyd reorients Madeline toward Gene Stewart, a lower-class cowboy who falls in love with Madeline before he meets her. Like Zane with his photo of Cavalieri, Stewart has a picture of Madeline from a newspaper that convinces him that she is the woman for him. When she takes over the Stillwell ranch, Madeline inherits Stewart as foreman. Though she notices him and interacts with him, he seems more a problem than a marriage prospect. As with most of Grey's stories, mishaps and misunderstandings keep the couple apart over much of the story, and in this novel they are caused by Gene's rambunctious behavior, and Madeline has to rescue him several times.

Gene's waywardness misrepresents the loyal, hardworking, natural leader that he really is. Madeline detects that there is more to Gene than she has realized when he gathers her onto his horse and speeds them away from a band of guerrillas after her.

> His arm, like a band of iron, held her, yet it was flexible and yielded her to the motion of the horse. One instant she felt the brawn, the bone, heavy and powerful; the next the stretch and ripple, the elasticity of muscles. He held her as easily as if she were a child. The roughness of his flannel shirt rubbed her cheek, and beneath that she felt the dampness of the scarf he used to bathe her arm, and deeper still the regular pound of his heart. Against her ear, filling it with strong, vibrant beat, his heart seemed a mighty engine deep within a great cavern. Her head had never before rested on a man's breast, and she had no liking for it there; but she felt more than the physical contact. The position was mysterious and fascinating, and something natural in it made her think of life. Then, as the cool wind blew down from the heights, loosening her tumbled hair, she was compelled to see strands of it curl softly into Stewart's face, before his eyes, across his lips. She was unable to reach it with her free hand, and

therefore could not refasten it. And when she shut her eyes she felt those
loosened strands playing against his cheeks (166–67).

This sensuality, with its own elements of wildness, inspires Madeline to reconsider Gene and her feelings for him. Over time, she finds him to be "an
object of deep interest to her, not as a man, but as part of this wild and wonderful West which was claiming her" (243). He completes her conversion
into a Westerner.

In causing his heroine to be transformed as men had been in his previous
stories, Grey fretted about a consequence that was not a problem for them:
Madeline might become too strong. He did not want her to become the
"Majesty" that is her nickname. Madeline's love for Gene causes her to realize not only that she needs and cares for him, but also that her influence,
rather like that of Jane upon Lassiter, impairs and debilitates him. Once Gene
has revealed his love to Madeline, he makes a determined effort to become
the respectable, peaceable cowboy that she wants him to be. When he is
charged with a crime that he did not commit and meekly submits to Hawe,
a corrupt sheriff he previously dominated, Madeline is upset by his docility
and worries correctly that his ignoble behavior results from the force of her
influence:

> The vague riot in her breast leaped to conscious fury—a woman's pas-
> sionate repudiation of Stewart's broken spirit. It was not that she would
> have him be a lawbreaker; it was that she could not bear to see him deny
> his manhood. . . . When the man Sneed [Hawe's assistant] came forward,
> jingling the iron fetters, Madeline's blood turned to fire. She would have
> forgiven Stewart then for lapsing into the kind of cowboy it had been her
> blind and sickly sentiment to abhor. This was a man's West—a man's
> game. What right had a woman reared in a softer mold to use her beauty
> and her influence to change a man who was bold and free and strong?
> (317–18)

The restless, homebound author who dreamed of this charismatic woman
as a diversion from the constraints of his wife, marriage, and family also conceived of her as sympathetic to his plight. Madeline's romance with Gene
helped Grey to formulate a concept that quickly became a cornerstone convention of the Western: a man grows weak and ineffectual when he commits
himself to one woman and her expectations.

While Grey was writing *The Light of Western Stars,* a glamorous approxima-
tion of Madeline entered his life. The same October 1911 letter in which he
informed Dolly that he had signed the lease for their New York apartment,

Zane mentioned that he was taking "your charming relative" to the movies.[63] He was referring to Lillian Wilhelm, Dolly's cousin, whom he met before his marriage and got to know better during his stay in New York City over the winter of 1911–12. Though she was born in Flagstaff, Lillian grew up in New York City. Her maternal grandfather sold his catering business to the famous New York City restaurateur Louis Sherry, and her mother had studied piano and opera in Switzerland. For years, her father operated a store on Broadway that imported fine European objets d'art. Lillian was ten years younger than Zane and the oldest of seven siblings; five brothers separated her from her sister Claire, the youngest. She was raised in a spacious three-story brownstone and attended by maids and governesses. However, a series of reversals over the 1890s eroded her father's business and left a cloud of gloom over the family. In her diary, Lillian would characterize her life from sixteen to twenty as the "Time of Trial." In a reflection on her unhappiness over the family's economizing relocation to New Jersey, she would declare, "I am burning to shake off all the trammels of conventionality and stand—alone—free and for Art!" This resolve motivated her to take up painting and to enroll at the School of Fine Arts of the National Academy of Design.[64] Zane had a long-standing interest in art—his drawings impressed one of his dental school professors and were used in the original edition of *Betty Zane*—and the fact that Lillian was a serious, trained artist made her even more attractive.

After Zane canceled his spring trip out West and following his summer return to Lackawaxen, he invited Lillian to visit. When she arrived, Zane was so energized that Dolly noticed, fretted, and in her journal wrote:

> Poor vain Lillian! She is so absolutely obsessed with her looks that she's painful and silly. It's partly Doc's fault, too, greatly, perhaps. He's flattering her till she thinks she's a beauty. When I remonstrate with him, he says, "But what harm is there; it makes her happy." Of course there is no harm, but the argument rather stumps me.

In this same entry, Dolly mentions that Lillian was accompanied by their mutual cousin Elma Schwarz. This was either the first time that Dolly met Elma or the first time that she had seen her in years because she refers to rumors about Elma's beauty and confesses an eagerness to judge for herself. After scrutinizing Elma's appearance and manner, Dolly is "disappointed," not just with Elma but also with Zane, who spends the whole day photographing the pair. Dolly is eerily reluctant to acknowledge the threat these women pose, but her avoidance and its consequences creep into her discussion of her children that follows:

> The more I feel, the deeper down I bury it. I wish I could bring some of
> my emotions more to the surface. I think I would be better liked. There
> is very little that is spontaneous about me and of late I have been fearing
> that that will militate against the friendship and companionship between
> me and my children. . . . The mother in me is satisfied, but then, I'm not
> all mother. Perhaps the loneliness was due to illness and nervousness. It
> is not good to be alone too much when one is not well.[65]

Obviously the children were not her only worries, but she was unwilling to
investigate the others.

Several months later, in late February 1913, Zane left for a third visit to
Long Key and took Lillian and Elma with him. They remained with him for
the duration of his six-week stay, and then accompanied him on the second
leg of the trip that produced his momentous first visit to the Rainbow Bridge.
Zane would justify his decision to take these two women as a professional opportunity for both Lillian and himself. He would develop his experience into
a novel, and Lillian would paint promising scenes and provide illustrations
for the novel. This professional justification glossed more personal reasons.
During his trips with Jones, Grey felt like an outsider and struggled to gain
acceptance. His instinctive wariness of strangers and need for companionship
increased the importance of his family and spurred him to include R. C. in
his recent trips. However, Grey's compulsive trips were also motivated by an
equally strong need to get away from the claustrophobia of his family circle.
Even more pertinent to his invitation of Lillian and Elma were his two years
of dreaming of beautiful women; now he had two willing companions who
were attractive, interested in the outdoors, and responsive to his needs.

Whatever the justification, Dolly was presented a final decision and left to
accept it. Her first letter to Long Key reminded her willful husband of the risk
he was taking. "This is my first letter to you," she observed. "Whether it will be
the last is still a matter of conjecture on my part." Deep down she still loved
Zane and certainly did not want to end their marriage. However hard it was
to believe that he loved her in return, she dared to trust that he did. Thus her
initial challenge was blunted with an ensuing account of her conscientious
dealings with his publisher.[66] The long letters that followed were peppered
with more complaints and criticism, and then similarly diluted with news
about her efforts on his behalf and reassurances of her loyalty. Although he
was a derelict father, she remained a devoted wife and conscientious mother.
"I am sorry to be compelled to intrude upon your dream of bliss," she opened
another letter filled with news about her negotiations and their children.[67]

Elma Schwarz and Lillian Wilhelm (reclining) in Lackawaxen, 1912. (Courtesy of Loren Grey.)

Both directly and indirectly, she kept reminding him that his companions would never understand him as well or ever do as much for him.

Since Zane was not available for important decisions, Dolly went ahead and made them on her own. Concluding that New York City was a poor place to raise children, she broke the lease on their apartment and relocated to a comfortable rental on Main Street in Middletown, New York, where R. C. and Reba had been residing for more than a year. Meanwhile, she shopped for a house to buy. When an imposing residence at 101 South Street became available and Zane was out of touch, she went ahead and arranged the purchase.[68]

Meanwhile Dolly hid her wounds. She would vent her anger, but not her anguish—she would be industrious and resourceful, never weak and incapacitated. These vulnerabilities she reserved for the privacy of her journal. In a year-end reflection on the strains of 1913, she wrote:

> This last hour of the old year I shall devote to a brief retrospect or whatever it may meander into. . . . Several times I have thought myself at the breaking point, always to discover that we are not given more than we can bear. Human nature is elastic.
>
> The great bitterness, the great hardening came when my husband announced to me that he would take the latest—what shall I call her—inamorata?—and her cousin (also my cousin) on a long and unusual trip through the south and southwest with him. It began with the statement that I was unable to go with him now, and therefore the other arrangements. The bottom fell out of the world for me then. Stupidly I said, "But I will go with you": to be told, "But I don't want you." Those words burned themselves on my brain.

After this admission of the pain that she had been suppressing and denying, Dolly proceeds to worry that her estimate has been too harsh. Later, she doubles back and decides that Zane deserves more compassion and a broader understanding:

> Oh, why write all this miserable stuff? After all, to be absolutely fair, I would have to get on all sides of the question, take up all points of view and that is impossible. A mere statement of cold fact makes a bad case for my husband. But he can't be looked at from that angle. Doc is a dreamer, a smiler, an intense egotist. In the same breath he can tell me that it's agony for him to leave me and the children and then that he can't keep from the things in N.Y. Very frankly he tells me that when he's miserable or sick or needs help, he comes home, but his good times he likes with the others. . . . I am getting deeper and deeper, and I feel it's all wrong—what I'm writing. If anyone should read this, ever, it wouldn't be fair to Doc. After all, he can't help it, he was born so, and for better or worse, I must stick to him.

Dolly wraps up her reflection with several resolutions for the upcoming new year, the chief of which is *"Keep your mouth shut."*[69]

In early April 1913, Zane, Elma, and Lillian left Long Key for Arizona. En route, they stopped in El Paso several days for Zane to gather information about the Texas Rangers for a future novel. There he interviewed the former Ranger Captain John Hughes who provided important historical background for the *The Lone Star Ranger* (1915).[70] When they arrived in Flagstaff, they were met by Al Doyle and his son, who had horses and provisions for the ride to Kayenta. Prior to their departure on April 26, Doyle told a Flagstaff newspaper that the Indians around there were "the most isolated and remote from civilization and railroads than any other tribes on the continent. They are nearly 200 miles from any white civilization, and are indeed pioneers on the last real frontier of the American continent."[71] In a reflection years later, Grey related that at the time of his initial visits, Kayenta was "in the heyday of its existence, colorful, bustling, primitive, beautiful, [and] dominated by the splendid spirit of the pioneer Wetherill."[72]

Both John and Louisa Wetherill came from pioneers who settled the Mancos River area in the southwest corner of Colorado. During a search for stray cattle up a canyon near the family's Alamo Ranch in 1888, John's brother, Richard, discovered the cliff dwellings of Mesa Verde. The whole family participated in the excavation of the site and researched its mysterious occupants, but their findings went unnoticed until the discovery of a mummified child became big news in Denver and brought visitors. In 1893, their collection of artifacts was included in the Colorado exhibition at the Columbian Exposition in Chicago. Afterward, scientists, geologists, and archeologists sought out the Wetherills and agreed to pay for information and guiding, but not enough to provide them a livelihood. In 1900, after four years of marriage, John was weary of his struggles with ranching and agreed to manage a trading post in Ojo Alamo, near Navajo Mountain and the Arizona-Utah border. To make ends meet and allow him to pursue his passion for Indian sites, John drove freight wagons, and left Louisa to manage the post. Her quick acceptance by the local Utes and Navajos and her facility with their language yielded valuable information and facilitated their opening a new post in Olajato at the western edge of Monument Valley in 1906. In 1910, following his trip with Cummings to the Rainbow Bridge, John Wetherill relocated his trading post from Olajato to near Kayenta.[73]

Wetherill's trading post was a low-lying outpost surrounded by desert waste, but Louisa had worked hard to make the interior attractive and accommodating. She had a long-standing interest in Indian arts and crafts and utilized them in her decoration. Lillian's fascination with them quickly made them fast friends, and they remained so over the next thirty years that Lillian lived and painted in Arizona. A surviving photograph from this trip of her and Louisa, along with Elma and Louisa's daughter, shows the interior of the trading post and a band of Yei figures on the wall near the ceiling that Lillian would later replicate in three of Zane's residences.

The Grey party's weeklong journey from Kayenta to the Rainbow Bridge commenced with a nervous crossing through the quicksand of Laguna Creek and a long day's ride northward through blowing sand and blistering heat. The first night, they camped on the edge of Monument Valley, which was illuminated first by lightning during a twilight thunderstorm and then by a glorious sunrise the next morning. In "Nonnezoshe," his account of this trip, Grey describes his ride around Mittens and the other spires as though it were his first encounter with Monument Valley. From there, the group looped to the southwest and entered the mazelike branches of Tsegi Canyon that affirmed Wetherill's guiding skills and brought them to Keet Seel, "the place of broken pot shards." The following day, Zane went to Betatakin, which inspired him with a "strange feeling that *Riders of the Purple Sage* was true" and "my dream people of romance had really lived there once upon a time."[74] His description of this visit makes it difficult to tell whether this encounter was a return that confirmed the accuracy of his recollection, or a first meeting that validated what he imagined from photographs and his memories of Thunder River, but he had an eerie sensation that his fiction was true and that he was now living it. While the others were off investigating the site, he sat and recalled Bess and Venters, "who had lived for me their imagined lives of loneliness here in this wild spot" (5–6). Though he had brought Lillian along to be his Bess and she was as enthusiastic about this outing as Madeline Hammond would have been, he preferred to be by himself reflecting on "my past, my dreams, my very self" (6).

Leaving behind the shelter and vegetation of Keet Seel, Betatakin, and Surprise Valley, the group worked its way around the great bulge of Navajo Mountain and came to a panoramic overlook of the washboard configuration of the landscape ahead. The views from inside the canyons proved even more awesome. As the challenges increased and the scenery grew stranger, the trip shaded into a reckoning with primal elements and cosmic forces. Grey writes:

> I imagined there was no scene in all the world to equal this. The tranquility of lesser spaces was here not manifest. This happened to be a place where so much of the desert could be seen and the effect was stupendous. Sound, movement, life seemed to have no fitness here. Ruin was there

Interior of Wetherill Trading Post, 1913. Right to left: Elma Schwarz, Louisa Wetherill, her daughter, and Lillian Wilhelm (kneeling). (Courtesy of Pat Friese.)

Wetherill, Lillian, and Elma at Betatakin, 1913. (Courtesy of Pat Friese.)

and desolation and decay. The meaning of the ages was flung at me. A man became nothing (8–9).

Cautiously, they picked their way over great expanses of slick rock with little secure footing. One of the horses slipped and was saved from plunging over a precipice by a heroic exertion from one of the wranglers. The canyons turned monotonous, treacherous, mesmerizing, and exhausting, and time became meaningless. Grey wore down, and other members dropped even further behind. Finally, Wetherill, with Nasjah Begay alongside him, announced, "Nonnezoshe," and, in his account, Grey provides this eloquent description of the sight:

> This rainbow bridge was the one great natural phenomenon, the one grand spectacle which I had ever seen that did not at first give vague disappointment, a confounding of reality, a disenchantment of contrast with what the mind had conceived.
>
> But this thing was glorious. It absolutely silenced me. My body and brain, weary and dull from the toil of travel, received a singular and revivifying freshness. I had a strange, mystic perception that this rosy-hued, tremendous arch of stone was a goal I had failed to reach in some former life, but had now found. Here was a rainbow magnified even beyond dreams, a thing not transparent and ethereal, but solidified, a work of ages, sweeping up majestically from the red walls, its iris-hued arch against the blue sky (14–15).

Earlier in the same account, Grey states proudly and inaccurately that "my party was the second one, not scientific" (3) to visit the arch. Even though he may not have been aware of them at the time, at least four other parties had already visited the Rainbow Bridge between the first visit of the Cummings-Douglas group and that of his group.[75] However, Grey did know that, three months *after* his trip, from mid-July to the end of August 1913, Theodore Roosevelt hired Jim Owens to take him hunting for mountain lions in the Grand Canyon, and afterward had Wetherill guide him to the Rainbow Bridge.[76] By specifically mentioning Roosevelt's trip at the outset of his article, Grey lets his reader know that the venturesome ex-president was following his tracks, but carefully avoids any mention of the two women who completed the arduous trip with him.

In late May 1913, after an absence of almost five months, Grey returned to Lackawaxen and immersed himself in writing. Eager to make headway with his fiction, he postponed writing about his experience; his uncharacteristically brief account, "Nonnezoshe," did not even appear until February 1915, eighteen months after his return and five months after completion of his novel.[77] *The Rainbow Trail* (1915) was the closest of all Grey's Westerns to his actual experience. Not only did he present actual places like Red Lake, Moencopie, Tuba, and Kayenta, but the names of Preston and Wetherill were amended only slightly and that of Nas Ta Bega was only a variant spelling. The conclusion of the novel recycles his own trip to the Bridge. His location of the "sealed wives" of the Mormons in Fredonia causes more than a little confusion since it is north of the Colorado River and many miles away from these other places.[78] This disparity is telltale evidence of the contrived connection between the two novels. *The Rainbow Trail* was supposed to be a sequel to *Riders of the Purple Sage,* but the two works were inspired by different trips to opposite sides of the Colorado River.

In "Nonnezoshe," Grey explains that during his visit to a Surprise Valley just beyond Betatakin he "climbed high upon the huge stones, and along the smooth red walls where Fay Larkin once had glided" (65). This nimble, daring Fay Larkin resembles the young woman in *Rainbow* more than the child in *Riders.* Ever since this inspirational visit, Grey conceived of *Rainbow* as a sequel exploring what became of Fay after Lassiter closed the access and sealed himself, Jane, and Fay in Surprise Valley of *Riders.* The protagonist of *Rainbow,* John Shefford, is a clergyman from Illinois and a friend of Bess and Venters, who have married and lived nearby for the past twelve years. They have told him about Lassiter, Jane, and Surprise Valley, and he is so captivated by Fay, who would be seventeen or eighteen by this point, that he leaves to find out about this alluring woman of his dreams.

Grey provides this quest another impetus that is equally important. Initially, Sheffield wanted to be an artist, but was pressured by his father to become a minister instead. This has caused mounting unhappiness and led to disaster. His narrow-minded congregation has eroded his belief in religion and God, and finally forced him to leave Illinois. During his trip from Red Lake to Kayenta, which opens the story, this earlier background emerges as a set of fragmented recollections he prefers to forget. Unlike Grey's previous protagonists who were ailing or wounded, Sheffield is sound physically but emotionally troubled, and his distressed state of mind influences his response to his new surroundings. He is willfully seeking "some wild life" to escape the "easy, safe, crowded, bound lives" of preachers.[79] By focusing his description upon what Shefford sees, smells, and hears, Grey implies that his character is living by sensory responses in order to avoid festering thoughts and emotions from his haunted past. Shefford's immersion of himself in his experience functions as both therapy and defense against inner demons.

Following a mishap along the way, Shefford is told that the desert is a place for wanderers, not missionaries. By the time he reaches Kayenta, this advice has become self-definition. He tells the owner of the trading post there, "My thoughts put in words would seem so like dreams. Maybe they are dreams. Perhaps I'm only chasing a phantom—perhaps I'm only hunting the treasure at the foot of the rainbow" (45). Shefford's "foot of the rainbow," Grey's original title, is at this point only a figurative definition of his directionless wandering and vague, undefined hopes.

En route to Kayenta, Shefford is saved from a menacing nighttime intruder by the fortuitous arrival of Nas Ta Bega.[80] Shefford's deepening alienation from whites predisposes him toward this Piute with the same name as the one who accompanied Grey to the Rainbow Bridge. Shefford senses an immediate brotherhood with this "sage and a poet—the very spirit of this desert" (93). As they become better acquainted, Bega's Indian heritage and mysticism reverse Shefford's disillusionment with religion and reorient him toward a more fulfilling alternative.

This compensatory theme of kinship and spiritual regeneration was so important to Grey that he modified the actual Nasjah Begay to fit it. Begay did not speak English. During his first trip with Byron Cummings to the Rainbow Bridge, he used hand signals to show the way. Unlike the son of a chief in Grey's story, the real Begay was an uneducated sheepherder who learned about the Bridge during his upbringing on his father's farm in a remote canyon midway between the Bridge and Olajato. The Nas Ta Bega of Grey's story not only speaks English, but also shares Shefford's discontent with white culture. He tells Shefford that years before, soldiers ignored the appeals of his parents and sent him to a mission school in California. After his successful completion of college fourteen years later, he decided that the "white-man's God" was not for him, and returned to his roots. Although he has come back to the land and beliefs of his people, he, like Shefford, is despondent—in his case, over all the damage done by whites. This Indian contains more than a little resemblance to Jim Thorpe, the Native American who went to the Carlisle Indian School in Pennsylvania, starred in football, and returned to his roots in Oklahoma for several directionless, unhappy years. Grey and the rest of the country learned about Thorpe and his past after he returned to Carlisle in 1911 for more football. There he won All-American honors, and then starred in the 1912 Olympics, where King Gustav of Sweden pronounced him the "greatest athlete in the world."

If the noble Nas Ta Bega was a bold new character for Grey and a precursor for the later hero of *The Vanishing American* (1925), Grey's villains continued to be Mormon polygamists. Shefford's search for Fay Larkin carries him beyond Kayenta to a hidden Mormon village of "sealed wives." Over the twelve years that have passed since the conclusion of *Riders,* laws have been passed against polygamy, and federal agents are aggressively enforcing them. Mormons have established secret towns across state lines and beyond the jurisdiction of federal agents in order to preserve their multiple marriages. During the day, only women live in these Arizona towns; at night, their husbands sneak across from Utah to be with them. Here Shefford meets Sago Lily and does not suspect what most readers do—that she is really Fay Larkin. After the two become friends and steal away for secret meetings, Fay reveals her identity and explains that she agreed to be a sealed wife two years before in order to save Jane and Lassiter. While Shefford is at her house one evening, her husband comes to visit, presumably to complete their still-unconsummated marriage. The next day, following a confusing chain of events, he is discovered dead from a chest wound.

As he was writing, Grey fretted that Mormons might be offended over his continuing depiction of them as harsh, close-minded fanatics and recalcitrant polygamists. In order to make these husbands appear more "normal" at the government trial of them for polygamy, Grey has Shefford acknowledge that many men want more than one wife:

> His judgment of Mormons had been established by what he had heard and read, rather than what he knew. He wanted now to have an open mind. He had studied the totemism and exogamy of the primitive races, and here was his opportunity to understand polygamy. One wife for one man—that was the law. Mormons broke it openly; Gentiles broke it secretly. Mormons acknowledged all their wives and protected their children; Gentiles acknowledged one wife only. Unquestionably the Mormons were wrong, but were not the Gentiles still more wrong? (97)

Later, another character presumes upon the dreaming that the desert inspires to make a similar point:

> See here, son, look things square in the eye. Men of violent, lonely, toilsome lives store up hunger for the love of woman. Love of a *strange* woman, if you want to put it that way. It's nature. It seems all the beautiful young women in Utah are corralled in this valley. When I come over here I feel natural, but I'm not happy. I'd like to make love to—to that flower faced girl. And I'm not ashamed to own it. I've told Molly, my wife, and she understands (112).

Even more surprising than Grey's inclusion of these passages is his failure to include more of them. Anyone aware of his ongoing involvement with Lillian and Claire cannot help wondering why he was not more sympathetic toward Mormons and their polygamy. Ever since his first visit to Fredonia, Grey was obsessed with the polygamist elders there. At the time and for years afterward, he had a compelling need to tell others about these strange men without ever plumbing the reasons for his preoccupation. Grey's reversal of his original intent *not* to "roast" Mormons is indeed strange. When Dan Murphy, his agent, offered the completed manuscript to an editor for serialization, he forthrightly acknowledged the story's anti-Mormonism and explained that Zane would moderate it, if necessary,[81] and for the novel version, he did eliminate some of his more outspoken comments. Apparently the editors at Harpers worried less about his depiction of Mormons than Fay's child, since this proved to be Grey's most significant modification of his original manuscript.[82] His elimination of this child had the effect of making Fay appear to be a virgin when she meets Shefford and her husband of two years arrives for his late-night visit. Grey's fascination with Mormon polygamy was strong enough to suggest an obsession, one too fraught with allure to relinquish but too dangerous to condone. Casting Mormon elders with their "sealed wives" as his villains kept Grey's story solidly positioned on the side of the approved and acceptable. His limp gestures of support for polygamy sparked no suspicions about his secret life, but they also stifled important inspiration, kept the romances in his novels conventional and wholesome, and checked his inclination toward the erotic and taboo.

The concluding trip to the Rainbow Bridge starts as flight and turns into pilgrimage. Nas Ta Bega and Shefford rescue Fay, who has been wrongly suspected of murdering her husband, and the trio flee to Surprise Valley where they find the much older Jane and Lassiter.[83] Aware that they are being pursued, the group heads for the Rainbow Bridge with Bega as their guide. After hanging back to fend off the enemy, Shefford catches up in time to hear Bega announce "Nonnezoche," and is awed by his first glimpse of the Bridge. Nas Ta Bega stands motionless, silently saying a prayer, and refuses to pass under it. This ritual, which the real Nasjah Begay performed for the groups he guided, accentuates the profound spirituality of the Bridge that Shefford has already sensed, one he does not fully comprehend until he and Fay behold it together, a scene that Lillian depicted in the frontispiece for the first edition of the novel:

There was a spirit in the canyon, and whether or not it was what the Navajo embodied in the great Nonnezoshe, or the life of the present, or the death of the ages, or the nature so magnificently manifested in those silent, dreaming, waiting walls—the truth for Shefford was that this spirit was God.

Life was eternal. Man's immortality lay in himself. Love of a woman was hope—happiness. Brotherhood—that mystic and grand "Bi Nai" of the Navajo—that was religion (344).

The Rainbow Bridge was so significant for Grey that he would return to it three more times. Whenever he wanted to take a special friend to a special place, he took him or her to the Rainbow Bridge. He took many photographs of the site. One of these was enlarged and hung over the fireplace in his study; several were used as illustrations for autobiographical accounts.[84] He favored shots of himself looking at the arch in poses meant to communicate his sense of awe and achievement. During his first visit, he inscribed his name and the date of his arrival—May 13, 1913—on a boulder near the northern base of the arch on which the members of the Cummings-Douglass group had scratched their names. This was done to create an enduring record that connected him both to the place and to these discoverers.[85] In both "Nonnezoshe" and *The Rainbow Trail,* he wrote the same sentence, "Only by toil, sweat, endurance and pain could any man ever look at Nonnezoshe." He really should have written "any man or woman." Years later, he would be dismayed and demoralized by the intrusion of development upon the sites he had visited when they were remote and pristine. But in 1913, he was so inspired by his successful journey to the Rainbow Bridge that he could not imagine—not even in his wildest dreams—that the Colorado River would one day be dammed and transformed into a lake, and that boats would comfortably whisk 300,000 visitors to the Rainbow Bridge each year.

5

Moviemaking and Button Fish: 1915–19

"I am an outcast. I am hunted. If I made you my
wife it might be to your shame and sorrow." . . .
"Take me," she cried, and the soft, deep-toned,
passionate voice shook Adam's heart. She would
share his wanderings.
"Good-by, Oella," he said huskily. And he strode
forth to drive his burro out into the lonely,
melancholy desert night.
—Wanderer of the Wasteland

During the spring of 1914, Grey sent Robert Davis an undated postcard on which he wrote, "You will be pleased to learn that the book you inspired me to write has been for a month the best selling book in the United States." He did not identify the novel, but his card was a piece of promotion for *The Light of Western Stars,* with an illustrated scene on the front and an exciting summary of the story on the back.[1] Besides urging Zane to write this novel,

Davis had agreed to serialize it in *Munsey's,* the magazine he edited, and he paid $3,000 for the rights. His contract with Grey stipulated that the serialization begin with the May 1913 issue and that the novel not appear until the run in *Munsey's* was completed. When Harpers published *Light* in January 1914, *Publishers Weekly* positioned it at number seven on its list for that month and number three for February.[2] The journal did not offer a list for March, and by April the novel had dropped to number eleven.[3] *The Light of Western Stars* made the *Bookman* list only once, number four for the month of April.[4]

Whether Zane was exaggerating or relying on an alternative source of information, *Light* was a gratifying success, and a first step toward more ambitious plans. At the time that Davis agreed to serve as Grey's agent for stage and film rights, he was convinced that Harpers had been slighting these alternative possibilities.[5] In the spring of 1913, Edwin Van Brunt, an aspiring playwright, contacted Grey and proposed a dramatization of *Riders of the Purple Sage.* When Van Brunt and Dolly went to Harpers to secure Hitchcock's approval for this project, the editor scrutinized them with "a fishy eye" and threw up roadblocks that made both uncomfortable. He insisted that Van Brunt pay Grey $1,000 for the rights and grant Harper and Brothers half of all proceeds. After Dolly intervened on behalf of Van Brunt, Hitchcock agreed to lower Harpers' return to a third.[6] A letter Hitchcock dispatched shortly after this meeting reminded Dolly that Van Brunt "seems to have no regular theatrical connection at present, and seems to have no play produced." "We are not interposing obstacles in any way," he insisted, but then added "as a matter of practice, the 'impecunious genius' very rarely places a book dramatization."[7]

Davis believed that Harpers was too obsessed with its own product and should have been doing more to encourage dramatizations of Grey's work. Alerting the young author to the handsome sums that might be realized, Davis urged him to plan his novels for this possibility. Unlike Grey, who preferred Lackawaxen and remote locations, Davis enjoyed New York and its diversions; he was an active theatergoer and attended the most popular plays. He was aware of the success of the 1904 stage version of *The Virginian* with Dustin Farnum in the lead and the Broadway production of *The Squaw Man* that opened a year later. Even more on his mind in his discussions with Zane was the enduring appeal of revivals of these plays, especially the January 1911 revival of *The Squaw Man* with Dustin Farnum in the lead and William S. Hart in the same role he played in the original production. Like Grey's Westerns, these two plays featured fugitives from civilization discovering the invigorating life of the West. In *The Squaw Man,* the male lead is an English lord whose drab life in England sharply contrasts with the boisterous conditions he discovers out West. These two productions convinced Davis that Grey's work had stage potential, that *Light* had special promise, and that he could get producers to pay handsomely for the rights.

Although none of Grey's novels reached the stage, Zane and Davis quickly grasped that their error lay in direction rather than thinking. The ensuing two years revealed that movies were outdrawing plays and presented far greater opportunity. Again *The Squaw Man* was a beacon. Following the successful stage revival, Jesse Lasky acquired the film rights. Young, unproven, but certainly not inexperienced, Lasky had been doing stage work for years, and recently had decided that movies were not the threat that many theater people feared. He believed that viewers would soon tire of two-reel displays of action and prefer the kind of drama that plays had always provided. Reassured by the stage success of *The Squaw Man,* he joined with his friends Cecil B. DeMille and Samuel Goldfish (later renamed Goldwyn) and they persuaded Dustin Farnum to play the lead with an appeal that their collective knowledge of the theater would result in a superior product.

In order to escape the legal outreach of the powerful Edison Company, which closely policed its many patents, the hastily assembled band of players and technicians elected to film *The Squaw Man* out West. After an aborted plan for Arizona, *The Squaw Man* began filming in late December 1913 and was released in February 1914. The six-reel result earned the distinction of the first feature to be made in Hollywood and its tenfold return on its investment validated all Lasky's hopes.[8]

The success of *The Squaw Man* showed the way to gold and touched off a rush of variations. Over the previous four years, Tom Mix had appeared in numerous one- and two-reelers about cowboy life, but nine months after *The Squaw Man*'s release, he completed his first five-reel feature, *In the Days of the Thundering Herd.* That same year, William S. Hart left the stage to play cowboys in films. After deepening frustration with his initial roles, he appealed to his friend Thomas Ince to allow him to make Westerns, and in December, he achieved his first success with a seven-reel feature entitled *The Bargain.* The short-action Westerns from before 1914 had rocketed Broncho Billy Anderson to stardom and gained him an annual salary that exceeded $100,000, but the surge of feature-length films prompted a reassessment of his limited acting skills, a cutback in his performances, and more involvement in producing. Two years later, he sold his interest in Essanay and by 1920, he was completely out of filmmaking.

Grey at the Rainbow Bridge. (Courtesy of Loren Grey.)

In a letter written to Thomas Ince from Long Key, Florida, in January 1915, Grey displayed an informed awareness of these developments:

> The enclosed letter is what prompts me to write you about my western stories, for which I have had many offers from moving picture people.
>
> I sold several of my earlier books, among them LIGHT OF WESTERN STARS, to Selig. They have been kept back because of their increasing value. This has opened my eyes. I am waiting for the right man. Maybe you happen to be that man. When he arrives I have a big proposition for him. And it concerns photographing RIDERS OF THE PURPLE SAGE, and a number of other books in that wild and magnificent country where I got the stories. It can be done, and the wonderful scenic possibilities would make these plays great.
>
> Does Mr. Hart know my work? I believe if you and he consider me long enough to look into the possibilities, you might see that I have a big thing.[9]

Grey believed that the Arizona-Utah settings for his novels were both essential and a slighted resource. For years he had been taking a camera on his trips, and his photographs filled his mind with images of spectacular backgrounds for film versions of his Westerns. His characters, like Zane himself, were inspired by desert waste, twisted gorges, and eerie rock formations, and his poetic descriptions realized their atmospheric potential. He was, of course, thinking in terms of drama, aesthetics, and verification, but his proposal contained a cost-saving feature that impressed producers even more. Again *The Squaw Man* pointed the way. Lasky originally intended his picture to be filmed in Flagstaff, but inclement weather and disappointing conditions necessitated a hasty relocation to a barn in Hollywood that would later became a famous landmark. Obviously, Lasky was hoping that the scenery around Flagstaff would give his film a Western look. Since the actual setting for the play was Wyoming, faithfulness to his film's source was not a concern. Flagstaff's convenient location along the train line to California was as important as its Western landscape. If Grey's novels effectively shifted the locus for Westerns from the lush plains and majestic mountains of Wyoming to the arid, dusty Southwest, Hollywood favored this shift because this scenery, whether it was stately buttes, scrub-brush arroyos, or merely weathered barns, was nearby and affordable.

Though his Westerns were best sellers and thus "presold properties," Zane greatly exaggerated Hollywood's interest in his work. Like today's dot coms, the companies that rushed into feature-length Westerns quickly discovered a new market environment that was both complex and treacherous. Less than two months after the opening of *The Squaw Man,* Selig released *The Spoilers,* a Western that would be long remembered both for its climactic fistfight between Tom Santschi and William Farnum and for the four remakes it inspired. Selig then purchased the rights to *The Light of Western Stars* for his next offering. Though *The Spoilers* fared better than the Westerns of his competitors, even Selig was forced to curtail his plans six months after his first Western premiered. On April 5, 1915, Selig, Lubin, and the Essanay Company (co-owned by Broncho Billy and George K. Spoor, the dominant business partner) affiliated with Vitagraph to form V-L-S-E, with hopes of releasing a new feature each month. The high cost of production and exhibition was not the only reason for this alliance. Initially, these moviemakers depended upon the established General Film Company to distribute their films, but they soon realized that General was not up to the challenges of the new features, and that they, as small companies, could not afford the greater expense and risk of these films. V-L-S-E was to be a superior alternative. Unfortunately, Vitagraph, the strongest member of the group and principal advocate of this strategy, was already in financial trouble and could not deliver on its end of the agreement.[10]

These developments derailed the filming of *The Light of Western Stars* and provoked this dejected letter from Grey to Davis on March 26, 1916:

> The bottom dropped out of the "Light of Western Stars" possibility.
> I might have spared you some trouble—and probable annoyance, by not bothering you. Pray accept my apologies.
> No doubt you sold Western Stars for as much as it was worth at that time. If we had held on to it—but regrets are useless. I have tried in every way to do something with these moving picture people. I am not equal to the task. It is a sort of lamb and wolf affair. I quite appreciate what you called me the other day—and by the way that was the second time, the first being in front of my wife—and I am sure I deserve it. All the same it hurt.[11]

Zane was already demoralized because he had sold the rights to this novel for $500 in 1914. Selig had purchased them with a shrewd anticipation that their value would increase, but he did not intentionally hold them as an investment as Grey believed. Selig fully intended to make the film and actually started filming it in 1916, but the turbulence within the industry and V-S-L-E prevented him from completing it. Grey was even more dejected by postponement of a film that might have boosted his reputation and sales of his

Grey in Monument Valley, ca. 1920. From a series of photographs promoting the Valley for filming of his novels. (Courtesy of the Ohio Historical Society.)

novel. The film was not only shelved indefinitely, but even worse, his sale of the rights barred him from locating someone else to make it.

Davis argued that Grey should not concern himself with matters like this and embarrassed Grey in front of his wife because he had involved himself with what agents were supposed to do. Two days after his derogatory estimate of Grey's business sense, Davis sent him a letter with an even harsher demand that he stay away from all financial decisions, and leave those responsibilities to him:

> I have told you several times: you are a rotten business man, and I reiterate it here. The position you occupy in American fiction is a high one and you have earned it by sheer ability, plus courage. I still insist that if I could handle you for the next five years, the Grey family would have a winter and a summer home, built of fireproof material, a retinue of servants, automobiles, boats and flying machines. You never should be permitted to talk to anybody on a business proposition; and every time you go roaming around New York to have a commercial jag, you set yourself back from ten to twenty-five thousand dollars per annum. If I could hurt your feelings often enough to keep you out of New York, except to visit a few friends, there is nothing I wouldn't say.[12]

Before he ever posted this letter, two men arrived and furnished Davis prime examples of his conscientious efforts on Zane's behalf. In a hastily appended postscript, he scribbled that J. Packard, a motion picture broker, had come to his office and offered a $1,000 for the film rights to *Riders of the Purple Sage*. Davis explained that he scoffed at this offer, and told Packard that he would have to pay $10,000. This was followed by a second postscript relating that another man named Reynolds (perhaps Sidney Reynolds), from the Fox Film Corporation, had arrived shortly after Packard, and proposed $1,500 for the rights to *Riders* and $1,000 for *The Last Trail*. Davis characterized this offer as "brass tacks," and advised Zane to decide quickly.[13] He even posted a telegram stressing the matter's urgency.[14]

It is surprising that Davis scorned the first offer and then pounced on the second for only a slightly higher amount. However, he did so to demonstrate the critical importance of knowledge and judgment. The Packard offer had dismal prospects. Davis assumed that Packard did not have hard cash, and that his contract would be filled with contingencies. On the other hand, Davis knew the Fox offer was solid. Although the Fox Film Corporation had been making films less than a year, it had been exhibiting them over ten years (under different names) and, like Carl Laemmle's IMP, Fox had an imposing record of success. Davis was confident that he and Zane would get their money, and this film *would* be made. When Reynolds returned several months later with a similar offer for the rights to *The Rainbow Trail, The Last of the Duanes,* and *The Lone Star Ranger,* Davis again urged Zane to accept.[15] On an undated postcard from this period, Grey posted Davis a hasty expression of gratitude that anticipated the memorable line from *Titanic,* "I merely desire to express to you, concerning a matter you loomed largely therein, that *The World is Mine.*"[16]

As great as it was, Grey's excitement could not stave off second thoughts about these sales. He was never comfortable with the fact that, once rights were sold, filmmakers were free to do as they pleased. His acceptance of Fox's money allowed it to modify his story, cast whomever, pocket the profits, and even tarnish his reputation should its efforts miscarry. Several months after he sold the rights to *Light,* Zane deliberated the possibility of starting a film company of his own to protect his interests.[17] Amid the turbulence and uncertainties of the fledgling industry, there were few dominant studios and none was as powerful as several would be a decade later. However, the risks, demands, and ruthless competition intimidated Grey and kept him from acting on this wish. A year and a half later, during the summer of 1917, Benjamin Hampton approached him with a tempting alternative whereby he would use Grey's name and writings to attract financing, confer with him on projects, and personally supervise the filming. Hampton was an ambitious, well-connected entrepreneur who believed that greater size and better integration would solve the problems beleaguering the industry. With a March 1916 letter of commitment from Mary Pickford, whose contract with Adolph Zukor and his Famous Players Film Company was about to expire, he had assembled a formidable group of backers that included Percival S. Hill of the American Tobacco Company (where Hampton had been a vice president), Charles Sabin of the Guaranty Trust, John Prentiss of Hornblower and Weeks, and George J. Whalen of the United Cigar Stores. With their clout and cash, he had his eye on the foundering V-L-S-E consortium. He was preparing to seize control of it, Lasky's company, and several other vulnerable distributors, and consolidate them into a single large company.[18]

Meanwhile, Adolph Zukor learned about Hampton's ambitious plans and other lucrative offers for Pickford, and he decided that he had to move boldly and quickly. Convinced that the new features necessitated larger capitalization and greater consolidation, like the example of V-S-L-E, he envisioned a more vertical integration of operations under tighter management. He enlisted Jesse Lasky to join forces and take over the Paramount Company.

W. W. Hodkinson, the owner of this two-year-old film distributor, had furnished crucial seed funding for *The Squaw Man* and two-thirds of his company's business involved handling the films of Zukor and Lasky, who were increasingly unhappy with his demands and fees. Zukor believed that he could not afford to pay Pickford more unless he controlled Paramount. Over April and May, Zukor and Lasky pooled their stock in Paramount, acquired more shares until they had amassed a majority stake, and then forced a buyout upon Hodkinson.

On June, 17, 1916, these components—Zukor's Famous Players Film Company, Lasky's company, along with Paramount—were merged into the Famous Players–Lasky Corporation (renamed Paramount in the 1920s), with Zukor as president, Lasky as vice president in charge of production, Cecil B. DeMille as director-general, and Samuel Goldfish as chairman of the board. Five days later, Zukor signed Mary Pickford to a new two-year contract that guaranteed her a million dollars, a tenfold increase of her previous contract's salary. A month later, he opened up Artcraft Pictures Corporation to handle the release of her films.[19] For the time being, Zukor and Lasky were content with their much stronger company and their retention of Pickford, but several years later, they would add Zane Grey to their collection of stars.

This preemptive strike left Hampton with an embittered sense of lost opportunity. On August 11, 1916, he wrote to Percival Hill: "Re Pickford, I believe we lost at least a million dollars a year when we lost her. Famous Players and Jesse Lasky Company, on February 22nd, orally agreed to consolidate with us; on our present capitalization we could have had them with us on a basis of $6,000,000 of our stock. Mr. Zukor now states that he will not consider less than $12,500,000, and declares that a part of it will have to be in cash."[20]

On May 17, 1916, Albert E. Smith and J. Stuart Blackton took over Vitagraph, and Hampton and his backers supported this move with an infusion of $250,000, which gave them all the stock in V-L-S-E. In March of the following year, while Smith was away, Hampton's group seized control of Vitagraph and locked him out. In June, Smith's partner, J. Stuart Blackton, resigned. In August, Selig and Essanay defected to George Kleine and the Edison Companies, and deprived V-L-S-E of its S-E.

Hampton had taken over the helm, but his ship was listing badly.[21] He quickly struck an alliance with the deposed Hodkinson, who put up funds from the sale of his Paramount stock in return for responsibility for film distribution.[22] Hampton then recruited Grey, Eltinge Warner, the owner of *Field and Stream,* and Rex Beach, another popular novelist, in a final desperate quest to broaden his base of support. During a trip out west over the summer of 1916, Zane wrote to Dolly, "I have a proposition from this Mr. Hampton that is great. He is a partner of Rex Beach. He and Mr. Warner want to organize to exploit my name as they do Beach. It could mean $50,000 a year to me. . . . Beach is making $250,000 a year!"[23] Hampton explained that his company would film Grey's novels under the name Zane Grey Pictures and release them through Hodkinson. This arrangement allowed Grey to retain his film rights, participate in the process, share the profits, and still have ample time for travel and writing.

What Davis thought of this overblown scheme can only be conjectured. The collection of his correspondence contains no letters from 1917 and 1918, and the ones that follow reveal that his professional collaboration with Grey had ended. After 1918, the discussion in their letters is cordial and superficial, personal rather than professional. Meanwhile, upheaval, reconfigured plans, and financial uncertainties so disrupted film production that the earliest films of Grey's novels did not appear until 1918. The first of them, *The Border Legion* (1918), involved a novel from two years before and was released by Goldwyn under terms for which no records exist. This was followed by *Riders of the Purple Sage* (1918) and *The Rainbow Trail* (1918). Both were made by Fox and starred Dustin Farnum's brother, William, who came to Fox after appearing in Selig's *The Spoilers*.[24] In the spring of 1916, Selig started shooting *The Light of Western Stars* with Tom Mix in the lead role, but the erupting problems with V-L-S-E disrupted the filming and occasioned Grey's complaint to Davis that "the bottom dropped out" on *Light*. Following his split with V-L-S-E, Selig folded the footage from *Light* into *The Heart of Texas Ryan* and sold his film rights to the novel to Harry Sherman, who recruited Dustin Farnum to play Gene Stewart in a production that was distributed by United Picture Theatres of America in 1919.[25]

Desert Gold, the first Hampton-Hodkinson film for Zane Grey Pictures, opened in 1919, and Grey's letter of praise to Hampton illuminates his expectations. Much of the filming was done around Palm Springs, California, far from the Arizona-Mexican border setting of the novel and the areas of northwestern Arizona that Grey had been aggressively promoting for several years, but he nonetheless wrote:

> Let me congratulate you upon the fact that you have put the spirit, the action, and the truth of "Desert Gold" upon the screen. My ideas, wishes, even my hopes, have been fulfilled. This is something that I had despaired of ever seeing.
>
> Your elimination of the star system is going to revolutionize the motion picture business. You are making a picture of a story to please and thrill

the public—not destroying the spirit and plot of a good book to cater to the whim and egotism of a star. Just so long as stars insist on having all the strong scenes of a book, just so long will motion pictures be weak, the producers puzzled, and the audiences slowly growing cold. It is as simple as ABC. The public loves motion pictures. The secret of that instinct is as deep-seated as the instinct for everyone to play. It is love of a good story. It is desire to forget oneself. It is longing to live the ordeal of the hero and heroine. And that instinct is what makes audiences survive in spite of stars who mar the story and exploit only themselves. . . . Well as I love pictures, I would not pay my fifty cents to see any picture if I knew that this actor or actress, because of the bone-headed conceit of a star, was not permitted to do his very best. Right here is the secret of the dry rot in the movies.[26]

Grey's objection to "stars" represented a telling change. His 1915 letter to Ince expressed high regard for William S. Hart, who was already a star. Given the striking resemblance between Hart and Grey, it is a shame that Hart never appeared in a film adaptation of Grey's work. Hart impressed Grey because of his conscientious effort to look, dress, and behave like a real cowboy. Grey also liked Dustin Farnum in *The Light of Western Stars.* When he viewed some early rushes, he reported back to Dolly that Farnum was "very good."[27] Nonetheless, he realized that both these actors from the New York stage were far cries from Emett, Doyle, Wetherill, and the real cowboys of his Arizona outings. The circus stunts and spangled outfits that gained Tom Mix stardom made this disparity unbearable. Grey viewed Mix as the embodiment of everything that was wrong with movies, and his loathing intensified several years later when Mix purchased a residence in Catalina down the hill from his.

Grey liked Hampton's adaptation of his novels because he had not capitulated to Hollywood's star system. In Grey's galaxy, there was room for only one star—Zane. He objected to actors who thought that they were more important than their roles. One reason he preferred cowboys like the ones he knew personally was their respect for his books and his reputation. Stars were unimpressed and ungrateful. In July 1916, before the Fox films of his novels were released, Zane met both Farnums in Catalina, and R. C., with more than a little help from Zane, wrote an article about the event entitled "Fishing with Famous Fellows." Being more experienced and more accomplished, Zane urged that the two actors buy expensive, topflight tackle. After they did so, Dustin hooked a broadbill that made off with his equipment and nearly pulled him overboard. Although R. C. mentions that he too lost a marlin, he describes at some length the big one that he landed, and provides a photograph showing his 304-pound "record marlin."[28] This account of the Farnums was meant to be humorous, not uncomplimentary, but Dustin was not pleased with its depiction of him as an inept beginner and its disregard for the 322-pound broadbill that he caught that same season.[29] This article soured Zane's brief friendship with the Farnums and influenced Dustin's vengeful testimony against him several years later.

If Grey's aversion for stars was personal, Hampton's was financial. His meager, unsure financing placed them beyond reach, and caused his Westerns to fare poorly at the box office and do little to promote Grey's books. Ironically, the rights to the few novels that Grey sold outright went to companies like Fox that were better funded and solidly committed to the star concept, and their films attracted large audiences. Though Grey bemoaned the fact that he sold these rights too cheaply, got no profits, and lost them forever, the films that resulted *did* bolster his reputation and sales of his novels. Although *Riders of the Purple Sage* was the first of Grey's novels to make the best-seller list, it was not the grand success that many assume. By the early twenties, several of Grey's early novels were selling as well as *Riders,* and *Betty Zane* was doing much better. The recognition that *Riders* commands today probably owes more to its multiple film versions than to its qualitative superiority to Grey's other work. Because Grey sold the film rights to *Riders* early and outright, without any stipulation that they revert to him, as he quickly learned to demand, Fox was able to remake *Riders* three more times before World War II, most notably in 1925 with Tom Mix in the lead.

Grey's involvement with the film industry altered his novels. Pressed by Davis to think in terms of stage and films, he consciously increased the amount of dialogue as well as the circumstances calling for it. Grey also included more action sequences—chases, stampedes, shoot-outs, and, above all, kisses. Stories with these features diminished his personal involvement and started him down the road to mannered variations that were easier to write but less satisfying. As an example of this evolution, *The Lone Star Ranger* (1915) was a flawed story with a checkered past, and it taught Grey how to finesse writing problems with gunplay and romance. Back in January of 1914, Grey sent Robert Davis a completed manuscript entitled "The Last of the Duanes." In it, Buck Duane is forced into the perilous life of an outlaw gunman when he is wrongly blamed for a pair of killings. After a series of mishaps that are either bloody or menacing, Buck meets Captain MacNeely, who offers him a pardon to help the Texas Rangers eliminate a troublesome gang.

Davis himself rejected the story as a serial for *Munsey's* with an explanation that "death comes too fast and thick," and he referenced nineteen deaths to support his point. Conceding that Buck was interesting and unusual, he claimed that he was too "saturnalian" for MacNelly's proposition.[30] A month later, Ripley Hitchcock was put off by the amount of fighting, killing, and gunplay and counseled Grey to try a different tack.[31] Grey hurriedly reworked his material into an alternative story about a legendary outlaw recruited by the Rangers that Davis accepted as "The Rangers of the Lone Star" for serialization in the Munsey-controlled *Cavalier-All Story Weekly,* and the first installment appeared in May 1914. Meanwhile, Grey sold the serial rights to "The Last of the Duanes" to *Argosy,* and it commenced four months later, while "Rangers" was still running. Although "Rangers" had less "pistol play" than the original "Duanes," the story was weaker. In order to avoid offending Grey with another rejection, editors at Harpers encouraged him to combine the two stories into a single novel.[32] This consolidation eliminated the first-person narrative of "Rangers" and made Buck Duane the lead character throughout. Grey relied on intrigue and gunfights to gloss the ragged stitching of his splice, which is most apparent in his retention of the romances from both stories. In the first half, derived from "Duanes," Buck's girlfriend Jennie Lee simply disappears—and so too do his feelings for her—so that he is free and available for Ray, a consolidation of two girlfriends from "Rangers," whom he meets and woos in the second half of the novel.

Much to everyone's surprise, including Zane's, *The Lone Star Ranger* (1915), with its hastily arranged marriage of two disliked serials, was his first novel to reach the number-one position on the *Bookman* monthly list, and the first one to make the annual list, position number eight.[33] Although the original "The Last of the Duanes" did not have as much violence as *To the Last Man* (1922), it represented an important first step in this direction. Sensing that attention-getting action was more important to readers and filmmakers than plausibility, Grey injected more "Perils of Pauline" and "Jim Dandy to the Rescue" into his next stories, notably *The U. P. Trail* (1918).

Meanwhile, throughout his early discussions with Bob Davis about book ideas and movie contracts, Grey withheld discussion of his fishing. Finally, in a letter in September 1915, he erupted, "Bob, you never knew I was a fisherman. Dog gone you! I'll simply make you ill. I broke all the records. What's more I have the only photographs ever secured of the great swordfish in action. *One charging the boat!*"[34] Actually, Davis did know that Grey was a fisherman, and had even gone fishing with him, but these excursions dated from three years before when Zane was less experienced and more reticent. Several months prior to their first outing together in 1912, Grey wrote to Dolly from Long Key, "I don't *care* to fish like I used to. I hate to do it."[35] At the time he was discouraged because he kept losing fish that "brutes" with rude equipment landed easily and in great numbers. His first fishing trip with Davis was even more embarrassing. While Zane left his rod unattended to rummage in his gear bag for a piece of equipment, a fish hooked itself, bolted, and pulled his rig overboard.[36]

Later that same fall, Grey, Davis, Eltinge Warner, and several other experienced anglers went fishing out of Seabright, New Jersey. After several hours with no success, they spotted a school of porpoises and decided to strike one with a harpoon attached to a line from Grey's rod and reel. For an hour, he futilely strained the porpoise to the boat, and the fish kept towing their dory farther out to sea. When it eventually surfaced, one of the men shot it, causing the wounded fish to erupt into a palsied frenzy and go limp. After Grey exhausted himself hauling it to the boat, the porpoise suddenly revived and thrashed violently. More gunshots and a massive hemorrhage finally killed the fish and allowed Grey to prevail.[37]

Assuming the role of "historian for the first porpoise club," Davis wrote a humorous account of the experience for *Field and Stream,* and posted an advance copy to the Tuna Club in Catalina. As Davis anticipated, the club secretary found himself in an awkward position since the tactics of these anglers flagrantly violated its rules against harpooning, shooting, and maiming a catch. Had they been Tuna Club members, the catch would have been disqualified and they would probably have been censured. Unwilling to brand strangers ignoramuses, a club representative sent back a cautious letter noting that he too had caught a porpoise—with regulation tackle of a 16-oz. rod and 24-strand line—and that he knew of several porpoises that had been harpooned. Davis and Warner published the letter in the same issue that carried his article.[38] They, of course, knew about the rules, thought them silly, and were delighted with their exposure of the club's stuffiness.

This spoof was also an envious acknowledgment of the Tuna Club's stature and authority. At the time, Grey quietly sided with the pranksters, and said nothing about his earlier Tampico experiences. Later that same year, when he caught a ninety-pound tuna, he did not bother to inform Davis, but he did seek recognition for his accomplishment. Well aware that *Field and Stream* had recently expanded its coverage of "prize fish" to saltwater fish,[39] he persuaded Warner to proclaim him the winner of the "First Grand Prize—Atlantic Tuna Class, 1912," and wrote an article about the catch for the September 1913 issue.[40]

Grey's next two visits to Long Key increased his experience and bolstered his ambition. In 1913, he wrote Dolly from Long Key that he had caught three "swordfish."[41] Although these were probably sailfish, he was succeeding with large, acrobatic fish and eager to catch even bigger ones. Following his 1914 visit to Long Key, he decided to try Catalina that summer. Having been intimidated by the intense competitiveness of the Tuna Club ever since his first visit eight years before, he puffed his new confidence into a foolish swagger. Prior to his first day of fishing, he visited the official taxidermist for the Tuna Club and arranged a mounting for his first marlin. Taken aback by Grey's presumptuousness, Charles Parker advised him to catch one first. Grey soon discovered that the challenge far exceeded his expectation. After twenty-one days and 1,500 miles of trolling, he had not hooked a single one. Finally, on the twenty-fifth day, one snatched his bait, performed dazzling leaps, and broke free. When his allotted time was up, he sheepishly returned and canceled the mounting.[42]

Grey was chagrined over his failure, but he also realized that Catalina fishing involved a steep learning curve. Up to this point, his saltwater angling had been done from rowboats and the dories long favored by the commercial fisherman from Seabright, New Jersey. His articles on his porpoise outing and his record tuna contain photographs that illustrate not only the boats he used, but also the way he fished. On both trips, Grey held his rod and shifted his position in order to maintain a tight line and good leverage. One photograph shows him seated in the forward section of the boat,[43] and he would have relocated whenever he needed a better angle on the circling fish. Any oarsman attempting to reposition this cumbersome craft would have had enormous difficulty and frequently been in the way of the angler. Under such conditions, Grey had an awkward, unstable position that worsened whenever he stood or moved.

The photographs of Grey from Catalina present a radically different situation. In them, he appears in a "fighting chair" situated in the stern of the boat.[44] This centerpiece of saltwater fishing today and a recognized symbol of the sport originated in Catalina shortly before Grey's arrival in 1914. The earliest version was a stationary wooden seat with a back to support the angler while he was fishing, but soon this was built so that the back could be removed for fighting a fish. This seat was affixed to a solid base that swiveled as the fish moved, and contained a rotating support cup for the butt of the rod. The boat's inboard motor provided crucial assistance, aiding the stability of the angler and increasing his effectiveness. Early Tuna Club members fished from boats that resembled Seabright dories, but these quickly evolved into eighteen- to twenty-foot launches with small eight- to ten-horsepower motors situated midship that boatmen used to maneuver the craft and assist the angler.[45] Around 1910, these launches began to be replaced by longer boats with more powerful inboard motors and fighting chairs in the stern.[46] The newer boats elevated the importance of the boatman/captain and his navigational skills. By using the rudder and motor speed to shift the stern right or left, to run with the fish, or to steady the boat, he gave the angler much greater control and enabled him to battle larger fish. One of the first things Grey did following his visit to the taxidermist was to hire O. I. Danielson and his launch the *Leta D.* As he later explained:

> Boatmen at Long Key and other Florida resorts—at Tampico, Aransas Pass—are not in the same class with the Avalon men. . . . And the boats—nowhere are there such splendid boats. Captain Danielson's boat had utterly spoiled me for fishing out of any other. He had it built, and the ideas of its construction were a product of fifteen years' study. It is thirty-eight feet long, and wide, with roomy, shaded cockpit and cabin, and comfortable revolving chairs to fish from. . . . Danielson can turn this boat, going at full speed, in its own length. Consider the merit of this when a tuna strikes or a swordfish starts for the open sea. How many tarpon, barracuda, amberjack, and tuna I have lost on the Atlantic seaboard just because the boat could not be turned in time![47]

These improved motorboats spurred complementary advances in tackle. The equipment utilized by the founders of the Tuna Club was as primitive as their boats. Not only were rods heavy and inflexible, and frequently broke, but their reels posed an even greater problem. The handle was affixed to the spindle, and when a hooked fish bolted and pulled line, the angler had to release the handle and allow the spool to spin. If he did not seize the handle and start cranking as soon as the fish stopped, the spindle would continue and "overspin," producing either a slack line or a gnarled nest that froze the line and allowed the fish to break free. If he grabbed too soon, the spinning handle could mangle his fingers and/or hand. Such mishaps injured enough fishermen that early detractors referred to the club as a hospital. To reduce this problem, leather patches were applied to the outer edge of the turning spindle to create drag, but the need for better control spurred the vom Hofe tackle company to devise a "star drag" system that enabled the spindle to release line without turning the handle, and to exert a counterpressure as soon as the line stopped.

Despite the fame and prestige of the Tuna Club, Grey did little tuna fishing during his first two visits. The club was established in 1898 and dedicated to catching large tuna with rod and reel. During the first season of its existence, twenty-four members caught tuna in excess of a hundred pounds. The club sought to recognize this achievement with the award of a blue button, and established it as a goal for the other members to emulate.[48] During the first four years of its existence, the club presented sixty-six blue buttons. However, the numbers of large tuna dropped sharply over the years that followed. Excluding the sensational year of 1909, only twenty-six blue buttons were awarded from 1903 to 1916; for the period from 1912 and 1916, members received a measly two.[49] This lack of big tuna sent anglers elsewhere—after swordfish. The first marlin from Catalina waters was taken in 1903. Charles F. Holder, the source for this information, claims that it was caught by a shore angler fishing for yellowtail and that it "aroused interest in the possibilities of this sport."[50] Writing about swordfish five years later, Holder observed, "That such sport would become popular in Southern California is doubtful, as there is an element of danger to be considered—that of being rammed by the fish."[51] Nevertheless, intermittent catches stoked enough interest and hope that the Tuna Club was moved in 1909 to establish a gold button for marlin over 200 pounds.[52] Over the two years that followed, eighteen marlin were caught, and three members received gold buttons.[53] As aspirants learned from others' successes and experimented on their own, the number of catches surged. In 1911, thirty-four marlin were caught and four gold buttons were awarded, and the year following the number jumped to one hundred marlin and thirteen gold buttons.[54] For those after buttons—and most club members prized them—the prospects for a gold button were far better than those for a blue one. In 1914, Holder reversed his earlier position and announced, "This new sport—swordfish angling with rod and reel—is in a class by itself and, all and all, when the danger, the leaps and the spectacular play is considered, I should place it ahead of leaping tuna or tarpon."[55]

These developments prompted Grey's decision to concentrate upon marlin his first summer. Better boats and tackle not only made catching marlin possible, but they also revolutionized tactics that likewise improved catches. Boatmen learned that the best way to attract a strike from a marlin was to maneuver a line with a "teaser," a large wooden plug, in front of the fish from a long distance away. Initially, these boats used sleds for deflecting the bait or "teaser" one or two hundred feet away from the boat.[56] Boatmen quickly discovered that outriggers were more effective. Around 1910, William Farnsworth, perhaps the best of Catalina's boatmen, invented "kiting," an ingenious modification of these advances.[57] A flying fish was attached to the hook, and a kite was then affixed well up the line. The captain used his motorboat to raise the kite and maneuver the bait close to a distant marlin without spooking it. By varying the speed of the boat, he was able to lift and drop the kite so that the bait resembled the flying fish that marlin especially liked. When the marlin hit the bait, the line pulled free from the kite. The angler in the fighting chair reeled in the slack, and, as the boat assumed a favorable position, he struck and initiated the fight. William Boschen employed this technique to catch the first broadbill in 1913. Until then, this fish was assumed to be a big marlin, but this achievement caused anglers to realize that this was a larger species and, even better, catchable.[58]

These overlapping developments explain Grey's failure to land a marlin during his first season. Danielson used his state-of-the art boat and his skill with these new tactics to get his client's hook to a sighted fish, but Grey was so unfamiliar with the process that he struck too soon or too late, and sometimes he totally failed to respond. Although Grey was disappointed over his misses and his failure to land a single one of that season's many marlin, he realized that he had acquired an invaluable, hard-won education in Catalina's innovative equipment and tactics.

The next season, Grey returned more determined and was more successful. By way of preparation, he had E. J. Murphy, an accomplished rod maker in Catalina, construct him a special double, split-bamboo rod, and he acquired a new, state-of-the art B-Ocean reel manufactured by vom Hofe. He also hired Danielson to work for him exclusively. During the first three weeks of fishing, he hooked seven marlin, six more than the whole season before. On August 11, after a glorious, hour-long fight, he finally landed his first one. Though it weighed only 118 pounds, the catch was a momentous breakthrough. Over the next three days, he hooked four more and boated three.[59] In August, he left Avalon with Danielson and camped for the whole month on desolate, unpopulated Clemente Island. This decision implemented a favorite Grey strategy, one he had developed in Zanesville years before and would repeat many times in the future: go to a place where there were many fish and few fishermen. There, on August 28, he caught a marlin weighing 284 pounds that earned his first button, the gold.[60] Three days later, he had an unforgettable day on which he caught four marlin. His fourth topped the scales at 316 pounds.[61] At the time he incorrectly believed it to be an all-time record, and with bursting pride, he informed Dolly:

> Would it interest you to know that I have all the Tuna Club Anglers and every fisherman I ever heard of skinned to a frazzle? The nearest to me has 9 swordfish to his credit, taken since swordfishing became something a few anglers cared to tackle.

I have caught 15. And the biggest this year, and one as big as any year, if not bigger.

I'll tell you about it, when I see you. The jealousy and rivalry among these boatmen and fishermen out here is amazing.[62]

Grey was jubilant over his success and eager for recognition. In addition to his letters to Dolly and Davis, he sent *Recreation* magazine an article entitled "Swordfish, the Royal Purple Game of the Sea," one of his finest accounts about fishing and a pioneering contribution to the literature of the sport.[63] The editors at *Recreation* immediately recognized the article's merits and importance, and introduced it with Grey's photograph of the swordfish charging the boat and a headnote proclaiming: "Here is the biggest and best story ever written of hunting big game in the sea with rod and reel—in fact, the biggest sporting story in years."[64] Obviously the editors wanted to capitalize on Grey's reputation as a best-selling novelist and adventurous outdoorsman. Grey, in turn, was using this respected sports magazine to promote swordfishing and his success with it. "The sport is young—very little has been known about it. Scarcely anything has been written by men who have caught swordfish," he declares. "It was this that attracted me" (255). His detailed accounting of the defeats of his first season and his triumphant return is enlivened with colorful descriptions of battles that justified his bold assertion: "To the great majority of anglers it may seem unreasonable to place swordfishing in a class by itself—by far the most magnificent sport in the world with rod and reel. Yet I do not hesitate to make this statement and believe I can prove it" (255). His hyperbolic boast, that swordfishing could only be done by "a man of enormous strength and endurance" (260), would return to haunt him several years later.

Grey's successful summer in Catalina inspired him to recruit a skilled boatman from Seabright, Sam "Horse-mackerel" Johnson, to accompany him to Long Key for the winter of 1916. Zane wanted to tap Johnson's skill with motorboats, to apply his hard-won knowledge of swordfishing to sailfishing, and to become more adept with light tackle. On February 22, 1916, he posted Dolly another excited announcement of success, "Say Dol, yesterday I broke all the records here. Came in with four sailfish. *4!* And the largest ever caught—7 ft. 6 inches!"[65] Again he was seeking to best and impress locals. Afterward, he wrote another article in which he celebrated sailfish as "the gamest, the most beautiful and spectacular, and the hardest fish to catch on light tackle."[66] After noting that his catch of four in one day rivaled his record at Clemente, he again celebrated the charm of Long Key and complained about the visitors who wanted three kinds of boats, superhuman boatmen, and special tackle. He proclaimed this kind of angler to be "queer"[67] and blithely disregarded his own movement in this direction.

Grey's return to Avalon for the summer of 1916 ended his run of success. Though he landed the first marlin of the season, his regimen of daily outings was cut short by the breakdown of Danielson's boat. His catches following its repair did not approach those of the previous season. He salvaged an article about his eventful first day on which he hooked and lost two marlin. As support for his calm acceptance of defeat, he offered the surprising declaration: "I do not fish for clubs or records. I fish for the fun, the excitement, the thrill of the game."[68]

All this fishing convinced Grey that he needed a boat of his own. During his previous winters in Long Key, he had rented a boat, and for his 1916 visit, he hired Sam Johnson to work as his captain. After relying upon him to evaluate his needs and wants, he arranged for a twenty-six-foot launch to be built for him in St. Petersburg. Following a down payment of $750 in the late spring of 1916 to start construction, he discovered that he was so strapped for cash by September that he feared he might have to default. Meanwhile, Dolly wanted to acquire some adjacent property in Lackawaxen and to renovate the main residence. Her estimated cost of $2,000 equaled the amount outstanding on the boat, and even that $2,000 exceeded their available assets. Dolly believed her plans should have priority and went to Duneka at Harpers for an advance to cover them. Zane was mortified by this public revelation of their financial needs and the likelihood that this loan would place his boat beyond reach. He complained to Dolly, "That $750 was the first payment on a boat that, as I told you, was to cost more than $2,500. I did not see why I could not get a boat, the same as poorer men buy automobiles. And a good boat was life insurance, in a way. Now I can't get the boat and I lose the $750."[69] For a man who never learned to drive, this was compelling logic. In order to raise money for his boat, he sold *Blue Book* the rights to *The U. P. Trail,* entitled "East and West" at the time and serialized as "The Roaring U. P. Trail"; the sale brought him $6,000, a full $4,000 less than Hitchcock advised him to seek.[70] Dolly withheld comment at the time of this decision, but lashed out at Zane several weeks later over some shipping charges. "I *do* so enjoy paying express & freight bills," she wrote. "And the way you casually mention buying a few little things 'but don't worry; the bill can't be for more than $500,' makes me have dysentery. You're almost dead broke. Don't you *know* it? *Quit* buying so much."[71]

Contrary to Zane's insistence that his boat was a wise investment, the *Betty Zane* was a crushing disappointment from the moment he took possession of the craft. Following its maiden voyage at Long Key in January, 1917, Zane admitted to Dolly, "The boat is some 'tippy' believe me, and one by one we got sick and had to come in. Rome is afraid to take chances with his stomach. I wish the damn boat was on the bottom of the sea. It is more trouble than anything I ever had."[72] Five days later, the situation worsened. The engine seized and Grey learned that several pistons had cracked. Replacements were so difficult to locate and came from so far away that the boat had to be stowed. By the time the parts arrived, Zane had left for Arizona. Dolly did little for his state of mind when she complained about the payments to Captain Johnson who had no boat and nothing to do.

The distress and conflict provoked by the *Betty Zane* was symptomatic of deeper problems. Since his trip to the Rainbow Bridge in 1913 with Lillian Wilhelm and Elma Schwarz, Zane had steadily added to his circle of companions. A year later, when he returned to Long Key and Kayenta, he brought Lillian and her sister Claire, who was sixteen.[73] The decline in the family business and the poor health of her parents obliged Lillian and her five brothers to fend for themselves. Since Claire was the last born and twelve years younger, Lillian believed that she needed help, and she persuaded Zane to include both of them on his trips. Zane also added Polly Hunter to his entourage. The main objective of his 1914 trip was to investigate the San Francisco peaks. Believing the outing to be too strenuous for the girls, he arranged for them to stay with Louisa Wetherill while he left with Al Doyle.

On November 20, 1915, Dolly gave birth to another son. Initially, she and Zane decided to name him Zane too. Several months later, they reconsidered and named him Loren instead, a decision made so close to the issuance of the birth certificate that Zane had to be crossed out and Loren penned in above it.[74] Over the summer in Lackawaxen and fall in Middletown, Zane made a special effort to be an attentive parent to his other two children, a role he preferred to play with dutiful letters. In order to lighten Dolly's responsibilities while she recuperated, he hired two professionally trained secretaries, Mildred Fergerson, a local girl, and Mildred Smith, who had been working for a film company in New York City. At a local dance, he met the attractive, vivacious Dorothy Ackerman, who eventually became the central figure of this fluctuating retinue.

Claire's 1916 journal of her stay in Long Key reveals that Lillian, Elma Schwarz, and Mildred Fergerson were there too, and that Long Key was no longer the rude, hastily modified railroad camp that Zane first visited in 1911. Claire would note the visits of Andrew Carnegie, J. Dexter Biddle, and Jack Dorance, the owner of the Campbell Soup Company. She also reports

Grey and his children, Romer, Loren, and Betty, 1917. (Courtesy of Loren Grey.)

sighting the yacht of Edward L. Doheny, the Los Angeles oilman who built the railroad connection that carried Zane to Tampico. Doheny was in Long Key socializing and talking business with wealthy Easterners in flight from northern winters; he too was drawn to the camp's warmth and exotic charm. Zane's young, beautiful, well-dressed companions must have made a powerful impression on these visitors. Striking, animated, and outgoing, they would have been much noticed when they entered the communal dining room, lending flair to his table and facilitating access to the social activities—if he wanted. Since Grey was by nature reserved and antisocial, he often used his retinue as a barrier. "The Goelets, Vanderbilts, Dominicks, and other swells are here," he once informed Dolly. "And I would prefer in the moment to be somewhat detached."[75]

The 1917 visit that was marred by the breakdown of the *Betty Zane* brought Grey a harsh reminder that life with these women was not always glamorous and exhilarating. Over the preceding fall, he had a series of tempestuous disagreements with a young housemaid named Emmeline, who had been helping Dolly with the children and whom Dolly once characterized as a "wild erotic creature."[76] In August, 1916, Emmeline gave Dolly a journal in which she had recorded lengthy notations on her relationship with Zane. Dolly did not want to read it, but did so because Emmeline insisted. She then wrote Zane a long, remarkably calm letter. Stating that she had learned "terrible things," she insisted she would not be "a woman cheated" and "rant and tear and act *natural.*" Allowing that he may have helped some of the young women in his retinue, "those other bits of fluff," she charged that he had harmed Emmeline, and twice she urged him to give up his selfish desire to "own the girl body and soul" and be a friend instead.[77]

At the time, Grey was in Catalina with R. C., his wife Reba, and other friends. In Avalon, he had always stayed at the Metropole Hotel, but this larger group made him aware of its limitations. When he shared this with Dolly, she fired off a less understanding response:

> I haven't quite made up my mind whether or not you meant that letter seriously. Somehow I think you couldn't so insult my intelligence. And yet it sounds serious—it sounds like your childlike innocence. How can you be so supremely egotistical & selfish as to drag your tender young friends & sensitive relatives to a "hole" like Catalina where there is "no nice place to eat. No nice accommodations. No amusements—not one damned thing to do." You see I am quoting you. Poor Doc, poor Claire, poor Mildred Smith, poor Lillian, poor Elma, poor Mildred Fergerson, poor Reba, poor, poorer, poorest Rome. Oh, my God! How I pity and sympathize with them! Why did they ever leave their happy homes—or *your* happy home? Such a fate! I wonder if you remember your letter. It was a masterpiece. It should be published from an altruistic point of view. Think of all the wives left at home (I don't know of any) who would be infinitely comforted & uplifted by its contents.[78]

Three weeks later when Zane departed for Arizona with his entourage of women, his self-absorption provoked ever greater resentment and irony from Dolly:

> Dearly beloved One—love-of-my-life devoted Husband,
>   You are a wonder! You are the greatest man on earth! There
> never was anyone like you, even remotely resembling you
> (honestly). After they made you the mold was broken. If you
> wanted to, you could be the biggest writer in the United States.
> As an author you are preeminent, as a fisherman unexcelled, as
> a hunter (well, I couldn't swear you wouldn't climb a tree, if a
> bear got after you—you see I'm being strictly truthful) but any-
> way, as a hunter you are twice as brave, as a manager of the fair
> sex you are superhuman, and as a husband you are . . . PUNK!![79]

By this point Dolly's anger was besting her wit and detachment. Rather than try to defuse the situation, Zane was more inclined to go to war:

> As I understand you now, and better than ever, what you have never had
> and what you *want* in a husband. Well, I did my best, which was little
> enough, I suppose. And now I pass. You can have the freedom you want
> and you can get the husband you want. I hope to God you find him.
>   As for me, I'd rather go to hell than stand your scorn and bitterness
> and discontent any longer. If I must continue to be made to feel as you
> have made me feel lately, I do not want your love, or you as a wife, or as
> anything. For a long time I have seen the futility of my life. . . . This year
> you have been particularly bitter, hard, satirical, and mean and unjust.
> . . . The pity of it all is that I know I could have gone far, if I had been be-
> lieved in. But no *woman* will stand for anything that excludes her from
> all. She would rather a man be a failure, so long as he was bound to her.
> You have stood for more than any other woman ever did stand, but at
> the expense of my nerve, my dreams, and now my future. You have been
> rotten to me. . . .
>   My friends are not what you think them. They all have weaknesses, as
> indeed the whole race has. But they are worth it to me, all and more than
> I have given them. If as you say, they must fail me, one by one, then I
> say that when that day comes I am done for good and all. Nothing could
> have been any crueler, any more a mortal blow to me than for you to say
> that. These girls have kept something alive in me. And now it is dying.

He follows with an extended discussion of his relationship with Emmeline, and contends that she had written "emotional rot" and yielded to a "debauch of agony." He, on the other hand, had been good to her and never misled her. "She swore she would share me with my other friends," he defensively proclaims. "When she came to L- and found she was not the *all* she had sup-posed, then she failed me. Let her pass."[80]

Zane was hoping that Dolly would send Emmeline away and eliminate his headache, but it quickly got worse. Prior to his January 1917 departure for Long Key, Emmeline informed his other girlfriends about her mistreatment. Concluding that Emmeline had indeed been mistreated, Elma and Mildred turned against Zane. As he had unwittingly predicted, he soon was "done for good and all," and the breakdown of the *Betty Zane* simply added to his woes.

These developments altered Zane's feelings toward Dolly. The woman responsible for his grief in September was forgotten, and he beseeched her for support and solace. In familiar fashion, he appealed to her to ease his burden of woe and empowered her to rescue him. Immediately, she relinquished her attacks, redirected the blame, and salved his guilt:

> You are exceedingly unfair to shove the blame of your friends' defection off on me, or to say that E. poisoned them is ridiculous. Don't worry that they've gone back on you—if there was anything in that, they wouldn't be with you. And if they're making trouble for you, they are an exceedingly ungrateful bunch after all you do for them. And if, to quote you, "they might be so many rag-dolls" for all the good they do you, you'd better send them home. Rag dolls at the Florida prices are somewhat expensive luxuries.
>
> I say this—the girls know perfectly well what they are doing and what they are getting from you. If they didn't want to be with you, they wouldn't. For them to make trouble for you is ungrateful, to say the *least*.[81]

Dolly dispatched another long letter to Elma seeking to heal the rift and prevent her defection. On February 19, Zane responded, "I didn't ask you to write the girl, but I'm pleased that you did, and thank you now, that I can say. Things like that make me feel warm inside for you."[82]

Dolly's decision to act on behalf of her rivals rather than against them left her compromised, insecure, and unsatisfied. A couple weeks before Zane's departure from Long Key, she presumed upon the improvement in their relationship, and entered into a bantering exchange about "Kifoozling." "I am dying to be kifoozled—and nobody here to do it," she announced, and then added, "You have only an eye for fish."[83] Both liked the slang term and its sexual implications, and playfully used it to tease each other, but underlying tensions soon caused the joking to turn dark and antagonistic. On March 14, Dolly wrote, "Your amazing, amusing, *infuriating* letter came this morning on the wings of a large and untimely snowstorm. . . . Do you realize that you have offered me a mortal insult ? You say, 'Let's be good comrades this year without a great deal of "k———ing.'" You imply that I'm—well, something unspeakable—a—a mink or something like that. Know then, my dear man, that you'll have to crawl around on your knees before I'll ever allow you to approach me again from that direction. Besides my spiritual and intellectual nature is beginning to dominate to the exclusion of the physical."[84] "Yours of March 14 is at hand," Zane shot back, "And I would rejoice if I knew I were to go to H- before I ever receive another such letter from you."[85]

Dolly did not realize that Zane's offensive remark was prompted by a disintegration of his truce with the girls and an angry spat with R. C. In a fit of pique, he fired both Elma and Mildred and sent them home. As protection against his looming isolation, he wrote to Claire and Lillian and requested that they meet him at the train station when he returned to New York City. Dolly, who was already vexed, became more so when she learned this, and announced that she would not meet his train if Lillian and Claire were there. "I have been upset for days, and am now sick," he explained to Dolly. "If I am no better when I reach N.Y., I will go to a hotel. . . . I have lost my friend, and next will be my family. I seem to have a mortal deathly sickness within me. Poisoned! Ever since I came down here you have been satiric, bitter, and rancorous, except in one letter. And under the circumstances I think you had better not meet the train next Saturday."[86]

Although Zane and Dolly did connect, he did not remain in New York long. A week later, he was in Middletown visiting his mother, who was well, but cantankerous, and his sister Ida, who was cheerful and busy. When he was reminded that Ida was fifty, he was plagued with thoughts about the passage of time that kept him awake all night. When he left Middletown for Lackawaxen, the weather turned overcast and cold. Alone there, he plunged into a deep depression and wrote in his journal:

> Love of life, love of youth, love of beauty, love of passion, and their expression, that is my burden, my tragic doom, and the years roll by on fleet relentless wings. I know that I am too much a man to despair utterly under this inevitable blow, when it falls. But between that hour and this there is agony . . . I am all alone. No one understands, no one would care.

The looming prospect of war worsened his dejection. Recalling that he came from "a family of fighters" and a great-grandfather who fought in the Revolutionary War, he was tormented over his intense opposition to the current conflict. The young men who rushed to enlist following the declaration of war against Germany in April seemed foolish to him, and plagued him with vivid imaginings of destruction and carnage. The sight of rafters upon the flooding Delaware evoked happier times, but brought more gloom when a canoe overturned and a young girl drowned. The isolation that was supposed to inspire him rendered him unable to write, except in his journal, and left him with a "hopeless, morbid, sickening, exaggerated mental disorder."[87] In a recollection of this period a year later, Zane wrote to Dolly, "Let me forget my breakdown. I am ashamed that I hurt you by it."[88]

The arrival of his family in May helped, but it took Dolly and his alma mater to lift his spirits. Penn invited him back to its June 1917 commencement, and awarded him an honorary master's degree. This recognition brought him much-needed reassurance that his Westerns were respected and not merely popular. Following completion of *The Rainbow Trail,* he decided to resume *Shores of Lethe.* "And now I'm ready, after years and waiting and agony, to begin the great story," he wrote in his journal in March 1914. Keenly aware of the social criticism inherent to his early Westerns, he had wanted for many years to write a novel that would make it forthright and explicit. When he resumed his journal after a year of no entries, he confided, "I stopped writing because I was ashamed to chronicle the continued break-downs."[89] Desperate for familiar terrain and sure footing, he immersed himself in *The U.P. Trail,* but he was displeased with the results and had a hard time placing the serialization. Dolly's suggestion that they take a long trip together helped even more than his honorary degree from Penn. Since their second trip to Tampico, on which she had gotten so sick, Dolly preferred to stay at home and care for the children. However, Zane's recent depression convinced her that he sorely needed attention and another trip. She planned a complement to their honeymoon trip that would cover the northern half of the country. She proposed that they take the train from New York City to Chicago, turn north toward Minneapolis, cross the Dakotas and Montana to Seattle, and head south to California. Hoping to repair the damage from Long Key, she invited Mildred Fergerson and Dorothy Ackerman to accompany them.

Four days after the July 7, 1917, departure, the group left the train in West Glacier, Montana, for a week of touring Glacier Park and taking long boat rides out of Many Glacier and St. Marys. Next, they stopped for four days in Spokane. Before he left home, Zane wrote in his journal that he would be seeking "new material for my work" and hoping "to forget this awful war the world is struggling with." "I hate the ways of men and politics and business and war," he added.[90] Frustrated by a third breakdown with *Shores of Lethe* and his thwarted yearning to comment on contemporary developments, he proposed to write a modern Western that featured ranching conditions that his readers expected, but linked them to the ongoing war. Grey initiated research on this project at a luncheon with members of the Chamber of Commerce in Spokane, Washington. There he learned about the nearby wheat industry and met A. Duncan Dunn, a regent for Washington State University, then the state's agricultural college. Dunn informed him that discontent among laborers and their unreliability had become a major problem for local wheat growers. A Spokane newspaper reported that when Grey was told about local activities of the Industrial Workers of the World (I. W. W.), a militant labor union that had staged major strikes around the country, he asked, "What is it, a union?" and then wondered, "Can't the farmers harvest the wheat themselves?"[91] Later, he learned about the so-called Bloody Sunday of November 5, 1916, when several Wobblies, as members of the I. W. W. were called, were slain in Everett during a fight over free speech. By the time he resumed his trip, Grey had decided that Wobblies were a serious threat to wheat production and that he would make them the villains of his novel.

These labor disputes carried Grey afield of his usual subject matter. He knew little about labor strife, and did not bother to learn more. In *The Desert of Wheat* (1919), he makes little effort to explain the background or organization of the I. W. W. This union was merely an excuse for his anguished obsession with the war. The I. W. W. in his novel has been infiltrated and corrupted by German agents who promote strikes that undermine the war effort. Grey conceives of the union as an organization with many immigrants who avail themselves of American opportunity, but secretly hate its people and government. Local ranchers triumph over the union's subversive plotting by turning into vigilantes. After hanging its corrupt leader, they ship his band of outsiders away in freight cars.

The Desert of Wheat was the first of a series of novels set in the present that assessed the war's damage to homeland culture and beliefs. The central part of the story features another conflict between father and son, only here the conflict is due to opposing attitudes toward war. Chris Dorn, one of the wheat ranchers, is a German immigrant who believes that his homeland is misunderstood and that England has turned the United States against it. He feels betrayed by his son Kurt, who is ashamed of his German heritage and believes that he has to spill German blood, and perhaps his own as well, in order to prove that he is a true American. After he is wounded in combat, Kurt questions his xenophobic assumptions and lapses into depression. Into Kurt's reevaluation of his patriotic rush into war, Grey channeled his own reservations about the war, and this character would be the first of several wounded veterans who reconfigured his previously sick fugitives from civilization.

Lenore nurses Kurt through his recovery, saves him from disillusionment, and wins his love. She is another strong, independent woman eager to help the man she loves, but her reluctance to change Kurt sets her apart from Grey's heroines so far. Her father wants her to keep Kurt away from the war, and realizing that she has the power to do so, she instead allows him to go and to do as *he* wants. "No longer could she think of persuading him to stay home," she reflects at one point. "She must forget herself. She knew then that she had the power to keep him and she could use it, but she must not do so. This tragic thing was a matter of his soul."[92] Lenore's acceptance of Kurt's need to leave and his peculiar thinking bespeaks more than a little of Dolly's tolerance of Zane's misbehavior and his recent gratitude for her patience and support. Given this similarity, it is hardly surprising that Dolly was impressed by Lenore. In fact, Dolly's attachment to Lenore provoked an angry letter denouncing Zane's betrayal of his heroine with a demeaning flourish of sexuality:

> I'm worn out struggling with that awful chapter of yours where Lenore hands herself over to Kurt on a platter—so now you've got to at least share the agony with me. My God—what hit you when you wrote that chapter? It sounds just as if you'd had a *liebestod* session with Mildred Smith. Lucinda fades into insignificance—"cool, soft pressures, white soft hands, arms, shoulders, dim starry eyes, heavy eyelids, white graceful images, reeling senses, brutal hugs, exquisite gowns, palpitating bosoms, sweetness, sudden-flashing, incredible portents, tremulousness, tumultuous Lenore Anderson!" . . . I groaned & cussed and got violent & furious and disgusted. And I'd been looking forward to this particular passage because you'd spoken so much about it. I don't know what to do. Do you want to rewrite it? Or shall I try? It has some very good flashes, here & there, but most of it is the limit. You've made a beautiful character of Lenore all the way through—and just here, where she should reach her pinnacle, you've made a nasty little mink out of her. What possessed you when you wrote that chapter? It's erotic . . . She *was* a fine type of girl & in this chapter she ought to do herself justice. And he was a splendid man. The big love passage between them should be big & noble and clean—not a mere appeal to the sensual.[93]

Needless to say, Zane rewrote the scene. This letter is a rare example of Dolly pressing Zane for revision. The letters exchanged by Zane and Dolly from before their marriage confirm that she did suggest modifications to his early work, but these letters do not reveal what they were or what he changed. The handwritten holographic manuscripts of Grey's novels from 1915 to

1923 reveal varying amounts of revision from the extensive reformulation of "The Last of the Duanes" and "The Rangers of the Lone Star" into *The Lone Star Ranger* to minor corrections of routine copyediting. Although the dearth of hard evidence poses irresolvable questions about the reasons for these changes and the person(s) responsible for them, the editors at Harper and Brothers undoubtedly influenced him more than Dolly, and this kind of request was unusual for her at this point in Zane's career. That said, had Dolly and his editors actually encouraged him to write more descriptions like this *"liebestod* session" and Madeline's horseback ride with Gene, it is possible that Grey's romances could have become less conventional and better attuned to the future.[94] Of course, if Grey had channeled more of his sexual experience into his stories, his novels might also have been more controversial and less popular, and his fear of controversy may have contributed to the repeated breakdowns with writing his novel of social protest.

When Grey, Dolly, and the other members of their party reached San Francisco on July 24, 1917, he learned that his mother had died the day before in Lackawaxen. Although her health had been declining, her death was unexpected and upsetting. Realizing that it would take him almost a week to return to Lackawaxen, he advised R. C. to hold the funeral without him and proceeded with his original plans.[95] Dolly, Mildred, and Dorothy took the train east for Lackawaxen, and he went south to Los Angeles. There he was joined by Claire, Lillian, and Elma, and together they took the ferry to Catalina. This time he rented a house for the summer. While he awaited the girls' train, he dispatched Dolly a brief letter declaring, "I want to thank you for being such a brick on this trip. I never really knew how fine you could be, and I love you more than I ever did. It was splendid of you . . . [and] I'll not forget it."[96]

Whatever misgivings Grey had about his decision not to be deterred by his mother's death were allayed by news that the fishing was sensational. On the boat over, he and the girls saw large schools of flying fish. After dinner that night, William Boschen showed them a broadbill caught that day, and told about two others from the week before, one weighing 422 pounds that established a new record.[97] During his season of unproductive fishing back in 1914, Grey had watched Boschen catch a 300-pound marlin that jumped sixty-three times, and later commented that "it made me wild to catch one, of like weight and ferocity."[98] This longing made him ecstatic when he landed a 316-pound marlin a year later, but Boschen's success with broadbill also intensified his envy. In "Swordfish, the Royal Purple Game of the Sea," Grey describes his fascination with this formidable adversary and Boschen's epic battle with one:

> The broadbill swordfish is a different proposition. He is larger, fiercer, and tireless. He will charge the boat, and nothing but the churning propeller will keep him from ramming the boat. There were eight broadbill swordfish hooked at Avalon during the summer, and not one brought to gaff. This is an old story. Only two have been caught to date. They are so purposeful, so resistless, so desperate, and so cunning that it seems impossible to catch them. . . . Boschen fought a big broadbill for eleven hours. And during this fight, the swordfish sounded to the bottom forty-eight times, and had to be pumped up; he led the boat almost around Catalina Island—twenty-nine miles; and he had gotten out into the channel, headed for Clemente, when he broke away. This fish did everything. I consider this battle the greatest on record (259–60).

Later he confessed, "It is my great ambition now to catch a broadbill. That would completely round out my fishing experience. And I shall try. But I doubt that I will be so fortunate. It takes a long time" (260).

Realizing that twice as many broadbill had been caught during the final days of July 1917 than all the years before, Zane was chagrined over what he had missed, but he was also optimistic that this unprecedented opportunity was not over. Over the next week, he averaged three sightings a day and got many strikes, but he did not hook one.[99] On August 3, following a conversation with Zane about these sightings, William Boschen landed a 462-pound broadbill that bettered the record set the week before. The following day, Grey confessed to Dolly, "Had a horrible disappointment yesterday. Dan and I have been trailing a big swordfish for days. He has taken 6 baits from me, and we were sure we'd get him eventually. But I foolishly blabbed about him to Boschen, and yesterday Boschen quit his usual ground, invaded ours, and hooked and killed my fish. The world's record—462 pounds. It made me sick!"[100]

This misfortune was reversed that same day when Zane hooked and successfully landed his first broadbill. Though it weighed only 260 pounds, it provided a memorable four-hour fight that he described in "The Gladiator of the Sea." Claire Wilhelm was on board at the time, and likewise described the momentous event in her journal. Unlike Grey who eloquently reconstructed the dramatic fight and the skillful, well-coordinated responses of himself and the crew, Claire acknowledged the mayhem and near disaster. Her account is both vivid and different enough to merit quoting:

> It was all so quiet and smooth on the water that we were deathly afraid the fish would hear or see us. Mil and I were tense—He ignored the bait—

Zane Grey, his first broadbill (260 pounds), and O. I. Danielson, Catalina, August 4, 1917. (Courtesy of Pat Friese.)

we cursed him—we swore at him and we waited. Was it to be the same old story? We almost wept at the thought of it. But why give up? Capt. Dan said, 'Let the bait sink a minute and keep it still. He may come back. That's what my big fish did.' We were going to tantalize it till we chased it if nothing better. The fins disappeared. Our heads stood still. We didn't dare say farewell. What! A thrill went through Doc—the line twitched ever so little. Was he beating the bait with his strong bill? He dared not open his mouth—he was speechless in fact. Yes, the line gradually ran out and then of a sudden the reel sang. What music to our ears! . . . In one of his leaps the whole body quivered and it looked immense. It was the most beautiful thrilling sight I've ever witnessed. At times he would just remain still and then he would go down several hundred feet. When he'd come up we were all on the alert watching eagerly for another leap or sight of him. . . . About 4:30 Doc had him up to the boat—there he woke up. Out he swam and Doc swore. At 20 minutes of five we had him up to the boat again and he slashed about and beat his sword against the boat and made the water fly, some excitement! . . . Dan got the gaffs in him alright and Doc slipped the noose over his tail lassoing him. The blood covered the fish and discolored the water all around. He fought frantically. The gaff came loose and Dan yelled to us to all help pull the rope. Doc jumped up on the stern of the boat rope in hand and we pulled. Dan yelled to take in slack rope and we had a h— of a time even holding it for the fish was pulling out his end and we nearly had our hands torn off. For a minute I thought all was up—Doc and Dan just escaped being pulled overboard. I screamed with terror. All was bloody and slippery and the sea was getting rough and the boat rocking. Doc finally got the rope on the cleat and the very worst was over.[101]

This catch earned Grey a coveted white button. Despite his persistent claims that he was the world's unluckiest fisherman, his timing and luck were perfect this time. Immediately following this catch, the broadbill disappeared, but tuna showed up to replace them. On August 10, Zane caught two. One weighed ninety-five pounds, his biggest so far—five pounds shy of the 100 necessary for a blue button, but large enough to spark hope that the four-year drought of big tuna might have ended. Three days later, Zane introduced a former classmate from Penn to the challenge and excitement of tuna fishing. Dr. Riggin had previously been captain of the football team and was currently an anatomist at Penn's medical school. He arrived just after Zane landed his broadbill, and together they performed an elaborate autopsy on the fish. When the muscular Riggin hooked a tuna several days later, Zane reset the reel's drag so that he was strained to the point of exhaustion. This prank kept Grey from fishing several hours during a record-setting day on which fifty-six tuna were landed.[102] Though Zane landed seven that day, his catches averaged only seventy pounds, much smaller than his ninety-five pounder and well shy of the 100 pounds required for the blue button on which he had his heart set.

Four days later, Zane and the girls returned to Los Angeles and hopped a train for Denver. Lillian's exit in Flagstaff was emotional for everyone, especially Claire. Meanwhile, R. C., his wife Reba, "Fergie," and Dorothy Ackerman had coordinated their departure from New York City so that they arrived in Denver the same day. After a two-day tour of the city, the group headed west to Yampa, a small town midway between Steamboat Springs and Vail. From there, an outfitter named Teague took them into the Flat Tops Wilderness area. From a well-situated base camp, they passed a pleasant but rather uneventful month riding horses, exploring high peaks, trout fishing, and hunting. Grey drew upon this experience for *The Mysterious Rider* (1921), which he completed after *The Desert of Wheat*.[103]

When Zane returned to Lackawaxen at the end of September, his spirits were much improved, but his return to the circumstances of his spring depression revived the demons he had been fleeing. "My mother died here on July 23," he wrote in his journal on his third day back. "The news, reaching me in San Francisco, was a rude and severe shock. I cannot remember ever having been so affected. There was sudden shock, then slow bewildered thought—then numb pain. . . . She is gone. Autumn is here. The flowers are fading."[104] Three weeks later, a meeting with Elma convinced him that their spring rift had irreversibly damaged their relationship and that any future trips with her would never be what they once were:

> It is settled now—and we will never be the same again. Alas! Where is it gone, the glory and the dream? Five years ago this month I met her, and never had I seen a more beautiful girl. Will October ever come without my remembering her and the sweetness of her charm, the allurement of her beauty, and the dreadful certainty of the death of love? Not death, perhaps, but change![105]

These losses and work on *The Desert of Wheat* reactivated corrosive thoughts about the war. Over the winter, the devastating influenza epidemic intensified, as did Dolly's fears about its threat to her children. Grey agreed with his wife when he learned that the epidemic had killed Nasjah Begay and many other Indians.

By June, this fixation with mutability and loss colored his view of fishing as well. Following the completion of *The Desert of Wheat,* Grey wrote an article entitled "Avalon, the Beautiful" that appeared in the May 1918 issue of *Field and Stream* and was rerun on the front page of the June 4th issue of the Catalina *Islander.* Grey's title for this landmark essay anticipates a celebration of Catalina's pastoral beauty and magnificent fishing, and it opens with a long description of the previous summer's extraordinary run of fish. However, the article also contends that this bounty masked a looming disaster, and informs its reader about the devastation being caused by commercial fishermen, their round-haul nets, the canneries, and especially the fertilizer plants that were harvesting tons of kelp. This commercial exploitation was a menace to fish and their habitat, depriving big fish of staples in their diet. Conceding that fish populations were still strong, Grey argues that Clemente Island, beyond the three-mile limit of protection, is no longer the paradise of fish, especially the beautiful, sporting yellowtail, that it once was. He maintains that the war has worsened this situation, pointing out that Germany had supplied the country's need for potash for many years, but the outbreak of war had compelled farmers to resort to kelp as an alternative. He is equally disturbed by "Jap" fishermen who harvest tons of albacore. He charges that "aliens" hostile to the United States make millions from netting fish, and that these foreigners use this money to foster political corruption and revoke existing laws against such practices.

Although remarkably prescient today, Grey's predictions about fish declines were discredited by the fishing that followed. When he returned to Avalon for the seasons of 1918 and 1919, they proved to be two of the best ever—especially for tuna. The 362 tuna caught during the 1917 season were a decided improvement over the catches from his previous seasons, but 1918 yielded a far more impressive 639. William Boschen caught a staggering 102. Though Zane took only twenty-one, this more than doubled his previous best.[106] Even better, large tuna returned for the first time in a decade. In "Big Tuna," Grey relates that tuna did not arrive until late June; fishermen harvested abundant catches for a full six weeks before the first big ones appeared. On August 14, 1918, when he and Danielson first spotted them, Grey received thirteen strikes, broke off ten, and did not land a single one. "Yesterday was the most wonderful and tragically unfortunate day I ever had fishing, since I was a boy," he complained to Dolly.[107] The total disappearance of tuna over the week that followed was almost as demoralizing. Finally he spotted another school and was able to hook one, but this tuna was so submissive that he guessed it to be small and became dejected. A three-and-a-half-hour fight followed, and when it was over, he discovered that he had a 138-pound giant that finally ended his five-year quest for the blue button.[108] During the next season, an unprecedented 775 tuna were caught, and Grey earned the red button for catching one with light tackle.[109]

The numbers of marlin for these two seasons were equally impressive. Over the 1918 season, 155 were caught.[110] On August 31, during a ten-day campout on Clemente, the island that Zane claimed to have been depleted of fish, R. C. set a new record by landing seven marlin in a single day.[111] Although neither season produced a broadbill, Zane hooked a monster that he estimated to weigh over 1,000 pounds on July 16, 1919. The leviathan gave him a twelve-hour battle before it snapped his line to pursue some flying fish.[112] The exertion of this contest left him unable to move for days and he still hobbled two months later.

If this fishing and his improved relations with Dolly helped Zane over the emotional anguish of 1916 and 1917, his outlook was also brightened by a new woman who was more of a kindred spirit than anyone so far. Grey's rift with Elma excluded her from the Long Key trip in January 1918. Instead, he took Mildred Fergerson, Claire Wilhelm, and Dorothy Ackerman. Claire had already been with him on many trips dating back to her 1914 trip to Arizona with her older sister Lillian. As Zane added more women to his retinue, Lillian lost the privileged position that she originally held in 1912, and one of those to supplant her was her own sister. During this period of Grey's turmoil and rapidly changing allegiances, Claire and Dorothy became close friends. Their spirited, outgoing personalities and enthusiasm for the outdoors made them compatible from the moment they met. They loved riding horses, camping in the wild, and especially fishing. During the 1918 season at Long Key, both graduated from attentive deckhands to accomplished anglers. In February, Claire and Dot each landed big amberjacks, and Dot followed with a barracuda large enough to qualify for one of the buttons of the new club that Zane established.[113] Claire bested her catch with a thirty-seven-pound barracuda that proved to be the largest of the season.[114] Dorothy and Claire had more success the following summer in Catalina. Dorothy caught a 79-pound tuna and a 145-pound sea bass, and just before they left, Claire hooked the biggest fish of all but unfortunately failed to land it.[115]

Over the course of these outings, Dorothy became Zane's favorite. Even though her success came at Claire's expense, both women made a valiant effort to preserve their friendship. One sign that Zane had emerged from the extended depression of 1917 was a November entry in his journal of an "exhilarating" horseback ride with Dorothy Ackerman who looked like "a rosy country girl."[116] Claire's journal reveals that this budding involvement

Claire Wilhelm (left) and Dorothy Ackerman, Avalon, ca. 1918. (Courtesy of Pat Friese.)

had deepened and intensified by the 1918 visit to Long Key. At a dinner celebration of Zane's January 31st birthday, Fergie presented him "the picture of Dot he so much wanted." He displayed more interest in Dorothy's upcoming birthday than his own. When Dorothy briefly left the table, Zane showed the others a beautiful diamond ring he was planning to present her. At least one person was not impressed. Claire mentions "an unpleasant incident" that occurred during the celebration of Dorothy's birthday that left her despondent. Though Claire does not say what happened, R. C.'s long walk with Dorothy afterward suggests that Reba, his outspoken wife, probably criticized Zane's extravagant gift. When Dorothy won a big hand at a communal poker game later that night, Claire said of her friend, "I was glad Dot got it—just topped off the day and made up for all her losses."[117]

An earlier entry in Claire's journal reveals unexplained strains with Zane. Typically, Claire is tight-lipped about her relationship with him, but she acknowledges a heated confrontation during which "the blood was in my head and I wanted to bite."[118] Apparently both put aside their differences for the remainder of their stay in Long Key, but they flared up again in Catalina. Early in August, Zane informed Dolly that he was "thoroughly disgusted with

Claire and Mildred S[mith].[119] Dolly responded, "What on earth has Claire done now to incur your displeasure? Elma's and my letters [from you] reek with reference to her fall from grace, but the reason is not forthcoming, and I am consumed with curiosity. Was it a man? Of course, if a lady falls from grace, cherchez l'homme."[120] Zane explained that he had come upon Claire going through Dorothy's things.[121] It is quite possible that Claire was more jealous of Dorothy's involvement with Zane than she was willing to admit, but Dolly's conjecture was also perceptive. For over a year, Claire had been dating and writing to Phillips Carlin, whom she would marry three years later. This graduate of New York University had both a stellar academic record and strong feelings for Claire, but was currently working for a failing export company and reluctant to commit.

Whatever the reasons, Claire's fall from grace jeopardized her position within Zane's retinue, upset Lillian, who worried about her security, and elicited a long, impassioned appeal to Zane on her behalf:

> If I have one hope for Claire it is that eventually she will obtain a similar happiness and I realize that you wish that for her too—but there's no real substance to that wild hysterical love making—haven't I learned it? I have had several letters from her, and I think the jolt has gone deep. She realizes that she is a woman now—and how much she owes to you and your interest in her. That is one thing that I feel honestly expressed in every line. Doc—I dread to think of what would become of my little sis if you let her go now out of your life and influence. It is a crucial time and from her letters, I feel that she has had a terrible awakening to the reality of the situation and realizes all that she stands to lose, depending on your decision for the future. I beg you, think it over carefully. . . . She tells me that if she were engaged, which is *not* the case, she would not think of marrying for some years to come for she wants to make something of her life first.[122]

Zane reconsidered his decision to have Claire return to New York. When he left for a fall hunting trip into the Tonto Rim area of Arizona, he took both Claire and Dorothy. But after their outing ended in late October, Claire was sent to stay with Lillian in Crown Point, New Mexico.

Instead of returning to Middletown and the East after his hunt during the fall of 1918, Zane went to California, and joined his family at a house that he had rented on 2445 Southwestern Avenue in central Los Angeles. Earlier in March, Zane and Dolly had discussed the possibility of relocating the family to southern California. His confidence in this decision was strengthened over the summer by the terrific fishing in Catalina and the promise of his film company. "Mr. Hampton was over to see me," he informed Dolly. "I am beginning to feel better, and very hopeful, but I'll have to work as I never worked before. This big motion-picture deal is going to make me stick to work. I will write you more fully as soon as I know the facts. The contracts are being made in New York by Mr. Stern, the Author's League lawyer. When I get them and the details of the business to follow I will let you know at once."[123] Over the summer, Dolly sold the house in Middletown.[124] In September, she, the children, and Ida left Lackawaxen for Los Angeles. R. C. and Reba rented a house nearby. That same fall, Ellsworth, the eldest of the Grey brothers, married Ethel Stern from Middletown, and they relocated to Los Angeles following their honeymoon. For Thanksgiving, there was a big family gathering to celebrate the warm, bright sunshine and their upcoming winter together.

The final element of Grey's recovery was a renewed commitment to Westerns. During Zane's 1918 visit to Long Key, Dolly attended an evening presentation by a spiritualist named Anna Andre, who resided in Placerville, California. Dolly was so impressed she scheduled a private meeting. Upon learning that Andre was an avid reader of her husband's novels, Dolly commissioned an analysis of his character and arranged for it to be sent to him in early February. Although this contained predictable flattery and conjecture, Andre possessed an uncanny understanding of her subject:

> A noble pride—A generous friend—A just foe—Independent—Courageous—Very sensitive—Vivid imagination—intuitive. . . . A crying need for a mate—the one woman. . . . The wrong woman would wreck you—kill your ambition—destroy your hope—It is the face of suffering—pain—sorrow—sometime—somewhere a great trouble fell upon you—You drained a bitter cup—The taste will linger until it turns sweet in your soul. . . . You are now in the full glory of manhood ready to touch the souls of men with the pen of flame—I have not found your equal for delineation of character in all my years of reading authors. . . . No man can do this unless he KNOWS HOW and to know it he must walk over thorns himself in pain and despair—Not sin—but suffering—To suffer is to understand the feel of pain—TO UNDERSTAND IS TO SYMPATHIZE AND WANT TO HELP THE CRYING NEEDS. That's why reason tells me you have suffered—Instinctively I know you have.[125]

Zane was impressed with her assessment of his strengths and weaknesses and wrote back a long letter of gratitude that dwelled on the strains and discontents behind his success. Andre's interpretation would not have affected him so much had he not been so distressed by his women problems and his writing. "All these years my idea has been to win a public, and write the powerful psychological novels of love, passion, and tragedy that I am capable of writing," he explained. He alluded to his failure with *Shores of Lethe,* and admitted that his editors had urged him to publish this work under a pseudonym. Although everyone at Harpers "was delighted with the wheat novel,"[126] he worried that its social criticism clashed with the romantic style of writing he preferred and handled best. "No matter where I would go, or what I would do," he confessed to Andre, "I could never write Realism." Before the serialization of *Desert* even started in May, Zane concluded that he had taken a wrong turn, and credited Andre with inspiring him to return to what he did best:

> I did half lose faith in myself. This is a hard bitter sordid old world. How terribly it needs a love of beauty—an understanding of nature! But what it needs, it repudiates. I meant, I think, to put the best of me, my mature work, in novels of character.
>
> My ordeal is over.
>
> If it will be any pleasure or happiness for you to know that your letters have been the dominant force in my decision, you may have them. It is not strange to me that this inspiration should come from a stranger. My relief is immense. My obligation is great.[127]

That same day, he wrote to Dolly, "I have gotten *that* great hold on myself. Dolly, rejoice with me. As far as my work is concerned, my ordeal is over."[128] Four days later, he explained to his publisher Ripley Hitchcock, "You will remember how for years I have been torturing myself, and perplexing you, with an insistent passion to write another kind of novel. I regarded my western stories merely as practice to this important end. . . . My Ordeal is Over! The decision is made. I shall put all my soul into a future interpretation of the beauty, color, wilderness and passion of the West.[129]

Although he had regained confidence and committed himself to another Western, he did not actually begin writing until months later. During the fall he read George Parsons, *A Thousand Mile Desert Trip* (1918) and in December, he decided that his Western would be about a prolonged desert trek.[130] Over the New Year, he and Dorothy went to Palm Springs and stayed at the Desert Inn.[131] There they were joined by Sievert Nielsen, a rawboned Norwegian adventurer whom Zane had included on his first two outings in the Tonto Basin.[132] By mid-January, Grey was back in Altadena and ready to begin. In his journal he wrote:

Today after years of plan[ning], and months of thought, and weeks of travel, reading, I began the novel that I have determined to be great.

It was with singular fire, sweetness, life and joy that I began to write. None of that poignant worry, pain, fuss, or vacillation so characteristic of me at the outset of work! I have made a plan.

This novel will not be great unless I have absolute control and restraint; and I am absolutely determined that it will be a great novel.[133]

In mid-March of 1919, after two months of struggle and faltering progress, he went off again with Nielsen, who had assembled mules and supplies for an outing. At Death Valley Junction, they loaded and went for a relatively uneventful four-day outing into the area of Furnace Creek and the Panamint Mountains.[134] Two more months of hard work and bipolar swings enabled him to finish his new novel at midnight on May 29th.[135]

Wanderer of the Wasteland (1923) is one of Grey's finest Westerns, certainly the best from this period of his career. Using words the way an impressionist painter dabs his oils, he serves up a masterly portrait of the most forbidding environment in the Southwest. For fourteen years, his protagonist Adam Larey roams a vast unmapped desert that is parched, desolate, and menacing, but he discovers it to be colorful, invigorating, and accommodating— enabling him to flee his haunted past, to salve his tortured psyche, and to discover a wealth of adventure.

This story's imaginative, self-serving conflation of Grey's recent ordeal resonated with a personal significance that had been sorely missed in his recent efforts. Like Buck in *The Lone Star Ranger,* Adam is another alienated victim of injustice, but his prolonged quest for understanding and acceptance is sustained by the many women who fall in love with him. Early in the story, Adam falls in love with Margarita, but his devilish brother Guerd claims that he can steal her away, and does so with a few words of affection. Furious over this theft, Adam shoots him, and guiltily flees into the desert to become "Wansfell, the Wanderer." When a rattlesnake bite leaves him unconscious, a young Indian named Oella finds him, nurses him back to health, and welcomes him into her tribe. Adam is flattered when her father, the chief, consents to a marriage with his daughter, but he explains that he is an outcast and must leave. His decision breaks Oella's heart and she dies.

After eight years of wandering that harden him into a strong, resourceful man of the desert, he learns about a contentious husband and wife who live at the base of a mountain in a remote section of the desert. He goes to offer help, and bonds with the wife Magdalene, who tells him about her daughter by another man and the abuse her husband has inflicted as punishment. When her husband finally murders her, Adam kills him and resumes his wandering.

Next, he rescues a fourteen-year-old girl from bandit kidnappers, and returns her to her ailing mother. When the mother dies three years later, the daughter confesses her love for him, but he pushes her away with an explanation that he is old enough to be her father. During a chance meeting with Magdalene's missing daughter, she recognizes him as Wansfell, and asks him to take her to her mother's grave. Soon she too wants him to "make her a woman." Still too guilt-ridden to commit, he leaves, this time to hunt for the grave of his slain brother. Now, fourteen years after the terrible event that had turned him into an outcast and wanderer, he learns that his brother was never killed and is still alive. He suddenly realizes that his self-imposed exile and abandoned relationships have been "a terrible mistake." At this moment of discovery that concludes the story, Grey does not say whether Adam's ordeal is over.

Like the romances in *Riders of the Purple Sage, The Light of Western Stars,* and *The Rainbow Trail,* Adam's involvements were inspired and shaped by Grey's personal life, but few readers have ever sensed this connection because it is so indirect and so veiled. Grey was straining so hard to overcome his own torment that even he did not fully comprehend these self-serving murmurings from his unconscious.[136] On a conscious level, he was uncomfortably aware that his previous Westerns had not expressed anything important or meaningful to him. He was also upset over the current direction of American culture and deeply frustrated by his inability to complete his novel of social protest. Finally, in *Wanderer of the Wasteland,* he was able to speak his mind, channeling into Adam's ordeal the turbulence of his personal life. Later, when he drew upon his distress again to finish his novel of social protest, the result was much stranger.

6

Calamity:
1920–23

Days and days pass! I have been filled with remorse,
and obsessed by a driving passion, and prey to endless
pangs. Besides I have not been well. Ah! What a battle
life is! I am so full of wildness. I have only begun to
find strength, and then recurrent spells are more terrible
as the years go by. 1923! Year of loss and pain and
realization! What yet has it in store?
—Diary, 1923–39, November 24, 1923

By 1920, the forty-seven-year-old and still youthful Zane Grey was on top and in charge, and he had no inkling of disaster on the horizon. After struggling with rejection and disappointment for the first ten years of his writing career, and then capitalizing on his hard-won advances during the years spanned by World War I, he now confronted a clamoring demand for anything he wrote. During a visit to New York City in January 1920, he reflected in his journal on the intoxicating effect of the intense competition for his work:

I seem to find myself a name to reckon with in the world of publishers.
I have two offers, three perhaps, that are larger than any ever offered an

American writer. I am in the throes of struggle with Harpers—they to retain me at their figures, and I to get what I want and deserve, or go to someone else. They tell me that any publishing house would lose money, or could afford to do so, just to get my name at the head of their list. This to me seems exaggeration. But it thrills me. I believe my long-sought-for goal is in sight. And I shall work as never before![1]

Several days of meetings and negotiations with other publishers added to this euphoria. A representative from *McClure's* offered Grey $15,000 for the rights to his recently completed *Wanderer of the Wasteland.* Barton Currie, the editor in charge of the *Country Gentleman,* praised his recent work, and presented a package deal of $10,000 for serialization of a novel in 1920, $12,000 for one the next year, and $15,000 for one the year following. Currie also expressed interest in Grey's outdoor articles of five to six thousand words, and offered $800 for each. In his journal, Zane wrote, "This is extraordinary, and almost incredible."[2]

The *McClure's* offer of $15,000 for serial rights pressured the *Country Gentleman* to increase its fee to retain Grey as a contributor, and represented an astounding leap from the $1,000 that *Cavalier* had paid for serial rights to *The Lone Star Ranger* only six years earlier. After topping the annual bestseller list for 1918 with *The U. P. Trail,* and holding down the number-three spot for 1919 with *The Desert of Wheat,* Grey was on a roll; Currie realized that he would have to increase his previous payment of $7,000 in order to provide his readers a first look at Grey's next novel. Since 1911, when the Curtis Publishing Company took over the original the *Country Gentleman,* the magazine's circulation had rocketed from 20,000 to more than 400,000 by 1920, and this growth put Currie in a position to pay more money. Grey had figured prominently in Currie's efforts to convert the magazine from a journal for farmers into one promoting an interest in country life for a more general readership.[3] With Grey's novels regularly making the best-seller lists and with Hollywood confirming the enormous audience appeal of Westerns, Currie realized that Grey was not just popular—he was at the forefront of a cultural trend.

All this attention and reward caused Grey second thoughts. He wondered if Harpers might be slighting him and became annoyed at the treatment he was receiving:

Harpers have become keen to hold me, but they have not yet convinced me of their sincerity and efficiency. The strange feature of that situation is they will save at least $150,000 in five years by letting me go, instead of

The successful author, ca. 1925. (Courtesy of Pat Friese.)

meeting my demands. I am disgusted with some aspects of their work. My next book, "Man of the Forest," has a paper cover upon which is printed these words: "God's Country and the Woman" which is a direct copy of title and advertising used by another house for one of my contemporaries! Of all the bonehead blunders! It made me furious.[4]

This discontent had been building for several years. Back in August 1918, he fretted over Harpers' financing and wrote to Dolly, "I believe they are going to slip on our money. That would be awful."[5] The year before, he had complained to Harpers advertising department about its handling of *The Desert of Wheat* (1919), and insisted that the lack of dignity in its advertisements would not attract the readership of the *New York Times* to his novels. At that time, the editor in charge responded with a long letter of reassurance urging that he not "think for a minute that any of this advertising copy is put out hastily or without due consideration."[6] But when *The Man of the Forest* proved to be *the* best-selling novel of 1920, Harpers decided that it needed to be more responsive to Grey and more supportive with its advertising. The promotion department was allotted $75,000 for simultaneous displays of his novels at selected bookstores around the country for the week of June 2, 1921. Harpers teamed up with Curtis Publishing Company, Grosset & Dunlap (Grey's reprint publisher), and W. W. Hodkinson so that its bookstore displays were supported by posters at newsstands and movie theaters as well. As a professional trade journal reported, "During this week Zane Grey will receive more publicity than any other living author."[7]

Royalties were more important to Grey than promotion. There is no record of Grey's demands to Harpers, but his reference to a $150,000 saving makes clear that substantial sums were involved. In early March, Frank Doubleday approached Grey with a lucrative contract to defect and Zane wrote to Dolly, "I would not under any circumstances accept it. Yet I signed my name to such an agreement."[8] Meanwhile, Ray Long, the editor at *Cosmopolitan*, was reported to have offered Grey $100,000 for the serial rights to any new novel. This represented an astounding jump from the dazzling offers Grey had received only a few months before. However, *Cosmopolitan* was owned by Hearst Enterprises, and for its $100,000, it wanted rights to both the serial *and* the novel.[9] Knowing Grey's long-term contract with Harpers was up for renewal, Long hoped Grey would defect to Hearst, and Grey's remarks suggest that he was considering the possibility. In early April, he informed Dolly of a proposed $100,000 advance in his new contract from Harpers, and explained that his lawyers worried about its grave tax consequences and discouraged acceptance.[10]

The next day, Grey recorded in his journal that he had signed a new ten-year contract with Harpers. Though he did not mention the terms, he believed that it was "the largest contract ever offered an American author."[11] Over the previous four years, his annual income had risen at an unbelievable rate. As recently as 1916, it had been only $27,717.92. By 1919, it had jumped to $95,908.89. Although he realized in January that he would make even more for 1920, he never would have guessed that his income for the year would reach $178,454.88.[12] His new contract with Harpers, the lucrative serial rights for his new novels, and substantial payments for film rights ensured him a handsome income. His fame and the recent film adaptations of his novels so increased sales of his earlier books that his income would have approached $75,000 without new publications. On January 11, 1923, he realized that his earnings for 1922 would exceed $200,000, and he wrote Dolly, "I think I can see $480,000 in the next two years."[13] In actuality, he would make $546,633.[14]

As in the past, available money stoked Grey's desire to buy, only now he had far more to spend. Over the course of 1920, he would plow the bulk of his formidable earnings into three properties. These satisfied powerful, suppressed longings, but privileged *his* needs and worsened his insensitivity to others. His first priority was a residence. The two-year experiment with California living convinced the whole family to make the relocation permanent. Grey's deepening infatuation with Catalina prompted his first purchase. Over the six years of his annual visits, Avalon had grown and changed enormously. The raging fire of 1915 had devastated not only the town of Avalon, but also the Santa Catalina Island Company (CSI) that controlled the island's development. Reconstruction proceeded slowly, and by 1918, there was still widespread evidence of the fire's damage. In 1918, William Wrigley, Jr., president of the Wrigley Chewing Gum Company in Chicago, was attracted to the island, and he persuaded the CSI to sell him a large stake in the spring of 1919. That fall, the CSI allowed Wrigley to purchase additional stock and to gain majority control.

This infusion of capital had an immediate effect. When she returned to Avalon in 1920 after a two-year absence, Claire Wilhelm was stunned by the sweeping change that had occurred. She noticed the disappearance of the colorful tents that dated back to the founding of the Tuna Club, and the many new residences that replaced them. Two big hotels had sprung up, and they were bustling with guests. In the Sugarloaf area near the new St. Catherine Hotel, there was an imposing new casino that housed a dance floor large enough to accommodate 250 couples. Automobiles had finally arrived, and macadam streets as well. All this development spiked real estate values, and convinced Zane that a house purchase would be a wise investment. His love of Avalon and its fishing furnished more incentive.

First, he commissioned blueprints for a bungalow. Meanwhile, he contracted to rent the three-story house on Olive Street that he had secured for the family the previous year. In February, he learned that its owner, Capt. A. L. McKelvey, was preparing to sell the house. This made him fearful that it might sell during high season, and force him to vacate when rentals would be scarce. "I think I might buy the McKelvey place just to play safe," he told Dolly.[15] Since everyone liked the house and its location overlooking the harbor, he decided to buy it. In its August announcement of the closing, the *Islander* reported, "Dr. Grey is planning to make a permanent residence on the island,"[16] but this was not accurate. Prior to this purchase, Zane and Dolly had already agreed to look for a grander, more accommodating residence on the mainland. Since neither cared for the rented house on Southwestern Avenue or the one on Sunset Boulevard that they had tried briefly as an alternative, they decided to remain in the Catalina house and to search for a residence they really wanted, even if it meant staying all winter.

The annual departure of the summer crowd and Avalon's small, provincial school gave Dolly second thoughts about staying on the island, and she immediately went searching for a home on the mainland. She was drawn to Altadena, a hill town overlooking Pasadena, which she recalled from her memorable honeymoon trip to the top of nearby Mount Lowe. There she found a residence that fulfilled her expectations. Just prior to the turn of the century, two Midwesterners, Frederick Woodbury and Andrew McNally, founder of the Rand-McNally Publishing Company, had decided to build large homes in Altadena, and afterward they campaigned for their Chicago friends to relocate there. One person who did so was Arthur H. Woodward, the president of the International Register Company that manufactured cash registers. Motivated by poor health, Woodward was strongly influenced by the narrow escape of his wife and two children from the disastrous fire at Chicago's Iroquois Theatre in 1903. He was adamant that the house be completely fireproof. His architect, Elmer Grey (no relation to Zane), was an affiliate of Myron Hunt, who built the Huntington Library, the Rose Bowl, and the Pasadena Central Library. Woodward's Spanish-Mediterranean-style mansion, constructed during the winter of 1908–9, had solid masonry walls and reinforced concrete floors covered with oak hardwood. Its ten rooms comprised approximately 7,000 square feet, and the building sat on five acres of land, two blocks west of the McNally residence.[17]

By the time the Woodward house appeared on the market in September 1920, the grounds were elaborately landscaped, with fruit trees of every variety peculiar to California. Grey was especially fond of the area's rural tranquility and the spectacular views from the building's many windows. Two years after his purchase that fall, Zane had Elmer Grey design a third story and terra-cotta tile roof. As he later explained in an essay entitled "Why I Live in Altadena": "The greatest appeal to me has always been in the beauty that abides here. I need but to look out of any window to get a magnificent view. To the north the great mountains sweep on. On a clear day I can see south to the ocean and the peaks of Catalina. Everywhere is warm, dry sunshine, the fragrance of innumerable flowers."[18] Though Grey would claim, "In Altadena I have found those qualities that make life worth living," he never intended to spend more than a few months here or at his Avalon house. A local newspaper announcement of his fall 1920 purchase noted that "for many months each year he will be off on long trips conducted into the most remote parts of the globe."[19] This point was quickly verified when Zane departed to go hunting in Arizona in early September and left Dolly to arrange the move and purchase furnishings.[20]

On this fall hunt, Zane took his brother R. C. and his wife; "Lone Angler" Wiborn and his wife; Sievert Nielsen; Claire Wilhelm; Elma Schwarz; and Dorothy Ackerman. "Babe" Haught and his two sons, Edd and George, were contracted as outfitters and guides. This was Grey's third visit to the Mogollon Rim, which overlooked the Tonto Basin of east-central Arizona, and it was also his most ambitious outing. His initial visit in 1918 was cut short after less than three weeks by news of the spreading influenza epidemic. Anxious to return as soon as possible, Grey opted for a shortcut against the advice of Babe Haught, and got the group into an arduous trek. Nonetheless, he was so impressed with the area and its hunting possibilities that he returned a second time in 1919. Problems from the first trip convinced him to purchase several fine rifles, to ship his favorite horse, Don Carlos, and to hire George Takahashi, a chef who would remain with Grey for the next fifteen years.[21] For the third visit in 1920, Grey arranged for three wagons of supplies, twenty-one horses, and a party of more than a dozen. Even before Grey's outings assumed such size and extravagance, an outfitter once joked that guiding the famous author was "like moving a house plant."[22]

The base camp was situated high above the Verdant Canyon and near Beaver Dam Canyon, approximately 1,000 feet below the location of the 1919 campsite. His party enjoyed unseasonably warm weather for most of its stay and had great success shooting turkey, deer, lynx, mountain lion, and bear. The elaborate planning and equipment eliminated much of the hardship and adventure of the early trips, and Grey was ecstatic with the results.

The enthusiasm and active involvement of his three female companions contributed significantly to the trip's success. In her journal, Claire Wilhelm reflected on her experience and wrote, "Every day I become fonder of this wonderful place. I should like to return here every fall."[23] She was petrified but undaunted by a high-exposure climb to a breathtaking overlook and "thrilled" when R. C. included her on a turkey hunt. She was a rapt audience for Babe Haught's stories around the campfire, and was amazed at his ability never to repeat himself. Had she kept a more detailed accounting, an informed reader would undoubtedly recognize how these stories worked their way into Zane's novels.

One week before the party broke camp, a fast-moving storm dumped two feet of snow on the encampment. Rather than a deterrent, this snow yielded the trip's most memorable experience and this description by Claire:

> Tonight the snow in the moonlight and starlight glistened and shone. On the smooth surface it looked as though it had been dusted with diamonds. It was the most beautiful and wonderful night I've ever known or seen. Made me think of a fairyland scene. Before dusk the sky to the southward was a bronze gold again. The snow was a blue white in color from where the sun's retreating rays had vanished. In the afterglow, the ridge tops were a soft-golden hue.[24]

Overnight, the temperature plunged, and the thermometer failed. Because its quicksilver had completely retreated into its reservoir, Claire knew only that the temperature was well below zero. When she awakened, she noticed that "my hair was frosty and cold" and "crystals were on the upper exposed blankets," but she still judged it to be "a glorious, beautiful morning."[25] This dauntless enthusiasm won her high praise from the adventurous Nielsen. "He said I was the whole life and spirit of the camp, that I had a disposition that people could envy," she wrote in her journal. "I think Nielsen is truly sorry we are going to leave. Said the men would be a lot of cranky bear hunters—not afraid to say in the absence of ladies what they thought of each other."[26] Grey was so exhilarated that, prior to his departure for Altadena, he arranged for Haught to sell him three acres of land on his nearby ranch, and commissioned him to build a lodge for his visit next year.[27]

This colorful lifestyle and his best-selling novels made Grey a model of

American achievement for the 1920s. For its July 1924 issue, *Success* magazine profiled the popular author, and relied on his description of the year before to convey the success and glamour of his life:

> One year is a good deal like another with me now—at least the last ten of them anyway. Last year was typical of what I do by way of work and play.
>
> January and February, I spent at Long Key down in Florida where I wrote, read and fished and wandered about on the beach. . . . The Spring I spent at my home in Altadena, California, where I wrote and studied, and played with my family. . . . June found me at Avalon, Catalina Island, a place I have found as inspiring as Long Key, and infinitely different. Here I finished a novel and then began my sword-fishing on the Pacific. This is a strenuous game, a test of eye-sight and endurance. . . . In September, I took Mr. Lasky and his staff to Arizona, to pick out locations for the motion picture, *The Vanishing American*. . . . In October I went to my hunting lodge in the Tonto Basin. . . . November and December found me back again at Altadena—hard as nails, brown as an Indian, happy to be home with my family, keen for my study with its books and pictures, and for the long spell of writing calling me to its fulfillment.[28]

This portrait made good copy, but like most portraits of Grey since, it left out as much as it revealed. In November 1923, when he returned to Altadena "hard as nails, brown as an Indian, happy to be home with my family," Grey resumed the journal, in which he had not written since May, and confided:

> In Sept. when I went fishing and went to Arizona, I was under the doctor's care, and advised that I was not in condition to undertake hard riding. But I went. If he had known my mental condition he would have scouted my physical ills.
>
> Last spring and summer saw the climax of my troubles. I suffered betrayal and loss and remorse. Altogether I had the ordeal of my life and it was no help to realize that I had only myself to blame—that I had been savage—selfish—proud—intolerant and supremely egotistical. What I got I deserved. But that in no wise lessened my pangs. I learned what it was to endure the tortures I had visited upon others.[29]

The reasons for Zane's plunge into his worst depression ever are not easily explained. Despite his candid admission of his mistakes and the careful analysis of his emotional anguish in his journal, he is frustratingly reserved about its causes. In his compulsive need to record the nuances of his black moods, he trusted his memory for the specifics, but may have worried that someone else might read his entries. The surviving evidence suggests two important points about his torment: (1) it was not provoked by any single person or event, and (2) it sprang from reversals with his women, writing, and fishing that spanned several years. Over the summer and fall of 1923, these problems converged and grew much worse.

The volatile ingredients for this devastation were stable when Grey went to Long Key following his exhilarating meetings with publishers in January 1920. From there, on the occasion of her birthday, he dispatched Dolly a letter of best wishes and gratitude for her loyalty and support: "It seems to me you have made a grand success of your life; and meanwhile have been my prod; my inspiration. The travail you went though is nothing to the result. Only a means to an end! Think of the women who suffer as much, and fail miserably. It makes me happy just to *think* of you."[30]

Six weeks later, on his last day in Long Key, he penned a long entry in another of his journals that records an aspect of his life left out of the *Success* profile. His long description of a final beach walk reveals the potentially explosive disparity between his public persona and his covert private life:

> It was my privilege to walk through this grove and along the shore with D—. Picture indeed she made, suitable for a Spanish romance of Campeche shores. She wore a white plissé shirtwaist [dress] that answered to the winds. Her hair blew back across her brown face, and her eyes shone dark as night. Neck and arms and hands showed golden brown with tan, and when we waded in the shallow water feet bursting crabs, her shapely feet and ankles shone as brown as her arms. Wind and sun had kissed warm tropic color into her flesh. Watching her was a constant delight for me. And walking with her under the palms and along the lovely shore was the unfolding of new stories . . . at times my heart swelled with the harvest of my riches. All this was mine, by right of heart, labor, and understanding.[31]

The "D—" to whom Grey refers was, of course, not Dolly, but Dorothy Ackerman. Since 1917, when Grey withdrew from Claire and focused upon Dorothy, Dolly had been well aware of what was happening. After years of pain and anger over these relationships, she had resigned herself to them and to Zane's insistence that they were necessary "inspiration." His productivity and success validated these claims. Though his outings were longer and more frequent, he always returned and reassured her of his commitment to their marriage. His continuous displays of need and gratitude for her unique understanding nourished and sustained her love. As late as October 26, 1920, the thirty-seven-year-old mother of his three children was still able to write to him in Arizona:

> I could not help being happy that you were homesick for me, but the unhappiness your letter expressed made me long passionately to put my arms around you and comfort you, to teach you what was real in life, and what would bring you peace. Often I feel as if you were like a child that needed me most, that I had to protect and shelter from the world. I do believe you need me more than even the youngsters do, and that is one of the sources of my perennial love for you. After all, the filling of a definite need is a very important thing in a woman's sense of happiness.[32]

During the early months of 1921, Grey fell in love with Louise Anderson, and his affair with this teenager toppled the quixotic balance of his life and sorely strained his marriage. Exactly where and when Grey met this attractive young woman is unclear, but she was the person who inspired this February 3, 1921, entry in his personal journal:

> It seems that I ought not to put off longer the great task of trying to record what a marvelous thing happened to me in New York, during the days Jan. 5 to 8. Even now I shall never be able to catch a thousandth part of the strength and strangeness and passion and splendor of my emotions . . . it is not possible even to estimate the magnitude or permanence of the emotions. But I must try now before the memory crystallizes into a less sharp unforgettable simplification of fact. I should have written it all out at the time. That however was impossible. . . .
>
>   This girl seemed a creature born of my imagination—a composite of Mescal [*The Heritage of the Desert*], Lucy [*The Spirit of the Border*], Fay Larkin [*Riders of the Purple Sage*], Allie Lee [*The U. P. Trail*], & Columbine [*The Mysterious Rider*], yet infinitely stronger and sweeter, and closer to me, than all of them. It seemed something long unconsciously waited for. Anyway, it came and life and sentiment was transformed, revived, intensified, beautiful beyond all words for me . . . the vision I see in my mind is one of loveliness—a slender, infinitely graceful girl, whose every line was beautiful—whose eyes were dark and eloquent, smoldering with latent fire—whose mouth was strangely sweet and sad, small, full-lipped, imperfect of contour—whose face was pale olive-dark, oval in shape, haunting with a beauty of youth, fire, discontent and melancholy—whose bonny head was small and sleek, covered with many tresses. . . . Whatever it was that happened was only a star on my horizon when I was lost in vague gloom. Whatever the folly of it, the pity of it, the strangeness and terror

Zane Grey and Louise Anderson, summer 1922. (Courtesy of Loren Grey.)

of it—it is true. By these things I know myself. And surely a little of my real nature dare appear in these records. Sometimes love and inspiration are synonymous in any faculty of creative labor. I began that way. So I must end. Then I have the boy's romance linked with the watered passion and wisdom of the years. What I needed I have found. How many · years have these notebooks recorded my agonies!

It does not matter about the fortunes of this last and crowning love of youth, beauty, life, nature, mystery as presented by this girl. I may never see her again or I may never have her affections. Or I may lose them and her. No matter what! A white living flame has come into my heart.[33]

Grey does not mention Louise by name here or in his other journal references to her, but following his visit to Zanesville, he did write in his secret code:

[I went there to meet Louise Anderson; never was there a sweeter or more fateful meeting.][34]

A month after his February 3 journal entry, Zane left Altadena for New York City. The ostensible reason for this quick return was a grand celebration that had been scheduled for him in Zanesville.[35] As he conferred with editors and readied himself for this first return to his hometown since the promotion of his first novel, Grey informed Dolly of his plan to bring Louise back with him to California for an extended visit. In her response, Dolly wrote, "Don't know that I can say much as regards your decision of bringing Miss A. back. It hit Dot pretty hard and I don't like it a bit." Dorothy was with Dolly at the Altadena residence, and both immediately comprehended the significance Zane's request that Dorothy be relocated into Ida's bedroom so that Louise could have a private room of her own. After cheerfully informing Zane she and Dorothy were having a good time together, Dolly admitted her disappointment that Zane had not taken her with him to the Zanesville celebration, and her suppressed anger came spilling out. Referencing a $10,000 check that accompanied his request that she "say a few calm, soothing words to Dot," she wrote, "Glad you place such value on my services. However, the things I've done for you can't be paid for in cash."[36]

During his Zanesville visit, Grey stayed with the Andersons, Louise's parents, and Mrs. Anderson hosted a reception for him and fifty former classmates.[37] In his journal, Grey wrote, "I was met at the station by an old friend—an old sweetheart (on my side, if not on hers)" and was taken to Maple Lawn Avenue where the Andersons lived.[38] Mrs. Anderson's death certificate reveals that she was born in Zanesville in 1873 (a year after Zane), that her given name was Nelly Dennis, and that she had a brother named Ralph.[39] In all likelihood, she was the Nelly from Grey's autobiography, whose brother Ralph circulated the lie that got him expelled from the dancing club. Angered by this injustice, Zane had given Ralph a thorough beating, and then unsuccessfully tried to win Nelly back by claiming that he "cared terribly" for her.[40] She is undoubtedly the one who mailed him a letter in November 1920 and was described in Grey's journal entry as "an old sweetheart, who in the tumultuous days of my youth, 30 years ago, turned cold eyes upon me when I needed friends, and encouragement and sympathy."[41] When they reconnected, whenever and wherever that was, Mrs. Anderson deployed her considerable charm to rekindle his adolescent feelings. When Zane did not respond, and she noticed his attraction to her precociously attractive daughter, she conspired to get them together.[42] For his Zanesville visit, she arranged for Louise to give a dramatic reading of a piece entitled "Gold" at a dinner party and for a newspaper announcement that Louise was going to California to "study literature under the direction of the noted author, Zane Grey."[43]

Zane's escalating involvement with Louise and her animated enthusiasm for everything he did quickly earned her the inauspicious nickname "Calamity" (as in "Calamity Jane"). She traveled with him back to California and remained there for the summer. During 1922, she accompanied Zane on his Long Key visit, went with him on a spring return to the Rainbow Bridge, and again spent the summer in Avalon. These adventures provoked a widening estrangement between Zane and Dolly. In May 1921, two months after Zane's return with Louise, Dolly left for her first significant trip without Zane. She took Betty and Loren with her for a cross-country drive, a summer stay in Lackawaxen, and a leisurely return. This trip included a stop in Zanesville during which she introduced herself as Mrs. Grey, and boldly corrected Zane's earlier exclusion of her. That fall, she wrote Zane, "But this—I beg of you—if you take the trip to N.Y., please go very soon after you get here. It is too hard for me—it's a situation to which I have never yet been able to callous myself—that of not seeing you for a long time & then when you come back, to have a snob around. It's requiring something almost superhuman of me! I can get away with the situation, but I suffer too much."[44]

A February 23, 1922, letter from Dolly to Zane in Long Key reveals other ways that this affair was unraveling their fragile accord. With a cheery opening to "Ducky Darling," she responds to a trip proposal in his previous letter: "Well, I'm glad you have so much enthusiasm. Whether it's good sense is another matter. It's nice of you to want to include me, but I don't think I could do it. In the first place, after being away from the kiddies so long, I'd be wild to get back to them." She voices concern that this trip could adversely affect his work schedule, and she urges him to keep that his top priority. "All your life," she advises, "you have pandered to your own desire. Pander now, for a little to your work. It will repay you so infinitely more so." To her closing protestation of love and longing for him, she adds more than a slight qualification: "The wildness is gone, the sex perhaps, the qualities in it that caused me bitterness and agony, (not altogether tho)."[45]

The waning of sexual relations between Dolly and Zane warranted only a passing comment here,[46] but over the next year, Dolly's uneasiness about the termination of their intimacy escalated into a fear that their much-tested marriage might be ending too. In the late spring of 1922, when Zane took Louise to the Rainbow Bridge, both Zane and Dolly were delinquent with their usual letters and when Dolly finally wrote on April 28, she charged Zane with distance and neglect:

> The fact of your having failed to write me from Kayenta as you had promised had a pretty bad effect on me—for of course I know the cause of your negligence. I'd climbed a long way up the hill to peace and happiness between us; but this thing caused me to take a tumble that hurt pretty badly. And it was some time before I could gather myself together to start climbing again. In my *fury* and resentment, I want to go tobogganing clear down to h—![47]

When Zane characterized Louise as "young and innocent" in a letter to Dolly, his thirty-nine-year-old wife shot back, "Bunk! I'm younger and innocenter than anyone you know, old dear! Do you remember the morning (in bed) when you said to me, 'Dolly, you're the youngest thing I know.' It's true absolutely. I know it, too. But don't fall in love with me again. I couldn't stand the shock!"[48] The ensuing fall, Dolly observed, "In the last seven months we've seen each other less than seven days—and the future doesn't promise much more." She then added, "I'm wondering whether we ought to keep up the physical during the negligible periods when we are together. I can't conceive how you can have any such emotion for me any more."[49]

Dolly's complaints had little effect upon Zane, and by the spring of 1923, she plunged into a Zane-like depression and decided that *she* now needed a trip to recover. On May 6, she informed him that she had played golf "to drive away some of the congestion from my brain," and she added that she had "been so seriously depressed that I saw a doctor about it."[50] This brief mention of her condition presumed that Zane knew about her dejection, and that these developments would not surprise him.[51] She also did not mention her hastily formulated trip plans. A week later, Dolly departed for a leisurely drive across the United States, a monthlong stay in Lackawaxen, a summer tour of Europe, and an automobile return that kept her away until the middle of October. By January 1923, Zane was sufficiently aware of this deepening rift to remark, "I fear my dear old Penelope is at last finding me not worth writing to or loving me any more."[52]

Zane's involvement with Louise produced other cracks in his base of support. Up to this point, Zane's paramours were limited to Dolly's relatives and kindred spirits. The surprising friendship that existed between Dolly and these women derived from their shared admiration for Zane's artistry and their commitment to doing all they could to alleviate his dark moods and to keep him productive. Likewise, their loyalty was sustained by his confessions of need and displays of gratitude for their help. However, Zane's defection to this much younger outsider left them feeling alienated, unappreciated, and resentful. Since her marriage to Westbrooke Robertson in November 1917, Lillian had remained close friends with Zane. He arranged a variety of art assignments for her in order to augment Robertson's meager salary from his administrative position with the U.S. Bureau of Indian Affairs. She prepared a series of colorful posters for the 1921 promotion of his novels. She also painted ornamental Indian figures on the walls of his Lackawaxen, Altadena, and Payson residences, and she was working on the library in Altadena when Zane first returned with Louise. She wrote to Claire, "Good 'ol Doc—I wonder if he remembers how lonely it was before poor Cal[amity] appeared on the scene. That's the worst of this old world, isn't it honey?— nothing lasts."[53] Though her own marriage to Robertson was disintegrating by this point, Lillian withheld her problems and kept a safe distance away from Zane. Lillian accompanied Zane on the 1922 trip to the Rainbow Bridge and another one a year later, but her handling of some business matters angered him and strained their relationship.[54]

Unlike Lillian, Claire opted to act upon her estrangement from Zane. Back in 1918, when Zane's attention had shifted to Dorothy, Claire was pained, but she accepted her displacement. She also remained a close friend of Dorothy, whom she considered a kindred spirit. Meanwhile, she met and fell in love with Phillips Carlin. By 1920, they were discussing marriage, but Carlin's shaky job delayed the actual wedding until June 1921. Since Claire did not have a job and always enjoyed Zane's outings, Phillips encouraged her to accept Zane's invitation to come to his new cabin near Payson for the fall 1921 hunting trip. However, Zane was unhappy over her marriage and made little effort to get along. Claire grew increasingly resentful of this slighting and of Zane's ongoing mistreatment of Dorothy, and she decided to exact revenge. Well aware of his intense dislike of flirting, she struck with devastating effectiveness. "The reason I busted camp," Zane wrote to Dolly, "was C's monkey-business with my hired men. I was disgusted. She is nuts where men are concerned, like her sister. That writes Finis for the Wilhelms for me."[55] A year later, after he learned that Dolly had allowed Claire the use of Lackawaxen while she was in Europe, Zane curtly informed Dolly, "I do not want Claire and her outfit in my house."[56]

When Zane brought Louise back to Altadena from the Zanesville celebration, Dorothy bolted for the East and left Zane with a big hole in his emotional life. During his winter visit to Long Key, he missed her enough that he enlisted Dolly to repair the breach. Since Dorothy and Elma were skilled typists and adept at transcribing his handwritten manuscripts, their alienation created a problem for Dolly as well. Her own trips would be jeopardized if she did not have reliable help for Zane. Nonetheless, she realized that a negotiated peace would be problematic at best, and she responded:

> Can't quite get my responsibility in the matter of making up to Elma and Dot what you impose on them in the case of Louise. . . . Darling, how do you get that way? In all seriousness, you put it to me. Well I don't know whether I want to bring them back with me. Of course, I know what's happened. You've told them and from now on, they'll plague you. They'd rather do that than go anywhere with you. But this is info to *me*. And I'll have to think real hard and lots of other things before I make a decision like that.[57]

Reluctantly, she persuaded Elma and Dot to return with her on the car trip back from the East. As she anticipated, Zane was offended by their altered responses to him, and Dolly turned a deaf ear to his complaints. His efforts to mollify them with extravagant accommodations and fancy clothes accomplished little, and then backfired when Dolly noticed the bills and dispatched an angry letter.[58] Wary of his adverse response to Claire's marriage, Elma intentionally kept him in the dark about her budding involvement with Fred Nagle, and quietly she prepared her own subversion for a later date.

Because Dorothy was "wistful and sad" over the Christmas holidays, Zane bought her an expensive brooch.[59] Initially she was overcome and became cheerful and animated again, but then restricted her availability. The week before his fall 1921 blowup with Claire, Zane wrote to Dolly from Arizona, "I've been having hell with the girls. E— has been hard to get along with. I have just about reached the end of my rope with her. And she has had a bad effect on D—. I might have to let D— go too. I refuse to be dictated to."[60]

* * *

Grey's women problems were matched by distress with his writing. His anguished state of mind generated corrosive doubts about his ability to sustain his phenomenal literary success and the writing schedule required by his contracts. In 1924, *Bookman* published an article entitled "Getting Into Six Figures" about Grey and several other best-selling authors. Its author, Arnold Patrick, provides unintended insight into the drift of Grey's tortured thinking. Most of the information in this broad-stroke portrait of Grey was gleaned from publisher promotions and convenient newspaper files, but Patrick justifies his recycling with an introductory reflection on Grey's popularity. "Of the work of all living novelists," he asserts,"Mr. Grey's books taken as a whole probably have the widest sale and the greatest reading public." This causes him to ponder how few writers ever make the best-seller list, and among those who do, the even fewer who manage a repeat appearance. As he explains:

> Public fancy is hard to capture and, once gained, even more difficult to hold. The life of any sort of author is not easy; but the life of a successful author is fraught with many perils. He stands in constant fear of losing his great audience. He may turn it away by some thoughtless act of his life which puts him into the limelight and destroys a popular illusion concerning him. His viewpoint may change, so that whatever the magic of his writing was, it vanishes—and he always knows that it will take perhaps only one dull book to drive away his following.[61]

During this discussion, Patrick provides his reader a list of contemporary repeaters—Gene Stratton-Porter, James Oliver Curwood, Peter B. Kyne, Joseph C. Lincoln, and Frances Hodgson Burnett. Patrick was citing authors who were at the time almost as well-known as Grey, but today their names read like material for a quiz on the arcane, and serve as a bracing reminder of how ephemeral best-seller success truly is.

Grey began to worry about this problem during his January 1923 trip to Long Key. At first, all was well. There he was able to write in uncharacteristically "good spirit, with a slow sure grip on myself," and to make great progress on *The Code of the West*.[62] During a seat-flattening session of thirteen hours on his fifty-first birthday, Grey completed the novel.[63] Eager to capitalize on his exceptional productivity, he decided to push ahead with a new work to be entitled *The Thundering Herd,* but soon found himself unable to continue. Two weeks later, he was gripped by one of his depressions. In a rare journal entry that went beyond his normally terse mention of whether his writing was going well or poorly, he reflected, "There is something wrong with me. This time is it development or retrogration?"[64]

This doubt was prompted and aggravated by unfavorable reviews for his most recent novels and a percolating worry that he might be losing touch with his readership. *The Day of the Beast* (1922) was the completed version of *Shores of Lethe,* a novel that Grey had worked on prior to his marriage and unsuccessfully revised at least four more times. His most recent rewrite during 1921 represented a fierce determination to finish his novel of social criticism and to speak out about current social conditions. Like *The Desert of Wheat, Beast* features a protagonist, Daren Lane, who gets badly wounded in World War I. As in many Hemingway stories, this physical wounding acquires a psychological dimension as Lane has to reckon with radically altered postwar conditions and values, which has the effect of worsening his illness. Lane is a native of Middleville, a thinly disguised version of Middletown, where Grey had been so depressed over his mother's death and the unfolding war. He valiantly enlists to fight in order to protect the women of his hometown, but his wounding sends him back home and transforms his battle into one against disillusionment. Grey utilized Lane's return to attack the modernization that had been troubling him for years. Although his sweeping condemnation of emergent Jazz Age conditions is not surprising, his preoccupation with the promiscuity of young women and harsh denunciation of it is. Initially, Daren is bothered that the town's fifteen- to eighteen-year-old women care nothing about the war or his efforts on their behalf. He is upset more to learn that they are interested only in smoking, drinking, petting, and, almost worst of all, the widespread use of cosmetics. Having made themselves as alluring as possible, these sirens have no qualms about hopping into a car with a single male and going off to park outside of town. Daren doesn't speculate about what they do, but he imagines the worst. At one point when he believes that his sister has gone off to park with a rival, he is so enraged that he goes after them with his military revolver. Luckily, he discovers that the girl is not his sister and does not kill her male companion. Dancing upsets Daren as much as cosmetics and automobiles, and he believes that it excites participants into a sexual frenzy that leads to parking.

What was Zane thinking? Perhaps more accurately, was he thinking about his own involvement with Louise? Had he written the book after he had broken up with Louise, it might have made sense, but writing the book just before he met Louise and during the period of his most intense involvement bespeaks a strange psychology. This is especially true of his phobia about dancing. Back in 1915, shortly after meeting Dorothy Ackerman at a dance in Middletown, Zane took her dancing several more times, and afterward wrote in his journal:

> I have been going out with D— to dances and am enjoying myself and making pleasure for her. . . . My conscience is not wholly clear, but I seem to scorn the idea that *I* could stoop to feel a sensuous pleasure in the embrace of a pretty girl in a dance. That seems cheap to me. But it may be true. I certainly have been infatuated with dancing with several of these younger girls, and I am little ashamed of it. On the other hand, I enjoy a good dance and a good dancer, entirely apart from the sensual appeal.[65]

Both Dolly and his editors at Harpers had urged Zane not to publish *The Day of the Beast.* In April 1922, when it began to run as a serial in the *Country Gentleman,* Dolly reported that the reception was very negative, and she went on to explain, "They (his editors) don't want you in the reform class. Your public for Western fiction is absolutely universal, from the child to old men and women."[66] But Zane insisted upon publication of the book anyway. Weak reviews and lackluster sales kept *The Day of the Beast* off the annual best-seller list for 1922, and made it the first of his last six novels not to make the list. The reviewer for the *New York Times* was typical in his proclamation that "in none of the factors of fictional excellence does it compare favorably with his previous work."[67] Though warned of this prospect and therefore prepared, Zane was nonetheless dispirited.

His next offering, *Wanderer of the Wasteland* (1923), was undertaken and completed with much higher hopes. While the serial version was being prepared for publication, his editors at Harpers decided that the book was flabby and advised him to eliminate a hundred pages. He immediately responded that this request was the "hardest—the most heartless, stultifying, demeaning, and alienating shock I have ever sustained,"[68] but reluctantly he cut 60,000 words. When the novel came out in January 1923, Grey was in Long Key. Though he was sent only a few reviews, the criticism was harsh enough that he could no longer dismiss the flaying of *The Day of the Beast* as the consequence of a wrong turn. The reviewer for the *Boston Transcript* wrote:

> There is a fundamental simplicity about Mr. Grey's novels. They require all the attention of the reader, because of the excitement of the plot, but they do not leave him with any problem to consider. Undoubtedly Mr.

> Grey has found the secret of his own success to lie in his appeal to the child qualities in the minds of grown men and women. He asks them to give him their attention but he does not ask them to think for themselves.[69]

The reviewer for the Brooklyn *Daily Eagle* claimed that Grey had "dragged [his] story through the turgid waters of inanity," and he reiterated the *Transcript*'s indictment of Grey's readership with an assertion that "morons will flock to purchase this drivel."[70]

In spite of these criticisms, *Wanderer* reached the best-seller list, but *Bookman*'s listing of it at number three for March 1923 was accompanied by the following explanation: "Zane Grey has another book out; naturally it jumps from nowhere to a place very near the top of the list. If this proves anything it would seem to be that the age of realism in American literature has not yet quite arrived. A great many persons, apparently, still believe in fairies."[71]

The most worrisome review was one written by Burton Rascoe for the *New York Tribune* that anticipated *Bookman*'s assessment and probably influenced it, since it appeared several weeks before. Rascoe was a distinguished reviewer, and, up to this point, reviewers of his stature had treated Grey's novels as unworthy of notice. He broke with this stonewalling, and awarded *Wanderer* a long review. His avoidance of criticism throughout most of the review implied a circumspect and favorable estimate. However, the closing paragraphs reveal this to have been a setup for a final withering assault:

> But do Mr. Grey's readers believe in the existence of such people as Mr. Grey depicts; do they accept the code of conduct implicit in Mr. Grey's novels; do they like to think that in similar situations they would act as Adam does? If they do I bow my head in ignorance and in humility. I have been among ranchmen and cowboys of the Southwest and I have never seen such purple cows. I hope I never see one, but I can tell you, anyhow, I'd rather see than be one.[72]

The Literary Digest judged Rascoe's review important enough to reprint it in an abbreviated version. This was introduced with an account of the novel's sale of 100,000 copies "before publication" and Harpers' expectation to sell three times that number the first year after its appearance in print. Noting that "there is no better seller in America," the *Digest* presented Grey's success so that it worked *against* him. Given the enormous audience predisposed toward any new Grey offering, the *Digest* proposed its reprint of Rascoe's article as an experiment to see "how he [Grey] strikes a sophisticated editor of a New York newspaper . . . [who] comes from that part of the country dealt with in the story, and he brings a fresh appreciation of the author."[73] Unlike the other reviews of Grey's work, Rascoe's was much noticed and discussed within publishing circles. Two years later, when continuing criticism provoked Grey to respond with a piece entitled "My Answer to the Critics" that Dolly opposed and he elected not to publish, *Wanderer of the Wasteland* was one of the few novels that he specifically mentioned, and he did so only to comment upon Rascoe's review:

> He took me seriously. He really read my book. He wrote a wonderful review, which, as I perused it, seemed to repay me for all the stings and arrows of outrageous criticism. I believed my justification had come. I was unutterably grateful. But—the very end—in the last paragraph—he spoiled it all; he crucified me by saying he could not believe in purple cows.
> To such ends do brilliant critics stoop![74]

Though conditioned to negative assessments of his work, Grey believed that the reviews of *Wanderer* were exceptionally harsh. The assault of the critics upon his readers as devoid of intelligence threatened to drive them elsewhere. For over a year, he had been noticing an emerging bias within literary circles for a new realism sharply at odds with the pronounced romanticism of his work. Back in March of 1921, he had commented to Dolly about Sinclair Lewis's *Main Street* (1920): "It is interesting realism of commonplace, vulgar, raw people. I really think it is a big book. But it is disappointing, of course, most of all real life is. Not one of the heroines' dreams or ideals ever come true. . . . I dare say the critics give it place far ahead of mine. Why? Why do the critics repudiate romance?"[75] Grey accumulated so much experience as support and inspiration for his romantic novels that he considered them as realistic as they needed to be.

Immediately following his journal notation that "there is something wrong with me" and his questioning of whether his new novel was "development or retrogration," Grey mentioned that he had read Warner Fabian's popular, widely reviewed *Flaming Youth* (1923), and proceeded to discuss the agitated thinking that it provoked:

> What is the younger generation to me? Or rather what *was* it to me? My distress, or part of its origin, may be traced to the secret hidden in the above. There is no longer any use in deceiving myself. Developments of the last year or two, perhaps longer, have stricken me to the heart. What was the younger generation to me? It would take a volume to answer that.[76]

That Zane was upset with the sensational realism of *Flaming Youth* is not surprising. This controversial novel offered an eye-opening look at the emergent

Jazz Age and its radical alteration of the ways men and women related. The author, Warner Fabian, a pseudonym for Samuel Hopkins Adams, a reputable writer from Boston whose books had not sold well, later explained: "I knew it was a book that could make a helluva of a lot of money, but I didn't want my name on it."[77]

Flaming Youth was the *Primary Colors* of its day, although its inflammatory exposé of contemporary mores avoided politics. The chief character, Mona Fentriss, is the mother of three attractive teenagers. She is thirty-seven years old, but still beautiful, especially to her many male admirers. She is receptive to their advances and open to where they lead. For her, doing as one pleases is more important than doing as one should. At one point she asserts, "Don't you know better, after all these years, than to try to keep me from doing anything I want to do? I always get what I want" (9). When questioned about expectations for her daughters, she replies, "Not goodness; that's for plain girls. Nor virtue, particularly; that's more or less of a scarecrow. I want happiness for them" (80).

A significant portion of the novel is devoted to an objective, nonjudgmental account of the activities of the three daughters. They are free to do as they please and naturally inclined to be like their mother. They go out without chaperones, drink, smoke, and actively participate in petting parties. They engage in sex before marriage and afterward with men who are not their husbands. The conniving charm of these women endows them with power and they do not hesitate to use it. One states, "I've always done exactly what I liked and never done anything I didn't like" (164). When they find true love, they consummate it—or, more accurately, they have sex and discover love. The reader is oriented to this new thinking by one character's question, "But how am I to tell whether I am or not (in love) without letting him make love to me?" (210).

The fates of these women could have been used to indict their mother as a disastrous parent. Her two older daughters wind up in loveless marriages and one elects to have an abortion when she becomes pregnant. However, these melodramatic elements are ostentatiously purged of the condemnation that traditionally attended them. As presented, they are the facts of life.

The overt sexuality of Fabian's novel was particularly troubling to Grey because of the operative assumption that women should make their own decisions and rely on *their* wants as determinants. If Grey was attracted to the young "Calamity" because she reassured him that young people were still impressed with his novels and with his dedication to outdoor adventure, the criticism of his recent work and the attention lavished upon *Flaming Youth* left him unsure and worried. For years Grey had been insisting that women inspired his writing, but this thinking took a strange turn in his answer to the question "What is the younger generation to me?"

> But it can be partly answered by splitting the younger generation in half— keeping only the feminine. . . . I do not deplore so much the loss of—whatever it was that this generation held for me as I do the incontrovertible truth of materialism. I cannot feel longer that I am writing to a legion of eager romance loving dreaming girls. The movie, the motor car, the jazz and dance, the suggestive magazine and novel, have done away with that type. I am a faint little voice in the cataclysmic roar of the age![78]

What could have caused him to think of the readership for his Westerns as "a legion of eager romance loving dreaming girls"? Was this not a paranoia resulting from the recent defection of his girlfriends and his aversion for the unfolding Jazz Age? Were Grey's readers not male and solidly committed to the manly actions celebrated in his books? Perhaps, but he also knew that women *were* a major component of his readership, and he was justifiably worried about the sensational appeal of *Flaming Youth*.

Back in January of 1920 when he negotiated his lucrative, long-term contract with the Curtis Publishing Company, Grey was dealing with Barton Currie, the current editor of the *Country Gentleman*. Later that same year, Curtis promoted Currie to head editor of its *Ladies' Home Journal*. Keenly aware of Grey's contribution to the success of the *Country Gentleman,* Currie wanted Grey to come with him. To accomplish this, he wooed him with a sweetened contract that doubled his $15,000 fee for a forthcoming serialization of *To the Last Man* in the *Country Gentleman* and thereby tripled the $10,000 that he received only the year before.[79] When Grey accepted, Currie urged that he keep the readership for *Ladies' Home Journal* in mind when writing his next novel. The result was *The Call of the Canyon,* which commenced with the November 1921 issue.[80]

The Call of the Canyon features a woman from the East as the lead character and was meant to be an updating of *The Light of Western Stars*. Like *The Day of the Beast,* it is also set in the present, and contains impassioned attacks upon postwar American culture. Carley Burch is a wealthy young New Yorker who enjoys the liberated life of a typical flapper. When her fiancé, Glenn, returns from war wounded and troubled, he is so upset by Carley and the altered conditions of life in Eastern cities that he flees to the West. There he meets the loving, rustic Flo Hunter whose hard elemental life bears more than a little resemblance to Lillian's, and Flo provides Glenn the therapeutic healing that was by this point an overworked convention.

Carley decides that she likes Glenn well enough to visit him in Arizona. Surprisingly, she dislikes most of what she encounters, and she adamantly refuses to adjust or change. To a local dance she wears a fashionable, revealing dress that provokes Glenn to remark, "But, Carley, the cut of that—or rather the abbreviation of it—inclines me to think that style for women's clothes has not changed for the better. In fact, it's worse than two years ago in Paris and later in New York. Where will you women draw the line?" (42). Her disregard for this warning gets her assaulted by an uncouth local. When she declares him "crazy," the local explains, "Nope, I'm not crazy, 'an I shore said invitation . . . I meant thet white shimmy dress you wore the night of Flo's party. Thet's my invitation to get a little fresh with you, Pretty Eyes!" (148).

Frustrated by such problems, Carley goes back to New York City, but she finds herself discontented there. Her return to the West and bonding with Flo awaken her to the error of her Eastern outlook. When she subsequently encounters several women like her former self, Carley launches into a vitriolic tirade, much longer than the following excerpt that, like *Beast,* decries developments that were bringing about social change and undoing the taboos that pressued Grey to hide his secret life:

> "Nothing wrong!" cried Carley. "Listen. Nothing wrong in you or life today—nothing for you women to make right? You are blind as bats—as dead to living truth as if you were buried. . . . Nothing wrong when these young adolescent girls ape *you* and wear stockings rolled under their knees below their skirts and use a lip stick and paint their faces and darken their eyes and pluck their eyebrows and absolutely do not know what shame is? Nothing wrong when you may find in any city women standing at street corners distributing booklets on birth control? Nothing wrong when great magazines print no page or picture without its sex appeal? Nothing wrong when the automobile presents the greatest evil that ever menaced American girls? . . . Nothing wrong when some husbands spend more of their time with other women than with you? Nothing wrong with jazz—where the lights go out in the dance hall and dancers jiggle and toddle and wiggle in a frenzy. . . . Nothing wrong with you women who cannot or will not stand childbirth? . . . You doll women, you parasites, you toys of men, you silken-wrapped geisha girls, you painted, idle, purring cats, you parody of the females of your species—find brains enough if you can to see the doom hanging over you and revolt before it is too late!" (247–49)

Diatribe supplants story in this embarrassing transformation of Carley into the woman Glenn wants and finally marries. As an outpouring of the social protest that had been festering within Grey for years, this rant sorely lacked analysis and serious thought. Grey failed to realize that his girlfriends had more in common with the new women he was attacking than with the increasingly dated heroines of his stories. At the time that he created them, Betty Zane and Madeline Hammond were strong women ahead of the times, but by the 1920s, conduct like theirs had grown old-fashioned. Grey's efforts to keep his secret life out of his Westerns produced a strident, dissonant voice riven with conflict when it finally spoke. Not only did this outburst expose how reactionary Zane had become but, even worse, it also revealed that the capitulation of his long-standing alienation to the expectations of his culture had left him out of touch with it. Having a hidden life more attuned to the Jazz Age than the editors of *Success* magazine ever imagined, Grey responded to those conditions with anachronistic condemnation.

Although the final installment of *The Call of the Canyon* ran in *Ladies' Home Journal* in March 1922, the novel version did not appear until January 1924. By June 1923, Grey was filled with misgivings about the novel's looming publication. If *Flaming Youth* caused Grey to worry that *Call* might be behind the times when it appeared, *The Code of the West,* which he was completing when he read *Flaming Youth,* intensified this anxiety. Rascoe's denunciation of "the code of conduct implicit in Mr. Grey's novels" made this title a poor choice. However, the story line was an even greater problem. Georgiana is the lead character and an obvious variation of Carley. She is sent West to live with her sister by her mother who worries about her flirtatious behavior and hopes the West will cure her. Unfortunately, Georgiana, like Carley, is too accustomed to the behavior she has learned in the East. Her openness to kissing fosters fights, firings, and rumors of promiscuity. In order to save her and her reputation, a cowboy named Cal Thurmond forces her to marry him. This makes Georgiana very unhappy, but she eventually discovers that he is a fine person and that he really does love her. Gradually she learns to give into love and to relinquish her foolish ways. Her concluding assertion "I want to be your real wife!" completes her conversion into a Westerner. When he was working on *Code,* Zane did not worry about this novel's pronounced resemblance to *Call* because it was contracted to run in the *Country Gentleman,* not *Ladies' Home Journal.* However, this carryover helps to explain why *The Code of the West* was the first of his serializations not to follow as a novel. Harpers elected not to publish *Code,* and this Western did not appear as a book until almost a decade later.

* * *

Ironically, the third reason for Grey's distress was his compulsive fishing, which had been a long-standing source of consolation. Most of the trips mentioned in his interview for *Success* involved fishing. For years, Grey had been defending these trips as a necessary stimulus for his writing. Besides using them to escape from the demands and distractions of home life, he believed that his articles about his experiences bolstered his reputation as a sportsman and validated his authority on matters relating to the outdoors. However, his mounting investment of time, effort, and money in his fishing adventures produced problems other than Dolly's complaints. His determination to be innovative and accomplished made him increasingly competitive, contentious, and disliked.

On July 26, 1920, during his summer stay at Avalon, Grey landed his second broadbill, an impressive 418-pound specimen that challenged him with a grueling ten-hour battle. The only larger broadbill that had been caught with tackle was the 462-pound monster W. C. Boschen boated in 1917. Grey's catch justified his preparatory regimen of rigorous physical exercise and his hyperbolic proclamation: "Let no fisherman imagine that he can land a fighting swordfish with soft hands."[81] Grey was so exhilarated that he declared this battle to be the most taxing of all his adventures so far:

> R. C. and I believe that the 1920 season was not only the hardest ordeal we ever endured, but the most dangerous experience of any kind we ever had. Lassoing mountain lions, hunting the grizzly bear, and stalking the fierce tropical jaguar, former pastimes of ours, are hardly comparable to the pursuit of *Xiphias gladius*. It takes more time, patience, endurance, study, skill, nerve, and strength, not to mention money, of any game known to me through the experience of reading.[82]

Grey's triumph vindicated his repeated claims that *Xiphias gladius* was the most challenging game fish in the ocean and so increased the stature of the broadbill that the Tuna Club felt pressured to reconsider its bias toward tuna.

This success inspired Grey to acquire a special boat for broadbill. Even though he had already spent a staggering amount during 1920 on his properties in Avalon, Altadena, and Arizona, he wanted this boat too badly to hold back or economize.[83] After obtaining a set of blueprints that accommodated his special needs, he took them to the Wilmington (California) firm of Fellows and Stewart and contracted for the boat to be finished for the next season.

Residents of Catalina had witnessed more and more powerboats over the preceding five years. Claire's record of changes in 1920 begins: "All summer long the bay has been full of boats—yachts and launches and skiffs of every description. The island seems to have drawn a bigger and gayer crowd this year."[84] This surge of boatbuilding was started by fishermen and driven by revolutionary fishing tactics. George Michaelis's *Juanita,* Tad Gray's *Ramona,* and James Jump's *Ranger* confirmed the greater range and maneuverability of these boats, and altered the relationship of boatmen to their clients.[85] As wealthy members of the Tuna Club acquired powerboats of their own and contracted captains for them, other boatmen were pressured into acquiring new boats in order to preserve their business and independence.

Like these other fishermen, Grey had his new boat designed to take full advantage of the latest tactics, tackle, and boat technology. The expensive new powerboats also offered important statements about their owners' success. In 1921, when Wrigley started bringing his Chicago Cubs to Catalina for spring training, the "gayer crowd" noticed by Claire quickly became more evident and more ostentatious. The prominent businessmen and Hollywood celebrities drawn to the island were buying boats to keep others apprised of their wealth and success.

Since his return to Catalina in 1914, Grey had regularly hired Captain O. I. Danielson and repeatedly mentioned both him and his wonderful boat in his articles.[86] In 1920, this association suddenly ended. In one of his published articles, Grey explained that this parting was caused by his late arrival and an unexpected surge of demand that had most of the captains already contracted,[87] but the true reason for the split was Danielson's acquisition of a new boat. At the end of the 1919 season, Danielson decided that his *Leta D* was sufficiently outdated to arrange for Fellows and Stewart to build him a new *Leta D II.*[88] Arthur Parsons and Dan Phillips, two wealthy businessmen-turned-fishermen, financed this purchase in order to lure Danielson away from Grey.[89] Grey was not especially bothered over the loss of Danielson; his published references to Danielson contain telltale hints of friction with him. On the other hand, the hiring away of Danielson by fellow Tuna Club members *was* upsetting.

In his article entitled "Xiphias Gladius," Grey claimed that he hired Sid Boerstler as a replacement for Danielson because Boerstler lacked broadbill experience and Grey wanted someone he could train.[90] Actually, Boerstler was both an accomplished boatman and a second choice. During May, Zane fished with A. E. Eaton and became frustrated when Eaton's smelly, old, unreliable *Leona* kept breaking down.[91] Grey decided to hire Boerstler because of his *Blue Fin* not just because the boat was more reliable, but also because it had recently been built for him by Fellows and Stewart.[92] Fellows and Stewart was not the only boatbuilding company in southern California, but it definitely commanded the greatest respect among Catalina fishermen. As the name of his boat implies, Boerstler thought of himself as a tuna fisherman, but his willingness to deploy his skills and new boat according to Grey's wishes enabled them to catch more marlin than any other boat their first year together.[93] By season's end, Grey was so convinced of the advantages of the *Blue Fin* that he contracted Boerstler to work for him exclusively, and then arranged for Fellows and Stewart to build him an even better powerboat of his own.

Grey wanted his *Gladiator* to avenge the piracy of Danielson, to proclaim his success as a writer, and, most of all, to make him Catalina's most accomplished fisherman. Its name, derived from the broadbill's Latin designation *Xiphias gladius,* was meant to broadcast Grey's recent decision to "fish exclusively for swordfish."[94] The surviving records of Fellows and Stewart furnish revealing insights into his thinking about this project. The contracts for the *Leta D II* and *Blue Fin* have disappeared, but they undoubtedly resembled the boat ordered by George Farnsworth, the most respected among Catalina's captains. He was at the helm when Boschen landed his record broadbill, and Boschen bequeathed $10,000 to him when he died suddenly and unexpectedly in 1918.[95] The contract for Farnsworth's *Grey Gull* specified a twenty-eight-foot launch that cost $4,300. The contract Grey signed on October 7, 1920, called for construction of a fifty-three-foot hull. The $9,000 requested in that contract paid only for the wooden frame and shell. On December 15, 1920, Grey agreed to pay an additional $7,260 for furnishings, fittings, and motor.[96]

The *Gladiator* was meant to make a big impression, and it did. The boat was the talk of Avalon well before its arrival on April 11, 1921, and that event occasioned a centrally positioned article and accompanying photograph on the front page of the *Islander,* the local newspaper. This article recounted the innovations pioneered by Catalina fishermen as important background to the significance of this new boat: "There seemed nothing more to be desired. But now comes the fifty-three-foot palatial craft of Zane Grey, fitted with every contrivance that the builders, Fellows & Stewart, and angling experience could suggest. . . . It marks a new era in fishing enthusiasm."[97] R. C., again with Zane's assistance, would bolster this promotion with an article for *Field and Stream* entitled "Tuna Fishing Yesterday and Today." Opening with a recollection of the dories from a decade before, it summarizes the history

Launch of the Gladiator *at Fellows and Stewart Shipyard, San Pedro, California, March 1921. (Courtesy of Dan Brock.)*

of the powerboat's radical alteration of sportfishing. Again the *Gladiator* is characterized as new zenith in the surge of boat building.[98]

Mindful of the risk in these ambitious claims, Grey was determined that his *Gladiator* deliver. Consequently, on June 19, after battling a giant broadbill for seven and one-half hours until it broke free, Grey quickly informed the local newspaper of his epic contest. With another front-page photograph of the *Gladiator* topped by the headline "Deep Sea Battle Catalina," the *Islander* reported: "If the true fish tale is ever written of the thrilling fight with a monster swordfish that lasted more than seven and a half hours, the writer of western fiction will tell of the hope and expectancy, the extensive preparation, the long search and fruitless efforts; then of the grueling misery and physical torment that all resulted from a thread that was strained."[99] Over that same summer, Zane, R. C., and Boerstler boated many marlin, but the broadbill lived up to its reputation for elusiveness. The big one that got away remained their greatest success.[100]

On October 13, 1921, two weeks after Grey and his friend, "Lone Angler" Wiborn, left to go hunting in Arizona, Mrs. Keith Spalding landed a 426-pound broadbill after a fight of an hour and twenty minutes. Her fish surpassed Grey's

1920 catch by eight pounds. Although it did not outweigh Boschen's record broadbill, hers was four and a half inches longer.[101] Though mismatched against her enormous adversary, Mrs. Spalding had substantial experience and verified skill. Born Eudora Hull, she had inherited the 5,000-acre Rancho Sespe near Pasadena, and later donated much of the property for Cal Tech's campus. She was married to Keith Spalding, who had come to California ten years before from Chicago where his family owned the A. G. Spalding Sporting Goods Company.[102] His future wife interested him in Catalina, and both became avid anglers. The year before her record broadbill, she caught a 116.5-pound tuna that should have qualified for a blue button because she followed club regulations for tackle and tactics.[103] However, she was not a member because the club did not admit women, and this policy was not changed when her husband was elected president of the club in 1921.[104]

The ripples set off by "the little lady and her big fish" spread to the mainland, where the *Los Angeles Examiner* made Mrs. Spalding's catch into a front-page story spoofing the sport's macho biases:

> Men, it's happened at last!
> Take off your hats and hand the angler's laurels to a member of the fair sex, and boast no more of the fish you've hooked . . . what makes the triumph all the greater for the gentler sex lies in the fact that Zane Grey, noted writer, and Arthur Parsons, wealthy San Francisco manufacturer, have been fishing all year for a broadbill with only a coat of sunburn to reward them for their efforts.[105]

A contemporary reader of *Field and Stream* might have expected the Grey brothers to be strong supporters of Mrs. Spalding's achievement. The July 1921 issue of the magazine had carried a lead article by R. C. entitled "Sea Fishing for Women," and his position was very similar to that of the *Examiner*. "The day has come when men can no longer corner outdoor sports nor hold all the records for outdoor achievements," it begins. "Women have taken their stand beside men in the open with the same success that they have met in the world of affairs. We are proud of them!"[106] After mentioning the large fish that Mrs. R. C. Grey had caught, the account dwells on the even bigger fish landed by "Miss Dorothy." With accompanying photographs of a fetching Dorothy Ackerman, the discussion recounts her success with sea bass and tuna. There is even a photograph of a long expanse of beach with a skirted figure in the distance that could have illustrated Grey's journal description of his walk there with her. Zane was indeed proud of his venturesome companion and her fishing successes.[107]

Mrs. Keith Spalding and her broadbill (426 pounds), Catalina,
October 13, 1921. (Courtesy of Mike Farrior, Tuna Club)

Since he was hunting in Arizona when Mrs. Spalding caught her broadbill, Grey did not learn about it until his November return, and the only record of his reaction dates from months later. In late June 1922, Dustin Farnum and Nelson Howard encountered him on the streets of Avalon and asked his opinion of Mrs. Spalding's catch. He replied that she was neither big enough nor strong enough to land such a huge fish. He maintained that her boatman, K. S. Walker, deserved most of the credit because he had maneuvered his boat to deliver the bait and then backed up to the hooked fish and gaffed it before it realized the threat and initiated a fight.[108] Although Grey was repeating what other fishermen had already said, he was speaking carelessly to Tuna Club members who disliked him and his outspoken opinions.

On July 1, Howard reported Grey's remarks to the board and called for a censure. After discussion of the problem and the awkward facts that Mrs. Spalding was married to the current club president but was not a club member, the board approved a motion that Grey be summoned to a special meeting on July 3rd.[109] In an account of this incident that was first published only four years ago, Grey wrote:

> I was not long in sensing the hostility of the majority of them, and that here, for them, was a welcome opportunity. . . . I must say that they tried to make the hearing rational and fair, but their voices were drowned in the insults of Mr. Howard and the ridicule of Mr. Ray Thomas. It was all so astonishing to me that I could not have said a word, even if they had given me a chance. I was not a practical person and knew little or nothing about business meetings and conferences. I was not slow to grasp, however, the hatred and maliciousness manifest by them.[110]

Nonetheless, Grey conceded the accuracy of Howard's report and his lack of proof for his claims. The board demanded that Grey retract his remarks and send Mrs. Spalding an apology. "Considering that the defendant was a lady," Grey explained, "and one whose courage I admired, I decided on that score to retract and apologize."[111]

Grey's account and surviving Tuna Club records agree on the main components of this episode, but differ sharply on what happened next. Grey claimed that he resigned the next day.[112] Tuna Club records show that he did not actually resign until March 31, 1923, a full eight months later.[113]

At the time of the club's censure, Grey's thinking gravitated to his longstanding membership in this prestigious organization and its enormous influence upon the history and development of sport fishing. Despite his complaints about the damage of commercial fishing, Catalina still had the most challenging fishing in the United States, and the club was central to that challenge. Even though Zane had long disliked the Tuna Club's stuffiness, elitism, and intense competition, Catalina and the club were key factors in his 1918 relocation to California and his 1920 decision to purchase a residence in Avalon. Belatedly, he realized that he had offended many Club members with his published characterization of Boschen as an angler who "horses in [a fish] before he wakes up to real combat," and his statement that Boschen's record broadbill offered no fight because he had been hooked in the heart.[114] Anonymous phone calls following Mrs. Spalding's catch urging Grey to try Jergens, a popular hand lotion for women, caused him to realize the hostility and jealousy that his fishing articles had provoked. Locals as well as club members believed that Grey's success as a writer got his articles published and that he did not merit the reputation they had brought him. When Will Dilg's wife wrote an article about Mrs. Spalding's catch and published it in her husband's *Izaak Walton League Monthly*, Grey was so outraged that he nearly ended his friendship with Dilg and his support for the league.[115] Amid the agitation of the moment, Grey decided that he did not want Mrs. Spalding's fish and these annoyances to spoil everything. Club affiliation was too important to both himself and Dolly for him to contest the decision, refuse to comply, or terminate his association.

But the animosity and humiliation inherent in the board's action left Grey with festering resentment and second thoughts. The 1922 season added to his frustration. Although they hooked numerous broadbills, neither he nor R. C. landed one. The *Islander* reported that R. C. had lost his seventh broadbill that year.[116] Ever since R. C. had caught seven marlin in a single day back in 1918, his persistent failure with broadbill provoked worsening embarrassment.

By season's end, Grey was convinced that the Tuna Club's rule limiting the strongest line to twenty-four threads was unfair and outdated. Ever since the Tuna Club was founded, fishing lines had been made from interwoven strands of linen thread; more threads made the line stronger, but also less maneuverable. Because many threaded lines were unwieldy and allowed fish little chance to escape, Tuna Club founders established rules that cued the number of threads to the size of the fish and limited the largest usable line to twenty-four threads.

Back in 1917 when he caught his first broadbill, Grey was a solid supporter of the Tuna Club's rules about line. During his 1918 visit to Long Key, he made a concerted effort to use "light tackle," involving 9-thread line, and was so successful that he wrote several articles encouraging fishermen to use it.[117]

That same year, he founded the Long Key Fishing Club, and in his role as its first president, established several buttons for light tackle. However, his intensifying quest for broadbill and his belief that they could reach a thousand pounds convinced him that anglers could not land a potential record if they were restricted to 24-thread lines. This thinking placed him at odds with Catalina anglers who were moving toward even lighter tackle. Support was building within the Club, and outside as well, for a revival of the defunct "Light Tackle Club" that favored "3-6" (6-thread line, 6-foot rod, 6-oz. tip). James Jump's remarkable success with fewer thread lines convinced locals that he represented the future for sportfishing.

The Spalding matter left Grey determined to act on behalf of his controversial beliefs. Starting with the 1923 season, come what may, he resolved to fish a 39-thread line for broadbill. As support for his rebellious course, Grey commissioned J. A. Coxe to build him a special 18/0 reel. If his main objective was a quality reel capable of holding 400 yards of 39-thread line, he also wanted it to surpass the currently available products. Several years before, Coxe was sufficiently disenchanted with vom Hofe's highly respected B-Ocean reel that he designed a reel that functioned better and was more resistant to breakdown.[118]

By 1923, Coxe had been making reels for only two years, but they were already superior to the B-Ocean.[119] The one Grey commissioned involved greater complexity; the intricacy and precision of its gearing was watchlike. For years, it would be his personal favorite. Coxe built only one more of these reels, which he kept on display in his shop, and that one has disappeared. The $1,500 that Grey paid Coxe would make it an expensive reel today, but perhaps the best measure of this price at the time is the fact that Grey could have purchased five new Model-T Fords with that same amount and still had money left over.[120] Here was another example of his willingness to spend exorbitant sums on innovative products for his avid pursuit of big fish.

During the early spring of 1923, Zane was invited to add his name to the list of prominent anglers who supported "The Light Tackle Club" and he pointedly refused.[121] When he later learned that the Tuna Club had appointed a tackle committee to review the current regulations, he submitted a petition requesting that the club allow 39-thread for large swordfish, large tuna, and broadbill. At a meeting on February 12, the tackle committee affirmed its long-standing rule that limited heavy tackle to "24 thread linen line manufactured from the grade of linen yarn known in the trade as 'No. 50.'"[122] Grey was not surprised, but he knew that the time for him to quit had arrived. On March 15, 1923, two months before Dolly left for Lackawaxen and Europe, Grey resigned from the Tuna Club.[123] Unlike Zane, his brother R. C. was both liked and respected as a fisherman by the club membership, but his long-standing loyalty to his brother and his dependency upon Zane's boat and tackle for his fishing placed him in an impossible position. On May 31, 1923, he too resigned from the Tuna Club.[124]

* * *

Over the summer of 1923, Zane's distress over his women, his writing, and his fishing overlapped, intensified, and delivered a series of blows that left him battered and stumbling. At the time of her June departure for Europe, Dolly was characteristically upbeat and reassuring of her love, but she also knew that she was leaving Zane with all the responsibilities that she had been dutifully shouldering. From abroad she wrote him long, cheerful letters about her activities, her love for him, and a handsome European nobleman who kept showing up at the same places. Zane's early letters were equally positive. "You are now on the big ship leaving your native land," he stated for her embarkation. "It was hard to let you go. Be as careful as possible and have the best time that you can. This is your opportunity. All fine here. The kids are happy and improving. I am well & in good spirits. Life is particularly good to us."[125]

These acknowledgments of Dolly's importance took on more sincerity and urgency as he updated her on all that was going wrong and his darkening mood. A couple of weeks before Dolly's departure, Zane was visited by John Pritchett, an editor from *American Magazine,* and when Pritchett left, he wrote in his journal "The reality of publishing MS, against the vision of my dreams, gave me a sense of disappointment and disillusion." This unpleasant experience revived his January fears and several weeks later he was regretting the forthcoming appearance of *Call of the Canyon* and wishing that it could somehow be postponed. Having sent *Ladies' Home Journal* his recently completed *The Thundering Herd,* he informed Dolly that he very much wanted her to read it and that he was "deathly afraid that you don't like it."[126] A week later, he announced to Dolly, "Bad news. I'm sorry to have to tell that I am sunk." Barton Currie had "roasted h-" out of *Herd,* informed him that his recent stories were "inferior to those before," and demanded that he rewrite his novel's conclusion.[127] Initially, he refused, but his position was undermined by the appearance of a long, negative article on *Wanderer* in the *New York Evening Post.* Contending that the account was filled with "stinking ridicule" and "the most villainous thing I ever read," Zane confessed that "it made me ill."[128] What would he do, he wondered, if held out against Currie and readers agreed that the conclusion to *Herd* was weak?

"The situation here with Louise is intolerable," Grey added in the same letter about the *Post* article. A week earlier, she had been "sick with her ridiculous fears" about local gossip,[129] and now she was cheerfully awaiting the arrival a boyfriend from Zanesville and, even worse, eager to go dancing with him. "I am sorry that I must distress you with my troubles," he concluded. "But if you were only here! I need you so badly."[130] Several days into this awkward situation, Zane and Louise had a violent argument, and he sent Louise back to Zanesville. He immediately contacted Dorothy and invited her to accompany him on his upcoming trip to Arizona. Initially, she accepted, but then reneged a few days later.[131] Meanwhile, Elma sent him an announcement of her upcoming marriage to Fred Nagle. With undisguised anguish and self-absorption, Zane complained to Dolly:

> If she had trusted me, and had told me I would have taken it well enough. But a deliberate double-cross like this is a humiliation I have never suffered before. She *writes* as if she expected me to be pleased as punch, and do favors for her.
>
> You, with your great heart and understanding of the frailties of humanity, and the inevitableness of life, will be sympathetic and get her point of view. But if you could have a look at me *now,* after 24 hours of shame, you would not be so sympathetic, I imagine.[132]

Shaken by this crashing of his pillars of support, he appealed to Dolly to contact Dorothy and persuade her to return with her to Altadena. "If you don't, I will not have anyone left," he moaned. "I'll be unable to work."[133]

In August, Currie wired back his satisfaction with the rewritten conclusion to *The Thundering Herd,* Grey wrote Dolly with tinges of doubt, "That's a turn of the tide, I hope," but he added, "Things have been tough for me. I'll have a tale of woe to unfold that will harrow up your soul."[134]

On August 13, five months after Grey's resignation, Dan Phillips told fellow Tuna Club members that he saw Zane fighting a swordfish that R. C. was credited with catching.[135] Since Tuna Club rules clearly stipulated that a person who hooked a fish had to fight it in order to receive credit for the catch, this was a serious infraction. Zane, on the other hand, insisted that Phillips's claims were untrue and slanderous. Coming on the heels of the Mrs. Spalding incident, these charges were upsetting, and the outcome even more so. The club, which had rushed to the defense of Mrs. Spalding, who was not even a member, now turned a deaf ear to his complaint, and blithely allowed one of its members to say what he pleased. Grey was even more vexed that the charge came from one of the pair who had lured Captain Danielson away from him and that his close friend Wiborn did not contest the lie. Since Wiborn was with Grey and knew what actually happened, he could have supported him, but did not; as with the Spalding incident, he chose to remain silent and neutral. "Wiborn sat right next to him (Phillips), according to what I can learn, and never said a word," Zane informed Dolly. "He has gone back to his cheap cronies. They are a cheap set."[136]

Grey's mounting distress was worsened by the poor fishing of that summer. During a two-week period of intense searching, he did not sight a single swordfish. Ninety-three days into the season he had managed to spot over a hundred, but he had received only eleven strikes, and he had not boated a single big fish. In his published account of this season, which he entitled "Herculean Angling," Zane admitted: "We had endured two months of bad luck, one way or another. I lost patience with Sid [Boerstler] and the little boat [*Gladiator!!*]. We were all downcast. It was impossible to be cheerful."[137]

During the final week of fishing, sunshine finally penetrated the thunderheads swirling around Grey. On August 21, he landed a broadbill, then a second one on the 22nd, and finally a third on the 31st.[138] However, his exuberance over this unprecedented achievement was restrained by the fact that two of these fish weighed less than 300 pounds, and the largest was only 360 pounds. Even worse, he learned from Dolly several weeks later that A. R. Martin, a Tuna Club member, had successfully landed a 474-pound broadbill, eclipsing Boschen's long-standing record, and dashing his hopes that his three broadbill would spite "the envious gang at the Tuna Club."[139]

This deepening angst sapped Zane's health and caused him to fear that he would be unable to take his upcoming trip to Arizona. Since December, Zane had been planning to meet Jesse Lasky and his crew for an on-location filming of *The Call of the Canyon, The Vanishing American,* and *The Heritage of the Desert.* This represented the fulfillment of two long-standing dreams. First, Grey badly wanted his novels to be made into first-rate movies. During 1922, he lost confidence in Hampton's handling of Zane Grey Pictures and hired James Forgey, a Los Angeles lawyer, to pursue funds that were past due. "I am amazed at the money coming from the Hampton outfit," he rejoiced to Dolly several months later. "I'll write Forgey, 'Congratulations, Keep after the Bastards.'"[140] When he belatedly realized that he could have made more money from sales of rights than he did from Hampton's films,[141] Grey delegated Forgey to break his contract with Hampton.[142] In December, he

Left to right: Richard Wetherill, Zane Grey, and Jesse Lasky, en route to the Rainbow Bridge, 1923. (Courtesy of Loren Grey.)

split with Hampton and immediately sold the remnants of his film company to the Famous Players–Lasky Corporation, currently renamed Paramount. Lasky badly wanted exclusive rights to Grey's new novels, and in addition to the purchase of Grey's film company, he agreed to pay Grey an outright fee of $30,000 for each and a modest percentage of the film's return.

Second, Grey had long wanted his novels to be filmed in the settings that inspired them, and Lasky guaranteed that his first three films would be. *The Call of the Canyon* was filmed in the Oak Creek area that Carley visited in the story. *The Heritage of the Desert* used the scenery around Gap and Lee's Ferry. *The Vanishing American* became the first Western to utilize the breathtaking scenery of Monument Valley. *Call* and *American* were also feature productions with handsome budgets and well-known stars—Lois Wilson and Richard Dix. Grey and Lasky agreed to confer about these productions during a fall trip to the Rainbow Bridge.[143]

Grey hoped this trip would mend his health, but everywhere he went there were more problems. The three hotels in Flagstaff were woefully inadequate for the large film crews. Heavy rains drenched his outing with Lasky and delayed shooting. Sets got washed away and had to be rebuilt. The director for *Heritage,* Irvin Willatt, accidentally shot himself in the leg and created more delays.[144] Grey had arranged for his outfitters there to be paid for providing livestock and provisions. He allowed Babe Haught and Lee Doyle to include his own horses in the herd they rented to the filmmakers. When agents for Lasky complained about excessive charges and he too received a steep bill for feeding his horses, Zane sought to renegotiate the fees and got embroiled in a bitter feud with his close friends.

The final blow was a letter from Louise. After denouncing his "childish threat" at their parting, she declared, "I am no longer a child," and announced, "We can no longer remain even friends, so I say good-bye."[145]

Zane was still in Arizona when Dolly returned from Europe. She dutifully complied with his request and persuaded Dorothy to travel with her back to Altadena. During their long hours in the car, Dorothy enlightened Dolly about Zane's disastrous summer. Although neither knew about his recent breakup with Louise, Dorothy provided Dolly enough information about their involvement to squelch the good will in her letters from abroad. She immediately posted this blunt account of her altered mood:

> There are many things about which I ought to write you, but I think I'll save them for your return. I was terribly put out about a number of things that had transpired about which I now can laugh; especially about your "little O.K.er," who was so absolutely indispensable to you, but really didn't get the credit for it etc. I was almost ready to throw up my job—but I guess your work still needs me more than anyone who has happened on the scene thus far. Any time you, however, find an indispensable "O.K.er" to take my place, let me know. No use or place for waste in my system. If I'm not indispensable to you, I can be to myself. Dot told me a lot about this summer which you never mentioned to me. You surely had some unpleasant experiences didn't you, but I guess we all have to reap our own sowing. My estimate of Mrs. A. was exactly right, it appears—but I cannot blame Louise.[146]

Needless to say, Zane confronted a chilly reception when he returned to Altadena. Though he badly needed the nursing regularly provided by the heroines of his novels, both Dolly and Dorothy were too offended to oblige. And he was too overwhelmed and preoccupied to make amends. When Thanksgiving arrived, he withdrew to his study, and wrote in his journal that 1923 was the worst year of his life. When he learned that Dorothy had been drinking with Claire during their stay in Lackawaxen the previous summer, he got into a violent quarrel that sent her packing. On December 15, he wrote in his journal in secret code, "Dorothy went home today. I may never see her again." Returning to normal prose, he elaborated:

> If there is one thing I cannot stand it is to see someone I care greatly for suffer on my account. It hurts, stings, wrenches me, and then rouses me to impotent fury and at last a coldness of despair. That is the way I have been lately.
>
> There is a constant pain in my breast, a recurrent memory of injustice and wrong, of a cruelty that deplored, but somehow could never avert.
>
> And now it is over—the daily sight of that pain I caused. But I can remember the pale face, the shadows, the lines of sleeplessness and tears, the dark sad eyes, and then the poignant words, expressive of the simple anguished soul.
>
> So I am wretched. I suffer. I cannot do anything.[147]

A few days later, he was so incensed by Romer's impertinence to him and Betty that he struck his son for the first time in years.[148] Desperate to escape the whirlwind of his destructive emotions, he pressured the family into celebrating its Christmas on the 24th and left early the next day for New York City.[149] In her letter to him there, Dolly commented on the wake of misery that followed his offensive departure:

> That was the most uninspiring farewell we bade each other this morning. You were cussing mad and exited with a most unpleasant expression on your face and I grabbed you and planted a kiss on all that wrath and sprinted madly home on a fool's errand. . . . And then I went down stairs and read what you'd written in the book and I wept some more. . . . If you are awake when the New Year comes in, I want you to think of me exclusively for a minute or two no matter who is with you.[150]

In New York, Zane could have consoled himself with the fact that he was still America's most popular author and one of its best-known anglers, but he was too distraught over his perilous lurching toward his father's embittered isolation. In his heart, he felt like the loneliest man on earth.

7

Movin' On:
1924–25

*The California conservationists have arrived late, maybe
too late to save the game and fish, but they have arrived!
And we want it distinctly understood that we are for
California and our children and grandchildren, to the
end of saving something of California's wild life for them
to enjoy and to live with. This is the main issue.*
—"California Game Fish: How Long Will They Last?"

Had Zane been able to foresee the future, he would have done nothing and
given thanks that his problems passed so quickly. Of course, he could not,
and in deciding to take action, he prolonged the healing process. Prior to
his departure for New York City, he mailed the Catalina *Islander* an article
entitled "Heavy Tackle for Heavy Fish," which ran on the front page of the
January 2, 1924, issue. This article opens with the declaration, "After years of
trial and experience I have come to the conclusion that the standard twenty-
four-thread line was not heavy enough for broadbill swordfish, not to mention big tuna." He reveals his decision of the previous season "to use tackle
which we were convinced was more sportsmanlike and fairer to swordfish,"

and to purchase the $1,500 Coxe reel that he had equipped with 39-thread line. He condemns the recently reaffirmed Tuna Club regulation limiting the strongest allowable line to twenty-four threads with a breaking strength of sixty pounds, and he advocates an alternative, custom-made 24-thread line with a breaking strength of eighty-eight pounds. Despite its $30 cost, he judges this line to be vastly superior to the "inferior grades" that cost only eight to twelve dollars. In support of these decisions, he argues that tuna frequently break standard 24-thread lines, become bloodied, and are devoured by sharks. He argues that boat captains, who work hard to locate big fish, are frustrated by the failure of the inadequate lines, and that many fishermen agree with his proposals. He quotes the words of support offered to him by the accomplished angler Harry Adams: "Now I want you to sell me one of your thirty-nine-thread lines. I'll use it, and when I catch a broadbill I will call a meeting of the directors of the Tuna Club and tell them flatly that you are right and they are wrong." R. C. not only used a 39-thread line for his first broadbill, but he also told Zane that he had "never had such a feeling of security as this tackle gave him."[1]

This airing of Grey's dispute with the Tuna Club worsened the rift. When he allowed "Heavy Tackle" to be reprinted in the February issue of *Outdoor America,* his disagreement turned into an open declaration of war. Even though his article appeared during the off-season, it elicited much discussion and little support, certainly not enough for the Tuna Club to reconsider its decision. Under pressure to comment, Harry Adams wrote a front-page article for the *Islander* urging that Grey's suggestions be considered, but he also insisted, "I have never used a thirty-nine-thread line on any fish."[2] Among the many letters of opposition, perhaps the most interesting was by "A. Westerner," who related Grey's position to his Westerns and parsed its ironic implications:

> I have just finished reading Zane Grey's article on heavy tackle, and my world has come tumbling down about me. I don't seem to be able to believe that there is a sportsman left! The whole charmed game is commercialized. The days of fast transportation, bodily comforts, gasoline, electricity and money have driven out of existence those old-time, hard-riding, clean-hearted men of the out-of-doors. . . . Now that is all ended, and it's bigger lines, heavier reels, more boatmen and more fish! Oh, the pity of it! Vale, Zane Grey, the ideal, 'Rest in Peace.'[3]

This controversy focused more attention upon the big fish being caught and whether the angler followed Grey's proposals or the Tuna Club regulations. Harry Mallen, a Tuna Club member loyal to its regulations, was handed a major role in the unfolding drama. On May 21, 1924, the *Islander* devoted the center section of its front page to a story headlined "Harry J. Mallen Lands 319-Pound Tuna on 24-Thread Line."[4] Previous reports either ignored line size or only mentioned it in passing. Suddenly the size of Mallen's line was as important as the size of his fish. His catch occurred in Mexico, far away from Catalina, and did not break any record, but it was judged newsworthy because of its verification that big fish could be caught with skillful use of 24-thread line.

The following summer, Mallen presented the Tuna Club an even better gift. On August 8, near Avalon, he landed a 528-pound broadbill that bested Martin's record of the previous year by a whopping forty pounds, and again he used a 24-thread line. This time the *Islander* did not headline the size of Mallen's line, but its relegation to a passing mention was accompanied by a quote affirming that Grey's pronouncements were far from forgotten:

> Earlier this season, Zane Grey, the author, landed a fish weighing 413 pounds; but I understand a thirty-nine-thread line was used, which disqualified his fish under the rules of the Tuna Club.
>
> "At no time during the fight did I feel that the twenty-four-thread line was insufficient to hold the big fish. I exercised the greatest care with the rod, but did not pay much attention to the thread as it cut into the water."[5]

Once more the existing broadbill record had again been broken, and again Zane was not the one who did it. Mallen's use of 24-thread line left him discredited, isolated, and embarrassed. Even worse, Zane was indignant over the way in which Mallen landed his broadbill. The *Los Angeles Examiner* reported that his battle lasted only forty-five minutes, and that the propeller of his boat had badly gashed his fish.[6] Since Tuna Club regulations disqualified a damaged fish, Grey was understandably offended over the club's acceptance of his catch and the *Islander*'s discreet elimination of this information from its report.

After the flap over Mrs. Spalding's catch and his proposal for heavy tackle, Grey was understandably wary of more controversy. Luckily, much of what he had to say was already in print. As support for "Heavy Tackle for Heavy Fish," a month later he published "Xiphias Gladius," an account of a broadbill caught four years before which he used to denounce unsportsmanlike tactics. Admitting that over these four years he had written several other articles about broadbill that were never published, he reveals why editors might have found these impolitic or intemperate:

> What does it mean to catch a broadbill swordfish in a fair battle? To sub-
> due him by dint of your own stalk, skill, strength, and endurance. . . .
> There have been innumerable instances of anglers fighting and losing
> broadbills after long hours. It used to be a joke on the pier. These must all
> have been fair fights. But a broadbill gaffed in a few minutes after being
> hooked—that is not to the credit of the angler. Nor is it a fluke! Nor can
> it be called good luck! A broadbill that swims to the surface in a half hour
> or so, to see what is the pesky thing bothering him—to look around—and
> has a harpoon, or three or four jabbed into him is most certainly not
> caught honestly or fairly. . . .
>
> R. C. pointed out to me how very easily a gaffed swordfish could make
> a surge, catch the gaff rope under the propeller and pull out half the stern
> of the boat.[7]

Grey's allusion to Mrs. Spalding's catch was uncanny in its anticipation of
the maiming of Mallen's broadbill that made his battle similarly brief. Zane
was too vexed to adhere to his initial silence.[8] In his *Tales of Swordfish and Tuna*
(1927), he included a short, previously unpublished piece entitled "The Deadly
Airplane-Wire Leader." This impassioned denunciation of airplane-wire as
leader for game fishing included a thinly veiled attack upon both Mallen and
Martin. Grey argues that airplane wires inflict deep wounds in the bodies of
fish, impair their ability to fight, and sometimes strangle them. He references
the record broadbills of 528 and 571 pounds—the catches of Martin and Mallen—and claims that the brevity of both fights was due to the damage caused
by their wire leaders. Grey's argument implies that Mallen's broadbill was
slashed, not by the boat propeller as the *Examiner* reported, but by his wire
leader. Besides naming Martin as the one responsible for introducing wire
leaders, Grey points out that he lost several fingers to coiled leader and that
he once landed a broadbill in a mere six minutes, presumably not his record
catch. These revelations are accompanied by five grisly photographs of badly
mutilated fish, and in one, Martin is shown standing alongside his maimed
catch.[9] As in his dispute with the Tuna Club, Zane held his tongue initially,
and then belatedly and intemperately he proclaimed his disagreement.

The fallout from "Heavy Tackle" did not wound Grey as much as it might
have because the main problems of 1923 were already behind him by the
time that it hit. In late January 1924, Dolly sent a letter to Zane in Long
Key that salved his wounds and facilitated his recovery. At the time of their
November reunion, she realized that his acute depression left him beyond
help; there was little that she could do for him, and little that she cared to
do. Secretly relieved that Zane's tempestuous affair with Louise was over,

she decided that her best strategy was to remain calm and detached until he eventually reached out for her, as she knew he would. In early January, Zane wrote to her from New York, "I miss you like hell. Something is wrong with me."[10] A week later, he confessed, "I have such dreadful fears, morbid some of them—that I might lose you or die away from you."[11] "I'd give all the money I sent you if I could just go to bed with you a while," he opened his next letter, an unusually long one. "I need to be soothed and reprimanded and sympathized with and talked to." He had met with Dorothy, Mildred, and Claire, but they had been cool toward him and critical of his behavior. "If I do not recover my balance and health and spirit in a very few days, I shall come home," he confessed.[12] "I feel that my anchor is slipping, or that I am skating on thin ice," he added in a letter that followed. "What is to become of me if I can no longer go to you with my troubles?"[13]

Sensing the need she had been anticipating and armed with the information that he had divulged, Dolly decided that the time to act had arrived. On January 18, she sat down, wrote a long letter, and mailed it so that it would be in Long Key when he arrived. "You don't know the longing that goes out from me," she opened, "to get my arms around you & comfort you and smooth things for you when you are sick, or distressed and worried." After initially vowing "I won't go into the matter of the girls again, it's useless," she paused for a quick observation that evolved into a searching analysis of Zane's unhappiness:

> Only this I say to you, no woman is ethical, can possibly be, in the relationship these girls are placed to you. So you will have to ignore that part of them & get what is worthwhile to you out of your personal contact with them. In a certain sense you have idealized every woman you have ever come in contact with—made her something to fit your momentary need, rather than grasped *at all* their real characters or relation to the world. It was when these latter considerations impinged on your "dreams of fair women" that the trouble began.
>
> Your friends have always been nice, more or less normal girls in the ordinary walks of life, but in their relations to *you* they have become just the biological "female of the species" and in that manner have reacted to each other and used their claws. . . . I find that the fighting spirit in the human species requires a blow for a blow, a hurt for a hurt. The Christ-like spirit of turning the other cheek never manifests in a battle of woman against woman for a man! That's where nature gets in her deadly work.[14]

Indirectly, Dolly was presenting herself as different from these needy, demanding women, and she was playing her strong suit of understanding and compassion. She was also consciously absolving Zane of guilt. Dolly realized that he had been castigating himself for weeks for all that had gone wrong, and she offered a new perspective that made *him* the victim—a victim of his romantic nature and of women turned cruel by their circumstances and natural instincts.

After reading this letter, Grey confided to his journal, "Today I received a letter from Dolly and it was medicine, strength, religion, [and] love. Something about my children delighted and thrilled me. Saddened me, too, because I see them so little."[15] The next morning, he dispatched Dolly a telegram proclaiming, "Bless you for wonderful sweet uplifting letter."[16] Having felt powerless, guilty, and alone, Grey was reassured that Dolly and his family were still behind him, even though they were, as usual, many miles away.

Two days after Dolly's uplifting letter, Zane received another boost from a more surprising source—a very positive review of his most recent novel. *The Call of the Canyon* (1924) was published that month, and ever since he had read *Flaming Youth,* he had worried that this Western might be viewed as even more reactionary and out of step with the times than his two previous novels. Like *Day of the Beast,* this novel featured a female protagonist whose chief adversary was modernization. Grey knew that commercial success was almost assured by the new plan that Lasky had devised, which had the film version open a month before the novel appeared. Recognizing that serialization actually increased sales of the novel, Lasky convinced Grey that movies would be even better promotion, shrewdly calculating that early access to Grey's latest novel would also greatly increase the box office for his film. This astute marketing strategy helped *The Call of the Canyon* to jump to number five on the best-seller list for January and to claim number six for the year. However, this aggressive commercialization left Grey understandably worried that reviewers might respond to it like bulls to a red cape and savagely gore his novel.

But this did not happen. In late January, the *New York Times* featured an unusually positive review in the Sunday *Book Review* that folded Grey's other novels into its discussion of *Call.* L. H. Robbins, the reviewer, cleverly recycles the *Literary Digest*'s introduction to its reprinting of Rascoe's *Wanderer* review: "Certainly his [Grey's] popularity is a phenomenon that cannot be ignored in any study of contemporary American life, social or literary." With a flourish of wit meant to show himself as sophisticated and cosmopolitan as Rascoe, Robbins praises Grey for his "honest workmanship," "clarity of thought," "strength of phrase," and, most of all, for his "corking good story." After judging his novels "as clean and fresh as a New England village after a three-day rain," he credits *Call* with "as thorough an understanding of the psychology of sex as any Washington Square production suppressed by the Anti-Vice Society." Relying on irony and condescension to qualify his praise, Robbins directs his criticism at Grey's detractors, branding them "sophisticates" who fail to appreciate the decency of his stories.[17]

The editorial staff that approved this review did so out of concern that the recent outpouring of condemnation for Grey's books sprang from a Jazz Age, metropolitan prejudice against popular readership and against subject matter that smacked of backwater, small-town culture. As calculated support for Robbins' estimate, they framed his review with an informal essay, unusual for the *Book Review,* in which Silas Bent returns to his Kentucky hometown to investigate reader preferences at the local bookstore. Bent is surprised to discover that its patrons are not much interested in trendsetting, avant-garde literature. They prefer classics and popular fare. Bent learns that a local flapper has just finished *Flaming Youth,* but the store owner informs him that more typically "[Joseph] Conrad [is] linked in popular demand with Zane Grey and Oliver Curwood." The most remarkable feature of Bent's nostalgic appreciation for heartland values was his disregard for the role commercialization played in such preferences, and his willful suspension of the critical acumen that would later make his *Ballyhoo* (1927) such a brilliant analysis of the culture of his day. Clearly, Robbins and Bent had been recruited by the *Book Review* to defend common, unpretentious readers, who wished only to read what they enjoyed, and to counterbalance the acerbic critics who were deriding their preferences.

These two articles help to explain why the mounting criticism of Grey's novels had little effect upon their popularity. When Grey's Westerns first appeared prior to World War I, they appealed mainly to an Eastern, urban-based readership that shared Grey's belief that city life caused sickness, and that rugged life in the unspoiled outdoors was therapeutic and invigorating. However, during the decade of his popularity, these assumptions underwent a profound change. The prosperity and industrial expansion of the 1920s endowed urban existence with renewed vitality and appeal. Glossy ads aggressively promoted new commercial products and associated them with glamorous, fashion-conscious cities where they were available. Outlying areas that lacked them were were staid, old-fashioned, and dull. As metropolitan culture embraced the latest clothing, conveniences, economic opportunity, and entertainment, the desire for these advances supplanted the dated longing to get away from them. Grey's outspoken aversion for flappers, cigarettes, and jazz arose from a reactionary sensibility that he had been harboring for years, but the changing times drew it out and made his voice shrill. He had good reason to worry that the renewed allure of cities might upstage the wholesome, elemental conditions that he had been celebrating as a preferable alternative.

On the other hand, those who continued to live in small towns and rural areas did not believe that city life was better, and they responded defensively to the urban derision for their tastes and mores. They embraced Grey as a successful writer who spoke out on behalf of their values and attacked the suspect thinking and living conditions of big cities. Though his West may have been far away, they accepted the premise of his stories—that the simple life away from crowds, tall buildings, and aggressive commercialization was better attuned to human needs. Although Grey retained a solid base of loyal readers in urban areas, this new readership from the rural heartland embraced his outlook *because* it was old-fashioned. Meanwhile, Zane worked feverishly to feed this demand with new variations and to ignore the widening disparity between the circumstances in his stories and those of his own life.

"Tonight I read a review of my new novel *Call of the Canyon* in the *N. Y. Times Book Review,*" Grey wrote in his diary. "It was the best review ever given me, wholly unexpected, and vastly inspiring. I feel grateful, humble, amazed, and thankful to the bottom of my heart. How I have longed for understanding! Not praise so much as appreciation of my efforts! Here they are, at last. I cannot say what incalculable benefit I shall derive from this Mr. Robbins' review."[18] "Did you like the Times review?" he wrote to Dolly the next day. "It just filled me with joy. And I immediately began to love you harder."[19] When his birthday arrived four days later, he elected not to work. Instead of writing away the day as he had done the year before, he took a break, enjoyed his newfound peace of mind, and gave thanks that the torment of the past year was behind him.[20]

At the end of his Long Key stay, Grey decided to forego his customary visit to Arizona and to fish the Everglades instead.[21] Dolly's letters inspired him to write more easily than he had in years, and she reassured him that his family would be there for him when he returned. Back in Altadena, he wrote in his diary, "After four months I found my family well and happy."[22] A month later when he went to Avalon, he jotted a lone entry in his journal that said even more about his improved state of mind—"From violent anguish surely free."[23]

Grey's summer return to Avalon brought an uncomfortable reckoning with the ill-will generated by his Tuna Club resignation and his outspoken call for stronger lines. Warily, he accepted his alienation and committed himself to a disciplined regimen of writing and fishing. The 413-pound broadbill that he landed on July 16 vindicated this decision and inspired him to believe that fortune again favored him. But the summer was not without problems. Zane learned that Tom Mix had purchased the Wiborn house down the hill from his, and Mix immediately covered its roof with a mass of glaring red lights.[24] From Wiborn, Mix learned that the staircase to Grey's residence extended across his property. Claiming that he did want his land used for a public thoroughfare, Mix had the staircase torn down and fenced off Grey's access.[25] Forced to remain aboard the *Gladiator* while a replacement was built, Zane fumed and pondered a relocation to his undeveloped property farther up the hill.[26]

Meanwhile, Grey focused on his upcoming trip to Nova Scotia. For years he had been reading and dreaming about its legendary tuna. Back in 1919, when Robert Davis wrote that he was taking his vacation there, Zane had dispatched a flood of advice about tackle, and announced that he would be going there the following year.[27] Although other interests preempted these plans, his feud with the Tuna Club revived them. His defection to a 39-thread line automatically disqualified any large fish that he landed in Catalina waters. The *Islander*'s disregard for his large broadbill that summer and its bias toward catches conforming to Tuna Club regulations steeled Grey's resolve to go elsewhere. The tuna in Nova Scotia were reported to be four times the size of the largest Catalina tuna, and no one there bothered about how they were caught. Commercial fishermen considered the huge tuna a nuisance that tore up their nets and jeopardized their livelihood. They also believed that anyone presuming to catch one with rod and reel was foolish and doomed. Zane, on the other hand, was convinced that his years of fishing experience endowed him with the necessary knowledge and skill, and he was energized by the prospect of getting away from line restrictions and landing one of these giants.

The origin for this trip extended back to his meeting with Laurie D. Mitchell during a 1923 visit to Abercrombie and Fitch in New York City. Mitchell was a Canadian who had graduated from Oxford, and during the war he had served as a captain in the Royal Engineers on the Saloniki front in Greece.[28] Prior to his enlistment, Mitchell ran a guide service for fishermen in Nova Scotia. On Great Island, near Port Medway, he had a bungalow hotel and several skiffs for fishing. In 1914, L. Mitchell-Henry, an Englishman and no relation, hired Mitchell to take him fishing. Over the previous eight years, Mitchell had helped fishermen to hook seventy-nine tuna, but none had been landed. After a four-hour fight on his first day of fishing, Mitchell-

Henry landed a 520-pound tuna that he proclaimed to be "the first tunny ever caught on rod and line unaided, in the open sea."[29] Since he had designed and constructed his own reel, Mitchell-Henry credited his unique success to his tackle. Conversely, when he lost ten fish over the days that followed, he attributed his setback to defective hooks. On his final day, he caught another large tuna that was forty pounds lighter, and he was so grateful for Mitchell's help that he lent him his spare tackle when he departed. As he was boarding his train to leave, he learned that Mitchell had successfully landed a 710-pound tuna, a local record that endured until Grey's visit.[30]

The challenge of this fishing made earning a living as a guide so difficult for Mitchell that he sought work in New York at Abercrombie after the war. When Grey came to purchase tackle and met him, Mitchell's unique fund of information about Nova Scotia convinced him to go fishing there and to hire Mitchell as his advisor.[31] During visits to New York City during 1923 and the early months of 1924, Grey had a series of meetings with Mitchell in which they formulated plans rivaling those of a military invasion. Grey learned that the skiffs used by locals were either rowed or powered by slow engines without a reverse gear. After a thorough review of their advantages and drawbacks, he commissioned Mitchell to return to Liverpool and supervise construction of two boats, one eighteen feet long and the other twenty, with a variety of special features that included spoon-shaped bottoms. Grey's Florida and Avalon experiences convinced him that he also needed a power launch. Initially, he intended this to be built in Nova Scotia as well,[32] but Bob King, a Long Key captain, argued that a Fort Myers firm could provide a superior product, and he agreed to supervise its construction. During his spring trip into the Everglades, Grey stopped in Fort Myers to sign a contract for a twenty-five-foot boat with two engines, two propellers, two rudders, and two Catalina fighting chairs.[33] As the boat neared completion that summer, King journeyed to California to confer with Grey and Boerstler about tackle and strategies, and he returned to the boatyard in Florida with a long list of special modifications.[34] Several weeks before King left to pilot the new boat to Nova Scotia, Mitchell arrived there to arrange a network of commercial fishermen that would relay information back to them about fishing conditions from all over the area.[35] With three boats, three captains, and a battery of local advisors, Grey was as prepared as he possibly could be.

Given Zane's substantial investment of time, energy, and money, it is hardly surprising that he was buffeted by doubt and anxiety as the date of departure approached. Back in Altadena and packing for Nova Scotia, he wrote in his journal: "I am tired and depressed, full of doubt and misgiving, uncertain whether or not I want to go away on another trip. . . . The love and reminder of my wife and children stops my heart. The passionate pursuit of adventure, romance, of all that drives me, begins to pall."[36]

To allay his fears of a relapse into loneliness and isolation, he arranged for R. C., his son Romer, Lillian, her new husband Jess Smith, and Mildred Smith to accompany him. This trip settled his evolving relationship with Lillian into a friendship that would never again be more than that. During Zane's return to the Rainbow Bridge with Jesse Lasky in the early fall of 1923, Lillian had been included in his party, and she fell in love with Jess Smith, one of Al Doyle's wranglers. In May 1924, she obtained a final divorce from Robertson, and quickly married Smith.[37] Her open displays of affection for Smith upset Zane, and Dolly had to reassure him: "Sorry you were fussed about Lil but if you want her around you'll have to put up with her idiosyncrasies—as with everyone else's. Lil has her maddening qualities, but also her very good points. I'd find her easier to live with than Mildred. I'm glad she is crazy about Jess—let her sleep with him—that sort of thing wears off after a while, but it's very thrilling while it lasts."[38] Despite his initial misgivings, Zane was able to accept Lil's marriage and discovered that her relationship with Jess actually improved his friendship with her.

Mildred Smith, ca. 1925. (Courtesy of Loren Grey.)

Grey's third trip to the Rainbow Bridge altered his relationship with Mildred Smith even more. She had been his secretary since 1916, when she came to work for him from the Worcester Film Company in New York City.[39] Although Zane became involved with her shortly afterward, she quickly realized that he was fonder of Claire and Dorothy, and she concentrated upon becoming an indispensable secretary and organizer. However, Zane's involvement with Louise reconfigured their relationship.[40] When Louise returned to Ohio and Dorothy spurned his offer, Grey was left without a companion for his Arizona trip. At this point he invited Mildred; she accepted and was with him the whole time until his return to Altadena. That fall, he presented her with the gift of an album containing 629 photographs of the places they visited together, and he inscribed it "To Mildred: This is a photographic record of your wanderings from May until November 1923."[41]

However, the unfolding tempest of 1923 that intensified Grey's relationship with Mildred also strained it. Even though she was willing to replace Louise, Mildred felt insecure and vulnerable. In June 1923 when Zane presented her with a brooch as a gesture of his affection, she realized that it was the same as the one he had given Dorothy, and she became very angry.[42] During the trip to the Rainbow Bridge, she learned for the first time that Louise had gone there with Zane the summer before, and she stopped speaking to him for several days.[43] Mildred objected strongly to Dorothy's return to Altadena, and berated Zane for attempting to reconnect with her during his January visit to New York City. When Claire and Elma informed Mildred that Dolly did not want her in her home, Mildred pressed Zane to stand up for her. When he cautiously appealed to Dolly to be nicer, she shot back:

> And so I say to you, because you want one to view Mildred Smith through the same rose-colored glasses through which you are seeing her, that you are doing Dot a bitter injustice. You don't have to go on with her, but at least be fair to her, and consider the position in which she was placed. Neither do I want you to give up Mildred Smith if she fills a present need for you. But don't, unless you want me to lose what little respect I have for her, let her & Lil & Clare form a combination to injure Dorothy in your eyes.[44]

Dolly's insistence that Mildred was "not a very peaceful or peaceable person" was validated when she infuriated Zane by brazenly smoking in his presence when he failed to get Dolly to treat her better.[45]

Despite these complaints and feuds, Mildred stayed with Zane through this trying period when all his other friends were leaving him. As Dolly sensed before Zane included her on the trip to Nova Scotia, Mildred was now his new favorite. At thirty years old and as stout as Dolly, Mildred was a striking departure from the young beauties that Grey had long preferred. For the past several years, he had been decrying flappers and their selfish preoccupation with their own wants and needs. Louise's preference for a visiting classmate over him was a painful lesson in the fickleness and unreliability of younger women. The recent marriages of Claire and Lillian and the defection of Dorothy exposed the instability of multiple involvements. Mildred was neither exciting nor compliant, but she understood Zane's peculiarities and accepted them. Like Dolly, she was competent, steadfastly loyal, and forgiving. Though she did not share Zane's passion for fishing and outdoor adventure, she did like traveling, and she did a superb job of managing the arrangements. Over the years that followed, Mildred would openly declare that she was Zane's mistress and usually behaved around others as though she was quite content with this role—even though her interaction with him did not always accord with this pose. Zane, on the other hand, did briefly (and unsuccessfully) pursue Nola Luxford, a beautiful, thirty-year-old actress from New Zealand.[46] Since she was well aware of his wandering, Mildred accepted these dalliances and concentrated her energies upon retaining her improved status. She convinced Zane to take her with him on every one of his trips from 1924–29, even the trying boat ride down the Rogue River, and she orchestrated the returns so that she was always nearby. Dolly knew that the woman behind her husband's request for better treatment was actually seeking a stronger commitment from him, and she wisely understood that this woman threatened her marriage more than Louise or Dorothy ever did. Hence, her unusual coolness toward this paramour.

When Grey rallied the members of his party in Nova Scotia in early August, the normally mild weather had turned rainy, foggy, and cool, and it stayed that way for the next two weeks. The fishing was poor, and so too the prospects for improvement. Zane remained dauntlessly upbeat and persistent, even after a big tuna snapped his muscular 39-thread line. Finally, on August 13, after a draining six-hour fight, he landed a 684-pound tuna. Although this trophy made his trip a success, Grey was determined to take full advantage of his allotted time, and he continued to fish every day and to fine-tune his strategy for battling his quarry. He and the captain of his launch coordinated to keep a hooked fish away from reefs and to avoid a deep soundings that might allow it to escape.[47] On August 20, after a three-hour-and-ten-minute fight, Zane landed the 758-pound tuna. This catch easily bettered Mitchell's long-standing record of 710 pounds, and brought Grey his first world record.

This tuna was a full 500 pounds heavier than Col. Morehouse's still-unsurpassed Catalina catch that won international recognition for the Tuna Club back in 1899. Since Grey was fishing beyond the jurisdiction of the Tuna Club and employing a line that violated its regulations, the *Islander* ran only a brief notice of his catch that was relegated to a back page.[48]

Grey countered this indifference and sullen opposition with aggressive promotion for his record tuna. From Liverpool, he dispatched several telegrams about his catch to J. A. Coxe, the maker of his special reel, who circulated the news to area newspapers. Next, he persuaded *Field and Stream* to publish a photograph of himself being congratulated by Laurie Mitchell in front of his fish and beneath a headline "World's Record Tuna."[49] During a trip to New York City, he visited *Bookman* and persuaded this influential journal to run a promotional blurb that mentioned his "world's record for tuna fishing."[50] As usual, he wrote an account of his trip that was published in *American Magazine.*[51] "My Adventures as a Fisherman," as he entitled his account, was expanded into "Giant Nova Scotia Tuna" for inclusion in his *Tales of Swordfish and Tuna* (1927). Since "My Adventures" did not appear until almost a year after his catch, he got *Outdoor America* to publish a picture story of his trip headlined as "Zane Grey's World Record Tuna" in its February 1925 issue.[52] Finally, he wrote an account entitled "Taking the World's Record Tuna," and hid his authorship by presenting it as the work of Captain Laurie D. Mitchell for the January 1925 issue of *Field and Stream.*[53] Never before had Grey recycled an experience so many times and in so many different ways. Clearly his objective was to gain recognition for his world record.

The most significant product of this self-promotion was a simple notation that appeared in the October 1924 issue of *Field and Stream.* In a two-page spread entitled "World's Record Catches with Rod and Reel and Otherwise of 50 North American Popular Fresh and Salt Water Fishes," he and his Nova Scotia tuna were listed opposite the entry for *Thunnus thynnus.*[54] In this case, Grey's achievement was not just the listing but also the list itself. *Field and Stream* was the first major journal to publish a comprehensive, up-to-date list of record catches. Since 1911, the magazine had been sponsoring an informal, unregulated national contest for the largest freshwater catches, but this was its first coverage of saltwater and areas outside the territorial United States. Prior to this list, information about record catches existed informally and unreliably—word-of-mouth memories shared by local fishermen or irregular notations in logs at regional organizations. The Tuna Club and affiliates like the Port Aransas Club were, of course, notable exceptions, but their records favored their regions and members who conformed to their regulations.

Zane Grey and his 758-pound tuna, his first world record. Liverpool,
Nova Scotia, August 20, 1924. (Courtesy of Loren Grey.)

The authors of this new list were identified as John Treadwell Nichols of the American Museum of National History and Van Campen Heilner of *Field and Stream*. Nichols was a well-known ichthyologist on the museum's staff, and Heilner had worked as his research assistant while he was an undergraduate at Trinity College.[55] Heilner published his second book, *Adventures in Angling* (1922), at twenty-two, and it earned him positions as field representative for the Museum and as at-large correspondent for *Field and Stream*.[56] Believing that the growth of interest in saltwater fishing with tackle warranted a listing of the largest catches of the major species, he persuaded *Field and Stream* to publish this first list with an agreement that periodic updates would follow.[57] Meanwhile, with the assistance of Francesca La Monte, also a staff member of the museum, Heilner arranged for a display, in the museum's exhibit of game fish, of a volume that presented the world's record catches on loose-leaf pages in handwritten up-to-date entries.[58]

Heilner would later be one of the original founders of the International Game Fish Association (IGFA) in 1939, and would serve as its vice president. His lifelong passion for saltwater fishing extended back to his youth and his meeting Zane Grey in Long Key when he was sixteen years old, a meeting that led to a close friendship spanning many years.[59] In his foreword to the first edition of Heilner's popular and highly respected *Salt Water Fishing* (1936), Grey mentions "the wonderful years that I fished with Van Campen Heilner in Florida and California, and off Seabright, New Jersey."[60] Heilner had obviously collected information for his *Field and Stream* list before Grey went to Nova Scotia, but its appearance only two months after Grey's record tuna and during his period of aggressive promotion almost certainly was no coincidence.

Grey's dream of a public scoreboard, unencumbered by peculiar restrictions like those advocated by the Tuna Club, included a yearning for "virgin seas" and more record fish. Long before his trip to Nova Scotia, he worried that the locations that had long been so special to him—Arizona, Long Key, and Avalon—were no longer what they were when he first visited them. Increased population and development had altered their wild, pristine conditions, and the indigenous wildlife was diminished and wary.

For Grey, Nova Scotia represented both an alternative and the first step of more ambitious plans. Prior to his visit, he had contemplated the purchase of a yacht to carry him to remote, little-fished areas of the world, and he came to Nova Scotia knowing that it was a center for boatbuilding with a lower standard of living that made everything less expensive. Thus he went shopping for a boat during his first week there. On August 11, Lillian wrote to Claire that he was "very excited" and debating whether "to either clinch or give up the purchase of a 3 masted, sailing schooner, 185 feet long, 35 feet wide."[61] Registered as the *Marshal Foch,* this ship weighed 351 tons when the Ward's Brook shipyard in Cumberland County completed it in February 1919. The *Marshal Foch* had already crossed the Atlantic twice, and it currently held the record for the fastest run from Halifax to New York City. Though its original cost is unknown, a smaller 284-ton schooner built there the same year cost $62,000.[62] Since owners of the *Marshal Foch* were willing to accept $17,000, Grey considered the price a terrific bargain. He would have to arrange costly renovations, but they would achieve everything he wanted for much less than the cost of a new boat. Lillian informed Claire that Zane wanted the boat "for trips on the Pacific Coast and maybe New Zealand, Australia, etc." Unfortunately, he calculated that his modifications would take many months and would necessitate postponement of his plans to visit South America the upcoming spring.[63] Grey fretted over the purchase and these complications, and only after his record catch was he confident enough to commit.

At the time of his purchase, Grey wanted renovation of the *Marshal Foch* to be done in New York,[64] but a visit to the Smith and Rhuland shipyard in Lunenburg and its economical bid changed his mind. He arranged for his schooner to be outfitted with two Fairbanks-Morse engines, an electric generator for lights and fans, an air compressor to drain water, and an emergency engine. He had tanks installed for 5,000 gallons of crude oil, 5,000 gallons of water, and 2,500 gallons of gasoline. Below decks he created eight staterooms, four bathrooms, a large refrigerated storeroom, a dark room, and storage for tackle.[65] He transformed the central area into a joint saloon and dining area large enough to accommodate mountings of his two huge tuna on opposite walls.[66] Grey decided that he also needed two new power launches as well as extensive modification to the one recently built for him in Florida. After contracting McAlpine in Shelburne to do the work, he got Sid Boerstler to supervise the renovations, to monitor the positioning of the power launches, and to recruit a crew.[67] The biographical sketch of Grey prepared for his induction into the Hall of Fame of the International Game Fish Association states that "he was the first to use the 'mother boat' concept for keeping his smaller boats supplied without having to return to land." All these modifications cost Grey $40,000, more than twice the ship's purchase price.[68]

After Grey arranged the main components of this renovation with Boerstler and the boatyard, he left them to complete the job because his hectic schedule did not allow him time for the details. Two days after his return to Altadena in mid-September, he and a large contingent of friends and support staff departed in three automobiles for a third visit to Oregon. After fishing the Rogue River for the second time and spending several days at Crater Lake, which he first visited in 1919, Grey took his group to Klamath Lake, Klamath Falls, and the Modoc Indian reservation, and then headed back to Altadena. The most eventful moment of the trip occurred outside Bakersfield when a careless driver slammed his automobile into one carrying Jess and Lillian. Jess had five cracked ribs and Lillian sustained face lacerations, but doctors were able to patch them so that they were able to follow a few days later.[69]

In early October, Grey was off again for his late fall hunting trip in Arizona where he encountered a situation that took his mind off fishing, his new yacht, and even his hunting. In the North Rim area of the Grand Canyon, the deer population had swollen to the point that many people, including his old friend Will Dilg, were worrying that upcoming winter would kill thousands of them. Back in 1922, Grey had supported Dilg when he rallied fifty-four worried sportsmen and established the Izaak Walton League to fight the many menaces to wildlife. Even before this, Grey had become a committed conservationist, and he had written several articles denouncing the recent decimation of habitats for game and fish. When Dilg started the *Izaak Walton League Monthly* (renamed *Outdoor America* in 1924) to promote the league's cause, Grey allowed his articles to be reprinted without charge, and contributed new ones as well.

By 1924, Dilg was so concerned about the North Rim deer that he devoted the November issue of the league's magazine to it, and he wrote an introductory editorial about the urgency of the problem:

> Believing the Kaibab deer herd to be one of our greatest national assets, the Izaak Walton League is vitally interested in the recommendation recently made by an investigating committee that the number of deer, estimated at approximately twenty thousand, be reduced to one-half that number to insure sufficient forage for the remaining deer throughout the winter months. . . . The columns of this magazine are open to anyone who can suggest a plan that will save this marvelous remnant of outdoor America made possible by that farsighted sportsman and conservationist Theodore Roosevelt.[70]

When President Roosevelt declared the North Rim area a national preserve back in 1906, the year before Grey's first visit, rough estimates placed the number of deer at 4,000. At that time, supporters of the preserve judged these figures to be low enough that they banned deer hunting. They also viewed the number of the predators as so high and so ruinous to the deer population that hunting of them was both allowed and even encouraged with bounties.

During the fifteen years since Grey's two lion hunts with Jones, government agents calculated that 700 cougars, 500 bobcats, and 5,000 coyotes had been exterminated. Jim Owens, the game warden who hunted with Grey and Jones, claimed that he himself had killed several hundred mountain lions. This slaughter of "enemies" allowed the deer to flourish so that they currently threatened both the environment and their food supply. By 1924, Forest Service officials estimated the current number of deer at 20,000, and some locals believed that this estimate was low.

However many deer there were, everyone agreed that there were far too many of them. Acting in conjunction with the special investigative committee established by the secretary of agriculture, the Forest Service proposed a special hunt to thin its numbers. Despite pockets of support for this proposal, locals worried that it would set a dangerous precedent and jeopardize protection for the deer, and the National Park Service strongly opposed the plan.[71] The impasse of this debate prompted Dilg's special issue that included comments on the situation from the director of the National Park Service, the governor of Arizona, and the superintendent of the U.S. Forest Service.[72]

By late October when the magazine appeared, George McCormick, a Flagstaff rancher with a large network of friends, had already persuaded the regional supervisor of the Forest Service and the game warden for the State of Arizona to issue him a special permit for a massive deer drive. He proposed to herd the deer from the North Rim across the Colorado River to the South Rim where feed was more plentiful and winters were milder. In a contract signed on October 20, 1924, the State of Arizona agreed to pay McCormick $2.50 for each deer that reached the south side of the river, and authorized McCormick to remove neither less than 3,000 nor more than 8,000 head.[73] When Grey learned about this plan at his hunting lodge, he immediately contacted McCormick and offered his support. Their discussions revealed benefits for both and strengthened their alliance. Grey offered to make the drive even more lucrative for McCormick by offering him a lump sum for exclusive literary and motion picture rights to the event, which Zane had already convinced Jesse Lasky to underwrite.

In early December, McCormick rallied a band of locals from Flagstaff at the North Rim, and began work on two six-foot-high fences of wire and cheesecloth. They started these fences several miles apart and constructed them so that they gradually converged over a stretch of three miles to the place where the deer were supposed to cross the river.

Complications delayed the start of the drive until December 14. Reinforcements were slow in arriving, and far short of the numbers expected. Grey showed up with a band of experienced wranglers, but his priority was a favorable position for his camera crew. Worst of all, inclement weather arrived with biting temperatures and low visibility. At the outset, the motley crew of wranglers and Indians formed a long wavelike line, and moved slowly forward, using soft whistles to get the deer moving without spooking them. On the second day, as the drive entered the area of the fences, horsemen saw hundreds of deer ahead and realized that they were already hesitant and fidgety. That night a snowstorm hit and worsened the situation. The following day, as the fences checked their movements, the deer picked up the scent of the cameramen ahead and started bolting through gaps in the line. By day's end, the bulk of the herd had escaped to the rear; Grey was struck by a fleeing deer and almost knocked from his horse. No deer reached the river, let alone the other side, and the cameramen did not get any usable footage. Lasky honored his agreement, and paid Zane $30,000 for the film rights, but he did not bother to complete the film. Grey received $35,000 more from *Country Gentleman* for the serialization of his novel about the drive, *The Deer Stalker,* but Harpers judged the story so weak that it did not published the novel until after his death. Grey responded to this fiasco with a statement claiming that a restoration of predators might be a better solution. As predicted, the next two winters took a heavy toll on the deer population.[74]

Though the outcome embarrassed Grey, his involvement fulfilled a strong wish to act on behalf of his conservationist beliefs. While he was writing *The Thundering Herd* in January 1923, he had asked himself, "What is the younger generation to me?" and answered, "I am a faint little voice in the cataclysmic roar of the age." Since 1917 and *The Desert of Wheat,* he had set his novels in the present, and used them to criticize current developments, but the success of *Flaming Youth* and condemnation of his work had left him feeling out of touch and over the hill. Fearing that he and his Westerns might be passé, he identified with the past, and began to use it as the setting for his stories and to campaign on its behalf. If citizens forgot the past, he asked with more than a little defensiveness, would not the present be diminished and the future imperiled?

The Thundering Herd (1925), which was published a month after the hunt, supported this reasoning with a return to the 1870s when vast herds of buffalo still roamed the open plains. Grey presents this reversion to better times with an aggravated consciousness of looming disaster as whites come to hunt the buffalo. These brawny animals test the prowess of these hunters and fill their pockets with money, but Grey portrays the greatest challenge as comprehending the vulnerability of the animals before it is too late. Tom Doan, the chief character, is a young Buffalo Jones, and Grey even has him meet Jones at one point. When he initially decides to become a hunter, Tom is uneasy about his decision, but the hunting, handsome pay, and zealous application of himself dispell his reservations: "Tom felt that he hated to kill that glorious and terrifying beast, yet he was powerless to resist the tight palpitating feverish domination of his blood" (63).

Milly Fayre revives Tom's misgivings and alters his priorities. She and Tom fall in love early in the story, but are kept apart by a variety of impediments, including the fact that she, like Louise when Grey was writing the novel, is only seventeen and cannot marry until she is "of age" (118). Although Milly does not demand that Tom convert to her visceral opposition to the killing, she voices her objections, and Tom's deepening love has this effect. A massive stampede precipitated by hunters reunites them a final time, and a forlorn, motherless calf left behind turns Tom against hunting for good:

> The calf scarcely noticed him. It smelled of its hide-stripped mother, and manifestly was hungry. Presently it left off trying to awaken this strange horribly red and inert body, and stood with hanging head, dejected, re-signed, a poor miserable little beast.... Thousands and thousands of beautiful little buffalo calves were rendered motherless by the hide-hunters. That was to Tom the unforgivable brutality (372–73).

Tom decides to marry Milly and to take up ranching instead.

Although Grey hoped this ending would sensitize his readers to the impending extinction of these wondrous creatures, the best parts of his novel are the hunts and the hunters' lust for them. Also, the noble cause of the ending was compromised by Grey's lucrative alliance with the motion picture industry. The film version of *The Thundering Herd* opened two months after publication of the novel, and Jesse Lasky had discussed this project with Grey when he took over his film company and obtained exclusive right to his novels. At the time, Paramount was preparing two novels by Emerson Hough—*The Covered Wagon* (1923) and *North of 36* (1924). Lasky's production team increased the appeal of these stories of western settlement with stirring montages of wagons trains and cattle herds. Lasky urged Grey to invent similar scenes for his novel, and he obliged with the stampede.[75] Unfortunately, the problem uppermost in Grey's mind almost prevented his finale; there were so few available buffalo that Lasky had to appeal to Yellowstone Park officials for access to the herd there.[76] The cooperation of park officials made the filming possible, garnered valuable publicity, and alerted Grey and Lasky to the cinematic opportunity in the North Rim deer drive, a spectacular variation that could never have been arranged.

Grey's *The Vanishing American* (1925) appeared as a novel and a film later the same year. Originally written before *The Thundering Herd,* this work was far more controversial than either *The Day of the Beast* or *The Call of the Canyon,* and both versions were delayed over two years for changes and modification. With the deer drive and *The Thundering Herd,* Grey's lucrative alliance with the film industry posed no real threat to his commitment to conservation, but *The Vanishing American* intruded a harsh reminder this capitulation had some very painful costs. Grey's revision of *The Vanishing American* left him feeling compromised and betrayed.

The Vanishing American was the first of Grey's Western to make a Native American the main character. While the novel involved another component of the national heritage threatened by the advance of civilization, Grey was so aware that the demise of the Indian was an overworked convention that he intentionally situated his protagonist, Nophaie, in contemporary Arizona, long after the familiar battles had ended. If Grey did not want his novel to be reconfigured Cooper, he was not averse to reworking his own material. In the same way that *The Call of the Canyon* and *The Code of the West* updated *The Light of Western Stars, The Vanishing American* recycled *The Rainbow Trail.* Like Nas Ta Bega, Nophaie is the son of a chief whom whites have taken away from his tribe and educated in their culture. When he returns to his roots, he too gets slammed by a wave of modernization. His people have relocated to a reservation that is controlled by Christian missionaries and government agents. Unable to identify with the debased culture of his people or the exploitive one of whites, Nophaie feels like the defrocked Shefford, unhappily searching for direction and spiritual redemption. His grim future, his "vanishing," arises from the fact that he is unmarried and has no offspring, but Grey implies that his crisis is essentially one of faith: "That was Nophaie's tragedy—he had the instincts, the emotions, the soul of an Indian, but his thoughts about himself, his contemplation of himself and his people, were not those of the red man."[77]

Believing that his Indian blood makes him a warrior, determined to avenge the mistreatment of his people by German missionaries, and longing to escape his tortured thinking, Nophaie enlists to fight in the war. Like the protagonists in Grey's recent novels, he gets wounded and has to battle disillusionment when he returns to Arizona. There he discovers that 3,000 members of his tribe have been killed by the influenza epidemic, and he too contracts the illness. Nophaie's physical infirmity mirrors his spiritual condition, and he treats his illness by striking out for the canyons of Naza where he discovers an awesome arch that cures him as the Rainbow Bridge did Shefford. Grey presents this encounter as a resolution of the conflict in his Indian and white thinking, but Nophaie's hybridized faith is transparently Christian at its core:

> In this deserted, haunted hall of the earth, peace, faith, resurging life all came simply to him. The intimation of immortality—the imminence of God! That strife of soul, so long a struggle between the Indian superstitions of his youth and the white teachings forced upon him, ended forever in his realization of the Universal God of Indian and white man [and his acceptance of Christianity] (302).[78]

This climactic communion with nature, so characteristic of Grey, exposes how little Native American culture Nophaie actually possessed. His experiences and responses were so similar to those of Grey's other protagonists, and so different from those of his tribe, that he is a token Indian at best. Although Nophaie's needs and thinking were supposed to make the character comprehensible and engaging to white audiences, Grey quickly discovered that his journey into Indian country was fraught with more peril than he anticipated. With his previous novels, Grey's outspoken complaints provoked little opposition. Although his fulminations may have weakened the appeal of his novels, critics flayed them for other reasons. Grey's strident attacks had so little effect that he sorely underestimated their potential offensiveness. To him, missionaries and government agents were more examples of misdirected modernization; *they,* not he, were ones who misunderstood Indians and exploited them. However, when the serialization of *The Vanishing American* started to run in *Ladies' Home Journal* in November 1922, the magazine was deluged with angry letters from religious groups, and the Bureau of Indian Affairs vehemently denounced his depiction of their efforts.[79]

Other readers were offended by the blatant miscegenation in his romance. Marian is a white missionary and her involvement intruded not just a cultural difference but a racial one as well. In the original manuscript, Grey was determined not to mute this problem. During their discussion of marriage, Nophaie voices concern that their children would be half-breeds, and Marian indignantly replies: "You mean the white people who have damned the Indian? The civilization that sends men like Blucher and Morgan to *improve* Indians? So they would call our child a half-breed. Let them! And I would fling in their faces that I thanked god he *was* half Indian, this red blood might be proof against white blood he must inherit from me."[80] At the story's conclusion, the couple beholds a mass of "broken Indians" from a failed revolt moving toward the reservation and the setting sun, and Nophaie observes: "It is . . . symbolic, Marian. . . . They are vanishing—vanishing. My Nopahs! Only a question of swiftly flying time! And I too—Nophaie, the warrior! In the end I shall be absorbed by you—by your love—by your children. It is well!"[81]

The firestorm of objection to this social criticism and miscegenation worried Lasky that it could jeopardize his big budget production of *The Vanishing America,* and during their trip to the Rainbow Bridge he entered into delicate negotiations with Grey about amending the story. Through well-orchestrated appeals and production delays extending through the summer of 1924, Lasky gained concessions and shrewdly waited for the original controversy to settle and disappear. When the film was released in October 1925, Grey's missionaries and bureau agents were consolidated into a single villainous trader, and Nophaie ended up dead. Initially, the staff at Harpers capitalized on these developments to delay the novel, and then cautiously urged that it too be changed. Beleaguered and defensive, Grey wrote to his editor in May 1925 that the requested modifications were destroying the honesty and integrity of his work:

> This is the first time in my life I have been driven away from the truth, from honor and ideals, and in this case, from telling the world of the tragedy of the Indian. It is a melancholy thing. I wonder what effect it will have upon me.
>
> I sent back to you most of *The Vanishing American* novel, cut as much as I could bring myself to do it. The remainder, which was fine, I destroyed upon receipt of Briggs' letter. I will rewrite the conclusion and strain every faculty to give the novel a tremendous climax.
>
> It is a very good thing for my publishers that I am able to do this and not fall prey to morbidness and gloom and hopelessness, such as would affect most writers confronted by this situation.[82]

His rewrite did not eliminate the mistreatment of the Indians by missionaries and government agents, but it was greatly reduced. In his amended conclusion, as in that of the film, Nophaie dies from a gunshot wound. His final exchange with Marian in the novel was reduced to three sentences, and they contained no reference to marriage. Despite his outspoken objections, Grey once again did rewrite. However, this capitulation was more momentous. Grey turned away from social criticism in the Westerns that followed and ever more toward women and distant places to satisfy his needs.

Grey compensated for this disappointment with fence mending. On the heels of the letter of understanding that so lifted Zane's spirits, Dolly sent him another one in which she revisited his strained relations with his girl-friends and counseled, "You'll be much happier, if you try to take people as they are—for the best in them—than in trying to constrict them to an impossible ideal."[83] Dolly's generous defense of her rivals counseled her husband to be more accepting of the women who had offended him. Sensitive to the trauma of his recent depression, she urged him to be less possessive and less judgmental. Once again, she was modeling the advice she was offering, and the first improvement was her own marriage. Over the months that followed, she and Zane spent little time together and their reunions seldom lasted more than a few days. If they were, by tacit agreement, avoiding each other, their letters bubbled with an outpouring of affection and their pen-pal marriage was again a happy one.

By following Dolly's advice and emulating her example, Zane found his relationships with Mildred and Lillian also improved, and they too encouraged him to be more forgiving. After many months of silence, Zane suddenly wrote to Claire in June 1924, confessed that Lillian and Mildred had "jumped all over me for neglecting you since you were married," and proceeded to explain:

> If I have hurt your feelings by not writing or seeing you, I'm sure sorry and haven't a single excuse to offer, but lack of time. My intentions were always good. I can see, of course, that your marriage would not make the least change in your old friendship for me. Nor should it make one in me. But now that I've gotten a look at the thing I find there is a difference. For years when I came to N. Y., I'd find you thin, sick, frail, biting your finger-nails, etc., and all at once drag you out of that situation and put you on your feet again. It was the best of reasons why I should think of you. Now all that is past. You are well, happy, you have a fine husband, and you do not need me any more. There are others who do. That, and that only, is why I have not been as formerly. I have not changed in the least. It is *life* that has changed.[84]

During the 1923 Christmas season, Claire was hit by an automobile while crossing a street in New York City. Her right leg sustained multiple breaks and her doctors feared that the leg would have to be amputated. In March, as the leg responded to treatment but Claire still faced a long recovery, Zane wrote, "I sure hope that by this time your cheerful, optimistic spirit has had an opportunity to get busy again." As a gesture of goodwill intended to bolster her spirits, he offered her $100 a month to do secretarial work for him.[85]

When her rehabilitation went well and her marriage did not, Claire accepted Zane's offer and she was such good company on the fall trip to Oregon that Zane invited her to come along with Jess and Lillian on his trip to South America.

Prior to the abortive deer drive, Grey learned that his schooner was ahead of schedule, and that its renovations would be completed in time for the spring 1925 trip to South America that he originally planned. In early December, the finished ship, renamed *Fisherman,* left Nova Scotia for the Panama Canal. Several days into the trip, it ran into a raging gale and had to battle menacing seas for twelve days until it reached Santiago, Cuba. On the second day of the next leg, the new captain from Nova Scotia overruled his officers, cut between two dangerous reefs, and ran aground. The stranded yacht quickly attracted a crowd of natives intent upon looting. Fortunately, their attack was repulsed and high tide freed the ship. In Panama, a thorough inspection revealed a damaged keel, but it did not take much time to repair. Grey immediately hired Boerstler to replace his incompetent captain.[86]

On January 15, 1925, Zane, Claire, Lillian, and Jess left from San Pedro on a commercial steamer to connect with the refurbished *Fisherman* in Panama and strike out for the Galapagos Islands. Their entourage also included Mildred Smith; George Takahashi, his cook; Chester Wortley, a professional cameraman from Lasky Studios; Zane's son Romer and his friend Johnny Shields. At the time, Romer was fifteen years old and for several years had been exhibiting a headstrong, rebellious behavior that worried his parents. They had sent him to a military school, but he was unhappy and frequently in trouble there. For years, Zane sought to avoid a repeat his father's mistakes by not being a parent. "The children are beautiful—and all satisfying," he once wrote to Dolly and then candidly admitted, "Only I can't stand them long at a time. They disrupt me—separate me from my mind."[87] From his childhood memories, Loren is today able to recall only a single occasion on which his father spent the entire day with him.[88] With festering guilt, Zane speculated that his absence may have contributed to Romer's waywardness, and decided to include his son in his outings. On the trip to Nova Scotia, Romer missed only a few days of school, but he was so enthusiastic about the fishing that Zane decided to include him and his friend on the much longer trip to South America. This time, Romer missed most of his junior year in high school.

Grey's choice of the Galapagos Islands as his destination was strongly influenced by a trip recently completed by a team of scientists from the American Museum of Natural History and the New York Zoological Society. In 1924,

William Beebe supervised a book on the group's findings entitled *Galapagos, World's End.* The part of greatest interest to Grey was the chapter on game fishing written by Robert G. McKay, who had done deep-sea fishing in both Florida and Catalina. McKay reported that the waters around the Galapagos and the Cocos Islands contained swarms of bait fish, exciting mackerel, and many leviathans: "Several savage and unseen strikes carried away leaders or broke new hooks. What these were we have no means of knowing: we *do* know that they were too heavy for our frail tackle."[89]

Grey took special note of McKay's comment on swordfish: "We worked hard to find the sword-fish family. We saw them,—gigantic ones—but in the short time at our command we were not fortunate enough to land one."[90] The best part was his summary: "The fish have not been fished on these grounds and are abundant, have plenty of food, are consequently in excellent fighting condition and run to great size. The fishing grounds are not marked by charts and guides, as in Florida and this adds a pleasant factor,—here you are exploring and fishing at the same time."[91] In short, these distant islands were uncharted waters and a golden opportunity for more records.

Despite his luxurious accommodations, Grey conceived of his trip as an exotic adventure akin to his early trips to Mexico and Arizona. Even though he had spent countless hours aboard boats, he usually returned to port at day's end, and seldom remained on the water overnight. This would be the first time that he was out of sight of land for an extended period of time. During the first days of the voyage, he reveled in the grandeur of his yacht and the magnificence of the expansive ocean. Like the young Richard Henry Dana on his voyage from New England to pre–gold rush California, he could not take his eyes off the expanse of sail propelling him toward unknown possibilities:

> The motion of the ship was stately and beautiful, and the soft ripple of water, the creak of the booms, the flap of the canvas, were strange to me. I stayed on deck for hours. It was something staggering to realize where I was, and to look out across the dim, pale, mysterious sea. The worries and troubles incident to this long-planned-for trip began to slough off my mind and to leave me with gradually mounting sensations of awe and wonder and joy. I was going down the grand old Pacific; and there was promise of adventure, beauty, and discovery.[92]

Grey's scant record of his other days at sea suggests that once his initial intoxication wore off and he adjusted to the ship's roll, he retreated to his cabin and dutifully churned out manuscript. Still, his elegant stateroom was

The Fisherman, *ca. 1925. (Courtesy of Loren Grey.)*

not the comfortable refuge that his den at Altadena and his bungalow at Long Key had been. During a raging storm near Tower Island, a crew member reported a steamer nearby. When Grey's keen eyesight failed to locate it in the crashing darkness, he was tormented with imaginings of disaster. Claire wrote in her journal that the turbulence pitched her about the boat so that she "felt as though she had been beaten with a plank for my ribs and body ached and I was sore to the touch all over."[93] The peak of the storm paralyzed Zane, Lillian, and several others with fear, but the battered Claire was "quite thrilled" and fought her way up the steps "to see what I might see of the storm."[94]

Grey was much relieved when Boerstler and Mitchell successfully maneuvered his ship to its distant destination on time and without any course corrections. The lush vegetation of the Cocos and Perlas Islands, their cascading waves of flowers, and the erupting flocks of birds impressed him as truly exotic. On the other hand, the desolate Galapagos Islands were "one of the wildest and lonesomest places in all the Seven Seas" (56). Grey's strained efforts to convey the eerie beauty of these islands betray a discomforting awareness that they were *too* different from his beloved Avalon and Arizona. In a candid aside on the Cocos Islands, he admits, "It was one place where I would not have cared to stay long. There are places too primitive for the good of man" (42).

The fishing was even more disappointing. McKay's report had noted the ravenous sharks around the islands and their intrusion upon the fishing. As he explained, "Large fish are wary of attacking other large fish, but the moment either one seems to be in trouble or incapacitated he immediately becomes a victim. The attack seems more savage than the kill of the jungle, and the smell of blood arouses much the same instinct among fishes it does among the jungle carnivora."[95] Grey's concentration upon the positive initially caused him to discount this drawback as a familiar hazard. However, the fishing around the Cocos and Galapagos Islands left him increasingly shaken by the ferocity and menace of the numerous sharks. Any sizeable fish that he hooked immediately attracted predators and was devoured. One large fish was reduced to a grisly shredded head before he could be landed (29). When he hooked a wahoo, "fully six feet long, round as a telegraph pole," the onslaught of sharks so distressed Grey that he stopped his reel and broke off the fish (80).

Although the quantities of fish were as great as McKay had claimed, Grey was troubled by the absence of large game fish. Luckily, he did land "the largest dolphin I had ever seen" (55), and its weight of fifty-one-and-a-half pounds earned him a second world record. However, this was a large version of a small species rather than a big fish, and it brought him little sense of accomplishment. This drought, combined with the unappealing scenery, the torrid heat, and ever-present sharks, sapped his energy and exhausted his interest. As an outlet for their anger and frustration, Zane and R. C. turned to sharks, but the three they caught were sweaty, grueling work. They agreed that sharks were game fish, but Zane admitted that "I never had a moment's comfort" (84). In her journal, Claire records that she returned from a long outing to find a harpooned shark suspended from a yardarm of the *Fisherman.* Looking to her like a sailor that had been executed by a naval tribunal, she observed that the hanging was "the men's way of expressing their disappointment."[96]

In early March, the *Fisherman* arrived back in Panama and headed north. A week later, off the coast of Panama, a school of whales and numerous dolphins were sighted. Soon, sailfish appeared and became more numerous. On March 20, the day after the yacht reached Zihuatanejo, Zane spotted thirteen sailfish, hooked several, and finally caught the first one of the trip. "Doc is in a much happier condition of mind," Claire jotted in her journal. "I think the spell of ill-luck has been broken."[97] Over the next week, Zane and R. C. landed five large sailfish, each over 100 pounds, and Zane capped this good fortune with one weighing 135 pounds that eclipsed Keith Spalding's world record by three pounds.[98] The following day, while he was using light tackle, Zane hooked a giant black marlin. Estimating its weight at over 600 pounds, a world record for sure, he battled it valiantly for four hours before it finally broke loose.[99]

During his stop in Zihuatanejo, Grey had an "opportunity to study the natives" (138), and he presented his findings in a paragraph. He judged the men of the tribe to be violent, and he mentioned two killings by males over perceived interference with their marriages. He offered six decidedly "romantic" photographs as proof for his claim that the lives of these people were "most natural and romantic" (138). Claire, Lillian, and Mildred were far more interested in the villagers, and they spent most of their time in Zihuatanejo getting to know them. Claire found the women fascinating and admirable, and she questioned why the men elected to go fishing instead. Though her Spanish was rudimentary, she was so sincere and warm in her outreach that the native women referred to her as "*cara—muy cara.*"[100]

On April 8, the *Fisherman* reached the Gulf of California, and in Cabo San Lucas, the crew dropped anchor amid a congestion of commercial fishing boats and a yacht from Los Angeles. Grey beheld American goods being unloaded on the dock, and rejoiced at this first evidence of the culture that he had left behind. Ironically, at the most developed spot on his itinerary, he finally located the spectacular fishing for which he had been searching. On his first day, he caught eight large Alison tuna from the yellowfin family, three over 150 pounds and his largest a hefty 218 pounds. He lost three others almost as big, and broke the socket on his chair fighting one of them. R. C. and Mitchell did more damage to the chair with their large fish, eventually rendering it unusable. Grey was so exhilarated by the group's total of thirty-one tuna by the end of the second day that he questioned the captain of a commercial boat about their marvelous success, and he learned that his luck was not unusual. Unlike Catalina, where yellowfin had been declining for years, the numbers and size of them around Cabo had been strong for the previous eight years. The boatman explained that the situation in Catalina was not due to commercial fishing, as Grey had maintained in "Avalon the Beautiful," but rather to a shift in migration that kept the fish further south. This informant revealed that, south of San Diego, he had seen concentrations of albacore that extended a hundred miles, and fishermen had filled their boats to capacity without diminishing the populations.

On the third day of fishing, Grey landed a 318-pound Alison tuna that some have considered a third world record, although Zane never claimed it to be. Claire characterized the area as "a tuna paradise,"[101] and Zane wrote, "There was something wonderfully thrilling for an angler in this beautiful bay, with its wild shore line and the incredible number and size of the game fish. It was heart-satisfying" (184). His excitement intensified when he discovered that the gulf contained black and striped marlin. Efforts to catch them produced several dramatic fights, but the only one that Zane landed weighed a mere 180 pounds; a dozen of the tuna caught by the group outweighed it. Back at the dock, Grey was awed by a giant, 690-pound black marlin taken by a market fisherman. On an outing at the conclusion of their stay, the fishermen sighted a giant whale shark (*Rhineodon typus*). Since it did not flee and was impossible to catch with rod and reel, Grey decided to harpoon it. The men attached stout lines to the embedded hook, lashed them to the boat, and affixed empty casks to prevent the fish from sounding, but eight hours later, the leviathan initiated a sustained dive, broke free, and made off with their equipment.

Shortly after their departure for Los Angeles and the final leg of the voyage, the *Fisherman* ran into a punishing, relentless headwind that necessitated long tacks, and its progress north slowed to a crawl. Outside Mazatlan, as Claire finished typing Grey's account of the trip, a spar broke loose and

Zane Grey residence, Catalina, ca. 1925. (Courtesy of Loren Grey.)

crashed down onto his stateroom. Grateful to have escaped without injury, he decided to complete the trip by train. Leaving Boerstler and the crew with the ship, he and his guests cleared customs and purchased train tickets.

Shortly after their arrival in Los Angeles, Claire, Lillian, and Jess bade Zane farewell and headed east. This was a momentous parting with the Wilhelm sisters. After myriad trips spanning more than ten years, and after nine months on the go with him this time, Lillian and Claire left Zane for good and settled into their marriages. Lillian and Jess accepted jobs at guest ranches, and she arranged for her paintings to be displayed in the lobby of the Monte Vista hotel in Phoenix. Five years later, when the new Biltmore Hotel opened, she worked in the art shop in the lobby, where she was allowed to sell her paintings and her Hopi-style china.[102] Claire returned to New York City where Phillips met her train. After escorting her to a room he had reserved at the Plaza, he sat her on his lap and engaged her in a four-hour discussion that resolved the strains in their marriage. Several weeks later,

Zane Grey on Rogue River trip, September 1925. (Courtesy of Loren Grey.)

Laurie Mitchell wrote to her, "I miss your laughing face and jolly ways; you were surely the life and soul of the trip south."[103] Over the next three years, Claire had two daughters, and she gave up traveling until they were grown. Lillian and Claire saw Zane again only when his trips brought him nearby, and these visits were infrequent and brief.

Grey's decision to end *Tales of Fishing Virgin Seas* with a description of defeat—the whale shark that got away—was apt since his trip to South America fell short of his expectations. His experience in the Galapagos convinced him that McKay's glowing estimate of its fishing was overly optimistic. Zane was disappointed by the omnipresent sharks and absence of big fish; he caught his biggest fish at the end of the trip when he was closest to home. Had he gone to Cabo and devoted his time to fishing there, he probably would have caught a brawny marlin and broadbill, and perhaps set a world record that mattered. But this would have been following an already blazed trail. To his credit, Zane understood that the real achievement in his trip was the experience, not the fishing or his three world records: he had dared to journey far away from a culture he perceived as unreceptive to his values and beliefs. He had extended his range, reached the truly remote, and was now ready for somewhere even further away.

8

Fresh Starts and Farewells: 1925–30

Oh Dolly, the rooms are haunted. There are our spirits there. . . . Perhaps the strangest impression, of which I was not conscious at first, is that of going back after all these years—going back alone. I mean, and changed as I am.
—Zane Grey, Letter from Lackawaxen, late May, 1929

In its February 21, 1925, issue, *Publishers Weekly* ran an article about the one hundred best-selling authors from 1900 through 1924 and ranked Zane Grey number six. The five authors above him—Winston Churchill, Harold Bell Wright, Booth Tarkington, George Barr McCutcheon, and Mary Roberts Rinehart—started writing best sellers before 1910.[1] Since Grey did not make the annual list until 1915, he was more recent and would have been higher had the starting date been later. A follow-up article in 1927 entitled "The Most Popular Authors of Fiction in the Post-War Period, 1919–1926" ranked Grey first and the odds-on favorite to be the best-selling author of the decade.[2] However, there were telltale signs of trouble ahead. The February 21,

1925, issue of *Publishers Weekly* that carried its first article on best sellers announced the arrival of *The Thundering Herd* on its monthly list.[3] Although *Herd* remained on the list for three more months, it did not do well enough to make the annual list.[4] *The Vanishing American* was on the monthly list for two months during 1926, and also did not achieve the annual list.[5] *The Call of the Canyon,* which won third place for 1924, marked the last appearance of a Grey novel on the annual list.

Grey's 1925 absence from the list on which he had been a regular for nine of the past ten years was both significant and misleading. It is quite possible that the annual list for this year was flawed and underestimated the popularity of *The Thundering Herd.* That year, *Publishers Weekly* did not publish a list for April. Since its annual list was a weighted computation of the monthly listings, it is possible that *Herd* would have made the April list, and that the exclusion of this month skewed the annual computation against it. This possibility is upheld by *Bookman*'s "Monthly Scoreboard," which showed *Herd* at various positions for six months from January through June.[6] Grey's financial records furnish additional support. His initial royalty payment for the novel—the distribution from the publisher and normally the largest— was $32,000. *The Call of the Canyon* achieved the annual list for 1924 with a significantly lower first royalty of $29,000.[7] While the periods covered by these payments may have differed, *Call* may have also made the list only because its competition had weak sales too. Even today's more reliable list is based on relative sales and therefore is subject to similar variables.

Frank Gruber claimed that *Herd* and *Vanishing American* failed to make the annual best-seller list for 1925 because they were published the same year.[8] Although this is true, *Herd* came out in January, and *American* was not released until December, long after *Herd* had dropped from the monthly listings. Each enjoyed almost a full year of sales unopposed, and Harpers was too experienced and too protective of Grey to pit his novels against each other in a ruinous competition. In fact, *Herd* was more of a threat to *Call* since it appeared the same month that *Call* dropped from the list, but the staff at Harpers carefully orchestrated these releases.[9] In short, both *The Thundering Herd* and *The Vanishing American* did well enough to suggest that the sales of Grey's novels were leveling off rather than declining.

Meanwhile, his annual income continued to grow impressively. He earned $128,496 for 1921, $292,473 for 1924, and $323,948 for 1927.[10] Fees from his serializations continued to spiral ever higher. Back in 1920, he was surprised and thrilled to receive $10,000 for a serialization. Two years later, *Ladies' Home Journal* paid $20,000 for *The Vanishing American* and $30,000 for *The*

Thundering Herd. For *Nevada,* which ran in *American Magazine* over the fall of 1926, Grey received $40,000. The prices for movie rights to his novels were also rising, though not so dramatically. Lasky paid $20,000 for *The Call of the Canyon* and $30,000 for both *The Thundering Herd* and *Nevada.*[11]

The buttressing provided by the serial and movie versions spurred secondary sales of the novels and was crucial to Grey's becoming the decade's best-selling author. They also masked the fact that he was getting dangerously overexposed. As the increases from alternative sources overtook and surpassed first royalties from his novels, Zane discovered that he could make as much from a serialization as he got from a novel and an equivalent amount more from film rights. Unlike the staff at Harpers, neither Lasky nor magazine editors fretted about excessive supply. On the contrary, both clamored for as much as Zane could provide. Following the absorption of Zane Grey Pictures and its contract for exclusive rights to Grey's novels, Paramount filmed three of his Westerns over the summer of 1923. Lasky was so pleased with the cost saving and handsome returns of this trio that he ambitiously raised his investment. He allotted big budgets to *The Thundering Herd* (1925) and *The Vanishing American* (1925) and shrewdly cued their release to coincide with publication of the novels. Over the next two years, Lasky remade *The Light of Western Stars* (1925), *Desert Gold* (1926), and *Man of the Forest* (1926) even though Hodkinson had filmed these novels only six years before. He also filmed the serials *The Code of the West* (1925), *Wild Horse Mesa* (1925), and *Drums of the Desert* (1927), derived from the serial "Captives of the Desert" that was entitled *Desert Bound* as a novel. The appetite of audiences for these films was so insatiable that Fox capitalized upon the rights it had bought outright from Grey years before and remade *The Last of the Duanes* (1924), *The Rainbow Trail* (1925), and *Riders of the Purple Sage* (1925), with Tom Mix in the lead role. Over 1925, seven films of Grey's novels were released. Grey noticed the strength of this market, committed himself to writing more, and skirted Harpers' restriction of his output to a novel a year. He completed six chapters of *The Deer Stalker* in six days.[12] In order to finish another novel and have some free time over Christmas of 1915, he wrote forty-seven pages, over 10,000 words, in twelve hours of a single day.[13] The financial incentive for this kind of productivity was so great that he began to write stories exclusively for serialization. *McCall's* paid $35,000 for "Captives of the Desert." *Country Gentleman* paid $30,000 for "The Code of the West," $35,000 for "The Deer Stalker," and $35,000 for "Wild Horse Mesa," but Harpers did not publish any of these as novels until years later. Over 1928 and 1929, Grey published eight different serials, and Paramount speedily converted most of them into movies. Lasky was so receptive and so generous that Grey sold the rights to his name for *The Vanishing Pioneer,* which he presented only as a story idea that had little to do with the completed film. Grey's alternative sources of income grew even more important after *Nevada* (1928) for which first royalties fell to $20,000, but his combined return from the serialization and film rights were a record $70,000.[14]

All these developments added to Grey's fame and obscured the eroding appeal of his novels. Filmmakers and magazine editors noticed Grey's reputation more than the quality of his writing. They wanted Grey because the public recognized his name and flocked to offerings that carried it. Scriptwriters simply eliminated problematic elements like the missionaries and government agents in *The Vanishing American* and provided film crews whatever they wanted or needed. Often the end result had little resemblance to what Grey initially wrote. These lucrative opportunities stoked Grey's drive to write more—and to disregard his lapses into formulaic repetition and mannered styling; he was a moneymaking machine fueled by proven success. Recklessly confident that hard work could sustain his popularity, he fled doubt and worry and relied on trips to keep him motivated and productive.

Criticism of Grey's novels increased, but had so little effect that at least one critic decided to look beyond the quality of his work for answers to his success. In the February 7, 1925, issue of the *Saturday Review of Literature,* T. K. Whipple, a professor of literature at the University of California (Berkeley), published an influential article entitled "American Sagas." At the time, the *Saturday Review* was less than six months old, but it already had become a prestigious and influential literary journal. Its founding editor Henry Seidel Canby decided that Whipple's analysis was so timely that he featured it. Whipple asserts that Grey's appeal is evidence of the growing importance of the popular arts. "As everyone knows, the latest fad of the intelligentsia is discovering the United States," he proclaims at the outset. "This is the cult of which Mr. Gilbert Seldes is high priest." Seldes's *The Seven Lively Arts* (1924) had garnered widespread acclaim the year before for its impressive discussion of such diverse entertainers as Charlie Chaplin, Ring Lardner, and Florenz Ziegfeld. Seldes had argued that the success of these figures heralded the ascendance of new art forms ranging from musical theater to comic strips and that these arts deserved the same critical respect usually reserved for the traditional arts. In his acceptance of this challenge, Whipple does not bother with movies and magazine serials, but focuses instead upon the specific appeal of his Westerns as "tales of the American folk."[15] Insisting that "Zane Grey should never be considered a moralist," he claims that Grey's Westerns are modern versions of *Beowulf* and Icelandic sagas. Citing his "narrative power" and "powerful imagination," Whipple commends Grey for presenting "a battle of passions with one another and with the will, a struggle of love and hate, or remorse and revenge, of blood, lust, honor, friendship, anger, grief—all of a grand scale and all incalculable and mysterious."[16]

This estimate was as much a departure from "high brow" values as Seldes's study, but Whipple bundled his praise with asides that were as damaging as Rascoe's delayed condemnation of Grey's "purple cows." "His art is archaic, with the traits of all archaic art," Whipple explains, "His style, for example, has the stiffness which comes from an imperfect mastery of the medium. It lacks fluency and facility; behind it always we feel a pressure for expression, a striving for a freer and easier utterance."[17] Whipple does not speculate about what Grey might have been straining to say, but he does judge Grey's treatment of sex to be "simple and naïve," and says nothing about his condemnations of Jazz Age culture. Had Whipple been a bit more skeptical of the family man emphasized in Harpers promotion, he might have developed a different take on the sudden hesitations and plot turns that cut short attraction and keep the sexuality of his stories percolating but thwarted. If Grey had not made such a determined effort to eliminate his secret life from his fiction, he might not have seemed so "simple and naïve" about sex to Whipple. Because Grey capitulated to the advice of his editors at Harpers and kept his romances well within the bounds of propriety, his ritualized courtships *are* contrived, but they nevertheless do betray intermittent flourishes of an eroticism "striving for a freer and easier utterance."[18]

Seven months after the appearance of Whipple's article, the reasons for Grey's success sparked a heated debate between two prominent figures from the literary scene in New York City. In the October 1925 issue of the *Bookman*, John Farrar, its editor, devoted his regular column to "Clean Fiction," a title that echoed Robbins's praise for *The Call of the Canyon*. Farrar chastises Laurence Stallings for his harsh condemnation of the fall offering of new books and for ascribing to the same unreasonably high standards and negative bias of critics like Rascoe, Menchen, and Van Vechten. "Why should anyone be afraid to acknowledge that he likes to read, in his leisure moments, a *good story*?" he asks. During this attack upon the Algonquin circle, Farrar observes, "We should consider it foolish indeed to claim that Dreiser is a better influence upon Americans than Zane Grey."[19] Although Farrar meant his remark to be only an aside, it repeated several earlier endorsements of Grey. The year before, he had commented, "We should like to appraise Zane Grey as the modern Cooper and find what you think about it. Do you realize that Cooper, Poe, and Mr. Grey are the three American authors most read in foreign languages?"[20] The editors at Harpers noticed this rare example of praise and invited Farrar to develop it into a short article entitled "Zane Grey and the American Spirit" that they twice incorporated into Grey promotions.[21] Consequently, knowledgeable New Yorkers were already aware of Farrar's favorable bias toward Grey before his comment in "Clean Fiction."

Heywood Broun, a handsomely paid journalist and an outspoken proponent of lively criticism, quickly seized upon Farrar's remark and subjected it to withering ridicule in his September 30, 1925, column for the *New York World.* Referencing Farrar's equation of Grey with Dreiser, he announces, "I nominate John Farrar, editor of the *Bookman,* to be shot at dawn or even earlier." For Broun, Farrar is merely an excuse and his real objective is to assault Grey. "One of my chief complaints against Zane Grey is that he prettifies a wild and glowing country," Broun hisses. "It is a fine and thrilling land, but just the same the sage is not purple. It is much more a dun and dusty green like the belly of the snake after his indictment in Eden."[22]

Deciding that Grey's work presented too much opportunity for wit to settle for a single salvo, Broun opened his next column with an disingenuous apology that his damnation may have been unfair since, he admitted, he had never actually read any of Grey's novels. As a test case and as material for more columns, he proposed to read and report on *The Call of the Canyon.* "It may be that I am neurotic because I have read too much in the writings of sophisticated and cynical authors," he concedes to Farrar in feigned contrition. "I need the sanity, the strength and the wholesomeness which can only be found in one of the great popular authors of America." The reader anticipates a withering assault, but his hastily written columns offer mostly windy summary of the novel with two notable exceptions. Perceptively, Broun notices the eroticism in Grey's romances, which he dismisses as "a sort of ham D. H. Lawrence,"[23] and his social criticism, which he dubs "very precisely a Ku Klux philosophy."[24] Broun's blustery efforts to extend his discussion of Grey through six columns exhausted his sense of humor, but he understood better than Whipple those pressure points in Grey's writing with "a striving for a freer and easier utterance." However, it was not in these columns that Broun coined the single most famous criticism of Grey—"the substance of any two Grey books could be written upon the back of a postage stamp"—but they certainly anticipated it. The source for this comment is actually unknown, and it would probably be forgotten today had Grey not referenced it in his complaint against critics' mistreatment of his work.[25]

During the same fall of 1925 that Broun was writing these columns, Harry Scherman recruited him for his new Book-of-the-Month Club, which had 46,000 subscribers by the end of 1926, its first year of existence, and over 100,000 by 1929.[26] Broun and his associates on the selection committee profoundly influenced the club's selections, and they soon became the ones that made the best-seller list. Neither the Book-of-the-Month Club nor The Literary Guild, its rival, ever selected a Grey novel for their recommendations, and that eroded sales even more.

Meanwhile, when Grey returned to Avalon for the summer of 1925, he found a new residence completed and awaiting him.[27] At the time of his departure for Nova Scotia the year before, he had speculated that his summer at Catalina might be his last.[28] He was so vexed with Tom Mix and the Tuna Club that his mind was set on leaving—and he was oblivious to Dolly's plans for his hastily acquired property. Two weeks after his departure for South America, she wrote to say that she was already conferring about a new residence. She had met with a young architect who proposed an Italian villa and informed her that the size of house she wanted would cost at least $25,000. She also learned that she would have to pay Wrigley's Island Company an additional 25 percent. Realizing that Zane's priority was the lot's hilltop location and its dramatic views of the harbor and adjacent hills, Dolly was determined to get more for less and to have a house that "*fit* the topography." During a recent visit to the site, she recalled the "Indian buildings" that she had seen at the San Diego World Fair and at the Chula Vista golf club, and she decided that a Pueblo-style building with flat adobe walls and protruding beams would be beautiful and appropriate. Not only was this mission style traditional and fashionable, but its Western flavor complemented Zane's novels. Dolly's rough floor plan called for his study to occupy the highest position, with panoramic views in all four directions.[29]

Ed Bowen and Ken Robertson were with Dolly when she visited the site and they reminded her of the "Indian buildings" that they had seen together. Bowen came from a professional background in construction and had been working for the Greys for more than five years. Initially he did whatever was needed, but his conscientious efforts so impressed Dolly that she increased his responsibilities and allowed him to hire Robertson as his assistant. Both had accompanied her on her cross-country drives to Lackawaxen and her trip to Europe. Although both served as chauffeurs, Bowen's duties quickly evolved beyond this. He planned the itineraries for Dolly's trips, handled the reservations, and processed the bills. By 1925, he was her trusted advisor. Because Bowen had done such a good job supervising the third-story addition to the Altadena residence in 1922, Dolly trusted him to convert her ideas for the Catalina house into blueprints and arrange construction.

Dolly wanted the new residence built while Zane was away in South America, and to be finished and ready for him when he returned in late May of 1925. He had only to move in and do as he pleased—and that, of course, involved a lot of fishing. In "The Log of the *Gladiator*," he kept a daily accounting of his fishing over this summer. From June 9 until the middle of August, he and R. C. caught few fish, and Zane did not even spot a broadbill until August 4. A week later, R. C. landed a 343-pound swordfish and the fishing immediately improved. On August 24, both R. C. and Mitchell landed broadbills. The *Islander* reported that "Catalina experienced its greatest broadbill day in history,"[30] and Zane wrote in his journal that "I never experienced anything like this day, since 1914."[31] By the end of the month, the *Gladiator* had returned to Avalon with six broadbills.[32]

Apart from the fishing, things did not go so well. Dolly returned to Lackawaxen with Bowen and Robertson and left Zane on his own for the summer. Since his return from South America, Grey had been plagued by a series of colds that progressively worsened and threatened to turn into pneumonia. By mid-July he had failed to improve and his doctor advised him to have his tonsils removed. A week after the operation, he was still unable to swallow food, and his weight had plunged to 106.[33] On August 5, he went fishing for the first time, but he was so weak that he slept through most of the outing and returned exhausted.[34]

The new house brought Grey more problems. He was besieged by waves of tourists seeking to glimpse the famous author or to visit the new Indian museum. He posted a sign declaring that the house was a private residence, but no one heeded it.[35] "We are having our trouble with this Indian Museum of yours," he informed Dolly. Next, the water system failed, and visitors worsened the situation by entering unannounced and using the toilets. Three days before his jubilant comment about the fishing, Zane wrote in his journal:

> Avalon has changed. It is now a cheap, vulgar tourist-resort. The atmosphere has changed . . . I have grown tired of old sensations. Perhaps it would be well for me to try a change. The publicity now given to me is not pleasant to say the least. People flock up here to my Hopi house and many accost us in the street and wait for me at the pier. . . . This new house is a mark, a magnet for tourists and people who want to see me. They come, they mean well, but they annoy and distract me.[36]

In characteristic fashion, Zane relieved his aggravation by fastening his attention upon his upcoming trip, this time to Oregon. As soon as Dolly returned to Altadena, Ed and Ken started reloading the two family cars so that everything was ready when Zane arrived. Two days after his return, Zane, Mildred, Romer, Mitchell, and Takahashi headed north to link up with Wiborn and his wife.[37] During his visit to the Rogue River the year before, his third, Zane had learned that boats had never run the upper reaches of the river. Today, this type of river trip is popular enough to be commonplace, but people then viewed the river's rocks and rapids as too treacherous for boats. Part of the appeal of this adventure for Zane lay in arranging an appropriate boat. His previous conversations with a local store owner about the trip's feasibility involved boat design, and Zane was sufficiently impressed to arrange construction of four boats and to recruit a knowledgeable guide. Claude Bardon, whom the store owner suggested, was a commercial fisherman who had worked the lower river, and he showed up with four boats of his own. His twenty-three-foot boats with upraised bow and stern and flared gunnels were prototypes for the drift boats on Western rivers today, and Grey was wise enough to recognize their value and take them, too.

The ten miles and seventeen rapids that the group covered during the first day on the river were very emotional for Grey. The gentle water at the start allowed him to savor the magnificent beauty of the heavily timbered, mountainous terrain, but the narrowing canyon walls eventually funneled the boats into rapids so treacherous that he had to have Bardon run his boat through one stretch. Later, when Grey lost control through an easier stretch and grounded his boat midstream on a rock, he needed more help to avoid swamping, and his confidence was badly shaken. During a lining of the boats through another difficult stretch, he slipped and landed hard onto a rock. By the time he arrived at the campsite, he was bruised, starved, and exhausted.

Good food, magnificent scenery, and a two-night layover helped Zane to recover, but the trip's resumption quickly depleted his energy and convinced him that he had not yet recovered from his operation. Romer's reckless handling of a menacing rapid narrowly averted disaster and terrified his father. "Youth has no thought or fear of danger," Zane reflected afterward. "When I went down that wild jungle river of Mexico, the hot adventure had not been modified by cool reason."[38] Now fifty-three, fearful, and ever more dependent upon his guides, Grey worried about his vulnerability, and his state of mind colored his view of his surroundings: "But all wilderness dwellers, hunters and fishermen, and lovers of the forest hate automobile roads, and know they are one great cause, probably the greatest, of our vanishing America. The quail and the trout have vanished from California, and the forests are following. I am glad Romer can still see something of wild America, but I fear his son never will" (191).

Though he fretted about road-builders, loggers, and miners, Grey was so awed by the wild beauty of the river and the scenery that he mused about purchasing real estate, but his thinking was checked by the hard fact that he was in the middle of nowhere and the U.S. government owned everything in view. At Battle Bar and then at Winkle Bar, he noticed mining claims and realized that individuals owned this property and could sell it to him. Following a rapturous description of the open setting at Winkle Bar, its nearby stands of trees and its dramatic cross-river views, Grey wrote, "I fished all of one of the briefest and happiest days I ever had" (207). Though he had not seen a fish or gotten a single bite, he was so impressed by the site and the encompassing range of mountains that he arranged to buy it the following year, in July 1926.

Grey had poor fishing through most of the trip. "We are not having so good fishing as expected," he wrote Dolly from a midway point. He should have written "I" rather than "we." Later in the same letter, he mentioned, "Capt. M has caught over thirty steelhead. He's sure some fisherman."[39] "I am the most unlucky of anglers," he reflected at one point when everyone except himself had caught fish (192). This unusual acknowledgment of failure came from the fact that his freshwater fishing experiences had been very limited since he abandoned Lackawaxen for Catalina. Mitchell's success under these trying conditions transformed Zane into a serious student of his technique. On the thirteenth day of the trip, he finally caught his first steelhead and the last ten days of the trip went much better. He took six out of one hole and ended up with a respectable twenty-five, though far behind Mitchell's seventy-nine.

The final stretch of river was a relatively uneventful two-day push except for the rapids at Blossom Bar, which were the worst of the trip. Grey's description of the perils and Bardon's acrobatics in dealing with them read like a stirring moment from one of his novels. When he returned to Altadena in late October, he characterized his journey down the river as "one of the hardest trips of all my experiences," but he concluded that it had "left me richer by its marvelous contrast to the desert."[40]

While Grey was away, Dolly learned that Zane had sold a serial to *McCall's* without informing her. During the voyage to the Galapagos, he had helped Mildred with a novel entitled *Desert Bound*.[41] Following their return, she became so despondent over repeated rejections of her work and gossip about their relationship that Grey decided to submit it as a serial of his own to *Ladies' Home Journal.* When Currie was slow to respond, he went to *McCall's* and secured a prompt acceptance in order to lift Mildred's spirits before his departure for Oregon.[42] Dolly did not concern herself with the wisdom of Zane's decisions, but she did worry out loud about the potential fallout from this shift of allegiances. "Are you sure you're clear with Currie?" she asked and went on: "You said you wouldn't go into these things without consulting me, you know. I presume this is all right, but you do get into a lot of trouble you know." She conceded that *McCall's'* offer of $50,000 was impressive, but she fretted that Zane's hasty resort to a new outlet might offend the editors with whom they had had long-standing ties.[43]

Dolly's suspicion of trouble was confirmed quicker than either she or Zane expected. In November, Grey reflected in his journal, "The break I prompted between Editor Currie and me bears some vital significance." During the last four of their eight years together, Currie had served as editor at *Ladies' Home Journal,* and defensively, Zane sought to reassure himself that this break was for the best and that Currie "had begun to put the screws on."[44] True, Currie had advised Zane that the quality of his work was dropping and demanded major revisions to *The Thundering Herd* and *The Vanishing American.* He was also aware of the pioneering research studies of reader tastes commissioned by the Curtis Publishing Company, the magazine's owner, and could see from their findings that Grey's celebrations of elemental life and his condemnations of current social conditions did little to sell the products of advertisers. However, it was Grey's decision to take his work elsewhere that ended this deteriorating relationship. "This is another crisis of my career," Grey reflected. "But where there was once a note of despair in it, there is now victory. I am not yet marked for defeat. I want ten years of prolific writing, some of which will be my best."[45]

Confident of his productivity, Grey was not stressed by the break with Currie and *Ladies' Home Journal.* He was now free to sell his work to the highest bidder, and used his upcoming trip to New Zealand to keep the split out of his thinking. He had considered an excursion to New Zealand before purchasing the *Fisherman,* but it was Alma Baker who finally convinced him to go. Baker was a New Zealander from humble beginnings who married well and made a fortune from contract surveying, tin mining, and rubber planting in Malay. During the First World War, his expansion into aircraft construction added to his already substantial wealth and enabled him to travel the world and to pursue his lifelong interest in fishing. In 1919, Baker visited Catalina, and joined the Tuna Club when he returned in 1920. Grey met Baker at the Tuna Club and their conversations about their fishing adventures made them fast friends.[46]

In 1923, Baker returned to New Zealand for the first time in twenty-three years, and discovered fabulous fishing in the Bay of Islands off the north end of the north island.[47] Back in Auckland, he spoke so enthusiastically about his success to local newspaper reporters that government agents in the Tourist and Publicity Department solicited his advice on how to promote the country as a travel destination. Baker immediately thought of Grey, whose writings had popularized so many other areas, and suggested that he be extended an official invitation. Consequently, when Baker returned to Catalina during the summer of 1924, he brought Grey photographs of his catches and an invitation from the prime minister of New Zealand. Grey was impressed and quickly agreed to meet Baker in the Bay of Islands in the January following his Galapagos trip.

On December 29, 1925, Grey, Mildred Smith, Mitchell, and three truckloads of gear left Los Angeles for San Francisco, where they boarded the *S.S. Makura* for a voyage that took twenty-six days and covered 7,000 miles. In Urupukapuka, an uninhabited area a few miles beyond Russell, Grey set up camp with his own stoves, cots, tents, and even blankets. After commissioning several local boatmen for himself, including Francis Arlidge and his *Alma G,* Grey equipped the launches with his own fighting chairs and fishing tackle.

Over his three months in the Bay of Islands, Grey had the best fishing of his life. He caught a broadbill weighing 400 pounds (the first ever taken with rod and reel in New Zealand waters), a black marlin weighing 704 pounds, forty-one striped marlin (including one of 450 pounds that set a new world record), and seventeen mako sharks. He also landed a 111-pound yellowtail that set another world record.[48] *Tales of the Angler's Eldorado, New Zealand* (1926), his book about this trip, is perhaps his finest book about fishing—not because of the sensational fishing itself so much as his decision to present his success as a tale of woe in which he emerges as the Job of fishermen. This *Tales* opens with a rush of catches that exceed Grey's wildest expectations. Over the first two days, he raises six marlin and successfully lands one weighing 226 pounds. On the third day, this bounty becomes even more remarkable when Grey sights three broadbills and hooks one on his fourth pass. After a grueling fight of two and a half hours, the wearying fish manages to break free and Grey has this astonishing reaction, "I could not help deploring the usual manifestation of my exceedingly miserable luck as a fisherman" (43–44).

Given the propitious start to Grey's fishing, this echo from his Rogue River trip contains greater dissonance. On the Oregon trip, Grey had merely noticed that Mitchell caught more fish than he did, but Mitchell's greater success here has the effect of transforming the area's wealth of opportunity into a cruel trick upon Zane. After Mitchell lands a hammerhead shark hooked by the tail, Grey nicknames him "Lucky Mitchell" and explains: "That sobriquet of Lucky I had once given to Frank Stick, and it surely was deserved; but as Stick was not in the Captain's class for luck I had to switch the honor" (36). On a day that Grey elects not to fish due to the bad weather and choppy water, Mitchell returns with his first marlin. Zane again calls him "Lucky Mitchell" and calmly swallows his regret over not having fished. By the end of the second week, Zane has caught thirteen marlin and the fishing is so good that he hopes to catch a rare striped marlin. When he hooks a big one and it bolts in dramatic jumps, he is convinced he has done so, but it breaks free and he laments, "There was no disregarding my bad luck. The loss affected me deeply, as my most cherished ambition for New Zealand waters was to catch one of those great Marlin" (77).

When Mitchell lands a 685-pound black marlin the next day, Grey withholds comment and steels his determination. This rewards him with a 480-pound broadbill. "The broadbill created a sensation in the little town," he rejoices. "As late as eleven o'clock at night people were inspecting the fish with torches" (88).

When Mitchell loses a black marlin and is dejected, Grey counsels him to be pleased that he hooked the elusive fish, advice he himself did not follow when he was in the same position. "I was watching, you lucky fisherman," he could not resist adding. "Can't understand why your black Marlin did not jump aboard your boat" (90). An excursion to the Cavalli Islands sorely tests Grey's mixed emotions of excitement and regret. There he hooks and loses another large black marlin. The next day, as he probably should have expected by this point, he learns that Mitchell is battling a mammoth marlin that has towed his boat ten miles away from where he hooked the fish. When Grey's boat arrives, Mitchell's fish has yet to surface, but as he finally draws it up, everyone realizes that it is a black marlin and larger that his previous one. Zane does not fully comprehend the enormity of the fish until the next day when it is hoisted and shown to weigh 976 pounds. "What an unbelievable monster of the deep!" Grey exclaims. "What a fish! I, who had loved fish from earliest boyhood, hung around that Marlin absorbed, obsessed, entranced and sick with the deferred possibility of catching one like it for myself. How silly such hope! Could I ever expect such marvelous good luck?" (99). His letter to Dolly offered an even more candid admission of his anguish: "Yesterday I hooked one nearly as large and lost it through my cursed bad luck. Then to make it worse the Captain hooked another that took him to sea ten miles. But he got it—an appallingly beautiful and magnificent fish. . . . I don't think I'll ever recover from the sight of that fish and my miserable misfortune."[49] "I think I'd sell my soul to catch one like it," he added in a letter several days later.[50] This black marlin set a world record that would endure for more than twenty years.

At this point, Grey could not imagine that fate had worse in store for him, but a week later, he suffered a setback that was even more disheartening. Grey initiates his account of this tragedy with another large black marlin that refuses his bait and attacks Mitchell's. When Mitchell realizes what is about to happen, he wisely passes his rod to his frustrated boss who seizes it and quickly strikes. Just as the fish is solidly hooked, the boatman mistakenly pushes the throttle to full-speed reverse, creates slack in the line, and then severs it with the boat's propeller. "What a pang tore my breast!" Grey blurts. "I was frantic in protest against such horrible sudden misfortune" (111). Mitchell worries that Zane's misfortune and misery could cost him his job, and is as frantic as his boss for a change in luck. When another black marlin stalks his bait, Mitchell again hands his rod over to Zane, who settles into the fighting chair, positions himself, and slowly tightens the line. The fish's belligerent response initiates an epic battle that consumes thirteen pages. Grey's reel comes off his rod three different times, but he is able to refasten it each time without losing the fish. The great fish sounds a thousand feet and nearly exhausts his rod's resilience, but Zane finally triumphs.

Grey's 704-pound black marlin was only midway between the two that Mitchell caught, but it concluded his ordeal. A final excursion to Poor Knights Islands, twelve miles off the mainland coast, verified that his luck had indeed changed. The group arrived during a run of marlin, and over the course of a single day Mitchell caught five, while Zane hooked twelve and landed four. Grey captioned his photograph of their combined catches "World Record Catch for One Day."[51] Next, Zane landed a 450-pound striped marlin that gained him another world record and raised his marlin score to forty, happily placing him twenty ahead of Mitchell.[52] During the final week, he caught a 111-pound yellowtail that set another world record and placed him ahead of Mitchell in another category. "I thought gleefully of how thoroughly I had Captain Mitchell's eighty-pounder beaten," he proclaimed. "A little consolation was coming to me late!" (138).

Unfortunately, Grey's revived pride brought him other problems. In characteristic fashion, he aggressively publicized his success. Before his return to Auckland, where large celebrations were scheduled to honor him, local newspapers devoted extensive coverage to his new world records and offered prominently displayed photographs of his catches. Locals unaccustomed to press coverage of fishing perceived Grey as grandstanding and were offended. As one reported:

> He runs his fishing on circus lines. When he caught a swordfish he announced through a megaphone in grandiloquent tones, "Mr. Zane Grey has caught another swordfish: weight 273 lbs," as the case might be. Then there would be run to the mast head a pennant with "swordfish" printed on it.
>
> One Australian who regarded the procedure as swank, announced, when he caught a swordfish, that it weighed 6,000 pounds and in the place of the pennant ran up to the mast head his pajama pants instead.[53]

During his interviews with Auckland newspapers, Grey agreed to write a series of articles about his experiences for the *New Zealand Herald.* He considered this a gesture of goodwill, but he was so appalled by the primitive tackle and fishing tactics of New Zealanders that he could not resist castigating them: "The New Zealand angler, when he got a bite, merely held his rod up and let the boatman run the boat in the direction the fish wanted to go. He did not strike the fish hard, as we do. He did not bend the rod, or pump the fish hard as we do. He followed the fish out to sea, and several hours later returned with or without the fish, mostly without."[54] These observations were meant to be enlightening and helpful, but Grey did not recognize the condescension in his presumed expertise or anticipate the offense that it would cause. Letters of complaint poured into the *Herald.*

During this controversy, Alma Baker felt pressured to write letters to the newspapers defending Grey. Presenting himself as "the chief cause of Mr. Grey's visit," he sought to downplay the matter as an unfortunate misunderstanding arising from cultural differences.[55] Early in their stay at the Bay of Islands, long before the controversy, Baker sensed Grey's competitiveness and warily elected to camp and fish elsewhere.[56] As the force behind Grey's official invitation, Baker agreed to be with him more after the excursion to the Bay of Islands. Since government officials wanted Grey's visit to spotlight the country's resources for tourism, he and Baker were escorted by dignitaries to such attractions as the Waitomo Caves, the thermal geysers, and historic sites near Rotorua. Grey feigned interest in these, but was not animated until he was introduced to the country's freshwater fishing on

Lake Taupo and the Tongariro River. Grey, Mitchell, and Baker all caught trout over eleven pounds and many more in the six- to eight-pound range. Away from saltwater and the prospect of record fish, Zane was more relaxed and better company. The earlier controversy, however, kept locals alert to his faults, and stories circulated of guides being sent ahead to hold holes for Grey and of his attempts to purchase prime stretches of revered streams.[57] Sincerely flattered by the many New Zealanders who turned out to see him and to do all they could to make his visit special, Grey ignored this carping and tried harder to get along.

By the summer of 1926, Grey had returned to the United States and immersed himself in promotion of his New Zealand achievements. He again contacted Van Campen Heilner, informed him about the country's sensational fishing, and offered some specimens for exhibition at the Museum of Natural History. Grey explained that his collection of mounted fish had outgrown his storage space and proposed to donate it in the belief that a museum display would interest and educate visitors. Having been appointed field representative in the Department of Ichthyology the year before, Heilner was enthusiastic about Grey's offer and after conferring with superiors, wrote back:

> Was delighted to get your letter. Would like to hear some of the details of your fishing. Can you give me the dimensions of Mitchell's big marlin? What a *wow!* of a fish that was!
>
> In re. your fishes, the Museum will be delighted to get them. I will see that you get the *entire end* of the Fish Hall. This is the best position as it commands the entrance to the great Roosevelt Memorial Hall, soon to be constructed. As far as humanly possible the entire collection will be kept together. . . . You will be well pleased. It is the rightful place for your collection—the Museum will treat you right and it will be a *fine* thing for both of you. Thousands will see them that might not otherwise and they will be preserved for posterity.[58]

From his close association with Heilner, Grey had advance knowledge of planning for a new Hall of Fishes. He knew that his collection would make a handsome exhibit and greatly reduce the cost of purchasing specimens for the new hall. Realizing that a major exhibit could strengthen his position at the museum, Heilner encouraged Grey to contribute as many specimens as possible and persuaded the board that his collection would offer a unique sampling of the world's game fish. Over the past two years, Zane had caught and preserved many strange fish, like his exotic rooster fish from South America, along with seven that either were or had been world records.

Three weeks after Heilner's enthusiastic response, Grey increased his world records to eight. On July 2, 1926, he landed a 582-pound broadbill near Catalina. After two years of mounting frustration as anglers from the Tuna Club broke the existing record, he was finally able to claim the largest *Xiphias gladius.* Predictably, the Tuna Club refused to recognize his catch because his 39-thread line exceeded regulation limits. A brief announcement of the catch, hurried into the July 7 issue of the Catalina *Islander,* stated that the next issue would carry Grey's account of the battle, but it did not.[59] Although the newspaper ran a photograph of Grey and his fish on the front page, there was no article.[60] Neither Grey nor the newspaper wanted more controversy over whether the catch was legitimate. Grey believed that he would get better publicity by adding his broadbill to his museum exhibit. There, far more people would learn about his impressive catch.

Meanwhile, Grey hoped his upcoming trips would furnish more specimens for the exhibition, which was currently scheduled for the fall of 1928. His second trip to New Zealand over the first five months of 1927 included a two-month stay in Tahiti. Again Mildred and Mitchell accompanied him, but this time he also took R. C., Reba, and Romer. Zane's inclusion of him on this trip prevented Romer from starting college, and he never bothered to attend after he returned. Unfortunately, the forty-two days of stormy weather created impossible conditions and the only significant catch of the trip was a 640-pound thresher shark that Zane initially believed to be much smaller and allowed Romer to land.

Zane countered his disappointment over the New Zealand visit with hopes that Tahiti might bring him better fishing. Grey had intensely disliked Papeete, when his steamship stopped there on his trips to New Zealand. He objected to the easy availability of drink and women, believed that the romantic image of Tahiti had turned both natives and visitors into derelicts, and wished he could avoid the island. But when he subsequently learned about Tahiti's extensive reef formations, he speculated that their large concentrations of bait fish would attract large game fish. His research uncovered rumors of bizarre swordfish whose bill grew from the lower jaw, and of a shark that killed its prey by sucking out its blood. He also discovered an article in *Harpers* about Tahiti by Charles Nordoff, the coauthor of *Mutiny on the Bounty,* who had been living there for years. Nordoff's response to Grey's letter of inquiry assured him that Tahitian waters did indeed hold big fish and convinced him to try fishing there.

Unfortunately, the inclement weather and poor fishing in New Zealand so discouraged R. C. and his wife that they chose to forego Tahiti and head back to California. Zane was too committed to back out; both Nordoff and the refurbished *Fisherman* were awaiting his arrival.[61] At the outset of *Tales of Tahitian Waters* (1931), Grey caused considerable misunderstanding about this first visit to Tahiti by carelessly stating that he had arrived in Papeete on May 30, 1928 (instead of 1927). Though this was his fourth time in Tahiti as he claims, his previous visits had been brief layovers. On the other hand, he was forthright and accurate in acknowledging that the fishing was disappointing. Both Grey and Mitchell sighted and hooked promising fish, but they landed only nine midsized marlin, the first ever taken in Tahitian waters. Grey left believing that he had come at the wrong time and that the prospects for big fish were much better during the fall months.

Although these trips failed to produce any additions, the exhibit of Grey's fish at the American Museum of Natural History opened in December 1928. Grey's mounted fish filled two entire walls and were impressively lit. One showcase contained barracuda, sailfish, and grouper, and was topped by the smaller of his giant tuna from Nova Scotia. The opposite wall displayed his 582-pound broadbill positioned at the center, and his yellowtail from Cabo San Lucas pursued a flying fish off to the right, though both had by then been surpassed as world records. Zane's world-record tuna from Nova Scotia was located so as to invite comparison with his broadbill. Grey's 702-pound black marlin and his 2,000-pound "ocean sun fish" (harpooned in Tahiti) were also displayed. In its account of the new Hall of Fishes, the *New York Times* offered a secondary headline "Exhibit of Trophies of Zane Grey, author, Includes Catches in All Parts of the World," and characterized his collection as "one of the largest and most interesting exhibits in the new wing for the average visitor."[62] Another article about the collection by Francesca La Monte, a museum curator, stressed that the game fish "were caught in a sportsman-like way, with tackle strong enough to subdue the fish, and not to break off a number of hooked fish in an endeavor to catch one on a lighter tackle." Two months before the show opened, the October 1928 issue of *Field and Stream* came out with an updated list of world records and that cited Grey for his catches of dolphin, striped marlin, tuna, and yellowtail.[63] This exhibit of Grey's fish at one of America's foremost museums and in the city of greatest cultural influence effectively validated his preeminence as the country's most accomplished saltwater fisherman. During this same year, it is worth noting, Ernest Hemingway visited Key West and tried saltwater fishing for the first time.[64]

Grey did not attend the opening of the exhibit because he was back in Tahiti. His stay from July to December 1928 proved to be even more trying than the year before, perhaps his worst fishing trip ever. For this visit, Grey commissioned Collins and Bell in Auckland to build him two new launches, each thirty-four feet long. Since both were too large to be carried aboard the *Fisherman,* he had them freighted to Papeete and motored around the island to the remote, outlying islands he wanted to explore. Two months of determined searching and experimentation did not produce a single bite. To his dismay, Grey learned that the information from his previous trip was erroneous, and he had again arrived too soon for the best fishing. "We were deceived about the time to come here," Zane complained to Dolly. "Oct., Nov., Dec., were drummed into us last year. As a matter of fact, Dec., Jan. & Feb. are the months. That upset me much."[65] Torrential rains worsened the situation, and they were accompanied by an outbreak of influenza that killed many natives and gravely sickened several members of Grey's group. Finally, on November 14, after eighty-three days without catching a fish worth mention, Zane successfully landed a 464-pound striped marlin that bettered his own world record, the 450-pound striped marlin from New Zealand.[66]

This catch solidified Grey's commitment to Tahiti. Near the end of his previous visit, he had stopped at Flower Point in the southeastern corner of the island where his group camped for several days on an overlook of the ocean that was surrounded by a cloud-garlanded, heavily foliaged range of high peaks. In his *Tales of Tahitian Waters,* he judged this area to be "the most beautiful part of a beautiful Tahiti" (48) and used it as his base camp for the 1928 visit. While he was there, he negotiated purchase of a sixteen-acre plot of land and arranged construction of cottages, dining hall, cook cabin, and a power station.[67]

This purchase and his two new launches were part of a 1928 spending spree that rivaled the one in 1920. During his summer visit, he launched an ambitious program of renovations to the rude dwellings on his Winkle Bar property in Oregon. In September, Dolly purchased a 160-acre grapefruit orchard in Indio, California, that was renamed the Flying Sphinx Ranch. While he was in Tahiti, Dolly and Ed Bowen built Zane a lavish new office at his Altadena residence.[68] This two-story addition, known as the east wing, was connected to the main building by a narrow hallway. The ground level was used as an enormous storage area, and the upper level contained a spacious two-room den area measuring forty-eight by seventy-five feet. The first room served as a library for Zane's books and Indian artifacts, relocated there from the much smaller room downstairs that Lillian had ornamented with Hopi figures. The larger area beyond, intended for writing, featured some of his favorite memorabilia, including a large hand-painted photograph of the

Rainbow Bridge above the fireplace. The dark, exposed, rough-hewn ceiling beams that supported the roof gave the rooms a lodgelike atmosphere and were major items in the overall high cost of $28,000.

Another even larger expense was a new house in Altadena that Grey financed for Mildred Smith. She had accompanied Zane on all his trips to the South Seas, and during the second voyage to New Zealand in 1927, young Romer wrote his mother:

> I was just thinking. Honest! And this is what I was thinking about—
>
> Dad is too clear minded to realize what people think about him dragging friend Millicent [an alternative name Zane gave Mildred] all over the way he does—and I am wondering if you hadn't better put him wise. Good Lord what else could they think—the majority of people?
>
> In his innocence he makes some awful brodies. His and M. K. S.'s cabins in the steamship always across the hall from one another; always next to him at the table; the way she talks; her actions as hostess to visitors; imagine his secretary with *some* airs. It would be a miracle if people believed the truth. They would always think the worst.[69]

Mildred Smith's Altadena residence that Zane Grey financed, ca. 1928. (Courtesy of Loren Grey.)

Dolly sent the letter back to Zane along with a note stating, "This is a very sincere tribute to you from your son. I'm glad he thinks this way about you. If only he knew how often I had told you! After much deliberation, I decided to send you this."[70] Though she sometimes felt threatened by Zane's closeness to Mildred, she worried as much about the relationship's volatility and instability.

One major source of friction between Zane and Mildred was their literary collaboration. Over the many years of typing and editing his manuscripts, Mildred harbored intense longings to be a writer too. Realizing that she was as needy and as insecure as he was when he started, Zane encouraged and helped her. After she completed a novel entitled *White Harvest* during their trip to Nova Scotia, he tried unsuccessfully to place it with a publisher for her. In support of her efforts, he collaborated with her on a series of plays— *Three Tight Lines, The Courting of Stephen, Ports of Call,* and *Amber's Mirage.* This close interaction, combined with her failure to achieve any success, made Mildred both more critical of Zane's work and less sure of her own. A 1927 letter from Zane to Dolly illuminates the tension that resulted:

> I have absolutely kept my word to you about the writing, and I will never publish a word again that you do not go over. Part of the trouble with M- was that I refused flat to accept any change in my MS, or anything written in it by herself. It is all right for her to correct any errors, and to cut when necessary. But I absolutely refused to listen to her ideas of what was wrong here and there. So we quarreled. She has sworn a dozen times that she will quit her job upon arriving home. I certainly do not want her any longer unless she changes.[71]

Mildred's failure to find a publisher for *Desert Bound* left her so upset and despondent that Zane intervened and rewrote it. His hasty resort to *McCall's* for an acceptance not only offended Currie and ended his long association with *Ladies' Home Journal,* but also committed him to the dangerous practice of selling his serials to the highest bidder rather than to faithful clients who had purchased his work for years. When no one was willing to produce *Amber's Mirage,* Zane reworked the play into a novel and had to fend off complaints from Dolly about allowing his involvement with Mildred to influence his writing. "Again and for the last time I think you have exaggerated M's claims about my work," he wrote in defense of his decisions. "She acknowledged that she had claimed to be of assistance to me. But even if her friends or folks have augmented that claim to the extent of starting gossip, I doubt that it can ruin me. . . . I did take M's advice about a little of the rewriting. To be honest it helped me to get her point of view."[72]

Grey treats his indebtedness to Mildred as minor, but his financing of her new house suggests that it may have been greater than he was willing to admit. By 1928, she had been with Grey for over fifteen years and was his companion on the long, demanding trips of the previous three years. By his own admission, she was also more than a typist on *Desert Bound* and *Amber's Mirage,* which he sold as serializations for $70,000. Because Mildred wanted a house of her own in Altadena, she pressured Zane for financial support. As he explained in the same letter to Dolly in which he acknowledged Mildred's editorial help: "About the house in Altadena, she (Mildred) is in despair about the expense. And I really believe that I will have to take it off her hands, by giving her what she has paid out on it. Several thousand on building, and somewhat more on furnishings. And that's all."[73] Mildred's house was an adobe structure of 4,200 square feet and had a Pueblo styling similar to Grey's Avalon residence. Ed Bowen supervised its construction and Margaret Sears was hired as landscape architect. Clearly, Mildred's secretarial wages were inadequate for the mortgage payments. When she could not meet this obligation, Zane assumed her payments and covered the cost of her furnishings. In the absence of any recorded comment from Dolly, one can only speculate how "faithful Penelope" reacted to the grand new house across town that her husband had financed for the alternative woman in his life.

Grey's hectic, transient, unconventional life during the recent years contained ample amounts of frustration and discontent, but he no longer suffered from the debilitating depressions that had plagued his writing career through the crisis of 1923. In a March 12, 1928, entry in his personal journal, he reflected, "The old black mood rarely visits me now."[74] A month later, this realization spurred him to reread one of his journals and track the ebb and flow of his emotions in the past. Shocked to discover how dark and despondent he had been, he nonetheless rejoiced at how strange and unfamiliar those moods now seemed to him. "I find I have succeeded in rising above the old black moods," he exulted.[75]

Grey remark about the disappearance of his "old black moods" occurred following his return to Altadena from a stay in Long Key from January through March of 1928. This was his first visit in four years and, following a comment on his positive mental health, he wrote, "Beautiful as ever, but my travels in the Pacific have spoiled me for Florida. Even the fish looked amazingly small."[76] Grey's trips to the South Seas had not only carried him far away from Long Key, Lackawaxen, Catalina, and Arizona, but had also distanced him from the emotions associated with these locations. Although his disappointment here was neither great nor surprising, it was real and portentous since he never again returned.

A year later, in May 1929, Grey was in New York talking with editors and decided to take a side trip to Lackawaxen, which he had not visited since 1922. The fifty-seven-year old Zane encountered changes that disturbed him far more than the ones at Long Key. In a letter to Dolly about his experience, he explained that he had been struck by the passage of time when he boarded the train. The schedule and regulations were very different from the ones he had known, and because the new reservation system would not issue him a ticket, he had to use his influence to secure one. To his surprise, the train no longer stopped in Lackawaxen, and he had to get off in Port Jervis and take a car from there to his residence. The trees and foliage of the surrounding area had grown so much they seemed like a jungle, and his encounter with the old buildings set off a tidal wave of memories and emotions:

> I was overcome with the beauty, the sadness, the loneliness, the desertedness of it all. Oh Dolly, the rooms are haunted. There are our spirits there. I thrilled and I wept. I recalled everything. I felt the cold of the old cottage, I saw you in bed. I heard Romer's tiny wail. I heard the wind, the river. For the first time I went into the room where my mother died. Something strange came over me there.
>
> The dust, the dirt, the decay, the river reproached me. Why have we not taken care of those places? They are a first and great part of our lives. Love, struggle, work, children, all came to us there. . . . Perhaps the strangest impression, of which I was not conscious at first, is that of going back after all these years—going back alone, I mean, and changed as I am, drew me in a circle back to the days of struggle, of agony, of growth. It would be great for me to return there, and stay a while to roam, and walk, and dream, and ponder. It would be a spiritual consummation, a realization, a most splendid experience for my creative power.[77]

But he did not linger or ever return. In characteristic fashion, he bolted for somewhere else. A week later he was in Newfoundland fishing for salmon. Originally, he had planned to go to Norway on what would have been his first trip to Europe, but when he realized that Newfoundland was closer and offered better fishing, he canceled the Norway trip.[78]

In August, he went to Arizona in order to "show my West to Romer and Betty."[79] There he gathered not only his two children but also a large a group that included Mildred, Takahashi, and Bob Carney, a friend of Romer's who would marry Betty a year later. Zane had arranged an ambitious itinerary in-

Zane Grey in Lackawaxen, May 1929. (Courtesy of Loren Grey.)

volving Zion National Park, Bryce Canyon, the Grand Canyon, the Havasu-pai reservation, and a month of hunting at his lodge near Payson. The high point was to be a horseback excursion to the Rainbow Bridge.

When Grey arrived at Flagstaff, he was immediately struck by how much the city had changed. Cars and tourists had replaced the cowboys and horses that once filled the streets. The rude, dusty town in which he watched a jury of weathered locals deliberate the fate of Jim Emett back in 1907 had disappeared and been replaced by a bustling center of commerce best exemplified by the new three-story Monte Vista hotel.

Grey's dismay over this development and change was intensified during the automobile trip to Kayenta. He immediately missed the horseback rides of his previous visits, and his misgivings about the outing were confirmed when the cars had difficulty with several stretches of quagmire. When he encountered Indian men in coveralls and their women in cheap store-bought dresses, he saw cultural annihilation, and his dismay intensified when he learned that the area's wild horses had become diseased and had to be shot.[80] In the guest book at the Kayenta Trading Post, he penned a troubled reflection on how different the area was from eighteen years before when he first visited it:

> It was in the heyday of its existence, colorful, bustling, primitive, beautiful, dominated by the splendid spirit of the pioneer Wetherills. . . . Peace and prosperity pervaded Kayenta. Love of the Indian and service to him.
>
> In the succeeding years on each visit I saw a slow change working. Time is cruel. The years are tragic. The pioneers could not stay the approach of deadly civilization. In 1923 I felt the doom of the Navajo. 1929 showed me the truth of the vision I had felt—the ghastly truth of the vanishing American. . . .
>
> But the desert remained the same. The so-called civilization of man and his works shall perish from the earth, while the shifting sands, the red looming walls, the purple sage, and the towering monuments, the vast brooding range show no perceptible change.[81]

When he departed with his party for the Rainbow Bridge, Zane worried that Night, his horse, might be too spirited for him and opted for a gentler one. En route, he was drained by the heat and a severe case of diarrhea. The trip "damned near killed me," he confessed to Dolly,[82] and the emotional toll was greater than the physical. He was disturbed by the abandoned hogans along the way, and the only people he saw were white tourists. At the Bridge, the antics and lack of respect by the youngsters in his group left him questioning whether he should have returned. By day's end he was so troubled and depressed that he could not sleep. His insomnia spurred him to a final solitary visit to Nonnezoshe and to write this poignant, unpublished account of his final night at this special place:

> Sleep seldom visited me . . . [and was] quite impossible owing to the noisy youngsters. Nonnezoshe did not rouse my reverence in them. But at last they fell asleep. By midnight everyone in my party was asleep, leaving the lonely canyon, the bridge and a melancholy owl to silence and to me.
>
> Then I began my night quest. I prowled like a panther seeking prey, but that was only because I could not sit or stand long at one point. It seemed as if I was trying to find a place where Nonnezoshe would explain its mystery.
>
> After hours a belated moon, misshapen and weird, passed the ramparts alone and flooded the canyon with strange light, unearthly and beautiful, I watched this moon go down until again the mystic shadows dominated. It was three o'clock when I softly trod among the sleepers, lying prone. Betty with her fair face upturned to the sky. Romer with his dark face upturned to the sky. They slept the sweet deep sleep of youth, with no knowledge of my lingering over them in the dead of night, with the cursed, menacing shadows of Nonnezoshe hovering over me.
>
> I stole away back to my bed, where I sat under the cedar, looking up. And all seemed magnified. Between the moon-blanched cliff and the dead black wall, which reached to the stars, the glorious thing arched. The silence was so unbroken that I could hear the beating of my heart. Silence of stone! It was a sepulchre. At that hour it seemed the most sublimely lovely phenomenon of nature in all the world. Impossible not to dwell on the spiritual power in the rocks, or the beauty of life, or the meaning of God, and the certainty of immortality! Some day Nonnezoshe would crash. Someday the sands of the desert would bury its shattered remnants. But of what?
>
> Nas ta bega [dead since 1918] came to me then. He was there in the shadow—the soul of the Indian, I did not question or doubt. I grasped that truth to my living soul. He gazed up at Nonnezoshe with me, but while he understood, I could not pierce beyond the physical confines of that lonely canyon.
>
> The moon went down, the chasm darkened, the bridge took on spiritual form, gray in the hour before dawn. It changed, it lightened. Lo! Day had come, cool and wan. And I returned to the spectacle of giant walls connected by the crescent of stone, waiting through the ages to fall.
>
> My party was the first to visit Nonnezoshe during 1929, and here it was late September. It was unlikely that there would be another this year.

> And I would never come back. Airplanes might in the future zoom over
> Nonnezoshe Boco; grasping men, despoilers of beauty, might blast an
> automobile road down that canyon, but the Red Indian trail was fading
> forever.[83]

The hunting trip cemented Grey's decision never to return. As he was preparing to go to the Tonto Basin, he learned that the hunting regulations had been changed since his previous trip and that the season would not open until a month later. Since he had already arranged for a film crew to cover his hunt in October, he applied for a special permit to shoot some "pig-killing" bears near his cabin. His meeting with Tom E. McCullough, the resident game commissioner, went well and he left confident that the state game warden would approve his telegrammed request. However, the warden immediately called a special meeting of the game commission in Phoenix to deliberate the matter. The meeting attracted state residents who knew that the area was under review for game preserve status and vehemently opposed exemptions. Because the dispute involved a famous author, newspapers covered the hearings and made the situation worse for Grey. His request was denied, and he construed the decision as a personal vendetta.[84] "I was refused a special permit and insulted publicly by the state Game Warden," he complained to Dolly. "The Game Commissioner of Flagstaff, a two-faced-[word intentionally left out] who pretended to be friendly to me over there, got up in the meeting on October 5 and roasted me vilely." Grey explained that he wanted to cancel his plans and leave immediately, but decided to stay so that everyone with him was not inconvenienced and disappointed.[85]

As with his resignation from the Tuna Club, Grey initially stifled his vexation and belatedly decided a public statement of his position was necessary. On October 10, 1930, he wrote a letter to the *Coconino Sun* announcing that he would never again return to Arizona. He openly acknowledged his resentment over the handling of his special request, but stressed that this was not his only reason. He maintained that the deserts and forests of Arizona were being sacrificed to the commercial interests of lumbermen, ranchers, hunters, and especially tourists. Each was intent upon money and oblivious to the consequential depletion of precious resources. The agencies that were supposed to protect these resources were pawns for these interests, and the beauty of Arizona's wilderness was imperiled.[86] The Arizona that he had explored and loved for so many years would soon be gone forever, and henceforth, he would write without visiting the state that had long served as vital inspiration for his dreams and fiction.

9

Undone:
1930–39

No chance of selling a picture now—they're all retrenching
and laying off. Everyone is busted. Everyday one hears of
millionaires losing everything. You may have read many
things—they're all trying to spout optimism, but meanwhile
the rout goes on.
—Dolly Grey, Letter to Zane, June 8, 1931

Common understanding of Depression history holds that it began on October 24, 1929, when the stock market "crashed." On that day the Dow Jones Average gave up thirty-four points, or 9 percent, on trading volume that was three times normal. The selling actually started in September when the market hit a record high of 386. Black Thursday, as the 24th came to be known, saw an across-the-board plunge that erased paper profits for the year so far. Moreover, the decline continued through the rest of October and persisted into November. By November 13, the DJA had dropped to 198,which represented a 40 percent loss of its September value. Over the winter, stocks steadied, reversed, and gradually recovered almost 75 percent of the ground they had lost. When the DJA clawed its way back to 294 by April 1930, confidence revived, and many believed that prosperity would be back soon. A punishing, unremitting slide followed and pushed the DJA to a low of 41 on July 8, 1932. The specious hope of 1930 evaporated, as stocks fell to 25 percent of their 1929 high, and some were hit even harder.[1] This corrosive scenario, with its deceptive signs of hope and wrenching betrayal, helps to explain Grey's disregard for the state of the economy in 1930 and its catastrophic consequences.

In his first journal entry following the calamitous October week of 1929, Grey, either oblivious to the crash or too self-absorbed to be bothered, wrote, "I cannot get used to the great airplanes, roaring over head during the day."[2] He still perceived widespread prosperity, and wanted to use his wealth to get as far away as possible. For 1929, his total income reached $340,717. *Colliers* paid him $80,000 for serial rights to "The Yellow Jacket Feud," and *American Magazine* forked over $65,000 for "The Drift Fence." *Country Gentleman* got "Rustlers of Silver River" for only $50,000, but this was part of a package that guaranteed Grey similar payments for two more serials. Paramount sent its usual $40,000 for the film rights to *Fighting Caravans* and remained solidly committed to him.[3] Since Dolly owned few equities, the fall sell-off had little immediate effect upon her investments. The problem for her and Zane was spending rather than losing. "I am sorry you are broke," he complained to her from Arizona in October. "You always *are* broke unless at a time when I have just given you some money. Your big interests have absorbed all the cash and credit you can get, and threaten to absorb mine. But nothing doing anymore, my dear. It's more important (to me) that I buy stuff I want and take the trips I plan than for you to buy this and that for investment."[4] In order to sustain his extravagant lifestyle, Zane, like many well-to-do Americans, spent his earnings and ignored his indebtedness. He still owed money on his automobiles, boats, and properties, and relied on hefty advances from Harpers to make ends meet. Since the demand for his work was still strong despite the drop in sales for his new novels, he dismissed the worry about the economy as unwarranted.

The losses Grey noticed were his old friends. While he was in the East visiting publishers and Lackawaxen in May 1929, he looked up Elma and Claire in New York and Dorothy in Boston. Both Elma and Claire had married during his involvement with Louise, and Dorothy had returned to the East for good in November 1923. Prior to her final visit to Altadena, Dorothy started dating Nick Dalrymple, and in December 1924, they married.[5] By 1929, Zane was resigned to the fact that these friends of many years had moved on with their lives, but their indifference toward him hurt. "Do you know that you are the only person left in the East who ever writes me," he wrote to Claire in February 1930. "Dot is a rotten letter writer and there's no sense in looking for news from her and I don't want to hear from Elma."[6] The month before, he severed ties with Sid Boerstler, who had been his boatman since 1920. During the previous trip to Tahiti, Boerstler had offended Grey by taking up with a native prostitute and getting so far out of shape that he was unable to complete a hike to a mountaintop in Raiatea.[7] This trip was so taxing for R. C. that he resolved never again to visit the South Seas and cost Zane the friend he valued most.

The most distressing loss was Zane's breakup with Mildred Smith in October 1930.[8] Over the previous two years, they had argued many times about people, literature, and his decisions, but their relationship had somehow weathered these tests. Whether she got fed up with him or with his unshakable commitment to Dolly, Mildred launched a withering assault that finally drove him away. As Zane confessed to Dolly several months before their final breakup:

> She [Mildred] decided some time ago to quit me, and after burning under some of her rotten speeches, about my being a bore etc., etc., and a habitual disparagement of all that concerns me, I gave up the situation and I am through. This is the first time I ever came to that. . . . At first she meant to give back the house, and take what she actually spent on it herself, which was fair & ok. But lately she leans toward keeping the house—saying she will pay me for it. She can't, of course, not in years and I confess this jarred me considerably. But it has not hurt me and I do not care.[9]

Later he would admit that her defection pained him deeply,[10] and his wound was aggravated by her refusal to repay her loan and by her threats to publicize his letters to her if he took her to court.

In characteristic fashion, Grey looked to trips to alleviate his painful experiences in Lackawaxen and Arizona and to compensate for the loss of his friends, and by 1930 he was contemplating his most ambitious trip of all. Having completed three trips to New Zealand and two to Tahiti, he wanted to travel the world in quest of big fish. He envisioned a voyage starting from Tahiti and continuing along the atoll of islands to Fiji. He was captivated by the untested fishing in the straits of Carpiteria and around the Mauritius Islands in the Indian Ocean. From there, he planned to head through the Suez Canal for the United States.

Once again the centerpiece of Grey's planning was a boat, and he wanted this one to be his grandest as well. Over the course of his visits to the South

Seas, his thinking about boats had evolved, and he had concluded that the single most important feature of his new ship should be its ability to carry the burly launches he currently favored. During his first trip to New Zealand, Grey had enjoyed fishing from Francis Arlidge's *Alma G* and was even more impressed by the *Zane Grey* that Arlidge's brother purchased for Zane's second visit. However, these experiences also left Grey uncomfortably aware of how murderous the South Seas could be. Aboard these vessels, he learned that the area's violent storms frequently developed too quickly for even the fastest boats to outrun and that the area's huge sharks and swordfish were capable of overturning most fishing boats and devouring anyone plunged into the water. These menacing conditions heightened his appreciation for the size and sturdiness of these launches and inspired a preference for even larger ones.[11] For his third visit, he had Auckland shipbuilders build two even heftier boats, the *Moorea* and *Tahiti*.[12] Because he wanted these launches for Tahiti as well as New Zealand and they were too large for the *Fisherman* to carry, he arranged for them to be freighted for his fishing there. His attempts to use the *Fisherman* in Tahiti exposed other drawbacks. Fretting over its vulnerability to storms, Grey insisted that his yacht anchor inside barrier reefs and away from the open ocean. During one awkward maneuvering through a complex maze of reefs, the *Fisherman* ran aground. Luckily, the tides allowed it to escape, but several more equally close encounters convinced Zane that his ship was too limited for his more ambitious plans and that selling it there would save him valuable time, perhaps money too. "In a way the *Fisherman* has been great for me," he confessed to Dolly in early October 1928. "Probably added immeasurably to my reputation and, what is better, given me incalculable experience."[13] After several months of negotiations, he finally sold the ship to Father Rogier, a Frenchman who owned extensive coconut groves on Christmas Island. Rogier's plan for converting the *Fisherman* into a freighter for copra (dried coconut meat) returned the ship to its original use and restored her original name—*Marshal Foch*.[14]

Grey used some of Rogier's payment of $30,000 to buy R. C. a new Stutz that Christmas and plowed a larger amount into a new boat for his next visit to New Zealand.[15] Unwilling to freight the *Moorea* and *Tahiti* back and forth, he commissioned the Auckland firm of Collins and Bell to build him a more substantial version of the *Gladiator*. His *Frangipani* was forty-eight feet long and had a deep V-shaped beam of twelve and a half feet, a characteristic of New Zealand construction that made their boats exceptionally seaworthy. Its triple-layered "skin" of Kauri wood protected the craft against worms and dry rot, and its two 110-h.p. engines, its 4,000 gallons of fuel, and its sleeping accommodations for eight endowed it with enormous range and flexibility.[16]

Meanwhile, he searched for a replacement for the *Fisherman* suitable for his world voyage. Grey once estimated that he had owned fifty boats and had twenty-two built for him.[17] This was to be his biggest by far—and also his last. Prior to his 1930 return to New Zealand and Tahiti, he learned that a 180-foot, steel-bodied schooner with two large masts and powerful support engines was for sale. This imposing yacht, currently named *Kallisto,* was originally built by Krupps, the famous German arms maker, for the Kaiser Wilhelm II. The owners wanted only $40,000, but Grey realized that its renovations would be far more expensive than those for the *Fisherman.* After arranging a tentative commitment, he commissioned Lambry and Mabry, a firm of naval architects in Wilmington, California, to prepare blueprints with his modifications.[18]

In a letter written on the eve of his departure, Grey informed Claire that he had received several bids and the highest was $317,000 without engines.[19] "There is no use for me to dodge the facts," he wrote Dolly the same week. "I am crazy to have a ship and do these big things and I believe I'd be willing to mortgage my future to accomplish it." He also explained that he needed this much larger yacht to stay ahead of William Beebe. Since his book that inspired Grey's Galapagos expedition, Beebe had undertaken numerous Caribbean trips and pioneered deepwater dives in a bathysphere. This distinguished director of tropical research at the New York Geological Society was currently considering an expedition to the South Pacific, and Grey did not want his ambitious plans upstaged. "The trend is all toward the South Pacific and I am to blame for it," he confided. "As sure as God made little green apples, if I don't do something *big* and do it soon, I shall have shot my bolt and will be out of it."[20]

The *Kallisto* was certainly large enough, but Grey worried that she was too cumbersome and that the renovations would be too costly. "If the *Kallisto* can be made do, well and fine," he grumbled to Dolly. "But I'd hate to buy her and be disappointed."[21] En route to Tahiti in February 1930, he learned from Lambry and Mabry that he could have a ship with similar specifications built in Holland for $175,000. After several days of deliberation, he dispatched a wire and canceled his option on the *Kallisto.* He then fretted that a new ship would take longer to build and delay his trip until 1932, perhaps even 1933.[22]

Dolly complicated matters with news of trouble. First, the editors at *McCall's* requested that he eliminate the rape from "Robber's Roost." When apprised of this demand, Zane responded, "It never occurred to me that the motive was really rape. Most of the present day novels are worse than rape. But I'm glad I get a chance to correct the blunder."[23] A sudden reduction to his expected fee was harder to accept. With a new editor in charge, *Ladies' Home Journal* had accepted two sixty-page novelettes, "The Ranger" and "Canyon Walls," but the worsening economic situation had so devastated newsstand sales and advertising revenues that the acquisitions department demanded a renegotiation of its agreed-upon payment of $20,000 for each to $7,000, or the manuscripts would be returned.[24] Normally, Dolly would have rejected any discounting and taken the stories elsewhere, but she knew that other magazines were also paying less and grudgingly accepted. She also complained to Zane about Paramount's indifference to his recent work, and she debated whether she should propose a fee reduction or shop the film rights to another studio.

"So with the magazine profits eliminated and the motion picture income stopped," Zane shot back, "where in the world will I get $300,000 for a ship and trip?"[25] Part of his testy belligerence stemmed from his conviction that the country's failing economy was temporary and that Dolly was overreacting, as she had many times before. He was also frustrated with the poor fishing. In his belated recollection of the 1930 trip to the South Seas, he would confuse his 1929 and 1930 visits to Tahiti and incorrectly claim that during 1930, rather than 1929, he went eighty-three days without a bite.[26] Actually, the 1930 trip started well. During the first month of fishing, Grey landed a 618-pound silver marlin. Days later, he caught a 63-pound dolphin that outweighed his world record dolphin from the Galapagos trip by more than ten pounds.[27] However, a long stretch of inclement weather and fishless days followed. "It seems most selfish of me to ask you to see me through this thing," Zane appealed to Dolly during this period. "If you don't help me, I shall never be able to accomplish it."[28]

On May 17, several weeks after this letter, Grey successfully hooked and landed a giant Tahitian striped marlin that weighed 1,040 pounds. His description of this battle concluded his *Tales of Tahitian Waters* (287–98). After a grueling two-hour fight, as he hauled the weary giant to the boat and his double leader reached his reel, he felt a series of jerks and realized that sharks were attacking. Furious counterattacks failed to repulse them, and the sharks devoured large chunks from the marlin's tail section, a maiming that reduced its official weight approximately 200 pounds and constituted grounds for disqualification.[29] However, the authoritative list of records for 1933, prepared by Grey's friends at the Museum of Natural History, cited this

Zane Grey and his 1,040-pound striped marlin, Vairao, Tahiti, May 16, 1930. (Courtesy of Loren Grey.)

catch as the world record for striped marlin.[30] This first landing of a fish over 1,000 pounds on rod and reel brought Grey a euphoric sense of achievement. When he returned to Altadena and resumed his personal journal, his first entry jubilantly proclaimed, "I hit it once and that by catching the greatest fish ever landed on a rod."[31]

Grey's world record marlin and dolphin validated his long-standing belief that the South Seas held enormous fish and bolstered his confidence that even larger ones might be caught in the remote, unfished waters west of Fiji toward the Indian Ocean. Determined to have the yacht he needed and keep his original schedule, he wired owners of the *Kallisto* that he would close on the ship as soon as he arrived back in the United States.

Grey never imagined that his mammoth marlin and exceptional good fortune would be his downfall. This momentary fulfillment of his lifelong quest for *the* biggest fish blinded him to looming danger. Dolly and Ed Bowen unsuccessfully tried to warn him about the worsening economy and slackening demand for his work to prevent him from assuming more debt, but Zane ignored their appeals. In a letter informing Claire that Mitchell had gone to New York to bring the yacht back to California, Grey exulted, "She is a beauty, Claire. If you saw her you'd give a gasp and a yelp."[32]

During renovations over the late summer and fall of 1930, Grey settled in and wrote frenetically to complete *The Trail Driver, Thunder Mountain,* and *Knights of the Range.* In addition to acquiring bountiful supplies and tackle, he hired a new secretary. For the first time since 1913, when he hired Lillian and Elma to accompany him to Long Key and the Rainbow Bridge, he did not have a proven assistant whom he could entrust with his work. During his tempestuous involvement with Louise, who never worked as his secretary, he still had helpers who had been with him for years, but now even Mildred, who had served him loyally for almost fifteen years, was gone. As with his previous selections, he wanted someone who was young, attractive, and admiring. Dolly aided and supported his choice of Berenice Campbell because she was adventurous and qualified. She had fled a drab home life in the rural Midwest, and had spent almost a year hitchhiking her way to Los Angeles. Even more important to Dolly than her good looks, vivacious personality, daring, and secretarial skills was her acknowledgment of the critical need for lean budgeting and strict accounting. Amid the darkening clouds over the economy, Dolly interpreted Mildred's departure as a ray of hope, since she had always been overly generous with bills and staff requests. If she could not prevent the upcoming trip around the world, Dolly did not

Grey and Berenice Campbell, ca. 1931. (Courtesy of Loren Grey.)

want its mounting costs to become astronomical. Instructing Zane to be as frugal as possible, she arranged for Berenice to police the spending.

On December 17, 1930, Zane completed preparations for his departure and penned a final entry in his journal: "I am leaving soon on a great voyage, to be gone over a year. A year and more out of my life—away from home! It is fearful to contemplate and yet I am glad." Troubled by Mildred's defection and his financial difficulties, he drew reassurance from his recent completion of *The Trail Driver,* and vowed, "I shall try to make this trip the climax of all my life of adventure on land and sea. . . . In fact, it is almost a miracle that I have been able to stand loss and keep on."[33]

When Zane and Berenice left for Tahiti in early January, Mitchell was already there readying his camp. Zane's daughter, Betty, and Bob Carney, a photographer, who were scheduled to wed in mid-February, were to take another steamship with Loren and to use Zane's voyage for their honeymoon. Meanwhile, the *Kallisto,* renamed *Fisherman II,* was nearing completion and supposed to arrive in Papeete shortly after the newlyweds.

"The place looks exquisite," Zane informed Dolly when he reached Flower Point,[34] but trouble erupted quickly. Having spent so much on his yacht, he badly wanted to please Dolly and to stay within his budget, but he discovered that bills for his new launch and improvements to his property exhausted his checking account, and he had to write Dolly for a $5,000 transfusion.[35] To soften the blow, he cheerfully assured Dolly, "Berenice is just the dandiest girl I *ever* had around in every way."[36] Ten days of steady rain and bleak news from Dolly on the worsening economy elicited a long reply and this confession of remorse: "That I've got *you* into such a mental and physical state just flays me." Vowing to write fewer serializations that were better, he revealed that the Mitchells were behaving peevishly "caty." At the time of their departure, Zane had agreed to pay "Cappy" $950 for two months of service and a host of expenses. In Tahiti, Mitchell requested $450 more for some expenses that he had already billed. Mildred had never questioned this routine procedure, and Mitchell wanted to test Berenice's new program of austerity. As Zane related:

> There is a new regime here at Flower Pt. Berenice has taken over the finances, and things are happening. She has stopped the leaks, the graft, the needless expense. And she is going to cut the whole d— bunch. It is a novelty, for someone besides you, to try to save me money. What did you write this girl? She is inspired. She says, "I'll know where every D— red cent goes!" She's a wonder. . . . Everybody has to accept a cut,

or walk the plank! This was B's idea. My Gawd, imagine me thinking of such a thing![37]

To Mitchell's surprise and dismay, Berenice reimbursed him only $250. Knowing that Grey was awaiting a yacht that had cost more than $300,000, he was understandably vexed over this miserly quibbling. The Guilds, a New Zealand couple who had been caretakers for Flower Point for the past year, had several late-night meetings with the Mitchells to share grievances. When both couples avoided Grey and did not hide their ill will when they did run into him, Grey construed their animus as anti-Americanism from their Commonwealth backgrounds. But when another boatman informed him of Mitchell's derogatory comments and blatant disregard for his orders, Grey dispatched an angry letter firing him. Having already conferred with the British Consul and a local attorney, Mitchell responded with a lawsuit for wrongful discharge that threatened to impound Zane's boats and block his cruise. Shortly after Grey agreed to a stopgap measure of paying Mitchell $300,[38] Mildred Smith suddenly appeared and let everyone know that she was there to testify in support of Mitchell's complaint.[39] Fearful of a plot and an exposé, Grey pressed for a settlement that awarded Mitchell a lump sum of $2,685 and the title to his new launch *Sky Blue II,* which had cost $6,500.[40]

Grey hoped to be off as soon as this nasty business was settled, but storms and mishaps kept delaying the *Fisherman II.* Betty, Bob, and Loren, who had arrived before they were expected, were likewise chafing to be under way. The tension of the situation intensified when Tahitian law blocked Mitchell from reselling his launch and he went on a drinking binge.[41] The belated arrival of the new yacht and a hasty departure brought little relief. Three days out of port, the ship encountered turbulent seas and rolled so much that everyone became violently ill. Grey could not sleep, eat, or write, and Berenice "nearly died." The ship handled this modest challenge so poorly that Zane doubted its ability to withstand a punishing storm.[42]

Meanwhile, back in Altadena, Dolly was having an even harder time staying afloat. Delays and rejections deprived her of funds she desperately needed for the yacht, taxes, and other debt obligations. From Tahiti, Zane had sent her ninety-five pages of "The Lost Wagon Train," but she had been expecting a completed manuscript that she could shop. For eight months, *American Magazine* had been running advance notices for "West of the Pecos," but until the serial actually ran, she could not collect the $45,000. Meanwhile, Harpers had agreed to an advance of $60,000 for *The Trail Driver,* but when an editor discovered that the story contained a masquerading girl very similar to the one in *West of the Pecos,* the manuscript was returned and Dolly was unable to place it elsewhere. "All markets are dead," she complained, and she did not mean just for stories. She had no success with trying to sell her jewelry, her property, even her cars. Desperate to economize, she dismissed Takahashi, the family cook, canceled her upcoming trip to Europe, and dispatched Bowen to the Coin Exchange in New York to secure a $50,000 loan. Harpers agreed to underwrite the note, but it raised Zane's indebtedness to the publisher to over $100,000 and obligated him to post eleven manuscripts as security and to forego 75 percent of royalties until the debt was retired. "I feel like Job with the Lord piling on more and more and burden upon burden," she moaned.[43]

Dolly did not need the news that arrived from Suva in early May. Zane informed her that his yacht was "a white elephant" and that "there was something terribly wrong with it." His crew was the worst ever—by far. He found that they had borrowed money against his account without his knowledge or permission. The captain was a drunken incompetent "whore-master" who sailed perilously close to reefs and surely would have hit one had someone not frantically signaled him to change course. The inept chief engineer damaged six engine bearings and forced Zane to dry-dock his yacht in Suva for assessment and repairs.[44]

These tribulations strained Zane's relationship with Berenice. Conceding that she was "lovely to look at, sweet of disposition, honest and unselfish, conscientious about work, etc.," he complained that she had presented him "the most exasperating, most damnable situation I've ever had." She socialized too much, and her seasickness was violent and persistent. Her takeover manner had disintegrated, and several times he came upon her on her knees praying. Worst of all, she would have nothing to do with him, and claimed that he had exploited her. "I think she gave me encouragement enough at home in Altadena," he defended himself. "She was eager, responsive, passionate, and what not." Unsure of what to do, he speculated that he could "become a eunuch for her," but he did not think it would help. The voyage had deteriorated into such an ordeal that he considered ending it, and only reneged because Carney and his children vehemently objected.[45]

Before she received these laments, Dolly concluded that the financial situation was too dire for the trip to continue, and she wired Zane to return immediately. In a follow-up letter sent to Tahiti, she apologized for "hav[ing] to shut down on your trip," and explained that she was hiding from process servers. A demand from Harpers for additional security for their $100,000 debt forced her to post her jewelry, and she had recently dipped into their collection of silver dollars in order to pay for food. She was so frustrated over the objections to *The Trail Driver* that she contemplated changing the masquerading girl herself, but found the challenge too daunting. When *McCall's* offered her half of its previous payment to serialize it, Dolly immediately accepted and appealed to the editors to keep the fee a secret. Unfortunately, this $40,000 windfall still left her so strapped that she stopped attending movies. She estimated that their earnings for the year were already spent, and beseeched Zane to restrict his purchases to essentials. "I have been fighting for my sanity," she appealed. "Doc, if you don't help me, I can fight no longer."[46]

"Your letter to Bob [Carney, Zane's son-in-law] just about finished me," Zane responded:

> How in God's name you could owe $300,000 on this yacht simply dazes me. I'll about kill Bowen, and be liable to believe Mildred's claims about him. You were all insane to let the work go on, and send the yacht.
>
> My extreme figures—the farthest I dared go—were $100,000 after initial investment & engines. That included the whole cruise.
>
> I am knocked cold. But I'll defer any more until my return.
>
> The situation here is abominable. This d— little vile port lives on slander, gossip, rumor. Because we are returning and selling some supplies, it has gotten nosed about that I have failed and [am] ruined.[47]

Rumors of Grey's financial problems were so widespread in Papeete that he was unable to cash a check or run an account, and had to sell spare fuel and tackle in order to raise money. His belated realization that his "big trip" and ill-considered yacht were responsible for his plight crushed him. A year and a half before, he had blithely informed Claire about the $300,000-plus estimates for his renovations, but they were now so central to everything that was going wrong that he was unable to accept responsibility for them. Fortunately, second thoughts persuaded him that anger and blame were inappropriate and counterproductive. Confessing that Dolly's news "struck terror into my heart," he strove to be conciliatory and admitted that he had wrongly underestimated her fears about their finances. "All I ask," he concluded, "is that you stick to me in this most critical of my vicissitudes."[48]

Berenice and Zane hopped a steamship back to the United States and left Bob, Betty, and Loren in Papeete to return with *Fisherman II*. When he arrived back in Altadena in August 1931, he reopened one of his personal diaries and wrote:

The great cruise was a failure. M. K. S. [Mildred Smith] started me downhill in Oct. [1930] by her defection and poison talk. The Mitchells and Guilds did the same. Mitchell was crooked, and had been stealing from me for years. After fleecing me, he began to drink hard and died of heart disease in three months. [Mitchell died in Altadena a month before Grey's return.]

I was far better without these people. But the financial depression overtook me. I was forced home. And I may lose everything. The magazines and picture business have flopped for the time being.

I am deeply in debt, with no way in sight of raising money for notes due.

It is a critical time for me.[49]

As in the past, Grey decided that writing more novels would solve his problems, but the magnitude of his debt and the dearth of interest in his work withered his resolve; over the summer and fall of 1931, he was too despondent to write. Realizing that home life in Altadena confined him and worsened his depression, Dolly encouraged him to go fishing for steelhead in Idaho in September and then scraped together funding so that he could return to Flower Point for the first three months of 1932.

By departure time, Zane and Berenice had patched their previous rift, and she agreed to accompany him, but the heat and more sickness were another ordeal for her, and when they returned to the United States, she left Zane and moved to San Francisco. However, this parting was complicated by earlier agreements that added to Zane's woes. At the time that she initially informed him about her hitchhiking adventures, Berenice revealed that she hoped to convert them into a novel, and Zane encouraged her with helpful suggestions about structuring and developing her story.[50] When he later realized that her work was less promising than Mildred's, he took it over, reworked it, and sold it for serialization as "The Young Runaway" to the *Pictorial Review* for $30,000. Grey rewarded Berenice with a contract granting her 15 percent of royalties from the novel. Although *Wyoming,* the novel version of "The Young Runaway," did not appear until 1953, fourteen years after Grey's death, Berenice took her agreement to an attorney shortly after her relocation to San Francisco, and Dolly had to negotiate a settlement. She handled the matter so tactfully and so amicably that Berenice lowered her royalty to 5 percent in return for a typewriter and an automobile that Dolly deducted as a business expenses. "Hereafter, my dear," Dolly advised in a letter informing her husband of this agreement, "let the literary end of things remain strictly in the family."[51]

In May 1932, while Dolly was negotiating this settlement with Berenice, the sixty-year-old Zane wrote in his journal, "The December last I met a young woman who came to work for me and who has exerted a remarkably good influence."[52] He was referring to Wanda Williams, whom he had originally met four years earlier when she was dating Romer. Zane had considered her as a replacement for Mildred, but did not invite her to become his secretary until Berenice decamped. Wanda was a Christian Scientist, and her positive outlook greatly impressed him. Ever since he broke away from his father's fundamentalism, Zane had avoided denominational religion and fulfilled his spiritual needs with nature at undeveloped locations, notably the Rainbow Bridge. However, his recent reversals had so demoralized him that he was deeply grateful for Wanda's cheerfulness and optimism and he credited them to her religion. Although he balked at the religion's opposition to science, he perceived Wanda and her equally animated parents as products of its influence and grasped Christian Science like a lifeline: "To stop worry, doubt, fear, the thinking of evil, of injustice—the change to belief, confidence, power! I can attribute these to W— if not directly to Christian Science. I do not believe I can ever be a true Scientist. But I have gained some of its splendid truths, and I shall never let go of them. It is only when the tiger of my passions ambushes me—*and I do not think*—that I fail."[53] "I have been helped a great deal by W— in my attitude toward people, things, feeling, thinking," he observed in another journal entry about Wanda and her Christian Science religion. "I recognize its [Science's] single worth. It will take time for me in this regard. But I am sure that this and its influence have helped me out the darkened depth I was in."[54]

Grey's hiring of Wanda and a summer visit to Oregon enabled him to write again. Over the first half of 1932, he worked frenetically, and completed or rewrote "The Young Runaway," "The Lost Wagon Train," *Thunder Mountain,* *Knights of the Range,* and "Bitter Seeps." But the sustained exertion took a heavy toll on his fragile health. As he wrote to Claire:

> I had written steadily for 7 months, the hardest spell I ever put in. And that during the period of my trouble, the least of which, bad as it was, was only financial. Up in the Oregon woods, on the Umpqua, I fought it out. I was run down from all these things, so I was prey to poison oak and a severe cold in my chest; and I damn near died. Night after night I was out of my head part of the time, when I awakened alone in the morning, all my vitality was at lowest ebb. I would have to sit up in bed until the bad spell passed.[55]

In writing to Claire, Zane accentuated the positive and implied that his tremendous exertion had liberated him from his black hole, but several weeks later, he confessed to his journal, "It is a terrible time. I do not know what to think, what to do, which way to turn."[56]

Once again Zane trusted that long days of writing would be his salvation, but this time the inevitable return of his energy and optimism was long-delayed and short-lived—brief upturns in a relentless decline. Over the fall of 1932 and during the entire year following, Dolly could not place a single serialization. Magazines, hard hit by the plunge in advertising and subscriptions, were themselves strapped, and editors noticed that Grey's work had lost its freshness and appeal. Harpers continued to publish one and sometimes two Grey novels each year, but with the solitary exception of *Western Union* (1939), which appeared days before Grey's death, all were written before 1932. *West of the Pecos* (1937) and *Raiders of Spanish Peaks* (1938) derived from serials published in 1931, and *The Code of the West,* his only novel for 1934, dated from 1923. Harpers consigned his new manuscripts from after 1932 to its bulging store of collateral that was looking more and more like a graveyard.

These developments eroded Grey's authority at home and inspired Dolly to become more resourceful and independent. Years before, he and Dolly had agreed that she was entitled to half of his earnings, and she maintained records that carefully calculated her half. Basically this agreement acknowledged what California law would have granted her in a divorce and allowed her to hold bank accounts in her name, but bills and expedience kept her from living by this division. Although she and Zane bickered constantly over excessive spending, of which both were guilty, his huge income had always rescued them from a hard reckoning or ruinous conflict. However, the precipitous drop in his income and their staggering debt necessitated a stricter accounting and better enforcement. When Zane returned from the ill-fated voyage of *Fisherman II,* Dolly informed him that henceforth she would make monthly deposits to his bank account from the funds she received, and he would be responsible for all his bills. Because she was no longer able, she would not provide additional distributions or backup coverage.

Given Zane's long history of doing as he pleased and her own capitulations, Dolly realized that they could not alter their engrained behavior without a better system, and Ed Bowen helped her to develop one. Over his ten years with the family, Bowen had evolved from a majordomo on household matters to an overseer of Dolly's construction projects, and more recently into a trusted financial advisor. From his background in construction and the knowledge of business he acquired from Lloyd Wright, Grey's attorney, he was able to educate Dolly on the advantages of incorporating her husband's holdings. In the past, Zane had repeatedly fumed over his huge tax bills, and Dolly had recently withheld tax payments in order to make ends meet, but this strategy had simply worsened the couple's staggering debt. Bowen showed Dolly how incorporation could reduce Zane's tax rate and qualify him for more deductions. Given the worsening state of the economy, Bowen believed that the IRS would be more favorably disposed toward Grey as a failing company than as a failing individual. The biggest drawback to incorporation was its greatest benefit: in order to convert Zane Grey into Zane Grey, Inc., Grey's finances would have to be handled like those of a business and adhere to strict accounting rather than the vicissitudes of Dolly's largesse.[57]

The benefits of incorporation were too great for Zane to oppose, and he reluctantly signed the necessary paperwork during the summer of 1932. Within weeks, he was chafing at the consequential constraints and complaining about Bowen. Relieved to have the blame shifted, Dolly felt obligated to stand up for Bowen and did so in this August letter to Zane:

> I have no brief for Bowen. He has made just as bad mistakes as the rest of us, but he has learned and profited by those mistakes in experience to the point of not making them or any similar ones again. He has handled our creditors as no one else I know could or would have handled them. Even now they have continually to be placated and soothed. If you wish that job, you may have it. I *won't* do that. . . . If you are not satisfied with Bowen's conduct of the business, you are at perfect liberty to make any change you wish, but at least you must be fair to him and just not say you don't want to talk to him or see him or have anything to do with him. If you are dissatisfied, or wish to make accusations, or to kick him out, come out with it and be straight and above-board. It is your business and your corporation and you should be intelligent about it. . . . Possibly Bowen could get much farther than be connected with the Z. G. Corporation. He is not the kind to stand still, wherever he is, and in one way or another is going to make a name for himself. Perhaps I have been selfish in wanting him to stay on with us, because I know his possibilities, and at this writing I know of no one else that I think able to take his place, or do the things he has been doing.[58]

Unlike Zane, who buckled under pressure, Dolly acquired a new resilience and determination. "I shall no longer be motivated by fear, as I have in the past," she wrote in the same letter. "All of you [the family] have taught me a rather bitter lesson and that is, that I can get along alone. As a matter of fact, it's what I have been doing most of the time."[59] For years, Zane's trips and long stays away from home had caused her to feel like a single parent. Having long thought of herself as a mother first and foremost, she learned early in her marriage to fend for herself. Over the 1920s, she began to chafe at the obligations and constraints of this role and started taking trips on her own. Moreover, her years of handling Zane's finances and of dealing with his editors had gained her a wealth of experience far beyond that of most wives and mothers. Her local bank in Altadena recognized this, and in appreciation for her substantial business, appointed her its president, more an honorary position than a full-time job. As one of the very few female bank presidents at the time, Dolly used her position to learn about banking operations and the financial problems of others, but she developed no illusions of importance. Fearing that her conscientious efforts to be a loyal wife and good mother had impaired her, she complained to Zane, "I'm afraid that my life job has been too highly specialized for me to be good at anything else."[60]

The devastation of the unfolding Depression spurred Dolly to do something about her "specialization" and low self-esteem. Her awareness of her personal limitations led her to perceive the ongoing financial crisis as a healthy disruption of the existing social order and invigorating redefinition of achievement. "It's a new deal all around," she echoed Roosevelt. "Those who continue to wallow in the past and its errors are going to fall by the wayside."[61] Dolly worked to improve her confidence and outlook with surprisingly modest undertakings. The bank president decided that she needed to be her own secretary and to acquire the skills she had been paying others to perform. First, she worked to become a proficient typist. Back in 1924, she had tried typing, but quit when she realized that she could use Zane's secretaries and that they did a much better job. By the end of 1932, she was typing her own error-free letters, saving herself both time and money. Since she and Zane had relied on chauffeurs since they purchased their first car in 1917, she learned how to drive. She was not only pleased with the consequential cost-saving and convenience, but she also discovered that she preferred the economical Chrysler sedan over the fancier but unwieldy Lincoln.[62] During 1933–34, she conscientiously attended courses on public speaking and creative writing, and they too improved her confidence. Even though Dolly was learning only rudimentary skills and hardly equipping herself for the intensely competitive labor market, her initiative functioned as a reckoning with her personal limitations and gained her new confidence. As she explained in defense of her course on public speaking, "The whole thing is merely an inferiority complex and fear I have discovered, and I am systemically running my fears into the ground. It has become a matter of survival."[63]

These accomplishments equipped Dolly to manage Zane Grey, Inc., and this position, much more than her bank presidency, transformed her into a resourceful, determined, and successful businesswoman. She converted Zane's former study into her office and spent many hours each day coping with bills and clients. Up to 1930, her negotiations with editors had been polite and easy. When they complained about Grey's work or did not offer enough money, she proposed a reasonable compromise and the matter was settled. She seldom had to go elsewhere. However, the rejections and financial pressures of the Depression produced a momentous change in the devoted wife who had patiently reviewed her husband's work and hesitantly suggested changes. The woman who could not bring herself to modify the masquerading woman in *West of Pecos* in 1930 was by 1933 ready to do anything to sell a manuscript. When she judged "Horse Heaven Hill" to be a weak effort, she reworked it before submitting it to a magazine (but was still unable to get it accepted).[64] She also counseled her husband on the current preferences of editors and readers. She urged that "Twin Sombreros" not be a sequel to *West of the Pecos* but the start of a new series instead. She instructed that future submissions to the *Country Gentleman* should be limited to 40,000 words and structured as three installments.[65] Cuing these suggestions to her own program of self-improvement, she urged Zane to "readapt yourself to present conditions." Boldly declaring that he had "fallen into ways of self-indulgence, into vanities of position," she advised, "Believe me, no one is too proud to retrench these days. It is those who do not when they ought to who are looked down upon."[66]

By January of 1933, Grey's income had deteriorated to the point that he was receiving only $200–300 a month from Harpers and quarterly installments of merely $2,500 from Paramount. During that month, RKO lapsed into receivership, and Dolly feared that Paramount would default on its upcoming installment.[67] The payment did arrive, several weeks late, but Paramount-Publix, its theater chain, lapsed into receivership two months later, forcing out Lasky and jeopardizing both the studio and its contractual agreements. Dolly restricted herself and Loren to a budget of $50 a month.[68] By April, the total funds available in the checking accounts she and Zane held were only $1,393.01, and Zane's personal savings account had sunk to $1,250.[69] In May, Dolly wrote, "The last month has been the worst, financially, in our existence." Miraculously, Paramount sent its payment, and she was able to add $500 to Zane's savings account; but she dismissed his hope for $1,000 as the equivalent of $1,000,000 under current conditions.[70] By mid-1934, Grey estimated his debt to exceed $160,000.[71] That year, in its May issue, *Country Gentleman* published "Outlaws of the Palouse" (later renamed "The Horse Thief"), the last of his stories to be accepted and published by the slick magazines that once clamored for his work.

Dire straits necessitated radical action, and Dolly persuaded the makers of Camel to pay Zane $1,000 to endorse its cigarettes as "an ideal smoke for fishermen." This promotion of a long-standing aversion prompted Zane to remark, "I am ashamed to admit what I would allow for $1,000."[72] Bowen arranged for agent Tess Slessinger to represent Grey, and Slessinger secured him a contract for a comic strip about *King of the Royal Mounted* with the King Features Syndicate.[73] Embarrassed over this further tarnishing of his name for money, Zane delegated the assignment to Romer.

In 1932, several years after Zane had taken Lady John Cecil (Cornelia Vanderbilt) fishing in New Zealand, a young member of the Vanderbilt family asked to be included in one of his fishing trips, raising fresh hopes for funding for the world voyage, but the rich heir later backed out.[74] As an alternative, Zane wrote Ernest Hemingway and unsuccessfully proposed that they team up for a "giant world fishing trip to make a picture."[75] Sensing his fragility as these pipe dreams evaporated, Dolly scrimped so that he could return to the South Seas with Wanda for the first six months of 1933, but under severely restricted terms. Grey's boats, which were costly to maintain and impossible to sell, sorely strained his depleted resources. During an especially bleak assessment of the *Fisherman II,* Dolly informed Zane about a former millionaire who sank his palatial yacht because he could neither sell it nor pay its mooring fees and taxes.[76] Grey's interest in Tahiti and Flower Point waned now that he did not have a boat there and could not afford to have one built, as he had done so often in the past. Ironically, other problems solved this particular one. In New Zealand, the *Frangipani* was threatened with seizure for back taxes and bills. The arrival of the Depression there had inflamed such fierce anti-Americanism by his 1933 visit that Grey resolved never to return.[77] Unable to pay the cost of shipping as he did in 1928, he got Peter Williams to run the *Frangipani* to Tahiti.[78] This necessitated a daring crossing of 2,500 miles of open sea and a risky evasion of New Zealand authorities, but it got Grey's favorite fishing boat to Tahiti for the price of gas.

This venture was the trip's only success. "Again I was forced to come back from Tahiti because of lack of funds," Grey wrote in his journal back in Altadena. "I am not quite ruined financially, but I cannot see any hope of future trips, especially the big one. . . . If I quit now, writing, going, fishing, loving, romancing, I am through."[79] Unfortunately, his 1933 trip to the South Seas ended his relationship with Wanda. The heat and financial strains made this seven-month excursion as much of an ordeal for her as the two earlier trips to Tahiti had been for Berenice. Her seasickness was so violent and prolonged that Dolly openly questioned the power of her Christian Science.[80] However, it was Zane's waffling, more than her sickness, that provoked Wanda to decamp. As he explained in an October entry in his journal: "W's defection is the climax of terrible blows that have ruined me, almost broken my heart. To be sure she loves me. But I will have to marry her to hold her. That is impossible. I cannot alienate my children and crush my wife just because I have been madly in love with a younger woman."[81]

Zane's distress over the loss of Wanda was part of a much larger fear that his whole life was falling apart. His entry about Wanda began with speculation that he might never again write in his journal. He had always maintained his journals as testimonials to his much-tested-but-never-defeated faith in himself and his work, but here he dejectedly concedes that he has lost confidence and turned into a "madman." His catalogue of his reversals ends with the bleak, unprecedented admission, "At this writing I am sick and tired of life. I do not care to live any longer without the thrill, the adventure, the love, the passion, the achievement that I've had for twenty-one years."[82]

At this time, Grey compensated for the loss of Wanda with a flood of letters to Lola Gornall, a poet living in Australia. She sent him a first letter expressing her admiration for his books in April 1933 while he was in New Zealand. He responded to her from Tahiti and explained how the intense anti-Americanism had spurred him to leave New Zealand sooner than he planned.[83] By August, he felt that he knew her well enough to admit that his "wife and three children did not keep me from several terrible love affairs."[84] By the end of 1933, when Grey was back in Altadena with Dolly and therefore was not writing to her, this sporadic correspondence quickened to several letters a week, and their relationship evolved into a torrid literary affair; Grey taught Lola his secret code, and both used it to achieve greater intimacy. Between 1934 and 1938, he would send over 500 letters that included numerous newspaper clippings, cartoons, and tokens of affection.

In November of 1933, Grey attended a social event at the University of Southern California with a new acquaintance whom he described as "sophisticated, daring, a flirt, and pagan and intellectual."[85] He was referring to Brownella ("Brownie") Baker, who became his next and last secretary. She had been a sorority sister of Marge Bowen, Ed Bowen's wife, while they were attending USC, and Marge introduced her to Zane. Brownella reciprocated

Zane's show of interest, and in May 1934 he wrote in his journal, "Romance and love not only abide as always but seem more poignant and beautiful and vivid and sweet. Eternal gratitude to B. B.!"[86]

Brownie was another burst of sunshine upon Zane's gloom, but she, Lola, and a modest improvement in his financial situation were not able to mend his broken spirit. During 1935, as the movie industry emerged from the shadow of bankruptcy, Paramount resumed its quarterly payments for movie rights, even though they were down sharply from 1929. That year, Grey kept brief, daily entries in a calendar book left over from the year before. He apparently started this alternative journal on an impulse but then maintained it as a record of his moods and experiences. However, the book contains only entries from the first two months of the year because someone, probably Dolly, ripped out the pages for the rest of the year. Every three or four days in the pages that survive, Zane has drawn a heart alongside a date, presumably to record one of his assignations with Brownie, but even more revealing are his equally frequent notations of sickness and depression.[87] "I doubt that I ever will get back to the big magazines," he wrote to Alvah James during the same January of 1935. "They never forgave us because they once had to buy my novels, and I had the nerve and the poor judgment to allow my novels to appear in *Colliers, McCall's,* the *American,* and *Country Gentleman* at the same time."[88] The following July he confessed to Dolly, "I have not yet gotten hold of myself to work, or write, or fish."[89] Two weeks later, he added, "I am not keen about Australia or Tahiti or any place. This is serious."[90] The previous fall, on November 8, R. C. died suddenly, and the loss of his brother annihilated Zane. Having regarded R. C. as his closest friend since their childhood together, he was devastated by his belated realization that his compulsive traveling had sundered their relationship, grieving that they had spent little time together over the previous three years. He continued to mourn R. C.'s death through 1935, and two years afterward he wrote that his brother's death had been "on my mind ever since, in lonely hours, on the sea, in the forest, in the dead of night."[91]

Dolly believed that Zane's persistent depression, his lack of vitality, and his diminished interest in fishing were indeed "serious." She could see that the demise of his grand voyage impaired his responsiveness to alternatives; her sixty-two-year-old husband was, for the first time in his life, looking his age. In the past, trips, even the planning of them, had always lifted his spirits, but ever since the ill-fated voyage of *Fisherman II,* his trips to Oregon and Tahiti had failed to do so. She could see that it would take years for the sputtering improvement in their finances to realize the trip of his dreams, but she was determined to send him to Australia. Officials in the government there had extended several invitations like the one from New Zealand, which greatly reduced the prospective costs and offered him access to one of few areas of untapped promise he had yet to fish.

Zane's despondent admission to Dolly that he was "not keen" about even this prospect was aggravated by a festering realization that his stature as a fisherman, like everything else in his life, was declining. The 1928 exhibition at the Museum of Natural History was probably the apex of his reputation and his 1,040-pound marlin from 1930 had burnished it. But there had been no triumphs since. During his previous three visits to the South Seas, his only big fish was a 170-pound sailfish, which brought him another world record, but his experiences were either too uninteresting or too traumatic for him to complete his projected *Tales of Coral Seas.* The major magazines on sport no longer wanted his articles and he had to place them in relatively obscure journals like *Motor Boating.*[92]

Without new records and major publications, Zane had to rely on endorsements to sustain his preeminence. Since the mid-1920s, he had allowed the Ashaway Company to associate his name with its Swastika fishing lines. Though Ashaway gave him only free line in exchange for his endorsement, the company's promotion treated him like the world's greatest angler. In 1927, it distributed a slick booklet with a cover photograph of men unloading his world record tuna. A page inside contained a cluster of photographs of anglers who had previously held the world record for broadbill, while a picture of Grey with his current world record broadbill took up the entire page that followed. By 1932, the South Bend Tackle Company was offering a full line of Zane Grey lures. That same year, Arthur Kovalovsky asked Grey to try his state-of-the-art reel. He wrote Kovalovsky a letter proclaiming his enthusiasm for the reel and allowed it to be used for promotion.[93] Grey's most influential endorsement was for Hardy Brothers, England's premier maker of fishing tackle since 1873. Alma Baker spearheaded the firm's introduction of saltwater equipment and paved the way for Hardy's introduction of a Zane Grey reel in 1929.[94] Unlike endorsements today, Hardy's boost to Grey's reputation did little for his ailing bank account. Although the company sent him products to test and granted him a discount on purchases, it gave him only two free reels and insisted that he pay for his orders. Grey nearly withdrew his endorsement in 1933 when Hardy sent him a letter referencing his delinquent account and threatening legal action if he did not settle it soon.[95]

Hardy's promotion of its Zane Grey reel gained Grey's international recognition but also embroiled him in ruinous rivalry. By the late 1920s, the small but influential British Sea Anglers' Society had grown very optimistic that a world-class tuna would be caught off the northwest coast of England in the area near Scarborough. In 1930, one of its members landed one weighing 735 pounds.[96] In 1932, Col. E. T. Peel, another member, caught a 798-pound tuna that bested Grey's oldest record and brought England its first world record. Hardy took out full-page ads in the Society's *Quarterly* stating how both anglers had used Zane Grey reels.[97] On September 11, 1933, L. Mitchell-Henry surpassed Peel with a 851-pound tuna, and he emphatically did *not* use a Zane Grey reel.

Mitchell-Henry represented an expanding field of competitors who were replacing Grey on the current lists of world records and making him defensive and acerbic. Worry over his slipping authority had already tainted his articles about fishing, and in one, he had injudiciously attacked Mitchell-Henry for refusing to fish from a power launch and for employing a 72-thread line, forcing the fish to tow his dory until it died.[98] In a follow-up entitled "Some Arresting Facts about Modern Sea Angling," he invoked the current rules of the Tuna Club as a basis for more criticism of Mitchell-Henry.[99] Offended by these public denunciations, Mitchell-Henry struck back with an article in the April 18, 1931, issue of *The Fishing Gazette* that reviewed Grey's own account of his 1,040-pound black marlin according to the rules he had enumerated in "Some Arresting Facts about Modern Sea Angling" and found him guilty of four major infractions. *The Fishing Gazette* was an obscure English journal, but Mitchell-Henry reached serious fishermen with his book *Tunny Fishing* (1934) that discussed his world record tuna and included his article attacking Grey.[100]

Had Mitchell-Henry been a lone voice of opposition, Grey could have dismissed this catfight as a careless run-in with another fisherman who was as ambitious and opinionated as himself.[101] However, Thomas Aitken, the current editor of deep-sea fishing for *Outdoor Life,* upset Grey even more than this Englishman by ignoring him. Aitken, like Mitchell-Henry, believed that Grey's reputation as a fisherman was overblown and suspect. In "Swordfish . . . King of the Sea," written for the magazine's July 1935 issue, he discussed the catches of Boschen and Mrs. Keith Spalding, but did not mention a single one of Grey's. Even worse, in a large box in the center of his article, he offered a list of "World's Record Catches" that mentioned only Grey's 111-pound yellowtail from 1926. Blatantly dismissing Grey's three records on Heilner's most recent list, he accompanied his list with the statement: "confusion of species and failure to file complete data leaves records open."[102] The month following this article, Grey complained in his personal journal about the "discrediting of my fishing records by envious, jealous, and little men."[103]

Despite Zane's claims of indifference to Australia, Dolly pushed ahead and did all she could to make the trip possible. After persuading the Australian government to help with expenses, enlisting Cook and Manor to handle the bookings, and arranging for Peter Williams to come from New Zealand to be his boatman, she approved a plan for the fishing to be converted into a feature film and for Emil Morhardt and Gus Bagnard to do the camera work. She also sent Ed Bowen along to monitor finances. On the eve of his departure in late December 1935, Dolly handed Zane a letter to be read after he was under way in which she wrote, "There is no question that mentally and physically you have gone forward a great deal in the last year, that your fund of understanding of humanity has increased; and that this will manifest itself in increased richness and depth in your work. . . . I have never lost my faith in you and in your work; but I knew that adjustment might be a long and painful process. Now I am sure that you are ready to gird on your armor again and leap into the battle. My love and hope and faith go with you, and in this spirit."[104]

Grey arrived in Sydney in time to celebrate the New Year and left soon afterward for Bermagui, an enclave 275 miles south, already known for big fish although it had been fished for only three years.[105] He set up camp on a bluff overlooking the ocean in a grove of eucalyptus with plenty of open space. On January 11, his first day of fishing, he rolled two big marlin, drew a strike from another, and landed one weighing 300 pounds.[106] Although he had been advised that the fishing would not be good until February, this was an auspicious start, and his good fortune continued. Over the seven-week stay, Zane landed five more marlin between 250 and 300 pounds and a 480-pound black marlin that attracted a large crowd to see the biggest swordfish caught there so far.[107]

Sharks were so plentiful and so large that Grey decided to concentrate on them. Long before his disappointment in the Galapagos Islands, he had harbored a visceral hatred of sharks, and his new experiences in Australia convinced him they were "engines of destruction."[108] Because many scientists still believed that sharks were not man-eaters, Grey was gathering information for a book to be entitled *Tales of Man-Eating Sharks* that would recount the many deaths and maimings caused by sharks and discredit this scientific misconception.[109]

Convinced that sharks were also his best prospect for a new world record, Grey relocated from Bermagui to Bateman Bay, just south of Sydney, because it was reputed to abound with them. There he briefly hooked a whaler shark estimated at 900 pounds and landed a great white shark that weighed 840 pounds.[110] However, he did not land his biggest shark until he had returned to the Sydney area. Having learned about the enormous size achieved by tiger sharks, he enlisted the help of Charles Bullen, who had caught the largest tiger shark to date, and for three weeks they fished out of Watson's Bay. One day as they were plying the waters between the Heads of Sydney, Grey finally hooked his quarry. As cruise ships passed and passengers waved, he battled and prevailed over a 1,036-pound tiger shark and bested Bullen's record.[111]

Grey's preoccupation with fishing left him little time for Sydney itself. Even though his reception there was more enthusiastic and more gratifying than that of his first visit to Auckland, he was more interested in Lola Gornall. He had been writing to her for more than three years, and both were looking forward to their first meeting with high expectations and more than a little anxiety. He had offended Brownie by leaving her back in the United States, partly to save money but also to be free for Lola.[112] Although their meeting was the climax of hundreds of letters, it lasted only three days and did not go well. Lola parried Zane's advances, and he stormed off in a huff. Shortly after he arrived at Hayman Island near the Great Barrier Reef to complete his film, both missed their correspondence and resumed their pen-pal relationship. Since the action footage had already been shot, this location was used for filming the movie's story line. Although he did no fishing, Zane was intrigued with the myriad marine life of the reef and enjoyed his stay.

Back in the United States in August 1936, Grey wrote in his journal that the Australian trip was "a big success" and added, "I overcame many handicaps, my habit of keeping alone, of *being unfriendly*. I felt grateful to the thousands of my Australian readers."[113] But his content did not last. The rushes for *White Death* were disappointing; the film was released with little fanfare and quickly vanished. Grey blamed its poor showing on Bowen's penurious financing and angrily demanded that he be fired. Trapped between the fragility of Zane's health and her indebtedness to Bowen, Dolly campaigned for a compromise, but Zane's intransigence forced her to award Bowen a generous settlement and say good-bye to the last of their long-term staff.[114]

As part of the financing for the trip, Grey agreed to write a Western about Australia, which he postponed until his return from a fall trip to Oregon. In December 1936, he initiated a log about this project with an assertion of renewed determination: "I *want* to write this big novel. I have a keen poignant desire to make it great. I shall *love* the job." When he finished the novel in early March, he wrote, "I have just finished the largest, and perhaps the profoundest of all my novels." Ten days later, he finished rereading the entire work and confessed, "At first I thought it wasn't bad. But I think now it was."[115] The editorial staff at Harpers agreed and consigned the manuscript to its bulging collection of future possibilities. *Wilderness Trek* was not published until 1944, and the editors eliminated two-thirds of the original manuscript.

The same March that Grey completed his novel, Harpers published his *An American Angler in Australia* (1937). Grey's fishing books had always been presented in a large format with much finer printing than his novels. They cost almost twice as much and were targeted at an upscale audience of well-to-do sportsmen who were willing to pay more. *American Angler* maintained the same format, but paled by comparison. The text was much shorter, only 115 pages that required large print to achieve this length. As usual, there were many photographs, but they were not incorporated into the text as before. Harpers used an economical bunching of the photographs at the end, and there were no ornamental drawings. Grey had hoped that this book would resuscitate his reputation, but the book itself made him look diminished, and Thomas Aitken was ready to say that he was. His review for the *New York Herald* interpreted the trip as "a personal war on the sharks of New South Wales" and dismissed Grey's tiger shark as a "scavenger species" unworthy of any list of world records.[116]

On August 11, 1937, five months after completion of *Wilderness Trek* and the publication of *An American Angler in Australia,* Grey suffered a stroke. He had been fishing on the North Umpqua River, and when the temperature topped 100 degrees, he opted for a nap. When he awoke, he knew immediately that something was seriously wrong. Since he had fallen asleep in the sun, he thought he might have suffered sunstroke and retreated to his cabin. Overnight he was stricken with a second, more damaging stroke that left him conscious, but he was unable to speak or to move the right side of his body. The doctor at a nearby Civilian Conservation Camp diagnosed his stroke and recommended hospitalization, but Grey refused, and instead hurried back to Altadena on a train.[117]

Grey's recovery was hard and prolonged. For months he could not walk or write. Determined to keep working, he resorted to dictation. During the fall of 1937, Brownie transcribed his autobiography and the first half of *Western Union,* and she wrote to Lola Gornall on his behalf to explain how his setback had caused the abrupt hiatus in his correspondence. Meanwhile, he practiced his signature in order to regain his ability to write, but his first efforts were a ragged, barely legible scrawl. By the time he returned to Australia for the first six months of 1939, he felt well enough to fish and hooked

Grey with books and fishing tackle, 1938. (Courtesy of Loren Grey.)

an 800-pound great white shark. Everyone aboard his boat urged that the sixty-seven-year-old fisherman abandon the fight and not risk his fragile health, but he refused, even though his victory drained him and left him incapacitated for weeks afterward. That summer, he recovered full use of his right arm and leg. This progress, together with final repayment of his debt to Harpers and its decision to publish his recently completed novel, made Grey more optimistic than he had been in years. He wrote in his journal: "In th[e]se two years, I have dictated two novels and a fishing story. And now, as is evident here, I can write fairly well again. And I write resurgent—I shall rise again!"[118]

This was his last entry. On October 22, Grey celebrated the publication of *Western Union* with a book signing at Vroman's Bookstore in downtown Los Angeles. The day went smoothly, and he felt fine when he retired that evening with Dolly to their bed on a screen porch upstairs in their Altadena home. Early the next morning, he awoke gasping for air. When Dolly was unable to help, she contacted the family doctor and dispatched Loren to bring him to the house. Zane was dead of a massive heart attack by the time they returned.[119] Later that day, as she was grieving, Dolly picked up the copy of *Western Union* that he had inscribed simply, "To Dolly from Zane." With her pen she added, "Gone fishin' on October 23, 1939."[120]

Postscript

Zane Grey died during a resurgence of interest in the Western. Over the years of the Depression, the genre was kept alive by an outpouring of B-films for "double features" that the major studios offered, along with free china, to lure penny-pinching audiences to theaters. Nearly half of all the film adaptations of Grey novels were B-films from the decade of the Depression. These low-budget productions drastically reduced his revenues from film rights, but they, more than book sales, saved him from bankruptcy and inched him back to a modest income. By 1939, Westerns had regained enough popularity to become featured attractions, and moviemakers were again assigning them major directors, established stars, and handsome budgets. Henry King's *Jesse James* (1939), Cecil B. DeMille's *Union Pacific* (1939), and George Marshall's *Destry Rides Again* (1939) were quickly followed by William Wyler's *The Westerner* (1940), Fritz Lang's *The Return of Frank James* (1940), Wesley Ruggles's *Arizona* (1940), and Michael Curtiz's *Santa Fe Trail* (1940). Collectively, these films affirmed that the box office appeal of Westerns was stronger than it had been since the 1920s. In 1940, the film version of *Western Union,* based on the Grey novel from the year before, was budgeted as a main feature and directed by Fritz Lang with Robert Young, Randolph Scott, and Dean Jagger in lead roles.

Still, the most important of these Westerns, the one most attuned to the future, was John Ford's *Stagecoach* (1939), which was filmed in Monument Valley and vindicated Grey's long-standing belief in the valley's cinematic potential. Back in 1923, Jesse Lasky had approved Grey's request that the adaptation of his *The Vanishing American* be made there, giving this film the distinction of being the first Hollywood movie to be set in the valley. John Ford's *Fort Apache* (1948) and *She Wore a Yellow Ribbon* (1949) employed Monument Valley even more effectively than the earlier *Stagecoach,* and, in conjunction with *Red River* (1948), reoriented audiences toward a new "adult Western" that quickly gained unprecedented popularity. By the late 1950s, the Western dominated the cultural landscape—in 1956, 83 of that year's 272 features were Westerns and by 1961, eight of the top ten serials on television were Westerns, a popularity that is today hard to believe.[1]

Although the television serial "Dick Powell's Zane Grey Theatre" was a moderate success, Grey's books were not featured in this resurgence of the Western in movies and on television. If the movie version of *Western Union* raised hopes for more and better adaptations of his novels, it contained a telltale clue that filmmakers were thinking otherwise. Twentieth-Century Fox did this film, not Paramount, which had loyally filmed Grey's new novels for sixteen years. Paramount continued its B-productions, but its *Knights of the Range* (1940) and *The Light of Western Stars* (1940) were its last two Zane Grey films. When the major studios rushed into Westerns during the 1950s, they avoided Grey's stories, and only fringe studios on the brink of collapse, like Republic and RKO, pursued them, and then only because the rights were so steeply discounted.

Meanwhile, sales of Grey's novels soared, and in a few cases surpassed the returns of the original publication. Although this popularity was aided by the resurgence of Westerns in movies and television, its driving force came from the proliferation of paperbacks. Until 1939, none of Grey's novels had ever appeared in paperback. During the war, the Armed Forces Editions issued nine titles with paper covers in editions that ranged from 125,000 to 155,000 copies.[2] This modest but significant beginning gained more momentum when Bantam included *Nevada* in its first twenty paperbacks that were released in January 1946.[3] Although this Western had sold poorly when it was first published in 1928, it was the hit of Bantam's slate, and soon became Grey's top-selling novel.[4] Harpers persuaded Dolly to slow the release of Grey paperbacks until it had drawn down the unpublished novels in its backlog. Shortly after Dolly's death in 1957, Pocket Books convinced Romer and the other members of the Grey family to allow its Cardinal series to carry most of his Westerns.[5] By the 1960s, the shelves of paperback galleries bulged with Zane Grey Westerns.

Since its first one in 1924, *Field and Stream* had periodically published a list of world records, and the 1938 list credited Grey with four.[6] But in his 1935 article for *Outdoor Life*, "Swordfish . . . King of the Sea," Thomas Aitken initiated his own list of world records that openly disagreed with the *Field and Stream* lists. In 1936, he authored an article entitled "Let's Get Together on Records," and during 1938 and 1939, he published his own lists in hopes of provoking debate about standards and spurring the creation of a more reliable list of records.[7] Michael Lerner, the heir to the Lerner chain of department stores and a well-known figure in the new generation of big-game fishermen, agreed with Aitken. After financing expeditions to Cape Breton and Bimini for the Museum of Natural History, he encouraged and underwrote a major renovation of the two galleries of Grey's fish at the museum. The 1938 exhibition of "Giants of the Mackerel Family" featured an innovative display of the broadbill's skeletal structure and a record marlin caught by Lerner. It replaced the exhibit of Grey's fish and reduced his presence to a single photograph of him alongside his 758-pound tuna. During a trip to Australia and New Zealand a year later, Lerner and Dr. William Gregory met with officers from the major fishing clubs there, and discussed the establishment of a new international organization. On June 7, 1939, four months before Grey's death, Lerner, Gregory, Heilner, and Francesca La Monte, in association with a group of distinguished anglers that included Ernest Hemingway, founded the International Game Fish Association (IGFA) and based it out of the museum.[8] They immediately solicited input from fishing clubs around the world and formulated a new set of standards for world records.

In 1943, the IGFA issued its first list of world records, and Grey was credited with a single catch. Two of his records on the *Field and Stream* list for 1938 had been bettered. Meanwhile, ichthyologists determined that striped marlin did not grow to 1,000 pounds, which disqualified Grey's 1,040-pound catches as a misclassification. The IGFA accepted his 618-pound silver marlin until 1954, when it was superseded by one weighing 755 pounds, but ten years later, the IGFA ruled that "silver marlin" was not a legitimate classification and abolished this category.[9] For years, both the IGFA and the Tuna Club distanced themselves from Zane Grey and ignored his achievements. But in 1999, when the IGFA relocated to a handsome new building that institutionalized its authority on all matters relating to recreational fishing, it created a hall of fame that included Zane Grey in its first group of inductees. Two years later, it sponsored a special exhibit of his fishing.

At the time of his death, Grey believed that far away, in the waters north of Australia and west toward the Indian Ocean, virgin seas still existed, and he bitterly regretted that he never fished there. Although he had complained for years about the drop in fish populations around Catalina, most of the remote areas of the world that he had fished still held as many big fish as they had for centuries. But in 2003, the front page of the *New York Times* carried news of a comprehensive study revealing that 90 percent of the big fish have disappeared from the oceans of the world.[10] The plunge in stocks of these magnificent fish over the past sixty-five years is deeply troubling, and unless something is done soon to protect them, they, and the sport in which Grey was a true pioneer, will soon disappear forever.

When Grey left for the West in search of new direction for his writing career, the Grand Canyon was not a national park, Arizona was not yet a state, and the Western was not a recognized genre. Although he was born too late to be among the original explorers of the unknown, uncharted regions of the world, he was at the forefront of a new wave of recreational adventurers. Today, readers of *Outside* and *Adventure Travel*—backpackers and white-water rafters, along with their guides and outfitters—attest to the widespread popularity of experiences first championed by Grey almost a hundred years ago. The Haas family, the manufacturers of Levi-Straus jeans, purchased Grey's retreat at the Winkle Bar in Oregon, and Malcolm Forbes acquired Flower Point in Tahiti. Although these properties have been improved in ways that would probably have offended Grey, they are still revered for the beauty and remoteness that first attracted him, and serve as apt memorials to his venturesome spirit.

Although it was perhaps the most successful and most durable form of entertainment during the twentieth century, the Western today has truly become a product of the past. But Grey's vision of the West still endures. Although he was convinced that *his* beloved West had disappeared by 1929, his writings have nurtured and still sustain a belief, one impervious to modern development, that life in the West is somehow different and better, that it offers open spaces, breathtaking vistas, and untapped possibilities, and that the last best place still exists somewhere out there.

Appendix:
Grey's World Records

Because there is so much inaccuracy and misunderstanding about Grey's world records, I am providing a list of them. Since the International Game Fish Association (IGFA), the overseer of world records today, was not established until 1939, the year of Grey's death, there was no official list or rigorous verification over the years that he fished. However, Grey's records were not merely self-proclaimed, as some have charged. In 1924, the year of Grey's first world record, John Treadwell Nichols and Van Campen Heilner, a friend of Grey's, initiated a list of world records that gained immediate credibility from their affiliation with the American Museum of Natural History. This list was maintained and updated at the museum by Francesca La Monte in a loose-leaf notebook. Unfortunately, the replaced pages of information were not saved. However, their updated list was published intermittently in the influential journal *Field and Stream.* The entries below note the *F & S* lists that recognized Grey's records as well as his books in which they are mentioned. Since a new list sometimes took four years to appear, records, like Grey's 582-pound broadbill, two sailfish and his first silver marlin, were set and eclipsed between appearances of the lists. Grey's records were also influenced by evolution of the list itself. Early lists had only one category for tuna and did not distinguish the bluefin from the yellowfin. Consequently neither Heilner nor Grey considered his 316-pound yellowfin, from Cabo San Lucas in 1926, a world record, which it probably was. Conversely, Grey lobbied Heilner to add classifications for "silver marlin" and "tiger shark" in order to be credited with more records.

1. Tuna	758 lbs.	Port Medvey, Nova Scotia	Aug. 1924	*F&S*, 1924, and *Tales of Swordfish and Tuna*, 96–97
2. Dolphin	51½ lbs.	Galapagos Islands	Feb. 1925	*F&S*, 1928, and *Tales of Fishing Virgin Seas*, 38 (plate)
3. Sailfish	135 lbs.	Zihuatanejo, Mexico	Mar. 1925	*Tales of Virgin Seas*, 104 (plate) and 159
4. Striped Marlin	450 lbs.	Bay of Islands, New Zealand	Mar. 1926	*F&S*, 1928, and *Tales of the Angler's Eldorado*, 81 (plate) and 220
5. Yellowtail	111 lbs.	Bay of Islands, New Zealand	Mar. 1926	*F&S*, 1928, and *Tales of the Angler's Eldorado*, 132 (plate) and 220
6. Broadbill	582 lbs.	Catalina, California	Jul. 1926	"Landing the Record Broadbill"
7. Silver Marlin	464 lbs.	Vairao, Tahiti	Nov. 1928	*Tales of Tahitian Waters*, 137 (plate)
8. Dolphin	63 lbs.	Vairao, Tahiti	Mar. 1930	*F&S*, 1933, and *Tales of Tahitian Waters*, 185 (plate) and 235
9. Silver Marlin	618 lbs.	Vairao, Tahiti	Mar. 1930	*F&S*, 1936, and *Tales of Tahitian Waters*, 221 (plate) and 232
10. Striped Marlin	1,040 lbs.	Vairao, Tahiti	May 1930	*F&S*, 1933, and *Tales of Tahitian Waters*, 282 (plate) and 297
11. Sailfish	170 lbs.	Tonga Island	May 1931	Grey never finished his account of this traumatic, aborted trip.
12. Tiger Shark	1,036 lbs.	Sydney, Australia	May 1936	*F&S*, 1939, "World Record Tiger Shark"

Notes

Zane Grey was not only a prolific author of novels, but he also wrote almost as much about his personal life. In addition to the thirty-five Westerns published during his lifetime, he authored nine books about his travels, fishing, and outdoor adventures. Less well known and far more revealing are his many personal journals and the hundreds of letters to and from his wife that both conscientiously saved. When Dolly died in 1957, all of these letters, along with his journals and correspondence from his girlfriends, were still stored at his Altadena residence. Romer inherited the home and its collections, and he did nothing with them until 1968. That year, with the agreement of his siblings Loren (LG) and Betty Grosso, he donated a large number of manuscripts, photographs, scrapbooks, and ephemera to the Ohio Historical Society (OHS) and the Zane Grey Museum in Zanesville, Ohio (ZGM—Z). Sometime between this donation and Romer's sale of the house in 1970, Betty claimed more than half of the letters and several journals, and she elected to burn the letters from her father's girlfriends. In 1976, when Romer died, Loren inherited the remnants of his collection, much reduced by the donation, loss, theft, and the materials that went to Betty. Several years later, Bridget McMahon, Betty's granddaughter, typed a large number of Betty's letters (Bmms) with the intent of publishing them, but she never did. Meanwhile, Joe Wheeler (JW) and Candace Kant (CK), two professors researching

Grey, approached Loren and Betty and received permission to photocopy their journals and letters. Each copied large amounts and much that was the same, but each also secured items the other had missed and their combined holdings were well shy of the whole. Since their findings were never published, few outside a narrow circle of collectors and readers have ever known about Grey's secret life. Even George M. Farley, an avid collector and promoter of Grey, who had a photocopy of McMahon's typescript and later donated it to the Cline Library at Northern Arizona University (NAU), insisted up to his death that Grey's relationships with other women were paternal and platonic. However, this wall of silence began to crack in 1995 when the *Missouri Review,* a small journal specializing in original fiction and poetry, published a selection of letters from the McMahon typescript. When I encountered these letters during research into Grey's fishing, I contacted Professor Philip Rulon at NAU and he generously mailed me a copy of the McMahon typescript. This convinced me to write Grey's biography and sent me searching for as many letters and journals as I could find. I benefited enormously from the cooperation and generosity of Loren Grey, Candace Kant, Joe Wheeler, George Houle (GH), Pat Friese (PF), and Dan Brock (DB). Over the five years I spent researching and writing this book, the Beinecke Library at Yale University (BY) acquired an important Grey journal, a collection of his letters to Lola Gornall, the many lots of letters that Betty Grosso put up for auction (BY-G), and another large segment of letters that was sold independently (BY-G2). The footnotes that follow employ these parenthetical abbreviations. I have tried to provide the location of actual journals and letters, but sales and disappearance of many items since McMahon, Kant, and Wheeler accessed them have necessitated that I cite their copies instead. In all cases, I have permission from Zane Grey, Inc., to quote from these unpublished documents.

Abbreviations

BY	Beinecke Library, Yale University, New Haven, Conn.
BY-G	Grosso Collection (uncatalogued Mss. 261), Beinecke Library, Yale University, New Haven, Conn.
BY-G2	Additional Grosso (uncatalogued Mss. 529), Beinecke Library, Yale University, New Haven, Conn.
Bmms	Bridget McMahon Typescript
CK	Candace Kant (photocopies of Grey letters and papers)
DB	Dan Brock
GH	George Houle
JW	Joe Wheeler (photocopies of Grey letters and papers)
LDS	David Dexter Rust Papers (Ms. 1143), Archives, Church of Jesus Christ of Latter-Day Saints, Salt Lake City, Utah
LG	Loren Grey

NAU Ms. 230, Zane Grey Collection, Cline Library, Northern Arizona
    University, Flagstaff, Ariz.

NYPL Robert Hobart Davis Collection—New York Public Library

OHS Ohio Historical Society, Columbus

OHS 1262 Zane and Dolly Grey Papers (Ms. 1262), Ohio Historical Society

Mss 1262 Zane and Dolly Grey Papers, Letter from Diosus to Zane Grey, 29
    March, 1899: Ohio Historical Society

Mss 1262 Zane and Dolly Grey Papers, Letter from Diosus (D.B.B.) to Zane
    Grey, May, 1902: Ohio Historical Society

Mss 1262 Zane and Dolly Grey Papers, Letter from Diosus to Zane Grey, un-
    dated: Ohio Historical Society

Mss 1262 Zane and Dolly Grey Papers, Letter from Zane Grey to Fiancée, un-
    dated: Ohio Historical Society

Mss 1262 Zane and Dolly Grey Papers, Notebook of visit to Cave Dwelling:
    Ohio Historical Society

Mss 1262 Zane and Dolly Grey Papers, Letter from Zane Grey to Dolly Grey,
    6 February, 1920: Ohio Historical Society

Mss 1262 Zane and Dolly Grey Papers, Letter from Dolly Grey to Zane Grey,
    25 August, 1924: Ohio Historical Society

Mss 1262 Zane and Dolly Grey Papers, Letter from Dolly Grey to Zane Grey,
    19 February, 1927: Ohio Historical Society

Mss 1262 Zane and Dolly Grey Papers, "Fading Indian Trails": Ohio Histori-
    cal Society

PF Pat Friese

ZGM—L Zane Grey Museum, Lackawaxen, Penn.

ZGM—Z Zane Grey/National Road Museum, Zanesville, Ohio

Introduction

1. Lina Grey, Letter to Dan Beard, November 26, 1939 (Dan Beard Papers, Library of Congress, Washington, D.C.).

2. This information is taken from Gruber, *Zane Grey*, 1. He derived it from Hackett, *Fifty Years of Best Sellers*, 81–97.

3. Justice, *Bestseller Index*, 134.

4. This information was also headlined in the *New York Times*'s obituary of Grey. *New York Times*, October 22, 1939, 24. See also *Publishers Weekly* 136 (October 28, 1939), 1698.

5. *New York Times*, October 22, 1939, 24.

6. Rascoe, "Opie Read and Zane Grey," 8.

7. *New York Times*, October 24, 1939, 22.

8. *New Yorker* 15 (November 4, 1939), 9.

9. There are several other books that cover various aspects of Grey's biography,

but none are comprehensive biographies and the most recent ones are based largely on Gruber and Grey's published accounts of his experiences: Farley, *Many Faces of Zane Grey* and *Zane Grey: A Documented Portrait;* Kerr, *Zane Grey, Man of the West;* and May, *Zane Grey: Romancing the West* and *Maverick Heart.*

10. Zane Grey, Letter to Lina Grey, October 13, 1911 (NAU).

11. Lina Grey, Letter to Zane Grey, August 29, 1924 (BY-G).

12. Derks, *Value of a Dollar,* 184–85.

13. Zane Grey, Letter to Lina Grey, [1905?] (NAU).

14. Zane Grey, Letter to Lina Grey, March 18, [1922?] (OHS).

15. Farley, *Many Faces of Zane Grey,* 146. Also Ashworth, *Arizona Triptych,* 181, 208–9. May suspected that these relationships were sexual; see May, *Maverick Heart,* 81–84.

16. This large collection of photographs involves several hundred negatives and prints. Since most of the materials are a scrambled mass, it is impossible to tell if there are prints of all the negatives—probably not. Most of the photographs are of nude females, and involve more than a dozen different women. A small percentage of the photographs were gathered into ten separate envelopes on which the name of the woman inside was written in Grey's secret code. Among these names are four about whom I know very little. The early photographs date from Grey's college years, perhaps earlier, and imitate the nudes in paintings by the masters, but the ones from the 1930s are more pornographic. Only short portions of the ten diaries have been translated, but they make clear that Grey used them to record graphic descriptions of his sexual activities. There are four other notebooks from girlfriends and one of these contains a pornographic story entitled *The Harp of Sappho.* There is also an array of memorabilia—lockets, strands of hair bound with ribbon, a gold ring from "Golden Fleece" to "Doc Grey" imprinted with the inscription "till death do us part," etc. I was allowed to examine this collection for three hours and to offer this inventory, but not to quote from the journals or to publish any of the photographs.

17. Lina Grey, Letter to Robert H. Davis, January 4, 1935 (NYPL).

Chapter 1: Wayward Youth: 1872–90

1. Other than a few birth and death dates, there is very little verifiable information about the Zane family prior to Ebenezer. Much of what is known comes from family accounts dating from many years after the period being recalled. Bibliographies of useful sources can be found at the conclusion of the "Betty Zane" and "Ebenezer Zane" entries in *American National Biography,* vol. 24, 215–17, 218–19.

2. Farley, *Many Faces of Zane Grey,* 16. Grey's belief in his Indian heritage was reinforced by Isaac Zane's many years among the Wyandots and his marriage to Myeerah.

3. Eckert, *Dark and Bloody River*, 10–12.

4. A good reconstruction of the actual history of this battle can be found in Hintzen, "Betty Zane, Lydia Boggs, and Molly Scott," 95–109.

5. Although Grey depicts Betty's romance with Alfred Clarke in *Betty Zane* (1903), the actual Betty was only sixteen and unattached at the time of her heroic action. Several years after the battle, she became involved with a man named Van Swearingen and with him had an illegitimate daughter in 1784. Zane's source for his romance between Betty and Alfred, if he had one, is further complicated by the marriage of Ebenezer's daughter Rebecca to a John Clarke. I am indebted to Diane Nichols, a genealogist of the Grey family, for information about Van Swearingen.

6. Quotes are from "Ebenezer Zane," *American National Biography,* vol. 24, 218–19.

7. Schneider, *National Road,* 7–13.

8. Diane Nichols, Samuel Zane Geneology.

9. Liggett's name is sometimes spelled Ligget or Liggit, and Guttridge has been spelled Guthridge.

10. This information comes from a genealogy by Norris F. Schneider that was based on an earlier one by H. L. Johnson from Pike County.

11. Ida Grey, "Family History" (DB). The credibility of this history is undermined by Ida's inaccurate mention of the death of Lewis's mother shortly after his birth. A genealogy of the Gray family in the papers of Norris F. Schneider states that Lewis and Nancy were married in 1825 and had nine children. There exists a family photographs showing Lewis surrounded by his sisters.

12. Ida Grey, "Family History" (DB).

13. Norris F. Schneider, "Father of Zane Grey," unidentified newspaper article (Norris F. Schneider Papers, mss. 789, OHS). The Zane Grey collection at the OHS contains various clippings about Dr. Gray's activities in Zanesville dating from the 1860s.

14. Records of Woodlawn Cemetery, Zanesville, Ohio. The Grays saved a Bible given to Ella by her father as an early present.

15. Farley, *Many Faces of Zane Grey,* 65–67.

16. Lewis M. Gray, "A Short History" (Lewis Gray Papers, mss. 885, box 1, folder 1, OHS).

17. "The Living Past" was first serialized in the *Zane Grey Reporter* 1 (March, 1986) and 3 (March, 1988). It has never been published in book form. Grey's first account of his past appeared in a letter he wrote to a clairvoyant named Anna Andre on February 16, 1918 (BY-G). Grey expanded this information into a broadside for a Harper promotion of his books in 1921 and used it for "Zane Grey" in *My Maiden Effort,* 82. These two articles served as the basis for "Breaking Through," 11–14, 76–80. Zane Grey is identified as the author, but the article was actually

written by an editor named John Pritchett. For this, Pritchett solicited informa-
tion from other people besides Grey. "Breaking Through" was reprinted as "My
Own Life" in a Harper and Brothers booklet entitled *Zane Grey: The Man and His
Work,* 1–19. Grey drew upon these accounts for "The Living Past."

18. Grey, *Tales of Lonely Trails,* 185.

19. Mrs. H. H. Johnson, Letter to Zane Grey, January 8, 1906 (Humanities Research Center, University of Texas–Austin).

20. Grey, *Tales of Lonely Trails,* 66.

21. *Zanesville Signal,* July 24, 1905, n.p.

22. Lina Grey, Letter to Zane Grey, "Christmas, 1904," *Zane Grey Review* 12
(June, 1997), 8–9.

23. Zane Grey, Letter to Anna Andre, February 16, 1918 (BY-G).

24. Quoted in Farley, *Many Faces of Zane Grey,* 64.

25. Timmerman, "Just the Facts, Ma'am," 12.

26. Ida Gray, "Family History" (DB).

27. In a 1905 letter to Zane, a girlfriend expressed sympathy toward his need
for other women and wrote, "I know how you are fighting your inherited trouble."

28. Even Gruber was inclined to believe that Lewis Gray's financial reversal
was a soured investment. Gruber, *Zane Grey,* 22.

29. Mowrey, "From G-R-A-Y to GREY," 6.

30. Gruber stated that Zane changed the spelling of his last name to "Grey"
when he opened his dental practice in New York City. Gruber, *Zane Grey,* 35. This
inaccuracy has been much repeated in subsequent explanations of the name
change.

Chapter 2: Quest for Direction: 1890–1905

1. Since Zane lived in Columbus a full year longer than he acknowledges in
"The Living Past," this contact from the Dental Association may have occurred
later than he remembered. City directories from 1891–95 list Pearl Grey at 108
Lexington Avenue, the same address as the family's residence, and identify him
as "dentist." The 1893–94 volume also identify R. C. as a dentist for the first time.
The amendment of his position to "assistant" for the 1894–95 directory suggests
intervention by the Dental Association.

2. An early, unidentified clipping identifies this team as from the "Latin
School," perhaps a variant name.

3. Local newspapers reveal that the City League was not formed until a full year
later than Grey indicated and that he and R. C. did not play together on the team
as he claimed. *Columbus Dispatch,* May 4, 1893, 2; May 9, 1893, 2; June 12, 1893,
2; and June 13, 1893, 2.

4. Grey, "Breaking Through," 76.

5. Ebbeskotte, "Delphos (Ohio) Baseball" is a thorough, detailed account of this season.

6. *Delphos Herald,* August 31, 1893, 4.

7. In "The Living Past," Grey says that he was sixteen when he started high school (4, 11). This suggests that he may have been held back a grade, perhaps due to poor academic performance, and started high school a year late. His autobiography does not give his level in school when the family departed for Columbus, but it was probably the middle of his junior year. Despite widespread assumptions that Grey graduated from high school, Grey once admitted that he did not. *Zanesville Courier,* April 11, 1904, 5.

8. Ohio State University did not have a dental school at that time. See Kock, *History of Dental Surgery,* 417–617.

9. "Conditions of Admission," Department of Dentistry, *University of Pennsylvania Catalogue and Announcements, 1893–94,* 309 (Archives, University of Pennsylvania).

10. Kock, *History of Dental Surgery,* 484–86.

11. *University of Pennsylvania Catalogue and Announcements, 1893–94,* 299.

12. Clipping file, "Franklin Field" (Archives, University of Pennsylvania).

13. On Mondays and Tuesdays at 10:00 A.M. Grey had general chemistry with Professor Wormley. At 3:30 P.M. on Mondays and Wednesdays he had anatomy with Pierson; at 4:30 P.M., physiology with Reichert; and finally mechanical dentistry and metallurgy with Essig at 5:30 P.M. On Tuesdays and Thursdays at 4:30 P.M. he had operative dentistry with Darby, and on Wednesdays at noon he had histology with Formad. *University of Pennsylvania Catalogue and Announcements, 1893–94,* 302.

14. "Zane Grey" Harper Promotion [1921?]. Also Grey, "Breaking Through," 78.

15. Light, *Cultural History of Baseball,* 568–69.

16. Ortho, *History of Athletics at Penn,* 147.

17. *Pennsylvanian,* March 21, 1895, 1. Also Weston, *New Phillies Encyclopedia,* 24–26.

18. *Columbus Dispatch,* May 28, 1894, 7.

19. Timmerman, "America's Pastime," 2. Also *Delphos Herald,* August 9, 1894, 4.

20. *Delphos Herald,* August 8, 1894, 4.

21. Ibid., August 9, 1894, 4.

22. Ibid.

23. Timmerman, "America's Pastime," 2. Also Ebbeskotte, "Delphos (Ohio) Baseball," 13.

24. *Delphos Herald,* September 19, 1894, 4.

25. *Pennsylvanian,* May 3, 1895, 2.

26. Ibid., September 27, 1895, 1.

27. Timmerman, "America's Pastime," 2, and "Just the Facts, Ma'am," 12.

28. *Pennsylvanian,* February 10, 1896, 1.

29. Ibid., February 27, 1896, 1.

30. Clipping, Zane Grey, *Baseball Scrapbook* (Zane Grey Papers, mss. 296, box 12, folder 32, OHS).

31. *Pennsylvanian,* May 10, 1896, 1.

32. *Philadelphia Ledger,* May 19, 1896, 17.

33. Grey, *Baseball Scrapbook* (Zane Grey Papers, mss. 296, OHS).

34. *Philadelphia Ledger,* June 11, 1896, 16.

35. This certificate is at ZGM—Z.

36. Grey, *Baseball Scrapbook* (Zane Grey Papers, mss. 296, OHS).

37. Ibid. Also Wheeler, "Two Roads," 32–33.

38. Kock, *History of Dental Surgery,* 1022. This book reveals that this examination was first instituted in 1895.

39. This license is displayed at ZGM—Z.

40. Grey, *Baseball Scrapbook* (Zane Grey Papers, mss. 296, OHS).

41. Gruber, *Zane Grey,* 37.

42. Quoted in Wheeler, "Two Roads," 33.

43. *Newark Evening News,* April 28, 1898, 11.

44. Ibid., July 6, 1898, 2.

45. Timmerman, "America's Pastime," 2.

46. *Orange Journal,* June 25, 1898, 3.

47. Zane Grey, Letter to Anna Andre, February 16, 1918 (BY-G).

48. Ibid.

49. Diosus (D. B. B.), Letter to Zane Grey, March 29, 1899 (mss. 1262, OHS).

50. Interview with George Fruel, Pike County historian, October 10, 2002.

51. Aron, *Working at Play,* 5.

52. In chapter 6, Aron discusses the popularity of camping during the late nineteenth century. Aron, *Working at Play,* 156–77.

53. Grey, "My Own Life," 8.

54. Copies of this announcement are held at the OHS and ZGM—L. There also exists a nameplate from this office with the name "Dr. Zane Grey."

55. Grey did go by P. Zane Grey and Dr. Zane Grey in several early articles. The first edition of *Betty Zane* (1903) identified him as P. Zane Grey.

56. Many accounts report that Zane met Dolly while he was canoeing with R. C. near the confluence of the Lackawaxen and Delaware Rivers, but in a letter of hers for their first anniversary, Dolly wrote, "We were bound to meet at some time and some place and that it just happened to be Westcolong made it so much more." Lina Roth, Letter to Pearl Grey, August 29, 1901 (BY-G2).

57. Lina Roth, Letter to Pearl Grey, May 17, 1905 (GH).

58. Kaplan-Mann, "Dr. Pearl Grey—Miss Lina Elise Roth," 3.

59. Zane Grey, Letter to Anna Andre, February 16, 1918 (BY-G).

60. For a legal appeal over back taxes owed the IRS, Grey's attorneys prepared a legal petition with a pair of exhibits from Julius Blumberg, the attorney for these estates, detailing the financial distributions of Dolly's inheritance. This appeal sought to argue that the couple had always been a partnership and she was entitled to the income claimed in their returns. Zane Grey vs. Commissioner of Internal Revenue, October 26, 1931 (LG).

61. Gruber, *Zane Grey,* 38–39.

62. Lina Roth, Letters to Dr. and Pearl Grey, November 22, 1900, and December 5, 1900 (GH).

63. Lina Roth, Letter to Zane Grey, December 5, 1900 (GH).

64. Diosus (D. B. B.), Letter to Zane Grey, May 8, 1902 (mss. 1262, OHS).

65. Ibid., Letter, undated.

66. Ibid., Letter, [1899?].

67. Zane Grey, Letter to Lina Roth, October 16, 1905 (BY-G2).

68. "Gertrude," Letter to Zane Grey, January 20, 1904 (Humanities Research Center, University of Texas–Austin).

69. Zane Grey, Letter to Anna Andre, February 16, 1918 (BY-G).

70. Grey mentions that he read these and several other authors while he was growing up. Grey, "The Living Past," 5, 5, 6, 5, and 7, 5.

71. Diosus (D. B. B.), Letter to Zane Grey, May, 1902 (mss. 1262, OHS).

72. Zane Grey, Enclosure in letter to Lina Roth, September 14, 1905 (BY-G2).

73. Zane Grey, Letter to Lina Roth, January 31, 1903, *Zane Grey Review* 6 (February, 1991), 7.

74. "Shields, George Oliver," *American National Biography,* vol. 19, 837–8.

75. Zane Grey, Letter to Anna Andre, February 16, 1918 (BY-G). Gruber incorrectly states that Zane got the money from Dolly. Gruber, *Zane Grey,* 47.

76. Christian, "Zane Grey: Legacy," 155.

77. Lina Roth, Letter to Zane Grey, "Christmas, 1904," *Zane Grey Review* 12 (June, 1997), 8.

78. Lina Roth, Letter to Zane Grey, August 28, 1904 (BY-G).

79. Zane Grey, Letter to Lina Roth, September 15, 1901 (BY-G).

80. Zane Grey, Letter to Lina Roth, December 9, 1903 (BY-G2).

81. Lina Roth, Letter to Zane Grey, November 28, 1902 (BY-G).

82. Zane Grey, Letter to Lina Roth, undated (mss. 1262, OHS).

83. Zane Grey, Letter to Lina Roth, April 18, 1904 (BY-G2).

84. Zane Grey, Letter to Lina Roth, September 28, 1902 (Bmms).

85. Lina Grey, Letter to Zane Grey, November 29, 1904 (BY-G2).

86. Lina Grey, Letter to Zane Grey, November 8, 1903 (BY-G2).

87. Lina Grey, Letter to Zane Grey, December 27, 1904 (BY-G).

88. *Zanesville Courier,* May 25, 1904, 3.

89. Ida Grey, Letters to Zane Grey, January 22–26, 1904 (Humanities Research Center, University of Texas–Austin).

90. Grey, "My Own Life," 1.

91. Christian, "Zane Grey: Legacy," 174.

92. *Cultural Landscape Treatment Plan for the Zane Grey Property,* U.S. Park Service, December 16, 1999, 10 (ZGM—L). Prior to their 1906 wedding, Reba gave R. C. a diamond and ruby ring worth more than half the purchase price of the Lackawaxen property. Zane Grey, Letter to Lina Roth, September 7, 1905 (LG).

93. Zane Grey, Letter to Lina Roth, [fall, 1904?] (OHS).

94. Quoted in *Cultural Landscape Treatment Plan for the Zane Grey Property,* 10.

95. Zane Grey, Letter to Lina Roth, [fall, 1905?] (NAU).

96. Shi, *Simple Life,* 183–84.

97. Wagner, *Simple Life,* 109.

98. Lina Roth, Letter to Zane Grey, May 3, 1905. Quoted in Gruber, *Zane Grey,* 51.

99. Lina Roth, Letter to Zane Grey, May 9, 1905 (GH).

100. Lina Roth, Letter to Zane Grey, May 17, 1905 (GH).

101. Diosus (D. B. B.), Letters to Zane Grey, September 7, 1905, and November 6, 1905 (mss. 1262, OHS).

102. Clippings from the *Zanesville Courier,* July 24, 1905 (Norris F. Schneider Papers, mss. 789, OHS).

103. Grey, *Journal, 1905–10,* July 22 and July 23, 1905 (BY).

104. Zane Grey, Letter to Lina Roth, October 16, 1905 (BY-G2).

105. Interview with Loren Grey, January 9, 2003.

106. Lina Roth, Letter to Zane Grey, January 2, 1905 (BY-G2).

107. Lina Roth, Letter to Zane Grey, September 14, 1905 (BY-G2).

Chapter 3: Adventurous Apprentice: 1906–10

1. *Forest and Stream* 71 (December 5, 1908), 899.

2. *Zanesville Courier,* May 25, 1904, 3.

3. Grey, *Journal, 1905–10,* January 11, 1906 (BY).

4. Lina Grey, *Honeymoon Journal,* January 4, 1906 (BY-G2).

5. Anderson, *Living at the Edge,* 63, 84, 89, 97.

6. Ibid., 73, 94.

7. Lina Grey, *Honeymoon Journal,* January 16–17, 1906 (BY-G2).

8. Ibid., January 24, 1906.

9. For a fuller discussion of the early development of sportfishing at Catalina and the Tuna Club, see Reiger, *Profiles in Salt Water Angling,* 74–78.

10. Lina Grey, *Honeymoon Journal,* February 1–8, 1906 (BY-G2).

11. The next year when Grey returned for his trip with Buffalo Jones, a snowstorm delayed the start and they opted for a visit to Los Angeles. Grey wrote to Dolly that he hoped to visit Catalina again, but improved weather in Arizona

prompted them to return sooner and he probably did not get to Catalina. Zane Grey, Letter to Lina Grey, March 27, 1907 (CK).

12. Reiger, *Profiles in Salt Water Angling,* 91–93.

13. Lina Grey, *Honeymoon Journal,* February 15–18, 1906 (BY-G2).

14. Grey, *Journal, 1905–10,* February 27, 1906 (BY).

15. "Shields, George Oliver," *Dictionary of American Biography,* vol. 9, 106, and *American National Biography,* vol.19, 837–38. Also Mott, *History of American Magazines,* vol. 4, 381.

16. *Shields'* 4 (April, 1907), 280.

17. These articles are: "A Night in a Jungle," "The Leaping Tarpon," "Three Strikes and Out," "Byme-by-Tarpon," and "Cruising in Mexican Waters." In his *Journal, 1905–10,* Grey recorded no entries from December 1906 to June 5, 1907. His first June entry begins: "Whatever has become of the months since I wrote here last? Six months! I have been to old Mexico and to Arizona in that time."

18. Waddell, "Tarpon Fishing at Tamos," 234–36.

19. Davis, *Dark Side of Fortune,* 34–39 and 42–46.

20. "Alvah James, 79, Adventurer, Dies," *New York Times,* October 23, 1958, 33.

21. Zane Grey, Letter to Lina Grey, May 1, 1906 (BY-G).

22. This lecture may have been hosted by the Canadian Club, since James had a closer affiliation with it and it later hosted Jones's lecture about his outing with Grey. ZGM—L possesses a broadside for the Canadian Club lecture by Jones. Also Lina Grey, Letter to Zane Grey, March 6, 1909 (mss. 1262, OHS).

23. Grey, "My Own Life," 2.

24. Schmitt, *Back to Nature,* 45–55, and Brooks, *Speaking for Nature,* 210–15.

25. Grey, "My Own Life," 3.

26. Zane Grey, Letter to Lina Grey, May 1906 (BY-G2).

27. Grey, "My Own Life," 2.

28. Lina Grey, Letter to Zane Grey, March 6, 1909 (OHS).

29. In a February 15, 1911, letter to David Rust (LDS), Grey mentioned a fee of $5/day, which would make this figure a conservative estimate of his total cost.

30. Owens relied on the bounties for these predators as an important supplement to his salary. By 1913, he estimated that he had killed over 200, and later raised his estimate to 1,200.

31. Isenberg, *Destruction of the Bison,* 181.

32. Dary, *Buffalo Book,* 227–28.

33. Zane Grey, Letter to Lina Grey, "Sunday" [1907] (BY-G2).

34. Zane Grey, Letter to Lina Grey, March 27, [1907] (BY-G2).

35. Zane Grey, Letter to Lina Grey, Easter Sunday, 1907 (LG).

36. Zane Grey, Letter to Lina Grey, April 8, 1907 (BY-G).

37. A fuller account of this trial and its background can be found in Reilly, *Lee's Ferry,* 193–206.

38. Zane Grey, Letter to Lina Grey, April 12, [1907] (BY-G2).

39. Zane Grey, Letter to Lina Grey, April 8, [1907] (BY-G).

40. Grey, "Notebook of Visit to Cave Dwellings," 15 (mss. 1262, OHS). This journal, which is from Grey's 1907 trip to Arizona, is not accurately identified in the OHS cataloguing of it.

41. Grey kept notes on what he learned about Lee from Emett, "Notebook of Visit to Cave Dwellings," 24 (mss. 1262, OHS). Recently, several popular books have discussed Lee and the Mountain Meadows Massacre. Bagley, *Blood of the Prophets,* Denton, *American Massacre,* and Krakauer, *Under the Banner of Heaven.* See also Eakin, "Reopening the Mormon Murder Mystery," A19 and A21.

42. Grey, "Man Who Influenced Me Most," 52–54. Emett's marriages are discussed in Reilly, *Lee's Ferry,* 147–50. Grey claimed that Emett had eighteen children, but he probably did not know about two of Emma's children who lived only several months.

43. Zane Grey, Letter to Lina Grey, April 12, 1907 (BY-G2).

44. On two different occasions in her journals, Claire Wilhelm mentions Zane telling others about this polygamist.

45. Zane Grey, Letter to Lina Grey, March 29, 1907 (Bmms).

46. Anderson, *Living at the Edge,* 147.

47. Grey added a second *m* to the spelling of Emett's name. Reilly explains that Emett did, in fact, spell his name with a second *m* until the 1870s and then suddenly dropped it. Reilly, *Lee's Ferry,* 147.

48. Grey, *Last of the Plainsmen,* 16.

49. After the trip was over, Grant Wallace wrote to Grey that Jones was "thoroughly despicable, picayunish and a four flusher." At the outset of the trip, Grey reported that Jones kicked and shot at his dogs. "Everyone out here hates him [Jones]," he added. "And I've learned to do the same." During negotiations relating to the book, Grey became so exasperated with his "flippant attitude" and "many slights and unkindnesses" that he decided (briefly) to sever ties with him.

50. Grey, "Man Who Influenced Me Most," 54–55, 130–36.

51. Yost, *Buffalo Bill,* 25.

52. Zane Grey, Letter to Daniel Murphy, June 2, 1907 (Edwin Markham Collection, Wagner College).

53. Grey, *Journal, 1905–10,* September 1, 1907 (BY).

54. Grey's journal reveals that he actually received a letter of rejection from Hitchcock a week before this meeting. Grey, *Journal 1905–10,* February 8 and 14, 1908 (BY).

55. Grey, *Journal, 1905–10,* December 8, 1907 (BY).

56. Zane Grey, Letter to Lina Grey, March 6, [1908] (CK).

57. "Warner, Eltinge Fowler," *National Cyclopedia of American Biography,* vol. 53, 180. Also Mott, *History of American Magazines,* vol. 4, 332.

58. *The Nation* 87 (September 24, 1908), 287.

59. *Field and Stream* 13 (October, 1908), 543.

60. *Field and Stream* 13 (December, 1908), 724.

61. *Field and Stream* 13 (January, 1909), 731.

62. Grey, *Journal, Arizona, 1908* (NAU).

63. Zane Grey, Letter to Lina Grey, March 29, 1907 (Bmms).

64. Zane Grey, Letter to Lina Grey, April 20, 1908 (CK).

65. Grey, "Roping Lions," in *Tales of Lonely Trails,* 66.

66. Grey, *Journal 1905–10,* February 6 and 19, 1908 (BY). In a December 7–8, 1907, letter to Murphy, Dolly wrote, "The purpose of this letter is to make up for a disgraceful lapse of Zane's. I don't know how many times he has written you since 'The Desert' came and each time I remember telling him not to forget to thank you for us both" (Edwin Markham Collection, Wagner College).

67. Grey, "What the Desert Means to Me," 5 and 7.

68. Leopold, "Thinking Like a Mountain," 130.

69. *Field and Stream* 13 (December, 1908), 724.

70. Obituary for Will H. Dilg, *New York Times,* March 29, 1927, 25. See also "Will H. Dilg" in Stroud, *National Leaders of Conservation,* 126, and Ives, "Interview with Zane Grey," 6. Marguerite Ives was Dilg's wife and she mentions in this article that she and Dilg first met Grey on this trip. Grey confirmed this in various tributes to Dilg following his death.

71. Dilg, "When Woman Goes Fishing," 922. Marguerite Dilg's visits to Tampico for 1905 and 1906 are verified in letters about Tampico that were published in *Forest and Stream.* An entry from December 9, 1905, 476, records that she caught twenty-five tarpon. One from April 7, 1906, 555, notes that Dilg fished five days and landed twelve.

72. *Tarpon* was composed of a short letter by Grey and condensed versions of "Byme-by-Tarpon" and "Three Strikes and Out." *Nassau, Cuba, Mexico* was a short travelogue written by Grey about points of interest to passengers on the Ward line. *Moody's* reveals that during 1906–7, the Ward line underwent a major refinancing, a corporate relocation, and a change of corporate leadership. A. G. Smith, who had been the company's secretary, became its first vice president, a position he retained through three rapid turnovers of presidents. The extension of the line's service to Tampico resulted from these developments, and *Tarpon* was used as promotion for it.

73. Recently, several pages from Dolly's journal of this trip were auctioned by Butterfield's (December 11, 1997, lot no. 8286). The location of the journal itself is currently unknown. Dolly's earlier return is confirmed by a letter from Dolly in Lackawaxen to Zane in Tampico dated March 6, 1909 (mss. 1262, OHS). Zane once claimed that Romer was conceived in Alacanes, but Dolly's sickness suggests that she conceived earlier than this. On March 24, 1909, Grey wrote in his *Journal, 1905–10,* "Have just returned from a three months trip to Cuba, Yucatan, and Mexico" (BY).

74. Zane Grey, Letter to Lina Grey, [February, 1909?] (GH).

75. Zane Grey, Letter to Lina Grey, February 17, 1909 (GH).

76. Grey, "Down an Unknown Jungle River," in *Tales of Southern Rivers*, 177.

77. Grey, *Journal, 1905–10*, April 1, 1909 (BY).

78. Grey, *Journal, 1905–10*, May 22, 1909 (BY).

79. Grey, *Journal, 1905–10*, April 22, 1909 (BY).

80. Grey, *Journal, 1905–10*, July 18, 1909 (BY).

81. Grey, *Journal, 1905–10*, October, 31, 1909 (BY).

82. Grey finished *The Heritage of the Desert* on January 23, 1910. *Journal 1905–10* (BY). The novel was accepted by Harper and Brothers in early April and published in September that same year.

83. Presumably Grey's imagination, Betty Zane, and perhaps *The Squaw Man* inspired this character, but a photograph opposite page 165 in Grey, *Tales of Lonely Trails*, showing Grey on a mule in front of a comely, smiling Indian maiden, suggests that Mescal may have been based upon an actual person. This photograph may also date from a later trip.

84. Grey, *Heritage of the Desert*, 5.

85. Reilly claims that the villainous Holderness in *The Heritage of the Desert* was based on Charlie Dimmick, the foreman for the Bar Z Ranch. Reilly, *Lee's Ferry*, 206.

86. Tompkins, *West of Everything*, 157.

87. *Journal, 1905–10*, January 18, 1908; February 3, 1908; September 26, 1908 (BY).

88. *Journal, 1905–10*, December 21, 1908; April 19, 1909; June 30, 1909; and January 23, 1910 (BY).

89. White, *Eastern Establishment and Western Experience*.

90. Wister, *Virginian*, x.

91. Van Dyke, *Desert*, 22.

92. Austin, *Land of Little Rain*, 16 and 21.

Chapter 4: Pursuit of the Dream: 1911–14

1. Zane Grey, Letter to Anna Andre, February 16, 1918 (BY-G). Also "Zane Grey," a promotional broadsheet circulated by Harpers.

2. Zane Grey, Letter to Dan Beard, June 5, 1910 (Dan Beard Papers, Library of Congress, Washington, D.C.).

3. Grey, *Journal, 1910–12*, March 10, 1911 (JW).

4. Grey, *Journal, 1905–10*, April 18, 1909 (BY).

5. Ibid., October 16, 1908.

6. Ibid., July 15, 1910.

7. Grey, *Journal 1905–10*, May 19, 1910 (BY), and *Journal 1910–12*, October 10, 1910 (JW). In a 1917 entry in another journal, Grey discusses meeting "an old

sweetheart of mine" who was greatly changed from the beautiful woman she was "ten years ago." Given Grey's carelessness with dates, he may well have been referring to a girlfriend from before his 1905 marriage rather than from two years afterward.

8. Zane Grey, Letter to Lina Grey, "Sunday" [1907] (BY-G2).

9. Grey, *Journal, 1910–12,* November 9, 1911 (JW).

10. Ibid., January 8, 1911.

11. Grey, *Journal 1905–10,* July 2, 1910 (BY).

12. *Field and Stream* 15 (February, 1911), 1012. In April 1908, just following Harpers' acceptance of *The Heritage of the Desert,* Zane wrote to Dolly: "Mr. Warner tried to cut me down again in price, and I told him I couldn't let him have the Jungle stuff. I can get $580 for it from *Recreation.*"

13. Zane Grey, Letters to George Allen, August 7, 1910, and January 8, 1911, *Zane Grey Review* 13 (February, 1998), 18.

14. Zane Grey, Letter to George Allen, [March, 1911], 18.

15. Akin, *Flagler,* 220–21.

16. Zane Grey, Letter to Lina Grey, February 9, 1911 (LG).

17. Grey, "Sea-Tigers," 782.

18. Ibid., 791.

19. Zane Grey, Letter to David Rust, December 4, 1910 (LDS).

20. Ibid., March 26, April 4, and April 14, 1911 (LDS).

21. Ibid., April 20, 1911 (LDS).

22. *Coconino Sun,* April 21, 1911, 1.

23. Hassell, *Rainbow Bridge,* 43–65. See also John Wetherill, "Notes on the Discovery of Betatakin," April, 1955, Stuart Young Collection (NAU). In this account, Wetherill mentions that Cummings paid a local Indian five dollars to guide him to the site and was so pressured by his imminent Rainbow Bridge trip that he stayed only a single hour at Betatakin following its discovery.

24. The name of this Indian has been spelled various ways. Grey spelled it Nas Ta Bega. On the plaque installed at the site in 1927, his name is presented as Nasjah Begay and my references to this person employ that spelling.

25. Comfort, *Rainbow to Yesterday,* 18–23, 55–66.

26. Cummings, "Great Natural Bridges," 157–67, and Pogue, "Great Rainbow Natural Bridge," 1048–56.

27. Zane Grey, "The Painted Desert," 8 (unpublished, incomplete manuscript, ZGM—L). Pogue, on p. 1052 under a photograph of the Bridge, likewise noted that the Flatiron Building would fit under it.

28. Grey, *Journal 1910–12,* May 6, 1911 (JW).

29. "The Painted Desert," 11–14.

30. Grey stated in a journal entry that this first trip went "to Marsh pass." *Journal 1910–12,* October 1, 1911, 108 (JW). Whether he actually reached Kayenta and saw the attractions nearby is unclear. In "Nonnezoshe," Grey incorrectly states

that he made three visits to Kayenta before going to the Rainbow Bridge. His journals and letters from 1912 reveal that he intended to return there in both the spring and fall of 1912, but Dolly's difficulties with the birth of Betty and the demands of his work forced him to cancel both trips. Grey later incorporated a dozen pages from "The Painted Desert" into a 1924 article entitled "Down into the Desert" which recounted his 1922 trip to the Rainbow Bridge. The manuscript reveals that at the point that the group reached Marsh Pass, he abandoned the typewritten pages from "The Painted Desert" and started new handwritten pages. However, his description of Betatakin employs a typewritten section like the early pages and suggests that this description was from his 1911 trip (GH).

31. Grey, *Journal 1910–12,* May 11, 1911 (JW).

32. Grey wrote, "Some weeks back, when I finished my romance 'Riders of the Purple Sage,' I was tired out." *Journal 1910–12,* September 20, 1911 (JW).

33. Grey, *Riders of the Purple Sage,* 1–2.

34. Kant, "Zane Grey and the Mormons," 1, 8–10.

35. Zane Grey, Letter to David Rust, December 4, 1910, and February 15, 1911 (LDS).

36. Zane Grey, Letter to Dan Murphy, June 2, 1907 (Edwin Markham Collection, Wagner College).

37. Grey, *Journal 1912–15,* September 7, 1913 (GH).

38. John Tuska, "Foreword," Grey, *Riders of the Purple Sage* (2005), 7. Tuska believes that editors at Harpers made these changes without consulting Zane, but he does not provide any documentation to support his claim. Hitchcock's letter of acceptance (note 43 below) expresses no reservations and does not request changes. Several years later, when editors at Harpers did modify Grey's grammar and punctuation, he noticed and denounced their unauthorized tampering with his work. In defense of his staff, the editor-in-chief stressed that it had always made only minor formatting changes. Even later, when the editors did request changes, Grey was left to make them.

39. Grey, *Journal 1910–12,* October 1, 1911, 108 (JW).

40. Ibid., October 1, 1911.

41. Grey, "My Own Life," 18–19.

42. Ripley Hitchcock, Letter to Zane Grey, September 15, 1911 (LG).

43. Charles MacLean, Letter to Zane Grey, September 21, 1911 (LG).

44. Grey, *Journal 1910–12,* December 20, 1911 (JW).

45. Ibid., December 20, 1911.

46. Zane Grey, Letter to George Allen, October 27, 1912, *Zane Grey Review* 13 (February, 1998), 17.

47. Grey, "Baracuda of Long Key," 271.

48. Zane Grey, Letter to Lina Grey, January 30, 1912 (LG).

49. The best example of the "high brow/low brow" debate appears in Brooks, *America's Coming of Age,* 3–35.

50. For important background on these developments, see Mott, *Golden Multitudes,* 204–6, and *History of American Magazines,* vol. 3, 431–38. Also see Justice, *Bestseller Index,* 4–5.The two best-known books on the history of best sellers are Hackett, *Fifty Years of Best Sellers,* and Korda, *Making the List.* However, both say little about this important background and apparently were unaware of Mott's groundbreaking research. Justice excavated other elements in his *Bestseller Index,* but this important chapter of publishing history warrants further research.

51. *Bookman* 35 (March–August, 1912), 218–19.

52. Ibid., 321.

53. Ibid., 396.

54. Zane Grey, Letter to Lina Grey, February 10, 1912 (LG).

55. Grey, *Journal, 1910–12,* April 11 and 12, 1912 (JW).

56. Grey started *Desert Gold* shortly after he finished *Riders* and hurriedly wrote it during the fall of 1912. By early December, Harpers had the finished manuscript. It started as a serial in March 1913 and was published the month following. *The Light of Western Stars* was written from March to August 1912, started as a serial in May 1913 and was published in January 1914.

57. Grey, *Journal, 1910–12,* April 23, 1912 (JW).

58. Lina Grey, *Diary, 1912,* October 13, 1912 (CK).

59. Zane Grey, Letter to Ripley Hitchcock, July 28, 1912 (Fales Library, New York University).

60. This represented a change from an initial title of *Light Everlasting,* whose religious overtones Zane did not like. When he proposed the title *Under Western Stars,* Hitchcock informed Grey that Joseph Conrad had already published a book with that title and so the author changed it again—this time to *The Light of Western Stars.*

61. Zane Grey, Letter to Robert H. Davis, March 19, 1912 (Fales Library, New York University).

62. Grey, *Light of Western Stars,* 4.

63. Zane Grey, Letter to Lina Grey, Oct. 13, 1911 (NAU). On March 30, 1909, Zane sent Lillian a copy of *The Young Pitcher* along with the inscription: "There are some old friends of yours in it. I am hoping you will be glad to meet them again." Dolly also mentions Lillian in a letter to Zane Grey, March 6, 1909 (mss. 1262, OHS).

64. Ashworth, *Arizona Triptych,* 164–85. Ashworth quotes Lillian's journal (174) and she provides a fuller discussion of Lillian's family background and early life. She also claims that Zane knew Lillian long before 1909.

65. Lina Grey, *Diary, 1912,* October 13, 1912 (CK).

66. Lina Grey, Letter to Zane Grey, February 18, 1913 (BY-G2).

67. Lina Grey, Letter to Zane Grey, March 9, 1913 (BY-G).

68. During April and May 1913, Dolly wrote to Zane from 133 South Street, which was next door to the house that Ellsworth was renting at 135 South Street.

On September 7, 1913, Zane wrote in his journal, "I am here in this slow, dull, overgrown village and expect to make it my permanent home." Grey, *Journal 1912–15* (GH).

69. Lina Grey, *Personal Notes* (marked: "Private—do not read"), December 31, 1913, n.p. (CK).

70. Grey acknowledged his indebtedness to Hughes in his preface to *The Lone Star Ranger.*

71. *Coconino Sun,* May 30, 1913, 1.

72. Zane Grey, Entry dated September 21, 1929, Register of Kayenta Trading Post (Harvey Leake). Grey folded this description into "Fading Indian Trails" (mss. 1262, OHS).

73. For a fuller discussion of this background, see Hassell, *Rainbow Bridge,* 43–65, and Comfort, *Rainbow to Yesterday,* 62–68. Also McNitt, *Richard Wetherill,* 80–83.

74. Grey, "Nonnezoshe," in *Tales of Lonely Trails,* 6.

75. Wetherill guided Arthur Townsend and his sister to the Bridge weeks after his return with Cummings. By the end of 1910, he had already taken eleven people to the arch and six of them were women. *List of Visitors to the Bridge* (Rainbow Bridge Collection, Folder 17, no. 239, NAU). Also Hassell, *Rainbow Bridge,* 66.

76. Roosevelt published three articles in *Outlook* about his trip: "A Cougar Hunt on the Rim of the Grand Canyon," *Outlook* 105 (October 4, 1913); "Across the Navajo Desert," (October 11, 1913); and "The Hopi Snake Dance," (October, 18, 1913). All three were included in Roosevelt, *Book Lover's Holidays,* 1–97.

77. On October 14, 1914, Grey wrote to the editor of *Century* magazine offering his recently completed sequel to *Riders* for serialization. Because *The Last of the Duanes* started to run as a serial in May 1914 and the serialization of *The Lone Star Rangers* commenced in September, they were both written before *The Rainbow Trail,* and Grey probably did not start this novel until he returned from his trip to Arizona in the early summer of 1914.

78. Grey's idea for polygamists crossing state boundaries to visit their wives derived from his visit to Kanab, Utah, and Fredonia, Arizona, where he learned about the multiple wives of Deé Wooley and several other Mormons.

79. Grey, *Rainbow Trail,* 14.

80. During his 1913 trip to Kayenta, Grey stayed in camp while Doyle took the others on an outing. Before their return after dark, he was sitting alone by a fire when a menacing Indian rode into camp, but the sound of the group's approach frightened him away before he did anything. The next day, Grey learned from Wetherill that the Indian's name was Tse Ne Get and that he was very dangerous. The bad Indian Shadd in *The Rainbow Trail* was inspired by Tse Ne Get. Zane Grey, "Fading Indian Trails" (mss. 1262, OHS).

81. Dan Murphy, Letter to Ray Long, [Spring, 1915?] (BY-G).

82. Loren Grey, "Foreword," in Grey, *Desert Crucible.*

83. In this sequel to *Riders,* Grey made Lassiter too old to be a significant character and thus foreclosed the possibility of developing this hero of his original story into a central figure for a series of novels. Grey attempted to do this with Ken Ward in his novels for adolescents, but decided early that he did not want his Westerns bound by this proven but restrictive formula for success.

84. Grey sent the *Book News Monthly* two photographs of the Rainbow Bridge for its three articles about him in the February 1918 issue. He used another in his article "What the Desert Means to Me," 8. A fourth one was included in *Zane Grey: The Man and His Work,* 46.

85. Hassell cites governmental directives to Wetherill, who served as custodian of the Bridge, to remove all defacement of the site by visitors. Hassell, *Rainbow Bridge,* 63. However, Wetherill left the inscribed names of the Cummings' party and Grey's. A photograph of Grey's name dating from 1966 shows that it was still quite distinct then, but it is barely discernible today.

Chapter 5: Moviemaking and Button Fish: 1915–19

1. Zane Grey, Postcard to Robert Davis, n.d. [ca. Spring, 1914] (NYPL).

2. *Publishers Weekly* 85 (March 14, 1914), 905, and (May 2, 1914), 1435.

3. Ibid., June 14, 1914, 1923.

4. *Bookman* 40 (January, 1915), 484.

5. Zane Grey, Letter to Robert Davis, June 5, 1914 (NYPL). Initially, Grey awarded Davis one-quarter of the sale of the film rights to *Desert Gold* and one-half of the sale of film rights to *Light.*

6. Lina Grey, Letter to Zane Grey, February 18, 1913 (BY-G2). A few months later, Totten and Davies took over this project, and their option delayed Grey's sale of the film rights to *Riders.*

7. Ripley Hitchcock, Letter to Zane Grey, February 24, 1913 (BY-G2).

8. A fuller discussion of the background of *The Squaw Man* can be found in Tuska, *Filming of the West,* 59–62.

9. Zane Grey, Letter to Thomas Ince, January 28, 1915 (LG). On July 10, 1916, Grey wrote to Davis that the deal with Ince had fallen through because "he was afraid of the Mormon Church."

10. Slide, *Big V,* 65–67.

11. Zane Grey, Letter to Robert Davis, March 26, 1916 (NYPL).

12. Robert Davis, Letter to Zane Grey, March 28, 1916 (NYPL).

13. Ibid.

14. Zane Grey, Telegram to Robert Davis, March 28, 1916 (NYPL).

15. On June 5, 1914, Grey contracted Davis to be his agent for films of seven novels, including *The Last of the Duanes* and *The Lone Star Ranger,* but not *The Heritage of the Desert* and *Riders of the Purple Sage.* In an October 7, 1916, letter to Davis, Grey mentioned that rights to all his novels so far, except *The Border Legion,* had

been sold. Since Fox filmed five of his novels—*The Last Trail, Riders of the Purple Sage, The Last of the Duanes, The Lone Star Ranger,* and *The Rainbow Trail*—Davis undoubtedly sold the rights to the last three sometime between March 30, 1916, when he sold the rights to the first two Grey novels, and the October 1916 date when the rights to the other three were no longer available.

16. Zane Grey, Postcard to Robert Davis, [1915?] (NYPL).

17. Zane Grey, Letter to Robert Davis, November 26, 1915 (NYPL).

18. Slide, *Big V,* 67–68. Hampton described these efforts in his *History of the Movies,* 146–69.

19. This important chapter in Paramount's history has not been much discussed nor well documented. This summary has been derived from Irwin, *House That Shadows Built,* 179–221 and Whitfield, *Pickford,* 139–49.

20. Benjamin Hampton, Memorandum to Percival S. Hill, August 11, 1916. Quoted in Slide, *Big V,* 69.

21. Ibid., 67–70.

22. Clipping file on "Benjamin Hampton" (Herrick Library, Academy of the Motion Picture Arts and Sciences). Hampton does not discuss his involvement with Zane Grey Pictures in his *History of the Movies.*

23. Zane Grey, Letter to Lina Grey, June, 1916 (JW).

24. Originally Dustin Farnum was supposed to play Shefford, the lead in *The Rainbow Trail.* Catalina *Islander,* April 3, 1917, 1.

25. In a February 20, 1918, letter to Dolly, Zane included a wire from H. A. Sherman stating: "Bought *Western Stars* from Selig for our first production." Zane Grey, Letter to Lina Grey, February 20, 1918 (BY-G2).

26. Zane Grey, Letter to Benjamin H. Hampton, May 2, 1919 (Thomas Nelson Page Papers, Perkins Library, Duke University Library).

27. Zane Grey, Letter to Lina Grey, June 26, [1918] (BY-G).

28. Romer C. Grey, "Fishing with Famous Fellows," 255–62.

29. Macrate, *History of the Tuna Club,* 153.

30. Robert H. Davis, Letter to Zane Grey, October 17, 1913 (LG). This letter is quoted in full in Loren Grey, "Foreword," in Grey, *Last of the Duanes,* 8.

31. Ripley Hitchcock, Letter to Zane Grey, November 13, 1913 (LG).

32. Loren Grey believes that the editors at Harpers created *The Lone Star Ranger* from the two serials. "Foreword," in Grey, *Last of the Duanes,* 10. The consolidation of these serials involved changes far more extensive than those done to *The Desert Crucible* and *Riders of the Purple Sage.* It is hard to believe that any editor would ever accept a job demanding so much work and so fraught with risk of offending the author. Grey probably hurried this careless consolidation in order to appease the objections of his editors at Harpers and to get his two serializations published as a novel.

33. *Bookman* 42 (January 1916), 518, and *American Library Annual 1916,* 149–50.

34. Zane Grey, Letter to Robert H. Davis, [September, 1915?] (NYPL).

35. Zane Grey, Letter to Lina Grey, February 10, 1912 (LG).

36. Davis, "At Sea with Zane Grey," in *Bob Davis Again!,* 346–47.

37. Davis, "Porpoise on Tarpon Tackle," 878–82.

38. *Field and Stream* 17 (December, 1912), 898.

39. *Field and Stream* 17 (July, 1912), 622–23.

40. Grey, "Following the Elusive Tuna," 475–79.

41. Zane Grey, Letter to Lina Grey, March 23, 1913 (GH). In his article "Sailfish," Grey explains that "sailfishing is really swordfishing" and mentions how some anglers believe sailfish to be in the same family as Pacific marlin. Grey, *Tales of Fishes,* 75.

42. Grey, "Swordfish, the Royal Purple Game of the Sea," 256.

43. Davis, "Porpoise on Tarpon Tackle," 879.

44. A photograph of Zane Grey in the fighting chair that was included in the original magazine version of "Swordfish, the Royal Purple Game of the Sea" appears in *Tales of Fishes,* 33.

45. Holder, *Salt Water Game Fishing,* frontispiece and 89.

46. In the frontispiece photograph to *Salt Water Game Fishing,* Charles Holder is shown standing with a rod and a Catalina boatman behind him. A photograph (204) in his *Big Game at Sea* also shows him again standing with his rod, but behind him is a chair that was a precursor of the fighting chair.

47. Grey, "Swordfish, the Royal Purple Game of the Sea," 260.

48. Macrate, *History of the Tuna Club,* 14 and 17.

49. Ibid., 149. This drop in large tuna, along with improvements in tackle, prompted the Tuna Club to create a red button in 1906 for tuna over fifty pounds taken with "light tackle," consisting of a rod shorter than six feet and a 9-thread line with a breaking strength of twenty-six pounds.

50. Holder, "Catching Swordfish," 752. Macrate says that Edward Llewellyn caught a 125-pound marlin in 1903 on heavy tackle, but does not say if he was in a boat. Macrate, *History of the Tuna Club,* 127.

51. Holder, *Big Game at Sea,* 102.

52. Macrate, *History of the Tuna Club,* 68 and 162. The gold button was originally awarded to the angler who took the largest tuna for the year.

53. Ibid., 153.

54. Ibid., 153 and 162.

55. Holder, *Salt Water Game Fishing,* 147.

56. Ibid., 90.

57. Ibid., 143.

58. The Tuna Club established a white button for broadbill in 1909, but Boschen was the first to win it. Macrate, *History of the Tuna Club,* 127.

59. Grey, *Tales of Fishes,* 30–37.

60. Macrate, *History of the Tuna Club,* 153.

61. Grey relates his fishing experiences at Clemente in "Swordfish, the Royal Purple Game of the Sea," 259–61.

62. Zane Grey, Letter to Lina Grey, August 31, 1915 (BY-G).

63. William Boschen, who was among the first to catch marlin and broadbill and held the earliest records for both, wrote two articles about swordfish, but they did not appear until three years later. Boschen, "Marlin Is an Acrobat," 70 and 82, and "True Swordfish and Its Capture," 54 and 106.

64. Grey, "Swordfish, the Royal Purple Game of the Sea," 255. The editors also anticipated this article's appearance with a report the month before on Grey's record catch of season, his 316-pound marlin, and his vow beforehand to improve upon his setbacks the year before. *Recreation* 53 (November, 1915), 231.

65. Zane Grey, Letter to Lina Grey, February 22, 1916 (BY-G).

66. Grey, "Sailfish," *Tales of Fishes,* 85.

67. "Sailfish," *Recreation* 53 (December, 1916), 871. Grey deleted this comment from his article when he included it in *Tales of Fishes.*

68. Grey, "Two Fights with Swordfish," in *Tales of Fishes,* 58.

69. Zane Grey, Letter to Lina Grey, September 21, 1916 (BY-G).

70. Zane Grey, Letter to Lina Grey, January 23, 1917 (CK).

71. Lina Grey, Letter to Zane Grey, October 1, 1916 (CK).

72. Zane Grey, Letter to Lina Grey, January 25, 1917 (BY-G).

73. Because Claire was born in 1898, she was sixteen at the time of this trip. In an unfinished autobiographical sketch, she wrote about her first trip with Zane in 1914, "I was invited to go with Lillian, my sister, to Arizona when I was about 13 years old . . . [and] I had my 14th birthday on the trip" (PF). Like Zane, who lowered his age by three years, she consistently presented herself as two years younger than she actually was.

74. Interview with Loren Grey, January 18, 2002.

75. Zane Grey, Letter to Lina Grey, February 17, [1916?] (LG). By 1919, the membership list for Long Key included such prominent Easterners as J. S. Auchincloss, A. H. Canfield, B. W. Croninshield, I. A. Filene, Isaac Guggenheim, Gifford Pinchot, and Carl McFadden.

76. Lina Grey, Letter to Zane Grey, September 9, 1916 (BY-G2).

77. Lina Grey, Letter to Zane Grey, August 14, 1916 (BY-G2). The only surviving letter from Emmeline to Grey is a lengthy protestation of her love dating from three months later, November 1, 1916 (BY-G2). With it are two pages written in secret code, one of the earliest surviving examples of it.

78. Lina Grey, Letter to Zane Grey, August 21, 1916 (BY-G).

79. Lina Grey, Letter to Zane Grey, September 12, 1916 (BY-G2).

80. Zane Grey, Letter to Lina Grey, September 21, 1916 (Bmms).

81. Lina Grey, Letter to Zane Grey, January 25, 1917 (Bmms).

82. Zane Grey, Letter to Lina Grey, February 19, 1917 (BY-G).

83. Zane Grey, Letter to Lina Grey, February 28, 1917 (LG). Conscious of the

secret code Zane had been using with his girlfriends, Dolly sent Zane a letter with drawn figures enacting a message. Zane's letter of response included this interpretation of her meaning.

84. Lina Grey, Letter to Zane Grey, March 14, 1917 (LG).

85. Zane Grey, Letter to Lina Grey, March 17, 1917 (BY-G2).

86. Ibid.

87. Grey, *Journal 1917–22,* April 3–7, 1917 (JW).

88. Zane Grey, Letter to Lina Grey, February 16, [1918] (BY-G).

89. Grey, *Journal, 1912–15,* March 25, 1914, and March 21, 1915 (GH).

90. Ibid., July 7, 1917.

91. *Spokesman Review,* July 16, 1917, n.p.

92. Grey, *Desert of Wheat,* 239.

93. Lina Grey, Letter to Zane Grey, June 20, 1918 (LG). The section to which Dolly refers was excised from chapter 22 where Lenore admits her love for Kurt.

94. Grey's journals in secret code about his sexual experiences affirm his interest in erotic descriptions and his suppressed talent for them.

95. Funeral services for Alice Zane Grey were held July 25, 1917. *Middletown Daily Argus,* July 24, 1917, 6.

96. Zane Grey, Letter to Lina Grey, July 25, 1917 (BY-G).

97. Wilhelm, *Journal, 1917—Catalina,* July 27, 1917 (PF). Also Zane Grey, Letter to Lina Grey, July 27, 1917 (BY-G).

98. Grey, "Swordfish, the Royal Purple Game of the Sea," 255.

99. Grey, *Journal 1917–22,* July 27–August 3, 1917 (JW).

100. Zane Grey, Letter to Lina Grey, August 4, 1917 (BY-G).

101. Wilhelm, *Journal, 1917—Catalina,* August 4, 21–26 (PF).

102. Claire says that thirty-six tuna were caught that day and that August 13 was the most productive day ever. Ibid., August 13, 36.

103. Ibid., August 17–September 28. Also Grey, "Colorado Trails," in *Tales of Lonely Trails,* 18–56.

104. Grey, *Journal, 1917–22,* October 1, 1917 (JW).

105. Ibid., October 22, 1917.

106. Catalina *Islander,* December 4, 1917, 3; August 20, 1918, 1; and October 8, 1918, 1.

107. Zane Grey, Letter to Lina Grey, August 15, 1918 (BY-G2).

108. Grey, "Big Tuna," in *Tales of Fishes,* 239 and 249. Since "Big Tuna" was originally published in May 1919, Grey had to be discussing the 1918 season. Also Catalina *Islander,* August 20, 1918, 1.

109. Catalina *Islander,* June 10, 1919, 1. Tuna Club records say that Grey earned a red button on July 27, 1918, and was awarded the blue button July 22, 1919. Macrate, *History of the Tuna Club,* 149–50. This information is at odds with Zane's claims and information published in the Catalina *Islander.* Perhaps Macrate reversed the dates for the red and blue buttons.

110. Catalina *Islander,* October 8, 1918, 1.

111. Grey, "Swordsmen of the Sea," *Field and Stream* 23 (March, 1919), 820–25. Grey entitled this account "Seven Marlin Swordfish in One Day" when he included it in *Tales of Fishes,* 197–215.

112. Catalina *Islander,* July 22, 1919, 1.

113. Wilhelm, *Journal, 1918—Long Key,* 132–33 (PF). This same day, both women and Fergie dressed in middies and posed for the photograph with Zane on pages 12–13.

114. Ibid., 160–63. This achievement is credited to "Williams" in the first booklet of the Long Key Fishing Club, a modification of the German name of Wilhelm that was probably done to avoid the stigma provoked by the ongoing war. In an undated letter from around 1930, Zane wrote, "Claire, you were some punkins with a rod."

115. Wilhelm, *Journal, 1918—Out West,* July 13, 30; August 1, 65; and August, 22, 116 (PF). About this fish, Claire wrote, "I experienced the queerest sensations and thrills, [and] seemed to lose control of myself with excitement and my knees shook dreadfully."

116. Grey, *Journal, 1917–22,* November 26, 1917 (JW). Over the summer of 1917, Dolly recorded in her journal numerous visits by Dorothy to Lackawaxen.

117. Wilhelm, *Journal, 1918—Long Key,* 55–56, 61 (PF).

118. Ibid., 21.

119. Zane Grey, Letter to Lina Grey, August 13, 1918 (CK).

120. Lina Grey, Letter to Zane Grey, July 22, 1918 (LG).

121. Zane Grey, Letter to Lina Grey, July 30, 1918 (BY-G2).

122. Lillian Wilhelm Robertson, Letter to Zane Grey, August 24 and 26, 1918 (CK).

123. Zane Grey, Letter to Lina Grey, July 8, 1918 (BY-G2).

124. Lina Grey, Letter to Zane Grey, July 5, 1918 (BY-G2).

125. Anna Andre, "Character Reading," February 4, 1918 (BY-G).

126. Zane Grey, Letter to Lina Grey, August 21, 1918 (BY-G2).

127. Zane Grey, Letter to Anna Andre, February, 16, 1918 (BY-G). Anna Andre was very upset when *Wanderer of the Wasteland* was published and Zane dedicated the novel to his wife rather than to her.

128. Zane Grey, Letter to Lina Grey, February 16, 1918 (LG).

129. Zane Grey, Letter to Ripley Hitchcock, February 20, 1918 (BY-G).

130. Grey, *Journal, 1917–22,* December 5, 1918 (JW).

131. Zane Grey, Letter to Claire Wilhelm, January 12, 1919 (PF).

132. Nielsen's grandfather graduated from a naval academy in Norway and later became president of that country's Parliament. In 1913, after years of working on ships and sailing the world, he went searching for gold in western Mexico. When he read *Desert Gold,* Sievert wrote Zane about his adventures and Zane invited him to Catalina, probably in 1917 or 1918. North, "Zane Grey's Mysterious

Guide," 9 and 11. Also Grey, "Death Valley" and "Tonto Basin," in *Tales of Lonely Trails,* 188–89, 364–93.

133. Grey, *Journal, 1917–22,* January 19, 1919 (JW). This passage and Zane's notes for the next five months were reprinted with substantial editorial reduction in Gruber, *Zane Grey,* 140–53.

134. Grey, "Death Valley," *Tales of Lonely Trails,* 374.

135. Grey, *Journal, 1917–22,* May 29, 1919 (JW).

136. If Grey did not realize how self-serving his story was, he certainly was aware that his own relations with women were influencing it. During a period of despondency over how to proceed, he spent a day reviewing his collection of letters and photographs of his girlfriends. A month later, he reflected on the anguish channeled into this novel and wrote: "Have I loved and trusted and reverenced women in vain? It seems I have. . . . If there has been harm it is already done. Perhaps a few days or a week will lighten the darkness. Now comes my ordeal! It is even greater than ever. I imagined I had long ago reached and passed the worst. Alas! That was an illusion. . . . Live some of the struggles of my book people. *Write my agony in the novel I am now working on.*" Ibid., April 17 and May 17, 1919.

Chapter 6: Calamity: 1920–23

1. "Zane Grey Welcomes 1920," *The Zane Grey Review* 10 (December, 1994), 1.

2. Ibid., 3.

3. Mott, *History of American Magazines* vol. 4, 434–35.

4. "Zane Grey Welcomes 1920," *The Zane Grey Review* 10 (December, 1994), 3.

5. Zane Grey, Letter to Lina Grey, August 7, 1918 (BY-G2).

6. Thomas Wells, Letter to Zane Grey, April 23, 1919 (LG).

7. For this event, Grey wrote an article entitled "Why I Write Western Stories." It, along with a description of the event, appeared in *The American News Trade Journal* 3 (May, 1921), 3. See also Catalina *Islander,* June 7, 1921, 1, and *Zanesville Signal,* March 29, 1921, 5.

8. Zane Grey, Letter to Lina Grey, March 7, 1920 (Waverly Auction, February 6, 2003, lot no. 172).

9. Gruber, *Zane Grey,* 154.

10. Zane Grey, Letter to Lina Grey, April 10, 1920. Quoted in Gruber, *Zane Grey,* 170.

11. Grey, *Journal, 1920,* April 11, 1920 (GH).

12. Zane Grey, Financial Records (DB).

13. Zane Grey, Letter to Lina Grey, January 11, 1923 (BY-G).

14. Zane Grey, *Financial Notebook* (GH). In 1918, R. C. estimated that Grey would be earning $500,000 in five years, and Zane branded him "assinine."

15. Zane Grey, Letter to Lina Grey, February 27, 1920 (JW).

16. Catalina *Islander,* August 3, 1920, 3.

17. *Builder and Contractor,* August 25, 1908, 4, and June 3, 1909, 4.

18. Unidentified clipping, Altadena Historical Society.

19. *Pasadena Star News,* August 16, 1920, n.p.

20. Zane Grey, Letter to Lina Grey, September 19, 1920 (BY-G2).

21. Grey, "Tonto Basin," in *Tales of Lonely Trails,* 169–245.

22. Quoted in Ashworth, *Arizona Triptych,* 206.

23. Wilhelm, *Journal, 1920—Catalina and Arizona,* September 27, 1920 (PF).

24. Ibid., October 21, 1920.

25. Ibid., October 22, 1920.

26. Ibid., October 27, 1920.

27. Kant, *Zane Grey's Arizona,* 36.

28. Brett, "Zane Grey," 27–28.

29. Zane Grey, *Diary, 1923–39,* November 17, 1923, 51 (MIC 172, OHS).

30. Zane Grey, Letter to Lina Grey, February 6, 1920 (mss. 1262, OHS).

31. Zane Grey, "Long Key, Florida—1920," in *Zane Grey Review* 12 (December, 1996), 4–5. The manuscript of these pages is held by the OHS.

32. Lina Grey, Letter to Zane Grey, October 26, 1920 (BY-G2).

33. Grey, *Journal, 1917–22,* February 3, 1921 (JW).

34. Ibid., March 23, 1921. In Grey's code, "I went there to meet Louise Anderson" appears as "∕21422" 26724Q24 26⊙ 7424" 18⊙3 ∕204 161104820⊙22."

35. *Zanesville Signal,* March 28, 1921, 1.

36. Lina Grey, Letter to Zane Grey, March 21, [1921] (GH).

37. Zane Grey, Letter to Lina Grey, March 29, [1921] (GH).

38. Grey, *Journal, 1917–22,* March 23, 1921 (JW).

39. Death Certificate, Nelly Dennis Anderson, January 12, 1928, Bureau of Records, Zanesville, Ohio.

40. Grey, "The Living Past," 6–7.

41. Grey, *Journal, 1917–22,* November 15, 1920 (JW). Along with this notation, Grey wrote, "I cannot forget. I felt too bitterly. Thirty years is as yesterday."

42. Interview with Loren Grey, January 9, 2003.

43. *Zanesville Signal,* April 4, 1921, 7.

44. Lina Grey, Letter to Zane Grey, October 22, 1921 (BY-G).

45. Lina Grey, Letter to Zane Grey, February 23, 1922 (Bmms).

46. Back on July 22, 1918, Dolly had written to Zane, "I am sure that the physical relation has ceased to exist between you and me—that all of that kind of desire is dead. I cannot conceive of it any longer. But that is your fault." Lina Grey, Letter to Zane Grey, July 22, 1918 (BY-G). At this time, her assumption may have been premature.

47. Lina Grey, Letter to Zane Grey, April 28, 1922. *Zane Grey Review 12* (June, 1997), 10.

48. Lina Grey, Letter to Zane Grey, July 5, 1922 (CK).

49. Lina Grey, Letter to Zane Grey, October 22, 1922 (GH).

50. Lina Grey, Letter to Zane Grey, May 6, 1923 (GH).

51. On April 2, 1923, Zane wrote this characterization of Dolly's most recent letter: "There was a cry from your very soul. It seemed to me you were in an agony of longing. Driven! My dearest wife, I do not see why your heart should break. Is it so bad as that? Why are you so desperate?" (BY-G2).

52. Zane Grey, Letter to Lina Grey, January 13, 1923 (JW).

53. Lillian Wilhelm Robertson, Letter to Claire Wilhelm Carlin, March 30, 1921 (PF).

54. Lina Grey, Letter to Zane Grey, June 9, 1922 (CK).

55. Zane Grey, Letter to Lina Grey, October 30, [1921] (GH).

56. Zane Grey, Letter to Lina Grey, August 14, 1923 (BY-G).

57. Lina Grey, Letter to Zane Grey, February 3, 1922 (JW).

58. Lina Grey, Letter to Zane Grey, June 13, 1922 (BY-G2).

59. Zane Grey, Letter to Lina Grey, December 31, 1921 (BY-G2).

60. Zane Grey, Letter to Lina Grey, October 22, 1922 (BY-G2).

61. Patrick, "Getting Into Six Figures," 424.

62. Zane Grey, *Diary, 1923–39*, January 20, 1923, 3 (MIC 172, OHS).

63. Ibid., January 31, 1923, 15.

64. Ibid., February 16, 1923, 23.

65. Grey, *Journal 1912–15*, March, 1915 (GH).

66. Lina Grey, Letter to Zane Grey, June 22, [1922] (BY-G2).

67. *New York Times,* August 27, 1922, 17.

68. Zane Grey, handwritten draft in letter mailed to Lina Grey, July 7, 1922 (LG).

69. *Boston Transcript,* January 17, 1923, 8.

70. *Daily Eagle,* January 6, 1923, 3.

71. *Bookman* 37 (April, 1923), 225.

72. *New York Tribune,* January 21, 1912, 19.

73. "New York's Awe at Best Seller," *Literary Digest* 76 (March 10, 1923), 30–31.

74. Grey, "My Answer," 4–5.

75. Zane Grey, Letter to Lina Grey, March 11, [1921] (GH).

76. Zane Grey, *Diary, 1923–39,* February 16, 1923, 25 (MIC 172, OHS).

77. Kennedy, *Samuel Hopkins Adams,* 130–31.

78. Zane Grey, *Diary, 1923–39,* February 16, 1923, 25–26 (MIC 172, OHS).

79. Zane Grey, *Notebook on Income Sources* (GH).

80. In a prefatory announcement to one of his serializations, Grey wrote, "I would rather publish my stories in the *Ladies' Home Journal* than in any other magazine. It reaches the heart of American homes and is elevating and instructive in its influence. More over I have found that the *Journal*'s readers have an unusually keen interest in the Great West and the men and women of the open, the natural and primitive people of whom I write."

81. Grey, "Swordfish, the Royal Purple Game of the Sea," 256.

82. Grey, "Xiphias Gladius, 418 Pounds," in *Tales of Swordfish and Tuna,* 124.

83. Zane and Dolly were not only as profligate in their spending as Scott and Zelda Fitzgerald but were also given to periodic vows of reform that were never kept. "You would not believe, but I have already taken in $100,000 this year," Zane wrote to Dolly in August of 1922. "It seems unbelievable, especially considering the way it slips away. . . . I have on hand $3,000. I guess we won't starve. But, darling, you must try to save some money." This request did not deter Dolly from signing a $10,000 commitment several days later to have an additional floor and roof built on their Altadena residence.

84. Wilhelm, *Journal, 1920—Catalina and Arizona,* n.p. (PF); Overholt, *Catalina Story,* 26, 32.

85. R. C. Grey discussed the innovation and progress achieved by these boat in "Tuna Fishing Yesterday and Today," 430. This essay was reprinted in *Adventures of a Deep-Sea Angler.*

86. In one of his fishing articles published in 1918, Grey remarked, "Captain Danielson's boat had utterly spoiled me for fishing out of any other." Grey, *Tales of Fishes,* 44.

87. Grey, "Xiphias Gladius, 418 Pounds," in *Tales of Swordfish and Tuna,* 122.

88. Catalina *Islander,* June 22, 1920, 11.

89. Wilhelm, *Journal, 1920—Catalina and Arizona,* n.p. (PF).

90. Grey, "Xiphias Gladius," 10. Reprinted as "Xiphias Gladius, 418 Pounds" in *Tales of Swordfish and Tuna.*

91. Catalina *Islander,* May 25, 1920, 6.

92. Ibid., March 9, 1920, 6. R. C. Grey also mentions the reliance of Zane and himself upon this boat during the 1920 season in *Adventures of a Deep-Sea Angler,* 61.

93. Grey published this account of Boerstler's hiring: "I made a deal with Captain Sid Boerstler, comparatively a newcomer to the colony. He was an expert engineer, young, strong, willing, but had not any knowledge of swordfishing. This R. C. and I undertook to teach him. I hope it is not unbecoming to my narrative to mention here that in 1920 and 1921 Captain Sid caught the most swordfish." Grey, "Xiphias Gladius, 418 Pounds," in *Tales of Swordfish and Tuna,* 122.

94. Catalina *Islander,* July 5, 1921, 2.

95. Macrate, *History of the Tuna Club,* 127. Also Catalina *Islander,* December 3, 1918, 1.

96. Contracts for Stewart and Fellows (Archives, Los Angeles Maritime Museum).

97. Catalina *Islander,* March 22, 1921, 1, 2, 8. Also February 8, 1921, 6.

98. Romer C. Grey, "Tuna Fishing Yesterday and Today," 430–31. Zane encouraged another article by an unnamed author, "Noted Author Builds New Fishing Cruiser," *Pacific Motor Boat,* April, 1921, 25–27. This article provides blueprint diagrams and a full accounting of the *Gladiator*'s appointments.

99. Catalina *Islander,* June 28, 1921, 1. Because Grey's catch came so close to publication, the *Islander* offered only a brief notice. See Catalina *Islander,* June 21, 1921, 6. The long March 22 account of the *Gladiator* was authored by "Lone Angler," who was Grey's friend, J. A. Wiborn. Although the author of this account is not identified, the style is typical of Wilborn.

100. This was not the first time that Grey salvaged a big story from a lost broadbill. Back in 1919 he hooked an even larger broadbill calculated to weigh 600, perhaps even 1,000, pounds and lost it after an epic twelve-hour fight. This incident received front-page coverage in the *Islander* and Grey described it in "Record Fight with a Swordfish" that was published in the August 1920 issue of *Country Gentleman.* Grey even got the *Islander* to offer a third account of the broadbill he lost in 1921. See Catalina *Islander,* August 2, 1921, 1.

101. Catalina *Islander,* October 18, 1920, 1 and 7.

102. *New York Times,* June 26, 1961, and *Santa Paula (California) Chronicle,* June 26, 1961.

103. Catalina *Islander,* August 20, 1920, 1.

104. Ibid., June 21, 1921, 6.

105. *Los Angeles Examiner,* October 14, 1921, 1.

106. Romer C. Grey, "Sea Fishing for Women," 261.

107. This article brought Dorothy publicity to match that which Lillian and Claire received from the photograph of them, Zane, and several large barracuda that appeared in the *New York Herald* two years before. *New York Herald,* Graphic Section, December 14, 1919, 1.

108. Grey, "Resignation from the Tuna Club," 3. Grey's interpretation of Mrs. Spalding's catch is consistent with what the *Islander* reported in its October 14, 1921, story.

109. Memorandums of Tuna Club meetings, July 1, 1922, and July 3, 1922.

110. Grey, "Resignation from the Tuna Club," 3.

111. Ibid.

112. Ibid.

113. Memorandum of Tuna Club meeting, March 31, 1923 (Archives, the Tuna Club). The *Islander* reported that Grey was still attending social functions at the

Tuna Club weeks after its board demanded that he apologize. See Catalina *Islander,* July 26, 1922, 7.

114. Grey, *Tales of Fishes,* 252 and 187.

115. Ives, "Small Woman and a Big Swordfish," 270. Three years later, Dilg and his feminist wife parted in an acrimonious divorce and her article may have been a contributing factor.

116. Catalina *Islander,* July 19, 1922, 6.

117. Zane Grey, "Gulf Stream Fishing on Light Tackle," 205–9. This was converted into the conclusion for "Sailfish" when it was included in *Tales of Fishes.* Also Grey, "Light Tackle," 747. This was reprinted in the Catalina *Islander,* February 4, 1919, 1, and it concluded "Avalon, the Beautiful" in *Tales of Fishes.*

118. Grey's articles on fishing from before 1923 contain several mentions of his disappointment with the B-Ocean reel. In one instance, his companions frantically poured buckets of water onto his smoking reel in a doomed attempt to prevent its stressed gearing from melting. In another instance, the pressure exerted by the running fish caused the gearing to jam and break it free. Grey, *Tales of Fishes,* 33 and 57.

119. Catalina *Islander,* September 19, 1923, 6.

120. Grey "Heavy Tackle for Heavy Fish," 1. During the period 1920–24, the price of a Ford Model-T fell to $260. Derks, *Value of a Dollar,* 136.

121. Catalina *Islander,* April 23, 1923, 10.

122. Minutes of the Special Meeting of the Board of Directors of the Tuna Club, February 12, 1923 (Archives, the Tuna Club).

123. Ibid., March 15, 1923.

124. Ibid., May 31, 1923. On August 5, [1923], Zane wrote Dolly, "The Tuna Club mess I got out of by just pulling out, and making R. C. & Wiborn do the same. The faction opposing the present regime wanted us to do the fighting" (BY-G2). Wiborn did not resign.

125. Zane Grey, Letter to Lina Grey, June 11, [1923] (CK).

126. Zane Grey, Letter to Lina Grey, June 30, [1923] (BY-G2).

127. Zane Grey, Letter to Lina Grey, July 8, [1923] (BY-G).

128. Ibid.

129. Zane Grey, Letter to Lina Grey, June 30, 1923 (BY-G2).

130. Zane Grey, Letter to Lina Grey, July 8, [1923] (BY-G).

131. Zane Grey, Letter to Lina Grey, August 4, [1923] (BY-G).

132. Zane Grey, Letter to Lina Grey, July 18, 1923 (BY-G).

133. Zane Grey, Letter to Lina Grey, July 30, 1923 (BY-G).

134. Zane Grey, Letter to Lina Grey, August 1, [1923] (CK).

135. Zane Grey, Letter to Lina Grey, August 14, 1923 (BY-G).

136. Ibid.

137. Grey, "Herculean Angling," in *Tales of Swordfish and Tuna,* 159.

138. Grey described these catches in "Three Broadbill Swordfish."

139. Zane Grey, Letter to Lena Grey, September 2, 1923 (BY-G), and Sierks-Overholt, "New World's Record," 804–5.

140. Zane Grey, Letter to Lina Grey, February 21, [1923] (BY-G2).

141. Zane Grey, Letter to Lina Grey, January 3, [1921] (GH).

142. Zane Grey, Letter to Lina Grey, October 22, 1922 (GH).

143. *Coconino Sun,* September 14, 1923, 1.

144. Ibid., September 21, 1923, 1; October 12, 1923, 1.

145. Louise Anderson, Letter to Zane Grey, September 4, 1923 (CK).

146. Lina Grey, Letter to Zane Grey, October, 15, 1923 (GH).

147. Zane Grey, *Diary, 1923–39,* December 15, 1923, 58 (MIC 172, OHS).

148. Ibid., December 21, 1923, 60.

149. Ibid., December 24, 1923, 69.

150. Lina Grey, Letter to Zane Grey, "Christmas night, 1923" (GH).

Chapter 7: Movin' On: 1924–25

1. Grey, "Heavy Tackle for Heavy Fish," Catalina *Islander,* January 2, 1924, 1 and 2.

2. Ibid., April 23, 1924, 1.

3. Ibid., January 26, 1924, 1.

4. Ibid., May 21, 1924, 1. See also May 14, 1924, 1.

5. Ibid., August 13, 1924, 1.

6. *Los Angeles Examiner,* August 10, 1924, 3.

7. Grey, "Xiphias Gladius," *Country Gentleman* 89 (February 9, 1924), 10–11. This essay was published as "Xiphias Gladius, 418 Pounds" in *Tales of Swordfish and Tuna.*

8. When Dolly informed Zane of Mallen's catch, he wrote back, "For a novice to catch a fish like that in less than an hour is appalling. I'm afraid the aero-plane wire leader, that tangles these broadbills' tails and kills them without a fight, has ruined the sport." Zane Grey, Letter to Lina Grey, August 17, 1924 (BY-G2).

9. Grey, "The Deadly Airplane Wire-Leader," in *Tales of Swordfish and Tuna,* 193 and 195.

10. Zane Grey, Letter to Lina Grey, January 2, 1924 (BY-G).

11. Zane Grey, Letter to Lina Grey, January 9, 1924 (BY-G2).

12. Zane Grey, Letter to Lina Grey, January 14, 1924 (BY-G2).

13. Zane Grey, Letter to Lina Grey, January 19, 1924 (Bmms).

14. Lina Grey, Letter to Zane Grey, January 18, 1924 (Bmms). Dolly wrote an even longer letter on January 28 that offered more explanation and more solace.

15. Zane Grey, *Diary, 1923–39,* January 23, 1924, 67 (MIC 172, OHS).

16. Zane Grey, Telegram to Lina Grey, January 24, 1914 (BY-G2).

17. *New York Times Book Review,* January 27, 1924, 2 and 4.

18. Zane Grey, *Diary, 1923–39,* January 29, 1924, 70 (MIC 172, OHS).

19. Zane Grey, Letter to Lina Grey, January 28, [1924] (BY-G2).

20. Zane Grey, *Diary, 1923–39,* January 31, 1924, 71–72 (MIC 172, OHS). Also Zane Grey, Letter to Lina Grey, January 31, 1924, *Zane Grey Review* 12 (December, 1996), 7.

21. Grey described this trip in "Rivers of the Everglades," in *Tales of Southern Rivers,* 41–134.

22. Zane Grey, *Diary, 1923–39,* April 26, 1924, 80 (MIC 172, OHS).

23. Ibid., May 25, 1924, 84.

24. Zane Grey, Letter to Lina Grey, June 14, [1924] (BY-G2).

25. Zane Grey, Letter to Lina Grey, [May, 1924] (BY-G2).

26. Zane Grey, Letter to Lina Grey, June 5, [1924] (BY-G2).

27. Zane Grey, Letter to Robert Davis, January 10, 1919 (NYPL).

28. Obituary for L. D. Mitchell, *New York Times,* June 19, 1931, 33.

29. Mitchell-Henry, *Tunny Fishing,* 17.

30. Mitchell-Henry, *Tunny Fishing,* 17. Mitchell-Henry, who went fishing with Mitchell before the war, reports that Mitchell was then in charge of "a bungalow-hostel established for the accommodation of fishermen" on Great Island near Port Medway.

31. Heilner, *Salt Water Fishing,* 143. Also Grey, "Big Game Fishing," 11.

32. Zane Grey, Letter to Lina Grey, February 6, 1922 (mss. 1262, OHS). This letter seems misdated and probably should be 1924. Grey believed that his boat could be built more cheaply and better in Canada, and he estimated its cost at $2,000.

33. Grey, "Giant Nova Scotia Tuna," in *Tales of Swordfish and Tuna,* 14.

34. Lillian Wilhelm Smith, Letter to Claire Wilhelm Carlin, July 14, 1924 (PF).

35. Farrington, *Atlantic Game Fishing,* 23.

36. Zane Grey, *Diary, 1923–39,* July 22, 1924, 90 (MIC 172, OHS).

37. Ashworth, *Arizona Triptych,* 232.

38. Lina Grey, Letter to Zane Grey, July 30, 1924 (BY-G2).

39. Obituary for Mildred Smith Johnson, *Arizona Republic* (Sedona), January 12, 1974, C, 7.

40. Despite the intensity of his initial involvement with Louise, Grey already had had misunderstandings and feuds with her by the summer of 1921. His journals and letters hint that his relationship with Mildred was intensifying more than a year and a half before his final break with Louise.

41. This album was sold at the Waverly auction on February, 6, 2002, lot no. 130.

42. Zane Grey, Letter to Lina Grey, June 15, 1923 (BY-G).

43. Zane Grey, Letter to Lina Grey, August 4, 1923 (BY-G2).

44. Lina Grey, Letter to Zane Grey, January 28, 1924 (BY-G2).

45. Lina Grey, Letter to Zane Grey, January 18, 1924 (BY-G2).

46. For more discussion of Grey's pursuit of Nola and her cautious response, see Van Grondelle, *Angel of the Anzacs,* 66–78.

47. Grey, "Giant Nova Scotia Tuna," in *Tales of Swordfish and Tuna,* 79–86.

48. Catalina *Islander,* August 27, 1924, 6. A decade later, Mitchell-Henry refused to acknowledge Grey's record because he fished from a power launch. Mitchell-Henry, *Tunny Fishing,* 19.

49. "World's Record Tuna," *Field and Stream* 29 (November, 1924), 17.

50. *Bookman* 60 (November, 1924), 373.

51. Grey, "My Adventures as a Fisherman," 168–79.

52. "Zane Grey's World Record Tuna," *Outdoor America* 3 (February, 1925), 16.

53. Mitchell, "World's Record Tuna," 22–24.

54. Nichols and Heilner, "World's Record Catches," *Field and Stream* (October, 1924), 17.

55. File LB58 (Library, International Game Fish Association).

56. Reiger, *Profiles in Salt Water Angling,* 182–83.

57. *Field and Stream* 33 (October, 1928), 32–33, and 40 (January, 1936), 26–27.

58. Heilner, *Salt Water Fishing,* 319. I have searched unsuccessfully for the pages from this important book. A few from late 1930s are held at the library of the International Game Fish Association. Apparently, the early ones were never saved, but were they ever to turn up, they would provide an invaluable accounting of record catches from 1924 to 1939. Currently, one has to rely on the limited information from the intermittent lists in *Field and Stream.*

59. *New York Times,* July 13, 1970, 31.

60. Heilner, *Salt Water Fishing,* 7. Heilner states that he fished with Grey out of Seabright from 1912 to 1916, 146–47. See also Reiger, *Profiles in Salt Water Angling,* 182–83.

61. Lillian Wilhelm Smith, Letter to Claire Wilhelm Carlin, August 11, 1924 (PF).

62. Information provided by the Ralph Getson Maritime Museum, Lunenburg, Nova Scotia.

63. Lillian Wilhelm Smith, Letter to Claire Wilhelm Carlin, August 11, 1924 (PF). The *New York Times* reported that Grey purchased the vessel for a long-distance voyage to South America. Both Smith and the *Times* referred to the ship's name as *Mapleland,* which was probably correct even though this name was never officially registered. See *New York Times,* August 20, 1924, 11.

64. *New York Times,* August 21, 1924, 11.

65. Grey, *Tales of Fishing Virgin Seas,* 3–4.

66. Wilhelm, *Journal, 1925—South America* (PF).

67. Grey, *Tales of Fishing Virgin Seas,* 4.

68. Gruber, *Zane Grey,* 186.

69. Wilhelm, *Journal, 1924—Oregon,* September–October, 1924, n.p. (PF).

70. *Outdoor America* 3 (November, 1924), 14.

71. Clippings and Testimonials, "Deer Drive of 1924" (Archives, Grand Canyon National Park). The Rotary address of August 14, 1964, presented by James A. Blaisdell quotes many governmental memorandums and documents from the period and is *the* single best source of information about this event.

72. *Outdoor America* 3 (November, 1924).

73. Quoted in Blaisdell's address.

74. Unidentified clipping, Zane Grey, scrapbook of newspaper clippings (OHS).

75. When reviewers commented upon the resemblance of *The Thundering Herd* to these two earlier films, they were noticing not only the repetitive casting of Lois Wilson, Jack Holt, and Noah Beery in the lead roles, but also the same panoramic display of animals and action. See "A Buffalo Stampede," *New York Times* March 3, 1925, 20; "Western Movie of the Best in 'The Thundering Herd,'" *New York Daily News,* March 3, 1925, 25; and "The Miracle of the Bisons," *Brooklyn Daily Eagle,* March 2, 1925, 8.

76. *New York Times,* January 12, 1925, sec. 7, 5.

77. Grey, *The Vanishing American* (1925), 113.

78. This quote and the one above are the same in the original manuscript, except for the bracketed final phrase, which was eliminated for publication.

79. Loren Grey, "Introduction," in Grey, *The Vanishing American* (1982), v.

80. Grey, *The Vanishing American* (1982), 340–41.

81. Grey, *The Vanishing American* (1982), 342. This original ending was even altered for the serialized version of *The Vanishing American* in *Ladies' Home Journal.*

82. Zane Grey, Letter to William Briggs and Henry Hoyns, May 25, 1925. Quoted in Loren Grey, "Introduction," in Grey, *The Vanishing American* (1982), vi–vii.

83. Lina Grey, Letter to Zane Grey, February 16, 1924 (GH).

84. Zane Grey, Letter to Claire Wilhelm Carlin, June 11, 1924 (PF).

85. Zane Grey, Letter to Claire Wilhelm Carlin, March 5, 1924 (PF).

86. Grey, *Tales of Fishing Virgin Seas,* 2.

87. Zane Grey, Letter to Lina Grey, January 24, 1916 (LG).

88. Interview with Loren Grey, January 21, 2002.

89. Beebe, *Galapagos,* 235.

90. Ibid., 237.

91. Ibid., 238.

92. Grey, *Tales of Fishing Virgin Seas,* 7–8.

93. Wilhelm, *Journal, 1925—South America,* February 16, 1925, 117.

94. Ibid., February 17, 1925, 119.

95. Beebe, *Galapagos,* 235.

96. Wilhelm, *Journal, 1925—South America,* February 24, 1925, 156.

97. Ibid., March 20, 1925, 223.

98. On page 159 of *Tales of Fishing Virgin Seas,* Grey says that the fish weighed 135 pounds; a photograph of him and this fish appears opposite page 105. Spalding's record is noted in "World's Record Catches," *Field and Stream* 29 (October, 1924), 17.

99. Wilhelm, *Journal, 1925—South America,* March 23, 1925, 243.

100. Ibid., March 27–30, 1925, 246–49 and 263.

101. Ibid., April 11, 1925, 298.

102. Ashworth, *Arizona Triptych,* 242–49, 258.

103. Lawrence Mitchell, Letter to Claire Carlin, May 26, 1925 (PF).

Chapter 8: Fresh Starts and Farewells: 1925–30

1. Hart, "Most Popular Authors of Fiction," 619–20.

2. Hart, "Most Popular Authors of Fiction," 473–77.

3. *Publishers Weekly* 107 (February 21, 1925), 633.

4. *Publishers Weekly* 107 (March 21, 1925), 1130, and (April 18, 1925), 1373. For the annual list for 1925, see *Publishers Weekly* 109 (January 23, 1926), 228.

5. *Publishers Weekly* 109 (February 13, 1926), 519 and (March 20, 1926), 1065.

6. *Bookman* 61 (April–August, 1925), 240, 365, 494, 609, 717, and *Bookman* 62 (September, 1925), 98.

7. Zane Grey, *Financial Notebook* (GH).

8. Gruber, *Zane Grey,* 189–90.

9. *Publishers Weekly* 107 (February 21, 1925), 630, and (March 21, 1925), 1130.

10. Zane Grey, Financial Records (DB).

11. Zane Grey, *Financial Notebook* (GH).

12. Zane Grey, *Diary, 1923–39,* January 19, 1925, 97 (MIC 172, OHS).

13. Ibid., December 7, 1925, 107.

14. Zane Grey, Financial Records (DB).

15. Whipple, "American Sagas," 505.

16. Ibid., 505–6.

17. Ibid., 506.

18. For interesting discussions of this aspect of Grey's work, see Bloodworth, "Zane Grey's Western Eroticism," 5–14, and Nesbitt, "Uncertain Sex," 15–27.

19. Farrar, "Clean Fiction," 115–16.

20. *Bookman* 60 (November, 1924), 373–74.

21. Farrar, "Zane Grey and the American Spirit," 2. This short article was run as an introduction for the serialization of Grey's *Stairs of Sand* and then incorporated into *Zane Grey: The Man and His Work,* 20.

22. *New York World,* September 30, 1925, 15.

23. Ibid., 17.

24. Ibid., December 17, 1925, 15. See also October 15, 1925, 11; November 2, 1925, 13; and November 4, 1925, 13.

25. Grey, "My Answer to the Critics," 6. Gruber first cited this quote in *Zane Grey,* 164, and he is the source for the others who have repeated it.

26. Lee, *Hidden Public,* 29–30.

27. Catalina *Islander,* March 25, 1925, 8. See also March 18, 1925, 7; and January 7, 1925, 7.

28. Zane Grey, *Diary, 1923–39,* July 20, 1924, 89 (MIC 172, OHS).

29. Lina Grey, Letter to Zane Grey, August 25, 1924 (mss. 1262, OHS).

30. Catalina *Islander,* September 2, 1925, 1.

31. Grey, "Log of the *Gladiator,*" 9–11, 56–62.

32. Catalina *Islander,* August 26, 1925, 6.

33. Zane Grey, Letter to Lina Grey, July 27, 1925 (BY-G).

34. Zane Grey, Letter to Lina Grey, August 4, 1925 (Bmms).

35. Zane Grey, Letter to Lina Grey, July 3, 1925 (BY-G).

36. Zane Grey, *Diary, 1923–39,* August 25, 1925, 102 (MIC 172, OHS).

37. Ibid.

38. Grey, "Down River," in *Tales of Freshwater Fishing,* 201–2.

39. Zane Grey, Letter to Lina Grey, October 1, 1925 (Bmms).

40. Zane Grey, *Diary, 1923–39,* October 22, 1925, 103 (MIC 172, OHS).

41. Vickers and Myers, "Special Friendship," 3.

42. Zane Grey, Letter to Lina Grey, August 7, 1925 (JW).

43. Lina Grey, Letter to Zane Grey, September 2, 1925 (Bmms).

44. Zane Grey, *Diary, 1923–39,* October 22, 1925, 104 (MIC 172, OHS).

45. Ibid.

46. Macdonald, *Imperial Patriot,* 64–68.

47. Ibid., 64–68.

48. Grey, *Tales of the Angler's Eldorado,* 220. At the end of this book, Grey published a detailed list of the fish that he and Mitchell caught. He provided another tally in "Big Game Fishing in New Zealand Seas," 47. The figures in the article are slightly different from the ones in his book.

49. Zane Grey, Letter to Lina Grey, [February 22, 1926] (BY-G2).

50. Zane Grey, Letter to Lina Grey, February 28, 1926 (Bmms).

51. Grey, *Tales of the Angler's Eldorado,* Plate XLIV, opposite p. 80. This photograph shows ten marlin, although the text claims that they caught nine.

52. Ibid., 220.

53. *Smith's Weekly,* February 5, 1927. Quoted in Macdonald, *Imperial Patriot,* 70.

54. *New Zealand Herald,* February 16, 1926. Quoted in Macdonald, *Imperial Patriot,* 71.

55. Macdonald, *Imperial Patriot,* 71.

56. Ibid., 69–71.

57. Bryn Hammond, "Introduction," Grey, *Tales of a Fisherman's Eldorado*

(1989). This introduction shows that the animus of New Zealanders toward Grey has never died.

58. Van Campen Heilner, Letter to Zane Grey, June 4, 1926 (Library Archives, American Museum of Natural History).

59. Catalina *Islander,* July 7, 1926, 16.

60. Catalina *Islander,* July 14, 1926, 1. Grey, of course, did write an account of his catch. "Landing the Record Broadbill," 8–10. For some reason, he did not include this in *Tales of Swordfish and Tuna* (1927).

61. Although the *Fisherman* also went to New Zealand, Grey did not use her there and never intended to. When he learned that the Arlidges were having launches built for them in Auckland, he suggested improvements and then did his fishing from the new boats, which were named *Avalon* and *Zane Grey* in honor of him. See Wiffin, "Deep-Sea Angling," in Holden, *Golden Years of Fishing,* 233.

62. *New York Times,* December 6, 1928, 4.

63. Nichols and Heilner, "World's Record Fish," 32–33.

64. Baker, *Ernest Hemingway,* 191–92.

65. Zane Grey, Letter to Lena Grey, October 14, 1928 (Bmms).

66. Grey provides a photograph with this designation opposite page 137 in *Tales of Tahitian Waters.* The striped marlin Grey caught in New Zealand was cited in Nichols and Heilner's 1928 list. His Tahiti record was bested before Nichols and Heilner's third list appeared in 1933.

67. Grey, *Tales of Tahitian Waters,* 85.

68. Zane Grey, Letter to Lina Grey, September 17, [1928] (BY-G).

69. Lina Grey, Letter to Zane Grey, February 19, 1927 (mss. 1262, OHS).

70. Ibid.

71. Zane Grey, Letter to Lina Grey, May 16, 1927 (BY-G).

72. Zane Grey, Letter to Lina Grey, October 14, 1928 (Bmms).

73. Ibid.

74. Zane Grey, *Diary, 1923–39,* March 12, 1928, 121 (MIC 172, OHS).

75. Ibid., April 18, 1928, 128.

76. Ibid., March 12, 1928, 121.

77. Zane Grey, Letter to Lina Grey, June 2, 1929 (BY-G).

78. Audun Koren, Letter to Zane Grey, January 14, 1928 (GH).

79. Zane Grey, Letter to Lina Grey, September 30, 1929 (BY-G2).

80. Grey, "Fading Indian Trails" (mss. 1262, OHS).

81. Zane Grey, Entry dated September 21, 1929, Register of Kayenta Trading Post (Harvey Leake).

82. Zane Grey, Letter to Lina Grey, September 30, 1929 (BY-G2).

83. Grey, "Fading Indian Trails," 16–18.

84. Kant, *Zane Grey's Arizona,* 39–41.

85. Zane Grey, Letter to Lina Grey, October 15, [1929] (BY-G).

86. *Coconino Sun,* October 10, 1930, 1.

Chapter 9: Undone: 1930–39

1. Klein, *Rainbow's End,* xiii–xiv, 263, and 274.

2. Zane Grey, *Diary, 1923–39,* November 3, 1929, 131 (MIC 172, OHS).

3. Grey, *Financial Notebook* (GH).

4. Zane Grey, Letter to Lina Grey, October 14, [1929] (BY-G).

5. Dorothy remarried John Parshall in 1945 and lived with him in Nyack, N.Y., until her death in 1975. What happened to her first marriage is not known, but she did not have any children by either marriage.

6. Zane Grey, Letter to Claire Wilhelm Carlin, February 12, 1930 (PF).

7. Zane Grey, Letters to Lina Grey, January 8, 1929, January 14, 1929, and March 1, 1929 (JW).

8. Zane Grey, *Diary, 1923–39,* August 27, 1931, 139 (MIC 172, OHS).

9. Zane Grey, Letter to Lina Grey, March 1, 1930 (JW).

10. In a December 11, 1930, letter to Dolly, Zane wrote, "I am not ashamed of caring so much for M. K. S." Zane Grey, Letter to Lina Grey, December 11, 1930 (BY-G).

11. Zane Grey, Letters to Lina Grey, February 22 and February 30, [1930] (BY-G).

12. Grey, *Tales of Tahitian Waters,* 86 and 88.

13. Zane Grey, Letter to Lina Grey, October 2, 1928 (JW).

14. Grey, *Tales of Tahitian Waters,* 82–83. Also Romer C. Grey, *Adventures of a Deep-Sea Angler,* 185–86, and Zane Grey, Letter to Lina Grey, September 17, 1929 (JW).

15. Zane Grey, Letter to Lina Grey, September 30, 1929 (BY-G).

16. Grey, "Big Game Fishing in Southern Seas," 16–17. Grey provides a full description of the *Frangipani* in this article and also discusses it in "In Quest of Record Fish," 38–40. In neither does he say when it was built. It was probably commissioned during his 1929 trip to New Zealand when he decided to ship the *Tahiti* and *Moorea* to Tahiti. It may have been the boat under construction at a cost of $2,500 that E. J. C. Wiffin mentioned in his article about fishing with Grey in 1929. See Holden, *Golden Years of Fishing,* 233. Loren Grey claims that the *Frangipani* greeted Zane when he arrived at Vairao in 1930, Loren Grey, *Zane Grey: Photographic Odyssey,* 164.

17. Grey, "Big Game Fishing in Southern Seas," 16.

18. Blueprints for *Fisherman II* bearing a date of January 14, 1930, were recently sold at a Butterfield auction. See Butterfield and Butterfield, *Catalogue for Fine Books and Manuscripts,* March 20, 2002, lot no. 2043, 15.

19. Zane Grey, Letter to Claire Wilhelm Carlin, February 6, 1930 (PF).

20. Zane Grey, Letter to Lina Grey, February 2, [1930] (JW).

21. Zane Grey, Letter to Lina Grey, February 19, [1930] (BY-G).

22. Zane Grey, Letter to Lina Grey, February 26, [1930] (BY-G).

23. Zane Grey, Letter to Lina Grey, March 30, [1930] (JW).

24. "Cost of Editorial Material—*Ladies' Home Journal,*" Curtis Publishing Records (Archives, University of Pennsylvania).

25. Zane Grey, Letter to Lina Grey, March 30, [1930] (JW).

26. Grey, "Big Game Fishing in Southern Seas," 17–18.

27. Grey's silver marlin overshadowed his big dolphin, but he was so proud of this catch that he wrote a special article about it for *Natural History*. See Grey, "Dolphin at Tahiti," 300–302.

28. Zane Grey, Letter to Lina Grey, March 30, [1930] (JW).

29. Loren Grey incorrectly stated that this fish was disqualified for maiming. Loren Grey, *Zane Grey: Photographic Odyssey,* 164.

30. Heilner and La Monte, "World's Record Catches [1933]," 31.

31. Zane Grey, *Diary, 1923–39,* August 15, 1930, 137 (MIC 172, OHS).

32. Zane Grey, Letter to Claire Wilhelm Carlin, July 30, 1930 (PF).

33. Zane Grey, *Diary, 1923–39,* December 17, 1930, 138 (MIC 172, OHS).

34. Zane Grey, Letter to Lina Grey, January 4, 1931 (BY-G).

35. Zane Grey, Letter to Lina Grey, January 11, [1931] (BY-G).

36. Ibid.

37. Zane Grey, Letter to Lina Grey, February 4, 1931 (BY-G2).

38. Berenice Campbell, Letter to Lina Grey, February 6, 1931 (LG).

39. Zane Grey, Letter to Lina Grey, March 14, 1931 (JW).

40. Zane Grey, Letter to Lina Grey, March 15, 1931 (BY-G).

41. Zane Grey, Letter to Lina Grey, March 16, [1931] (BY-G).

42. Zane Grey, Letter to Lina Grey, April 16, 1931 (JW).

43. Lina Grey, Letter to Zane Grey, April 27, 1931 (BY-G).

44. Zane Grey, Letters to Lina Grey, May 11, [1931] (BY-G), and May 13, [1931] (BY-G2).

45. Zane Grey, Letter to Lina Grey, May 13, [1931] (BY-G2).

46. Lina Grey, Letter to Zane Grey, June 8, 1931 (BY-G).

47. Zane Grey, Letter to Lina Grey, June 22, 1931 (JW).

48. Ibid.

49. Zane Grey, *Diary, 1923–39,* August 27, 1931, 139 (MIC 172, OHS).

50. On January 12, 1931, Grey wrote Berenice three pages of advice on how to develop her novel. This letter was sold at Butterfield's. *Catalogue for Fine Books and Manuscripts,* May 27, 1999, lot no. 6166, 30.

51. Lina Grey, Letter to Zane Grey, June 9, 1932 (BY-G).

52. Zane Grey, *Diary, 1923–39,* May 15, 1932, 141 (MIC 172, OHS).

53. Ibid., October 8, 1932, 142.

54. Ibid., May 15, 1932, 141.

55. Zane Grey, Letter to Claire Wilhelm Carlin, September 2, 1932 (PF).

56. Zane Grey, *Journal, 1930s*, October 11, 1932, n.p. (JW).

57. The establishment of Zane Grey, Inc., altered the way in which Dolly and Zane maintained and stored their financial records. I have successfully located a whole range of financial records from prior to this date, but I have found none from afterward.

58. Lina Grey, Letter to Zane Grey, August 20, 1932 (BY-G).

59. Ibid.

60. Lina Grey, Letter to Zane Grey, March 13, 1933 (BY-G).

61. Lina Grey, Letter to Zane Grey, August 20, 1932 (BY-G).

62. Lina Grey, Letter to Zane Grey, May 6, 1933 (BY-G2).

63. Lina Grey, Letter to Zane Grey, June 29, 1933 (BY-G).

64. Lina Grey, Letter to Zane Grey, March 13, 1933 (BY-G).

65. Lina Grey, Letter to Zane Grey, June 29, 1933 (BY-G).

66. Lina Grey, Letter to Zane Grey, March 13, 1933 (BY-G).

67. Lina Grey, Letter to Zane Grey, January 27, 1933 (BY-G).

68. Lina Grey, Letter to Zane Grey, March 13, 1933 (BY-G).

69. Lina Grey, Letter to Zane Grey, April 9, 1933 (BY-G2).

70. Lina Grey, Letter to Zane Grey, May 6, 1933 (BY-G2).

71. Zane Grey, *Diary, 1923–39*, May 3, 1934, 149 (MIC 172, OHS).

72. Zane Grey, Letter to Lina Grey, June 28, 1932 (JW).

73. "King of the Royal Mounted" started as a Sunday strip on February 17, 1935, and was converted into a daily offering on March 2, 1936. In 1938, these strips were collected and brought out by the Whitman Publishing Company in a series of Little Books. It is possible a version began even earlier since Dolly refers to "the strip" in a January 27, 1933, letter to Zane (JW).

74. Zane Grey, Letter to Alvah James, Nov. 6, [1932] (ZGM—L).

75. Quoted in Baker, *Ernest Hemingway*, 271.

76. Lina Grey, Letter to Zane Grey, March 13, 1933 (BY-G).

77. Zane Grey, Letter to Lola Gornall, April 23, 1933 (BY).

78. Lina Grey, Letter to Zane Grey, April 9, 1933 (JW). Zane Grey described the *Frangipani's* voyage in "In Quest of Record Fish," 38–40.

79. Zane Grey, *Diary, 1923–39*, October 6, 1933, 144 (MIC 172, OHS).

80. Lina Grey, Letter to Zane Grey, May 6, 1933 (BY-G2).

81. Zane Grey, *Diary, 1923–39*, October 6, 1933, 145 (MIC 172, OHS).

82. Ibid., October 6, 1933, 145.

83. Zane Grey, Letter to Lola Gornall, April 23, 1933 (BY).

84. Zane Grey, Letter to Lola Gornall, August 31, 1933 (BY).

85. Zane Grey, *Diary, 1923–39*, May 13, 1934, 149 (MIC 172, OHS).

86. Ibid., May 13, 1934, 151 (MIC 172, OHS).

87. This journal was sold at a Butterfield auction, September, 2000, lot no. 9080, 24.

88. Zane Grey, Letter to Alvah James, January 6, 1935 (ZGM—L)

89. Zane Grey, Letter to Lina Grey, July 5, 1935 (Bmms).

90. Zane Grey, Letter to Lina Grey, July 17, 1935 (BY-G2).

91. Zane Grey, *Diary, 1923–39,* September 24, 1936, 163 (MIC 172, OHS).

92. *Motor Boating* published articles by Grey in its January, February, and April issues of 1934.

93. Farley, "Famous Kovalovsky Fishing Reel," 1 and 4.

94. The 8½" reel, the first, was intended to hold 1,500 feet of 39-thread line, though Grey loaded it with a combination of 500 feet of 39-thread and 1,000 feet of 50-thread line for his 1,040-pound marlin. Hardy expanded this reel into a broad range of sizes and continued to offer it until 1957. Drewett, *Hardy Brothers,* 477–80. Also Wheeler, "Zane Grey and the House of Hardy," 10–11.

95. In a January 6, 1934, letter to Dolly, Zane included Hardy's November 1, 1933, request for settlement. Waverly Auction, February 6, 2003, lot no. 180.

96. Hannam, "Tunny Fishing," 18–19.

97. *British Sea Anglers' Quarterly* 26 (December, 1932), iv, and 27 (September, 1933), iv.

98. Grey, "Big Game Fishing," 11–12, 64–65.

99. Grey, "Some Arresting Facts," 17–19, 83. Grey also criticized Mitchell-Henry in "Big Tuna," *Motor Boating* (April, 1923), 21–23.

100. Mitchell-Henry, *Tunny Fishing,* 100–109. In his excellent overview of Grey as a fisherman, George Reiger reprinted Mitchell-Henry's *Gazette* account as the most influential negative appraisal of Grey as a fisherman. *Profiles in Salt Water Angling,* 136–40.

101. Even his fellow members in the British Sea Anglers' Society found Mitchell-Henry hard to stomach and worried that he might be considered a spokesman for the club. "It is a very great pity," wrote the unnamed reviewer of his book for the Society's *Quarterly,* "that Mitchell-Henry should have loaded his book with so much bitterness and controversy." "Reviews," *British Sea Anglers' Society's Quarterly* (September, 1934), 92–93.

102. Aitken, "Swordfish," 46. See "World's Record Catches," *Field and Stream* 40 (January, 1936), 27. As support for this world record, Grey wrote, "World Record Tiger Shark," 9–11, 56–58. Aitken's opposition to Grey is likewise evident in two ensuing articles: "Half the World Fishes for Tuna," 48–49, and "When Is a Big Fish a Record?," 54–55.

103. Zane Grey, *Diary, 1923–39,* October 19, 1935, 161 (MIC 172, OHS).

104. Lina Grey, Letter to Zane Grey, December, 1936 (BY-G).

105. Grey, *American Angler,* 2–7.

106. Ibid., 8–19.

107. Ibid., 26–27.

108. Ibid., 56, 63.

109. Ibid., 79. Grey may have written this, perhaps only part of it, but so far no

manuscript has surfaced. On the other hand, he did write several articles about sharks for *Field and Stream* in 1937 and 1938 that may have been intended for this book.

110. Ibid., 71–76.

111. Ibid., 87–95.

112. Zane Grey, *Diary, 1923-39,* September 24, 1936, 164 (MIC 172, OHS).

113. Ibid., 164.

114. Ed Bowen, Letter to Lina Grey, November 9, 1936 (DB).

115. Grey, "Record of Writing," n.p., December 11, 1936; March 9, 1937; and March 17, 1937 (mss. 1262, OHS).

116. Aitken, "Review," sec. 10, 6.

117. Loren Grey, "Facts about Zane Grey's North Umpqua Stroke," 4.

118. Zane Grey, *Diary, 1923-39,* August 13, 1939, 171 (MIC 172, OHS).

119. Interview with Loren Grey, May 23, 2003.

120. Joe Wheeler discovered this final inscription. See Wheeler, "Zane Grey in Oregon," 11.

Postscript

1. Buscombe, *BFI Companion to the Western,* 427.

2. *Zane Grey Review* 12 (June, 1997), 21.

3. Tebbel, *History of Book Publishing,* vol. 4, 380–81.

4. Hackett, *Sixty Years of Best Sellers,* 16 and 41. The popularity of the Bantam paperback edition enabled *Nevada* to become Grey's best-selling novel by 1955.

5. Blake, "Zane Grey Paperback First Editions," 9–13.

6. Heilner, Schrenheisen, and LaMotte, *Field and Stream* 43 (January, 1939), 31.

7. Aitken, "Let's Get Together on Records," 40 and 73. His 1937 and 1938 lists were published in *Country Life* 73 (February, 1938), 55, and (February, 1939), 83.

8. *A History of IGFA* (published by the International Game Fish Association), 2–5.

9. For information about the IGFA lists, I am indebted to Gail Marchower, librarian at IGFA.

10. *New York Times,* May 14, 2003, 1.

Bibliography

This bibliography cites only the works by Zane Grey that are quoted, discussed, or merit a citation. A complete bibliography of Grey's novels, one that includes the exact publication dates of his books, even those published after his death, can be found in Farley, *Many Faces of Zane Grey,* 215–17. The bibliography of Grey's magazine articles and serials, in Farley, *Zane Grey: A Documented Portrait,* 97–109, is more thorough and more accurate than the one in Gruber, *Zane Grey,* 260–73. Even though Farley missed several items listed below, there are not enough additions to warrant another complete list here.

Aitken, Thomas. "Half the World Fishes for Tuna." *Outdoor Life* 76 (August, 1935), 48–49.
———. "Let's Get Together on Records." *Outdoor Life* 76 (February, 1936), 40 and 72–73.
———. "Review of *An American Angler in Australia.*" *New York Herald Tribune,* May 9, 1937, X, 6.
———. "Swordfish . . . King of the Sea." *Outdoor Life* 76 (July, 1935), 46, 48.
———. "When Is a Big Fish a Record?" *Outdoor Life* 76 (September, 1935), 54–55.
Akin, Edward N. *Flagler, Rockefeller Partner and Florida Baron.* Kent, Ohio: Kent State University Press, 1988, 220–21.
American National Biography. 24 vols. New York: Oxford University Press, 1999.

Anderson, Michael F. *Living at the Edge: Explorers, Exploiters, and Settlers of the Grand Canyon Region*. Grand Canyon: Grand Canyon Association, 1998.

———. *Polishing the Jewel: An Administrative History of the Grand Canyon National Park*. Grand Canyon: Grand Canyon Association, 2000.

Aron, Cindy. *Working at Play: A History of Vacations in the United States*. New York: Oxford, 1999.

Ashworth, Donna. *Arizona Triptych: A Story of Northern Arizona Artists*. Flagstaff, Ariz.: Small Mountain Books, 1999.

Austin, Mary. *The Land of Little Rain*. Boston: Houghton, Mifflin, 1903.

Bagley, Will. *Blood of the Prophets: Brigham Young and the Massacre at Mountain Meadows*. Norman: University of Oklahoma Press, 2002.

Baker, Carlos. *Ernest Hemingway: A Life Story*. New York: Charles Scribner's, 1969.

Baldini, Ralph. *Men, Fish and Tackle: The Story of J. A. Coxe*. Bronson, Mich.: privately printed, 1936.

Bederman, Gail. *Manliness and Civilization: A Cultural History of Gender and Race in the United States, 1880–1917*. Chicago: University of Chicago Press, 1995.

Beebe, William. *Galapagos, World's End*. New York: Putnam, 1924.

Blake, Kevin. "Zane Grey Paperback First Editions, U.S. Publishers." *Zane Grey Review* 11 (December, 1995), 9–13.

Bloodworth, William. "Zane Grey's Western Eroticism." *South Dakota Review* 23 (Autumn, 1985), 5–14.

Bold, Christine. *Selling the Wild West: Popular Western Fiction, 1860–1960*. Bloomington: Indiana University Press, 1987.

Boschen, W. C. "The Marlin Is an Acrobat." *Vanity Fair* 10 (May, 1918), 70 and 82.

———. "The True Swordfish and Its Capture." *Vanity Fair* 10 (April, 1918), 54 and 106.

Boyle, Robert H. "The Man Who Lived Two Lives." *Sports Illustrated* (April 29, 1968), 68–82.

Brett, Alden. "Zane Grey: His Life Story." *Success* (July 1924), 27–28.

Brooks, Paul. *Speaking for Nature*. Boston: Houghton Mifflin, 1980.

Brooks, Van Wyck. *America's Coming of Age*. New York: Huebsch, 1915.

Brown, Bill. *Reading the West: An Anthology of Dime Novels*. Boston: Bedford/St. Martin's, 1997.

Burroughs, John. "Red and Sham Natural History," *Atlantic Monthly* 91 (March, 1903), 298–309.

Buscombe, Edward (ed.). *The BFI Companion to the Western*. New York: Athaneum, 1988, 427.

Cawelti, John. *Adventure, Mystery, and Romance: Formula Stories as Art and Popular Culture*. Chicago: University of Chicago Press, 1976.

——. *The Six-Gun Mystique.* Bowling Green, Ohio: Bowling Green Popular Press, 1971.

Christian, Patricia H. "Zane Grey: The Legacy of His Lackawaxen Days." *Once Upon a Memory.* Equinunk: Equinunk Pennsylvania Historical Society, 1987, 151–74.

Comfort, Mary Apolline. *Rainbow to Yesterday.* New York: Vantage, 1980.

Cummings, Byron. "The Great Natural Bridges of Utah." *National Geographic* 21 (1910), 157–67.

Dary, David A. *The Buffalo Book: The Full Saga of the American Animal.* Columbus, Ohio: University Press, 1989.

Davis, Margaret Leslie. *Dark Side of Fortune: Triumph and Scandal in the Life of Oil Tycoon Edward L. Doheny.* Berkeley: University of California Press, 1998.

Davis, Robert, *Bob Davis Again! In Many Moods.* New York: Appleton, 1918.

——. "Porpoise on Tarpon Tackle." *Field and Stream* 17 (December, 1912), 878–82.

Denton, Sally. *American Massacre: The Tragedy of Mountain Meadows, September, 1857.* New York: Alfred A. Knopf, 2003.

Derks, Scott (ed.). *The Value of a Dollar: Prices and Incomes in the United States, 1860–1999.* Lakeville, Conn.: Grey House, 2002.

Dictionary of American Biography. 10 vols. New York: Scribners, 1935.

Dilg, Mrs. Will H. "When Woman Goes Fishing." *Field and Stream* 16 (January, 1912), 922.

Drewett, John. *Hardy Brothers: The Masters, the Men, and Their Reels, 1873–1919.* Middlesex, England: J & J Publishing, 1998.

Eakin, Emily. "Reopening the Mormon Murder Mystery." *New York Times,* October 12, 2002, A19 and A21.

Eames, John Douglas. *The Paramount Story.* New York: Crown, 1985.

Easton, Robert, and MacKenzie Brown. *Lord of the Beasts, the Life of Buffalo Jones.* Tucson: University of Arizona Press, 1961.

Ebbeskotte, Robert. "Delphos (Ohio) Baseball." *Zane Grey Review* 9 (December, 1993), 9–13.

Eckert, Allan W. *That Dark and Bloody River.* New York: Bantam, 1995.

Fabian, Warner (Samuel Hopkins Adams). *Flaming Youth.* New York: Boni, 1923.

Farley, G. M. "The Famous Kovalovsky Fishing Reel." *Zane Grey Collector* 1 (Winter, 1984), 1 and 4.

——. *The Many Faces of Zane Grey.* Private printing, 1991.

——. *Zane Grey: A Documented Portrait.* Tuscaloosa, Ala.: Portals Press, 1996.

Farrar, John. "Clean Fiction." *Bookman* 62 (October, 1925), 115–16.

——. "Zane Grey and the American Spirit." *McCall's* 55 (February, 1928), 2.

Farrington, S. Kip. *Atlantic Game Fishing.* New York: Kennedy Brothers, 1927.

Farrior, Michael L. *The History of the Tuna Club, 1898–1998*. Avalon: The Tuna Club Foundation, 2004.

Fenin, George, and William K. Everson. *The Western: From Silents to Cinerama.* New York: Orion Press, 1962.

Gilmore, Frances, and Louisa Wade Wetherill. *Traders to the Navajos: The Story of the Wetherills of Kayenta.* Albuquerque: University of New Mexico Press, 1953.

Grey, Loren. "The Facts about Zane Grey's North Umpqua Stroke." *New Zane Grey Collector* 1 (Fall, 1985), 4.

———. "Foreword." In Zane Grey, *The Desert Crucible*. Waterville, Maine: Thorndyke, 2004.

———. "Foreword." In Zane Grey, *The Last of the Duanes*. Waterville, Maine: Five Star, 1997.

———. "Introduction." In Zane Grey, *The Vanishing American*. New York: Pocket Books, 1982.

———. *Zane Grey: A Photographic Odyssey*. Dallas: Taylor, 1985.

Grey, Romer C. *Adventures of a Deep-Sea Angler*. New York: Harpers, 1928.

———. "Fishing With Famous Fellows." *Recreation* 56 (June, 1917), 255–62.

———. "Sea Fishing for Women." *Field and Stream* 26 (July 1921), 261–65.

———. "Tuna Fishing Yesterday and Today." *Field and Stream* 27 (August, 1922), 430–33.

Grey, Zane. *An American Angler in Australia*. New York: Harper and Brothers, 1937.

———. "Avalon, the Beautiful," *Field and Stream* 23 (May, 1918), 19–21.

———. "The Barracuda of Long Key." *Field and Stream* 17 (July, 1912), 270–86.

———. *Betty Zane*. New York: Harper and Brothers, 1903.

———. "Big Game Fishing." *Outdoor Life* (April, 1930), 10–12, 64–67.

———. "Big Game Fishing in New Zealand Seas," *Natural History* 28 (January–February, 1928), 47–52.

———. "Big Game Fishing in Southern Seas." *Motor Boating* (January, 1934), 16–17

———. "Big Tuna," *Field and Stream* 24 (May, 1919).

———. "Breaking Through: The Story of my Life." *American Magazine* 97 (July, 1924), 11–14, 76–80.

———. "Byme-by-Tarpon." *Field and Stream* 12 (December, 1907), 613–16.

———. "California Game Fish: How Long Will They Last?" *Field and Stream* (June, 1982), 64–65.

———. *The Call of the Canyon*. New York: Harper and Brothers, 1924.

———. "Canoeing on the Delaware," *Recreation* 18 (June, 1903), 415–17.

———. *The Code of the West*. New York: Harper and Brothers, 1934.

———. "Cruising in Mexican Waters." *Field and Stream* 12 (January 1908), 737–39.

———. *The Day of the Beast.* New York: Harper and Brothers, 1922.

———. "A Day on the Delaware." *Recreation* 16 (May, 1902), 339–40.

———. *The Desert Crucible.* Waterville, Maine: Thorndyke, 2004.

———. *Desert Gold.* New York: Harper and Brothers, 1913.

———. *The Desert of Wheat.* New York: Harper and Brothers, 1919.

———. *Diary, 1923–39* (MIC 172, Ohio Historical Society).

———. "Dolphin at Tahiti." *Natural History* 32 (May–June, 1932), 300–302.

———. "Down an Unknown Jungle River," *Field and Stream* 15–16 (March, 1911–January, 1912).

———. "Down into the Desert," *Ladies' Home Journal* 41 (April, 1922), 8–9, 43–46.

———. "Fading Indian Trails" (mss. 1262, Ohio Historical Society).

———. "Following the Elusive Tuna." *Field and Stream* 18 (September, 1913), 475–79.

———. "Gulf Stream Fishing On Light Tackle." *Field and Stream* 23 (July, 1916), 205–9.

———. "Heavy Tackle for Heavy Fish." Catalina *Islander,* January 2, 1924, 1. Also reprinted in *Outdoor America* 2 (February, 1924), 335–36.

———. *The Heritage of the Desert.* New York: Harper and Brothers, 1910.

———. "In Quest of Record Fish: Zane Grey Lands a Giant Marlin." *Motor Boating* (February, 1934), 38–40.

———. "James' Waterloo." *Field and Stream* 11 (September, 1906), 460–63.

———. *Journal, Arizona, 1908* (Ms. 230, Zane Grey Collection, Cline Library, Northern Arizona University, Flagstaff, Ariz.).

———. *Journal, 1905–10* (Beinecke Library, Yale University, New Haven, Conn.).

———. *Journal, 1910–12* (Joe Wheeler).

———. *Journal, 1912–15* (George Houle).

———. *Journal, 1917–22* (Joe Wheeler).

———. *Journal, 1920* (George Houle).

———. *Journal, 1930s* (Joe Wheeler).

———. "Landing the Record Broadbill." *Outdoor Life* 24 (October, 1926) 8–10.

———. "Lassoing Lions in the Siwash," *Everybody's* 18 (June, 1908), 776–85.

———. *The Last of the Duanes.* Waterville, Maine: Five Star, 1997.

———. *The Last of the Plainsmen.* New York: Outing, 1908.

———. "The Leaping Tarpon." *Shields'* 5 (September, 1907), 153–57.

———. "The Letters of Dolly and Zane Grey." *Missouri Review* 18 (1995), 115–76.

———. *The Light of Western Stars.* New York: Harper and Brothers, 1914.

———. "Light Tackle." *Field and Stream* 23 (February, 1919), 747.

———. "The Living Past." *Zane Grey Reporter* 1–3 (March, 1986–March, 1988).

———. "The Log of the *Gladiator.*" *Sunset Magazine* (April, 1926), 9–11, 56–62.

———. *The Lone Star Ranger.* New York: Harper and Brothers, 1915.

———. "The Man Who Influenced Me Most." *American Magazine* 102 (August, 1926), 52–54, 130–36.

———. "My Adventures as a Fisherman." *American Magazine* (April, 1926), 26–27, 168–79.

———. "My Answer to the Critics." *Zane Grey Collector* 8 (1978), 3–9.

———. "My Own Life," in *Zane Grey: The Man and His Work*. New York: Harper and Brothers, 1928.

———. *Nassau, Cuba, Mexico*. New York: New York and Cuba Mail S. S. Co., 1909.

———. "A Night in the Jungle." *Shields'* 4 (May, 1907), 296–98.

———. "Nonnezoshe," *Recreation* 52 (February, 1915), 63–67.

———. *Notebook of Visit to Cave Dwelling* (mss. 1262, Ohio Historical Society). [Journal of Grey's 1907 visit to Arizona.]

———. *The Rainbow Trail*. New York: Harper and Brothers, 1915.

———. Record of Writing, September, 1936–March, 1937 (mss. 1262, Ohio Historical Society).

———. "Resignation from the Tuna Club." *The Zane Grey Review* 15 (December, 1999), 1 and 3.

———. *Riders of the Purple Sage*. New York: Harper and Brothers, 1912.

———. *Riders of the Purple Sage*. Waterville, Maine: Five Star, 2005.

———. "Roping Lions in the Grand Canyon," *Field and Stream* 13–14 (January, 1909–August, 1909).

———. "Sailfish." *Recreation* 53 (December, 1916).

———. "The Sea-Tigers of the Florida Keys." *Field and Stream* 16 (December, 1911), 782–91.

———. "Some Arresting Facts about Modern Sea Angling." *Outdoor Life* (February, 1931), 17–19, 83.

———. "Swordfish, the Royal Purple Game of the Sea," *Recreation* 53 (December, 1915), 255–61.

———. "Swordsmen of the Sea." *Field and Stream* 23 (March, 1919), 820–25.

———. *Tales of the Angler's Eldorado, New Zealand*. New York: Harper and Brothers, 1926.

———. *Tales of a Fisherman's Eldorado, New Zealand*. Auckland: Halcyon Press, 1989.

———. *Tales of Fishes*. New York: Harper and Brothers, 1919.

———. *Tales of Fishing Virgin Seas*. New York: Harper and Brothers, 1925.

———. *Tales of Freshwater Fishing*. New York: Harper and Brothers, 1928.

———. *Tales of Lonely Trails*. New York: Harper and Brothers, 1922.

———. *Tales of Southern Rivers*. New York: Harper and Brothers, 1924.

———. *Tales of Swordfish and Tuna*. New York: Harper and Brothers, 1927.

———. *Tales of Tahitian Waters*. New York: Harper and Brothers, 1931.

———. *Tarpon, the Silver King*. New York: Ward Line, [1908].

———. "Three Broadbill Swordfish." *Outdoor America* 2 (February, 1924), 332–34, 389.

———. "Three Strikes and Out." *Field and Stream* 12 (July, 1907), 201–3.

———. *The Thundering Herd.* New York: Harper and Brothers, 1925.

———. "Tige's Lion." *Field and Stream* 13 (June, 1908), 117–22.

———. *The Vanishing American.* New York: Harper and Brothers, 1925.

———. *The Vanishing American.* New York: Pocket Books, 1982.

———. *Wanderer of the Wasteland.* New York: Harper and Brothers, 1923.

———. "What the Desert Means to Me." *American Magazine* 97 (November, 1924), 5–8, 72–78.

———. "Why I Write Western Stories." *The American News Trade Journal* 3 (May, 1921), 3.

———. *Wilderness Trek.* New York: Harper and Brothers, 1944.

———. "World Record Tiger Shark." *Field and Stream* 41 (February, 1937), 9–11, 56–58.

———. *Wyoming.* New York: Harper and Brothers, 1953.

———. "Xiphias Gladius." *Country Gentleman* 89 (February 9, 1924), 10–11.

———. "Zane Grey." In *My Maiden Effort,* edited by Gelett Burgess. New York: Doubleday, 1921, 82.

Gruber, Frank. *Zane Grey: A Biography.* New York: World Publishing, 1970.

Hackett, Alice Payne. *Fifty Years of Best Sellers: 1895–1945.* New York: R. R. Bowker, 1945.

———. *Sixty Years of Best Sellers: 1895–1955.* New York: R. R. Bowker, 1956.

Hammond, Bryn. "Introduction." In Zane Grey, *Tales of a Fisherman's Eldorado, New Zealand.* Auckland: Halcyon Press, 1989.

Hampton, Benjamin B. *A History of the Movies.* New York: Covici-Friede, 1931.

Handley, William R. *Marriage, Violence, and the Nation in the American Literary West.* New York: Cambridge University Press, 2002.

Hannam, F. B. "Tunny Fishing in 1931." *British Sea Anglers' Quarterly* 25 (December 1931), 18–19.

Hart, Irving Harlow. "The Most Popular Authors of Fiction between 1900 and 1925." *Publishers Weekly* 107 (February 21, 1925), 619–20.

———. "The Most Popular Authors of Fiction in the Post-War Period, 1919–1926." *Publishers Weekly* 111 (March 12, 1927), 473–77.

Hassell, Hank. *Rainbow Bridge: An Illustrated History.* Logan: Utah State University Press, 1999.

Heilner, Van Campen. *Salt Water Fishing.* New York: Knopf, 1943.

Hintzen, William, "Betty Zane, Lydia Boggs, and Molly Scott: The Gunpowder Exploits at Fort Henry." *West Virginia History* 55 (1996), 95–109.

Hitt, Jim. *The American West from Fiction (1823–1976) into Film (1909–1986).* Jefferson, N.C.: McFarland & Co., 1990.

Holden, Philip. *The Golden Years of Fishing in New Zealand.* Auckland: Hodder and Stoughton, 1984.

Holder, Charles Frederick. *Big Game at Sea.* New York: Outing, 1908.

———. "Catching Swordfish with Rod and Reel." *Outing Magazine* 44 (September, 1904), 752–54.

———. *Salt Water Game Fishing.* New York: Outing, 1914.

Irwin, Will. *The House That Shadows Built.* New York: Doubleday, 1928.

Isenberg, Andrew C. *The Destruction of the Bison: An Environmental History, 1750–1920.* Cambridge: Cambridge University Press, 2000.

Ives, Marguerite. "Interview with Zane Grey." *Izaak Walton League Monthly* 1 (June, 1923), 6.

———. "A Small Woman and a Big Swordfish." *Izaak Walton League Monthly* 1 (April, 1923), 270.

Jackson, Carleton. *Zane Grey.* Revised edition. Boston: Twayne, 1989.

Justice, Keith L. *Bestseller Index.* Jefferson, N.C.: McFarland & Co., 1998.

Kant, Candace C. "Zane Grey and the Mormons of the Arizona Strip." *Zane Grey Reporter* 3 (1988), 1, 8–10.

———. *Zane Grey's Arizona.* Flagstaff, Ariz.: Northland Press, 1984.

Kaplan-Mann, Marsha. "Dr. Pearl Grey—Miss Lina Elise Roth—A Romance." *Zane Grey Review* 10 (December, 1994), 3.

Keller, Betty. *Black Wolf: The Life of Ernest Thompson Seton.* Vancouver: Douglas & McIntyre, 1984.

Kennedy, Samuel V., III. *Samuel Hopkins Adams and the Business of Writing.* Syracuse, N.Y.: Syracuse University Press, 1999.

Kerr, Jean. *Zane Grey, Man of the West.* New York: Grosset & Dunlap, 1949.

Kimball, Arthur G. *Ace of Hearts: The Westerns of Zane Grey.* Fort Worth: Texas Christian University Press, 1987.

Klein, Maury. *Rainbow's End: The Crash of 1929.* New York: Oxford University Press, 2001.

Kock, Charles R. E. *History of Dental Surgery*, vol. 1. 3 vols. Chicago: National Art Publishing Co., 1909.

Korda, Michael. *Making the List: A Cultural History of the American Bestseller, 1900–1999.* New York: Barnes & Noble, 2001.

Krakauer, Jon. *Under the Banner of Heaven: A Story of Violent Faith.* New York: Doubleday, 2003.

La Monte, Francesca. "The Zane Grey Game Fish Collection." *Natural History* 28 (January–February, 1928), 94.

Lasky, Jesse L., with Don Weldon. *I Blow My Own Horn.* Garden City, N.Y.: Doubleday, 1957.

Lee, Charles. *The Hidden Public: The Story of the Book-of-the-Month Club.* Garden City, N.Y.: Doubleday, 1958.

Leopold, Aldo. "Thinking Like a Mountain," *A Sand County Almanac and Sketches Here and There*. New York: Oxford University Press, 1949, 129–33.

Light, Jonathan Fraser. *The Cultural History of Baseball*. New York: McFarland & Co., 1997.

Lutz, Tom. *American Nervousness, 1903: An Anecdotal History*. Ithaca, N.Y.: Cornell University Press, 1991.

Macdonald, Barrie. *Imperial Patriot: Charles Alma Baker and the History of Limestone Downs*. Wellington, New Zealand: Bridget Williams, 1993.

Macrate, Arthur. *The History of the Tuna Club*. Privately printed, 1948.

May, Stephen J. *Maverick Heart: The Further Adventures of Zane Grey*. Athens: Ohio University Press, 2000.

———. *Zane Grey: Romancing the West*. Athens: Ohio University Press, 1997.

McNitt, Frank. *The Indian Traders*. Norman: University of Oklahoma Press, 1962.

———. *Richard Wetherill: Anasazi Pioneer Explorer of Southwestern Ruins*. Albuquerque: University of New Mexico Press, 1957.

Mitchell, Laurie D. "Taking the World's Record Tuna." *Field and Stream* 29 (January, 1925), 22–24.

Mitchell, Lee Clark. *Westerns: Making the Man in Fiction and Fact*. Chicago: University of Chicago Press, 1996.

Mitchell-Henry, L. *Tunny Fishing at Home and Abroad*. London: Rich & Cowan, 1934.

Mott, Frank Luther. *Golden Multitudes: The Story of Best Sellers in the United States*. New York: Macmillan, 1947.

———. *History of American Magazines*. 4 vols. Cambridge: Harvard University Press, 1960.

Mowrey, Marshall. "From G-R-A-Y to GREY." *Zane Grey Review* 11 (June, 1996), 6.

National Cyclopedia of American Biography. 12 vols. New York: James T. White, 1971.

Nesbitt, John D. "Uncertain Sex in the Sagebrush." *South Dakota Review* 23 (Autumn, 1985), 15–27.

Netherby, Steve. "Zane Grey—Author, Angler, Explorer." *Field and Stream* 76 (January, 1972), 52–53, 85–88.

Nichols, John Treadwell, and Van Campen Heilner. "World's Record Catches with Rod and Reel." *Field and Stream* 29 (October, 1924), 16–17.

———. *Field and Stream* 33 (October, 1928), 32–33.

———. *Field and Stream* 37 (January, 1933), 31.

———. *Field and Stream* 40 (January, 1936), 26–27.

———. *Field and Stream* 43 (January, 1939), 31.

North, Dick. "Zane Grey's Mysterious Guide." *New Zane Grey Collector* 1 (Fall, 1985), 9 and 11.

Ortho, George W. (ed.). *History of Athletics at Penn.* Philadelphia: University of Pennsylvania, 1896.

Overholt, Alma. *The Catalina Story.* Catalina, Calif.: Catalina Island Museum Company, 1962.

Patrick, Arnold. "Getting Into Six Figures." *Bookman* 60 (December 1924), 424–29.

Pogue, Joseph E. "The Great Rainbow Natural Bridge of Southern Utah." *National Geographic* 21 (1911), 1048–56.

Rascoe, Burton. "Opie Read and Zane Grey." *Saturday Review of Literature* 21 (November 11, 1939), 8.

Reiger, George. *Profiles in Salt Water Angling.* Englewood Cliffs, N.J.: Prentice-Hall, 1973.

———. *Undiscovered Zane Grey Fishing Stories.* Piscataway, N.J.: New Century, 1983.

———. *Zane Grey: Outdoorsman.* Englewood Cliffs, N.J.: Prentice-Hall, 1972.

Reilly, P. T. *Lee's Ferry: From Mormon Crossing to National Park.* Logan: Utah State University Press, 1999.

Ronald, Ann. *Zane Grey.* Boise, Idaho: Boise State Press, 1975.

Roosevelt, Theodore. *A Book Lover's Holidays in the Open.* New York: Scribner's, 1916.

———. "Roosevelt on the Nature Fakers." *Everybody's* 16 (June, 1907), 770–74.

Rothman, Hal K. *Devil's Bargain: Tourism in the Twentieth-Century American West.* Lawrence: University of Kansas Press, 1998.

Schick, Frank L. *The Paperbound Book in America.* New York: Bowker, 1958.

Schmitt, Peter J. *Back to Nature: The Arcadian Myth in Urban America.* New York: Oxford University Press, 1969.

Schneider, Norris F. *The National Road: Main Street of America.* Columbus: Ohio Historical Society, 1975.

———. *Zane Grey.* Privately printed, 1967.

Schreuders, Piet. *Paperbacks, U.S.A.* San Diego: Blue Dolphin, 1981.

Scott, Kenneth W. *Zane Grey: Born to the West.* Boston: G. K. Hall, 1979.

Shi, David S. *The Simple Life: Plain Living and High Thinking in American Culture.* New York: Oxford University Press, 1985.

Sierks-Overholt, Alma. "A New World's Record." *Field and Stream* 28 (November, 1923), 804–5.

Simmon, Scott. *The Invention of the Western Film: A Cultural History of the Genre's First Half Century.* New York: Cambridge University Press, 2003.

Slide, Anthony. *The Big V: A History of the Vitagraph Company.* Metuchen, N.J.: Scarecrow Press, 1978.

———. *The New Historical Dictionary of the American Film Industry.* Metuchen, N.J.: Scarecrow Press, 1998.

Slotkin, Richard. *Gunfighter Nation: The Myth of the Frontier in Twentieth Century America*. New York: Atheneum, 1992.

Stroud, Richard (ed.). *National Leaders of American Conservation*. Washington, D.C.: Smithsonian, 1985.

Tebbel, John. *A History of Book Publishing in the United States*. 4 vols. New York: R. R. Bowker, 1981.

Thomas, George C., Jr., with George C. Thomas, III. *Game Fish of the Pacific*. Philadelphia: Lippincott, 1930.

Timmerman, Caroline. "America's Pastime." *Zane Grey Review* 11 (June, 1996), 2.

———. "Just the Facts, Ma'am." *Zane Grey Review* 11 (October, 1996), 12.

Tompkins, Jane. *West of Everything: The Inner Life of Westerns*. New York: Oxford University Press, 1992.

Tuska, Jon. *The Filming of the West*. Garden City, N.Y.: Doubleday, 1976.

———. "Foreword." In Zane Grey, *Riders of the Purple Sage*. Waterville, Maine: Five Star, 2005.

Van Dyke, John Charles. *The Desert: Further Studies in Natural Appearances*. New York: C. Scribner's Sons, 1901.

Van Grondelle, Carole. *Angel of the Anzacs: The Life of Nola Luxford*. Wellington, New Zealand: Victoria University Press, 2000.

Van Wagoner, Richard C. *Mormon Polygamy: A History*. Salt Lake City, Utah: Signature, 1989.

Vickers, Jim, and Ed Myers. "A Special Friendship: Zane Grey and Mildred Smith." *Zane Grey Quarterly* 1 (Winter, 1992), 3.

Waddell, J. A. L. "Tarpon Fishing at Tamos, Mexico." *Forest and Stream* (March 25, 1905), 235–37.

Wagner, Charles. *The Simple Life*. Mary Louise Hendee (trans.). New York: McClure, 1904. Originally published as *La Vie Simple*, 1901.

Weston, Rich, and Frank Bilovsky. *The New Phillies Encyclopedia*. Philadelphia: Temple University Press, 1993.

Wheeler, Don. "Zane Grey and the House of Hardy." *Zane Grey Review* (April, 1998), 10–11.

Wheeler, Joseph Lawrence. "Two Roads Diverged in a Yellow Wood." *Zane Grey's West* 7, 32–33.

———. "Zane Grey in Oregon." *Zane Grey Review* 14 (October, 1999), 1, 3–11.

———. *Zane Grey's Impact on American Life and Letters: A Study of the Popular Novel*. Ph.D. dissertation, George Peabody College for Teachers, Vanderbilt University, 1975.

Whipple, T. K. "American Sagas." *Saturday Review of Literature* 1 (February 7, 1925), 505–6.

Bibliography

White, G. Edward, *The Eastern Establishment and the Western Experience: The West of Frederic Remington, Theodore Roosevelt, and Owen Wister.* New Haven, Conn.: Yale University Press, 1968.

Whitfield, Eileen, *Pickford: The Woman Who Made Hollywood.* Lexington: University of Kentucky Press, 1977.

Wilhelm, Claire. *Journal, 1914* (Pat Friese).

———. *Journal, 1916—Long Key* (Pat Friese).

———. *Journal, 1916—Arizona* (Pat Friese).

———. *Journal, 1917—Catalina* (Pat Friese).

———. *Journal, 1918—Long Key* (Pat Friese).

———. *Journal, 1918—Out West* (Pat Friese).

———. *Journal, 1920—Catalina and Arizona* (Pat Friese).

———. *Journal, 1924—Oregon* (Pat Friese).

———. *Journal, 1924—Arizona* (Pat Friese).

———. *Journal, 1925—South America* (Pat Friese).

Wister, Owen. *The Virginian.* New York: Macmillan, 1902.

Yost, Nellie Snyder. *Buffalo Bill: His Family, Friends, Fame, Failures, and Fortunes.* Chicago: Swallow Press, 1979.

Zane Grey: The Man and His Work. New York: Harper and Brothers, 1928.

Index

THOMAS H. PAULY is professor and associate chair of the English Department at the University of Delaware. He is the author of books on Elia Kazan and the historical background of the musical "Chicago."

The University of Illinois Press
is a founding member of the
Association of American University Presses.

Composed in 9.5/13.5 ITC Stone Serif
with ITC Tiepolo display
by Jim Proefrock
at the University of Illinois Press
Designed by Dennis Roberts

Manufactured by Thomson-Shore, Inc.
University of Illinois Press
1325 South Oak Street
Champaign, IL 61820-6903
www.press.uillinois.edu